Poem for the Day

Poem for the Day

366 poems, old and new,
worth learning by heart

Edited by
Nicholas Albery

Assisted by
Peter Ratcliffe

SINCLAIR-STEVENSON

First published in Great Britain by
The Natural Death Centre, 20 Heber Road, London NW2 6AA
(tel 0181 208 2853; fax 0181 452 6434)

in association with

Sinclair-Stevenson, an imprint of Reed Consumer Books Ltd
Michelin House, 81 Fulham Road, London SW3 6RB
Auckland, Melbourne, Singapore, Toronto

Reprinted 1995 (five times), 1996 (three times)

All royalties from this book are going to The Natural Death Centre, a charity for the support of those who are caring for a dying person at home and for advising families who are arranging funerals themselves, with or without the help of funeral directors. More information about the Centre's work is given at the end of this book. The Natural Death Centre gratefully acknowledges the generosity of poets, publishers and agents who gave permission for poems to be published.

ISBN (paperback) 1 85619 499 X

Compilation copyright © The Natural Death Centre 1994
For copyright in individual poems see the acknowledgment pages

Printed by Clays Ltd, St Ives plc

A CIP catalogue reference for this book is available at the British Library

Foreword

Wendy Cope

Learning poetry by heart is easier for some people than for others. Nigel Molesworth, hero of Geoffrey Willans's *Down With Skool*, finds it hard. 'when i recite' he tells us, 'it is something like this:

> Tomow and tomow and tomow
> Um ah um ah
> Tomow and tomow and tomow
> Um – ah creeps creeps in the last syll –
> No!
> Tomowandtomowandtomow'

Molesworth is no lover of the art he consistently calls 'peotry'. Neither are many of the adults who remember making fools of themselves in a similar fashion. I would not welcome the revival of learning poems by heart as a compulsory task in our schools.

Learning poems as a voluntary activity is an entirely different matter, and I'm all for encouraging children and adults to do more of it. My own repertoire of memorised poems, though much smaller than Nicholas Albery's, is immensely valuable to me. It's wonderful to be able to take one's favourites everywhere, and to listen to them at any time. No Walkman needed, and no bag. I find them especially helpful in situations that scare me. As the aeroplane takes off, or the dentist drills into my tooth, I close my eyes and silently recite something by Shakespeare, Housman or Emily Dickinson. It doesn't banish fear but it helps prevent total panic. A time may come when I need memorised poems even more – if my eyesight fails, for example.

Most of the poems in my invisible library are by the three poets mentioned above. It is too small and too narrow, and I'm grateful to Nicholas Albery for inspiring a new determination to extend it. His idea is an exciting one, and his selection an excellent mix of the old and the new. Am I going to emulate him and learn a poem every day? Not a chance. But those of us who are daunted by the task Nicholas has set himself would gain a lot from just *reading* a poem a day, and maybe learning one a week, or one a month. I think I'll begin with those I half know already, such as The Charge of the Light Brigade.

> Har fleag har fleag har fleag onward
> Into the er rode the 600

That's Molesworth's attempt. At least I can do better than him.

(Wendy Cope's books of poetry include Making Cocoa for Kingsley Amis *and* Serious Concerns*, published by Faber and Faber.)*

Introduction

Nicholas Albery, editor

To explain how this *Poem for the Day* anthology came about:

I have been trying to learn a poem a day for the last couple of years, ever since I found myself without a newspaper on the tube, the Monday after returning from honeymoon. Sitting opposite the 'Poem on the Underground' card, with nothing better to do, I learnt the delightful Tennyson poem from 'The Princess', 'Now sleeps the crimson petal, now the white'. I enjoyed reciting this to my wife later, and since then I have learnt or relearnt a poem each morning, except for the days when I am deprived of this daily pleasure through pressure of work or pressure of holidays. I use poetry learning as a way of livening up my exercises. I dance around the bedroom to quiet music, learning the day's poem as I dance – it takes between five minutes and an hour, depending on the poem, and I find it a wonderful form of meditation for a speedy Westerner like me. Rather than sitting cross-legged, I am occupying my body with dancing and my brain with poetry, allowing a part of me to enjoy a timeless and inspired zone.

The snag with my middle-aged brain is that, within days, I have forgotten the poem that I had been able to recite faultlessly. I have tried reading the poems onto tapes, repeating each verse as I go, but find that I rarely have time to listen to them. So the idea of the *Poem for the Day* anthology is that by coming back to each poem once a year, the relearning will be easier and quicker each time and eventually all 366 will be recitable at will. Long poems can be learnt bit by bit, year by year. At the very least, the reader may like to learn the poem on his or her birthday, or to see what other poetry-related events happened on that day.

My criteria for choosing a poem have been simple: Did I feel attracted to learning it by heart? Did it inspire or intrigue me? Was it short enough? Did I agree, at least in certain moods, with its sentiments? Did it have rhyme, rhythm or at least resonance? Despite having built up an impressive library of poetry, I needed help, so I am grateful to all the poets, friends and relatives who sent me their favourite poems.

Many poets, including Ted Hughes, Carol Ann Duffy, Richard Wilbur, Anne Ridler, X. J. Kennedy, Robert Creeley, Denise Levertov, Charles Causley, Philip Gross, Sharon Olds, Gavin Ewart, E. J. Scovell, Adam Thorpe, Theo Dorgan, Dick Davis and Wendy Cope, kindly added comments to their poems, which we have placed in the commentary section at the bottom of each page. I am also grateful to Peter Ratcliffe and my other colleagues for assistance with the lay-out and lasersetting, with fitting the poems to their seasons and anniversaries and with compiling the notes.

This collection includes many of the great classics, although well over half the book is given over to this century's most learnable poetry. The statistics as to contents are as follows: There are 366 poems by 195 poets, 64% of whom are from this century, 27% of this century's poets in the book are women (rising to 37% if only those poets who are alive today are included), 30% of this century's poets in the book are American, and a total of 13 other countries make guest appearances, in translation where necessary. Biographical or other details have been added to each page, to encourage readers to delve more deeply into the works of poets who intrigue them.

But why bother to learn poems?

When I look back at everything that I studied at school, nothing fills me with as much pleasure as remembering the few poems I learnt there. My hope is that schools will use this book to encourage children (without any obligation being involved) to learn poems, and that schools will organise sponsored poetry recital events. One school raised over £2,000 for charity by organising a poetry week, where pupils and staff were sponsored to recite poems learnt by heart (see the back of this book for ideas on organising such events). The added advantage is that any child who knows a number of poems by heart will begin to feel at ease with English literature and should cope better with the English exams.

I wish that poetry learning were part of university English courses too. How dispiriting and arrogant it felt to me spending those years writing critical essays about poets and authors I couldn't even begin to emulate. It put me off literature for many years. Whereas if the course had focused on learning poetry and writing poetry and stories, rather than on studying what the critics had to say, what a joy it might have been. Now I find that immersing myself in poetry once again has encouraged me to start writing poems of my own.

For me, learning poetry has been a way of getting to know a poem in depth and almost automatically leads to the development of a critical appreciation. For instance, I find that the lines that are hardest to learn often turn out to be those where the poet's choice of words seems sloppy or the construction too contrived. Besides exercising the brain, I find that learning poetry elevates the spirit. It helps me to take delight in nature, it reaffirms my belief in the soul and love and all the important aspects of life, and it helps me to contemplate my own mortality. Nor am I surprised by Dr Robin Philipp's research at Bristol University, indicating that poetry reading is as good a cure for depression as pills.

All royalties from this book are going to the educational charity The Natural Death Centre, which assists families who are looking after a dying person at home or who are trying to arrange a funeral, with or without using undertakers. I am grateful to all the poets and copyright holders who have allowed their work to be used, and to Wendy Cope for all her help.

My vision is of a world swept with the same poetry-learning fever as has infected me, with a daily poem on radio and in the popular press, and with sponsored recital events and prizes. To that end, *Poem for the Day* organises a Poetry Marathon in London on the second Sunday in October each year – a chance to raise money for the charity of your choice by reciting your favourite poems (again, see the back of the book for further details). So, get in to training for this event. The brain needs exercising as much as the body. Happy learning! May this collection bring you as much enjoyment as it has brought me. If books were to be rated by the hours of pleasure they give, divided by the price, this book, even if I hadn't edited it, would be in my top ten – and I hope that soon it will be in yours too.

January 1

- A Midsummer Night's Dream *performed at Hampton Court January 1st 1603*
- *William Wycherley, playwright and poet, was imprisoned in the Fleet prison until King James II paid his debts, and died January 1st 1716*
- *In 1782 Burns was at a New Year carousal, when the shop burnt down, ruining his business prospects*
- *Poet Arthur Hugh Clough born in Liverpool January 1st 1819*

New Every Morning

Every day is a fresh beginning,
Listen my soul to the glad refrain.
And, spite of old sorrows
And older sinning,
Troubles forecasted
And possible pain,
Take heart with the day and begin again.

Susan Coolidge
(January 29th 1835 – April 9th 1905)

This poem has been used in a UK hospice to bring comfort to patients. Susan Coolidge (the pseudonym of Sarah Chauncey Woolsey) was born in Cleveland, Ohio, in January 1835. She composed three volumes of verse, wrote the *Katy* books and other unsentimental stories in a natural style for girls, and edited the letters of Jane Austen and Fanny Burney.

- Roman poet Ovid died in banishment January 2nd 17AD
- George Gordon, Lord Byron, married Annabella Milbanke,
  January 2nd 1815
- American author and poet Robert Nathan born January 2nd 1894
- Christina Rossetti, who died of cancer after a long illness, was buried
  at Highgate cemetery January 2nd 1895
- Cornwall-based poet and novelist Peter Redgrove born January 2nd 1932

Bloody Men

Bloody men are like bloody buses –
You wait for about a year
And as soon as one approaches your stop
Two or three others appear.

You look at them flashing their indicators,
Offering you a ride.
You're trying to read the destinations,
You haven't much time to decide.

If you make a mistake, there is no turning back.
Jump off, and you'll stand there and gaze
While the cars and the taxis and lorries go by
And the minutes, the hours, the days.

Wendy Cope
(July 21st 1945 –)

Wendy Cope notes: "When I wrote this, in 1987, I must already have been a bit short-sighted. Nowadays, if I'm wearing glasses, I have no difficulty in reading the destination on buses."

January 3

• Poet Padraic Fallon was born in Athenry, County Galway, January 3rd 1905
• On this day in 1924 Hardy thanked Charlotte Mew for her acknowledgement of his help in getting her a Civil List Pension
• Poet Anne Stevenson born of American parents in Cambridge, England, January 3rd 1933. Stevenson founded the Poetry Bookshop in Hay-on-Wye

Infant Joy

'I have no name:
'I am but two days old.'
What shall I call thee?
'I happy am,
'Joy is my name.'
Sweet joy befall thee!

Pretty joy!
Sweet joy but two days old,
Sweet joy I call thee:
Thou dost smile,
I sing the while,
Sweet joy befall thee!

William Blake
(November 28th 1757 – August 12th 1827)

There are children in Shakespeare and there were nursery rhymers aplenty, but Blake was the first poet to speak to and for small children in their own right, in their condition of innocence.

• On January 4th 1788, Burns met for first time Mrs M'Lehose, cousin of Lord Crag – in their letters Burns became 'Sylvander', she his 'Clarinda'
• A. E. Coppard, prize athlete, country-life writer and poet, born January 4th 1878, son of a tailor
• T. S. Eliot died January 4th 1965

From Preludes

1

The winter evening settles down
With smells of steaks in passageways.
Six o'clock.
The burnt-out ends of smoky days.
And now a gusty shower wraps
The grimy scraps
Of withered leaves about your feet
And newspapers from vacant lots;
The showers beat
On broken blinds and chimney-pots,
And at the corner of the street
A lonely cab-horse steams and stamps.
And then the lighting of the lamps.

T. S. Eliot
(September 26th 1888 – January 4th 1965)

Eliot insisted that "The essential advantage for a poet is not to have a beautiful world with which to deal; it is to be able to see beneath both beauty and ugliness; to see the boredom, and the horror, and the glory."

'Preludes' was the first of Eliot's poetry to be published – by Wyndham Lewis in the magazine *Blast* in July 1915. The world was opening up to Eliot: in June he had married Vivien Haigh-Wood, whom he had met in Oxford. Bertrand Russell described her as "light, a little vulgar, adventurous". Aldous Huxley argued that it was "almost entirely a sexual nexus" between her and Eliot: "one sees it in the way he looks at her ... she's an incarnate provocation."

January 5

• Poet W. D. Snodgrass, *author of the epic verse cycle* The Fuerhrer Bunker, *born in Wilkinsburg, Pennsylvania, January 5th 1926*

Poet-tree

i fear that i shall never make
a poem slippier than a snake
or oozing with as fine a juice
as runs in girls or even spruce
no i wont make not now nor later
pnomes as luverlee as pertaters
trees is made by fauns or satyrs
but only taters make pertaters
& trees is grown by sun from sod
& so are the sods who need a god
but poettrees lack any clue
they just need me   & maybe you

Earle Birney
(May 13th 1904 –)

This poem is a pastiche of the six-stanza poem 'Trees' by Joyce Kilmer, published in 1914, which starts "I think that I shall never see / A poem lovely as a tree" and which ends "Poems are made by fools like me, / But only God can make a tree."

Earle Birney grew up in Calgary and on a farm in British Columbia. In the 1930s he had to leave the States because of his involvement in Trotskyist causes. He served in the Canadian Army from 1942 to 1945, and was an active writer until a severe heart attack in 1980. His poetry collections include *Pnomes*, and *Jukollages and Other Stanzas*, his memoirs are entitled *Child Addict in Alberta* and he edited *Twentieth Century Canadian Poetry*.

• *Chicago writer and colloquial poet Carl Sandburg born January 6th 1878*
• *Poet P. J. Kavanagh born in Worthing January 6th 1931*

January 6

From Twelfth Night
Sweet-and-Twenty

O mistress mine, where are you roaming?
   O, stay and hear! your true love's coming,
   That can sing both high and low:
Trip no further, pretty sweeting;
Journeys end in lovers meeting,
   Every wise man's son doth know.
   What is love? 'tis not hereafter;
Present mirth hath present laughter;
   What's to come is still unsure:
In delay there lies no plenty;
Then come kiss me, sweet-and-twenty!
   Youth's a stuff will not endure.

William Shakespeare
(April 23rd 1564 – April 23rd 1616)

On this day in 1601 *Twelfth Night* was entered on the Stationers Register.

This song is sung by the clown Feste in *Twelfth Night*, to two of the comic characters, Andrew Aguecheek and Sir Toby Belch. Feste offers a love song, or a song of good life. Sir Toby replies, "A love song, a love song," and Andrew agrees, saying, "Ay, ay. I care not for good life."

Also on January 6th, in 1586, John Shakespeare, William's father, was deprived of his alderman's gown, as a consequence of his long absence from Stratford-on-Avon council meetings.

January 7

• On this day in 1807, Wordsworth completed reading 'The Prelude' to Coleridge, who in response penned his poem 'To Wordsworth'
• Catholic poet and French patriot Charles Péguy born the son of a peasant, January 7th 1873
• John Berryman committed suicide January 7th 1972 by jumping off a bridge over the Mississippi

Sonnet 115

All we were going strong last night this time,
the *mots* were flying & the frozen daiquiris
were downing, supine on the floor lay Lise
listening to Schubert grievous & sublime,
my head was frantic with a following rime:
it was a good evening, an evening to please,
I kissed her in the kitchen—ecstasies—
among so much good we tamped down the crime.

The weather's changing. This morning was cold,
as I made for the grove, without expectation,
some hundred Sonnets in my pocket, old,
to read her if she came. Presently the sun
yellowed the pines & my lady came not
in blue jeans & a sweater. I sat down & wrote.

John Berryman
(October 25th 1914 – January 7th 1972)

When Berryman was still a child, his father died of gunshot wounds, probably by suicide. Berryman won a scholarship to Cambridge University. At Princeton University, where he was a Creative Writing Fellow from 1943 to 1944, he completed many of the poems later published as *Berryman's Sonnets*. In *Dream Songs* (1969) he wrote: "I'm cross with God who has wrecked this generation ... he gorged on Sylvia Plath. That was a first rate haul. He left alive fools I could number with a kitchen knife." His novel *Recovery* admitted his struggle with alcoholism. He married three times.

• French poet Paul Verlaine, whose stormy affair with Rimbaud led to two years' imprisonment for immorality, died in poverty January 8th 1895
• Harold Monro opened The Poetry Bookshop (where Robert Frost and Ezra Pound met for the first time) January 8th 1913
• Poet and artist Charles Tomlinson born January 8th 1927
• Kenneth Patchen, the American poet who focused on injustice, died January 8th 1972

Lullaby

Lay your sleeping head, my love,
Human on my faithless arm;
Time and fevers burn away
Individual beauty from
Thoughtful children, and the grave
Proves the child ephemeral:
But in my arms till break of day
Let the living creature lie,
Mortal, guilty, but to me
The entirely beautiful.

Soul and body have no bounds:
To lovers as they lie upon
Her tolerant enchanted slope
In their ordinary swoon,
Grave the vision Venus sends
Of supernatural sympathy,
Universal love and hope;
While an abstract insight wakes
Among the glaciers and the rocks
The hermit's sensual ecstasy.

Certainty, fidelity
On the stroke of midnight pass
Like vibrations of a bell,
And fashionable madmen raise
Their pedantic boring cry:
Every farthing of the cost,
All the dreaded cards foretell,
Shall be paid, but from this night
Not a whisper, not a thought,
Not a kiss nor look be lost.

Beauty, midnight, vision dies:
Let the winds of dawn that blow
Softly round your dreaming head
Such a day of sweetness show
Eye and knocking heart may bless,
Find the mortal world enough;
Noons of dryness see you fed
By the involuntary powers,
Nights of insult let you pass
Watched by every human love.

W. H. Auden
(February 21st 1907 –
September 29th 1973)

On this day in 1937, Auden, soon to be leaving for Spain, met Benjamin Britten to say goodbye. Auden wrote out the poems 'Lullaby' and 'Danse Macabre' on the backs of two musical scores which Britten had brought with him. The gesture affected Britten strongly and he commented in his diary: "It is terribly sad and I feel ghastly about it … he gives me two grand poems – a lullaby, and a big, simple, folksy Farewell – that is overwhelmingly tragic and moving. I've lots to do with them."

January 9

• Connecticut-based poet (and translator of Apollinaire) William
Meredith – two of whose key themes have been loneliness and the
threat of death – was born January 9th 1919
• Scottish poet William Sydney Graham died January 9th 1986

Accidents of Birth

*Je vois les effroyables espaces de l'Univers qui m'enferment, et je me trouve attaché à un coin de cette vaste étendue,
sans savoir pourquoi je suis plutôt en ce lieu qu'en un autre, ni pourquoi ce peu de temps qui m'est donné à vivre
m'est assigné à ce point plutôt qu'à un autre de toute l'éternité qui m'a précédé, et de toute qui me suive* (Pensées
sur la Religion, *Pascal*). [1]

*The approach of a man's life out of the past is history, and the approach of time out of the future is mystery. Their
meeting is the present, and it is consciousness, the only time life is alive. The endless wonder of this meeting is what
causes the mind, in its inward liberty of a frozen morning, to turn back and question and remember. The world is
full of places. Why is it that I am here?* (The Long-Legged House, *Wendell Berry*).

Spared by a car- or airplane-crash or
cured of malignancy, people look
around with new eyes at a newly
praiseworthy world, blinking eyes like these.

For I've been brought back again from the
fine silt, the mud where our atoms lie
down for long naps. And I've also been
pardoned miraculously for years
by the lava of chance which runs down
the world's gullies, silting us back.
Here I am, brought back, set up, not yet
happened away.

        But it's not this random
life only, throwing its sensual
astonishments upside down on
the bloody membranes behind my eyeballs,
not just me being here again, old
needer, looking for someone to need,
but you, up from the clay yourself,
as luck would have it, and inching
over the same little segment of earth-
ball, in the same little eon, to
meet in a room, alive in our skins,
and the whole galaxy gaping there
and the centuries whining like gnats—
you, to teach me to see it, to see
it with you, and to offer somebody
uncomprehending, impudent thanks.

William Meredith
(January 9th 1919 –)

1. I see the terrifying spaces of the universe that enclose me, and I find myself attached to a corner of
this vast expanse, without knowing why I am more in this place than in another, nor why this little time
that is given me to live is assigned me at this point more than another out of all the eternity that has
preceded me and out of all that will follow me (*Thoughts on Religion*, Pascal).

- *Elizabeth Barrett and Robert Browning began a courtship by correspondence January 10th 1845 [1]*
- *Isolationist poet Robinson Jeffers, who lived at Carmel, California, in seclusion with his wife Una, was born January 10th 1887*
- *Poet Philip Levine born in Detroit January 10th 1928*
- *Anti-academic poet and Black Mountain College director Charles Olson died January 10th 1970*

Meeting At Night

The grey sea and the long black land;
And the yellow half-moon large and low;
And the startled little waves that leap
In fiery ringlets from their sleep,
As I gain the cove with pushing prow,
And quench its speed i' the slushy sand.

Then a mile of warm sea-scented beach;
Three fields to cross till a farm appears;
A tap at the pane, the quick sharp scratch
And blue spurt of a lighted match,
And a voice less loud, thro' its joys and fears,
Than the two hearts beating each to each!

Robert Browning
(May 7th 1812 – December 12th 1889)

On October 27th 1845, Elizabeth Barrrett saw 'Meeting at Night' in printer's proof and wrote to Robert Browning: "You throw largesses out on all sides without counting the cost: how beautiful."

1. Elizabeth Barrett was a 39 year old invalid confined by illness and a possessive father to the family house in Wimpole Street when Robert Browning first contacted her. Browning had read her poem 'Lady Geraldine's Courtship' containing a brief tribute to the humanity of his poetry and was moved to respond.

His letter begins "I love your verses with all my heart, dear Miss Barrett, – and this is no off-hand complimentary letter that I shall write". For a page or so the critical compliments continue until, quite suddenly, he insists "I do, as I say, love these books with all my heart – and I love you too".

On May 20th 1845 she agreed to allow him to visit her in her room, and on September 12th 1846 they were married secretly at St Marylebone Church, leaving almost immediately for the milder climate and cheaper living in Italy. Hearing news of the marriage, Wordsworth is reported to have commented "Well, I hope they understand one another – nobody else would."

January 11

• *William Blake acquitted of sedition and assault January 11th 1804*
• *Shelley's sonnet 'Ozymandias' first published January 11th 1818*
• *Thomas Hardy died January 11th 1928*
• *Arthur Guiterman, New York-based comic versifier, died January 11th 1943*

The Voice

Woman much missed, how you call to me, call to me,
Saying that now you are not as you were
When you had changed from the one who was all to me,
But as at first, when our day was fair.

Can it be you that I hear? Let me view you, then,
Standing as when I drew near to the town
Where you would wait for me: yes, as I knew you then,
Even to the original air-blue gown!

Or is it only the breeze, in its listlessness
Travelling across the wet mead to me here,
You being ever dissolved to wan wistlessness,
Heard no more again far or near?

Thus I; faltering forward,
Leaves around me falling,
Wind oozing thin through the thorn from norward,
And the woman calling.

Thomas Hardy
(June 2nd 1840 – January 11th 1928)

Hardy's strained marriage to his first wife Emma Gifford nevertheless resulted in moving love poetry after her death in 1912. At his own death in 1928, his heart was buried with Emma in Dorset and his ashes were placed in Westminster Abbey next to those of Charles Dickens.

• *Allegra, the illegitimate daughter of Lord Byron and Claire Clairmont (who lived with Shelley and his wife Mary), was born in Bath on January 17th 1817*

January 12

Don't Be Literary, Darling

Don't be literary, darling, don't be literary
If you're James in the morning you're Hemingway in bed
Don't talk of yourself in the style of your own obituary –
For who cares what they say of you after you're dead.

Don't be always a thought ahead and a move behind
Like a general reconnoitring dangerous ground,
This is a game it's much better to enter blind
And the one who wins is the one who is caught and bound.

If you can't be straight then just say nothing instead.
I'll know what you mean much better than if it was said.

Sasha Moorsom
(January 25th 1931 – June 22nd 1993)

Sasha Moorsom was one of the BBC's first woman producers. Encouraged by Dylan Thomas, she brought the poems of Ted Hughes, Philip Larkin and her friend Thom Gunn to a radio audience while they were still relatively unknown. The author of two novels, she also edited the education magazine *Where?* and had a regular column in the *The Listener*. Married to Michael Young (see his poem 'The Metronomic Moon' in this present volume), she became involved with many of his projects, including the Open College of the Arts and the Consumer's Association. As well as being a poet, she was a painter, photographer, sculptor and talented organiser. Her poems are published for the first time, jointly with Michael Young's, by Carcanet, in November 1994, entitled *Your Head in Mine*.

January 13

My life closed twice before its close

My life closed twice before its close –
It yet remains to see
If Immortality unveil
A third event to me

So huge, so hopeless to conceive
As these that twice befell.
Parting is all we know of heaven,
And all we need of hell.

Emily Dickinson
(December 10th 1830 – May 15th 1886)

On this day in 1854, Emily Dickinson wrote from Amherst to the Revd. Edward Everett Hale: "You were the Pastor of B. F. Newton, ... and I have often hoped to know if his last hours were cheerful, and if he was willing to die ... Mr Newton was with my Father two years ... [He] became to me a gentle, yet grave Preceptor, teaching me what to read, what authors to admire, what was most great or beautiful in nature, and that sublime lesson, a faith in things unseen, and in a life again .... [He] was an elder brother, loved indeed very much, and mourned and remembered."

Benjamin Newton had been a law student with her father, and she had been 18 when he left. He married and died not long after, in 1853. This has been conjectured to be the first 'parting' to which Emily refers in this poem. The second could be the loss of her much loved spiritual adviser, Revd. Charles Wadsworth, who left New York for California in 1862. As she put it in a letter to Thomas Wentworth Higginson, written when she was 32:

"When a little girl, I had a friend who taught me Immortality; but venturing too near, himself, he never returned. Soon after my tutor died, and for several years, my lexicon was my only companion. Then I found one more, but he was not contented I be his scholar, so he left the land."

- *Pastor Martin Niemöller born in Lippstadt, Westphalia, January 14th 1892*
- *Lewis Caroll (the pseudonym of mathematician Charles Dodgson), nonsense versifier and author of* Alice's Adventures in Wonderland, *died January 14th 1898*

First They Came for the Jews

First they came for the Jews
and I did not speak out –
because I was not a Jew.
Then they came for the communists
and I did not speak out –
because I was not a communist.
Then they came for the trade unionists
and I did not speak out –
because I was not a trade unionist.
Then they came for me –
and there was no one left
to speak out for me.

Pastor Niemöller
(January 14th 1892 – March 6th 1984)

German Lutheran pastor Martin Niemöller was an ace submarine commander in World War I and offered to serve in the German navy in World War II, despite his outspoken opposition to Hitler. In retaliation for his preaching against the Führer, his house was ransacked by the Gestapo and he was imprisoned for seven years in Sachsenhausen and Dachau concentration camps. His memoirs were entitled *Vom U-Boot zur Kanzel* ('From U-Boat to the Pulpit').

January 15

• Osip Mandelstam, "the greatest Russian poet of the century", born
into a Jewish leather family January 15th 1891. A poem
denouncing Stalin led to imprisonment, and he later died on the
way to the camps
• New Zealand poet Mary Ursula Bethell died January 15th 1945

The Second Coming

Turning and turning in the widening gyre
The falcon cannot hear the falconer;
Things fall apart; the centre cannot hold;
Mere anarchy is loosed upon the world,
The blood-dimmed tide is loosed, and everywhere
The ceremony of innocence is drowned;
The best lack all conviction, while the worst
Are full of passionate intensity.

Surely some revelation is at hand;
Surely the Second Coming is at hand.
The Second Coming! Hardly are those words out
When a vast image out of *Spiritus Mundi*
Troubles my sight: somewhere in sands of the desert
A shape with lion body and the head of a man,
A gaze blank and pitiless as the sun,
Is moving its slow thighs, while all about it
Reel shadows of the indignant desert birds.
The darkness drops again; but now I know
That twenty centuries of stony sleep
Were vexed to nightmare by a rocking cradle,
And what rough beast, its hour come round at last,
Slouches towards Bethlehem to be born?

William Butler Yeats
(June 13th 1865 – January 28th 1939)

The poem was written in January 1919, no doubt with the Russian revolution and the troubles in Ireland in mind. Yeats, in annotating this poem, wrote: "All our scientific, democratic, fact-accumulating, heterogeneous civilisation belongs to the outward gyre [spiral revolution] and prepares not the continuance of itself but the revelation as in a lightning flash, though in a flash that will not strike only in one place, and will for a time be constantly repeated, of the civilisation that must slowly take its place." Concerning Marxism, Yeats wrote to George Russell: "I consider the Marxian criterion of values as in this age the spear-head of materialism and leading to inevitable murder." And of the poem's beast he commented in his introduction to *The Resurrection:* "I begin to imagine, as always at my left side just out of the range of sight, a brazen winged beast that I associated with laughing, ecstatic destruction."

- *Edmund Spenser died January 16th 1599*
- *Canadian poet Robert W. Service born in Preston January 16th 1874*
- *Laura Riding born in New York January 16th 1901*
- *Anthony Hecht born in New York January 16th 1923*
- *Hardy was buried in Westminster Abbey January 16th 1928, with Kipling and Housman among the pall-bearers*
- *Irish poet Aidan Carl Mathews born January 16th 1956*
- *Translator and lyric poet Robert Fitzgerald died January 16th 1985*

My Love Is Like to Ice

My love is like to ice, and I to fire:
How comes it then that this her cold so great
Is not dissolved through my so hot desire,
But harder grows the more I her entreat?
Or how comes it that my exceeding heat
Is not allayed by her heart-frozen cold,
But that I burn much more in boiling sweat,
And feel my flames augmented manifold?
What more miraculous thing may be told,
That fire, which all things melts, should harden ice,
And ice, which is congealed with senseless cold,
Should kindle fire by wonderful device?
Such is the power of love in gentle mind,
That it can alter all the course of kind.

Edmund Spenser
(c. 1552 – January 16th 1599)

Spenser was the son of a clothmaker in East Smithfield, and became a 'sizar' or poor scholar at Pembroke Hall, Cambridge. He entered the household of the Earl of Leicester in 1579 and got to know Sir Philip Sidney. In return for crushing rebellion and settling Munster, he acquired Kilcolman Castle in County Cork. Sir Walter Raleigh visited him there and persuaded him to take the first three books of his epic poem *Faerie Queene* to Court. Spenser's previous published attack on Queen Elizabeth's match with the Duc d'Alençon helped prevent preferment, however (although he secured a royal pension), and he returned to his Irish 'exile'. A rebellion destroyed his home and he fled with his second wife and his children to London, where he died in poverty the following year and was buried in Westminster Abbey.

January 17

- *Sir Thomas Wyatt imprisoned in Tower of London, January 17th 1541, accused of misconduct in his role as ambassador to Charles V*
- *On this day in 1610, poet Thomas Lodge wrote to the British ambassador in Paris to thank him for enabling him to return to England (he had fled under suspicion as a Roman Catholic)*
- *Kansas-raised poet William Stafford born January 17th 1914*

I Am Not I

I am not I.
          I am this one
Walking beside me whom I do not see,
Whom at times I manage to visit,
And at other times I forget.
The one who remains silent when I talk,
The one who forgives, sweet, when I hate,
The one who takes a walk when I am indoors,
The one who will remain standing when I die.

Juan Ramón Jiménez
(December 24th 1881 – May 29th 1958)
translated by Robert Bly
(December 23rd 1926 –)

Jiménez was born in Moguer, Huelva, the setting for his story of the young poet and his donkey, *Platero y Yo* (1914). Giving up the law, he moved to Madrid. When the Civil War started he remained in the capital for a time, caring for the wounded and collecting children from the ruined streets. He moved to Havana and then to Florida, losing many of his manuscripts in the process. Influenced by Verlaine in his youth, he in turn influenced Lorca and other Spanish poets. He was awarded the Nobel prize for literature in 1957, the year before his death.

• A. A. Milne, *author of* Winnie-the-Pooh, *born January 18th 1882*
• *Poet and biographer Jon Stallworthy born in London January 18th 1935*
• *Rudyard Kipling married Carrie Balestier on this day in 1891 and died on this day in 1936* [1]

January 18

Gertrude's Prayer

That which is marred at birth Time shall not mend,
    Nor water out of bitter well make clean;
All evil thing returneth at the end,
    Or elseway walketh in our blood unseen.
Whereby the more is sorrow in certaine—
Dayspring mishandled cometh not againe.

To-bruizèd be that slender, sterting spray
    Out of the oake's rind that should betide
A branch of girt and goodliness, straightway
    Her spring is turnèd on herself, and wried
And knotted like some gall or veiney wen.—
Dayspring mishandled cometh not agen.

Noontide repayeth never morning-bliss—
    Sith noon to morn is incomparable;
And, so it be our dawning goth amiss,
    None other after-hour serveth well.
Ah! Jesu-Moder, pitie my oe paine—
Dayspring mishandled[2] cometh not againe!

Rudyard Kipling
(December 30th 1865 – January 18th 1936)

G. M. Young wrote: "Kipling, though short, was lithe and slim, with beautifully balanced movements. His most arresting feature was his heavy eyebrows, which shot up and down with his talk: under them twinkled bright blue eyes."

1. Kipling made clear his attitude to death in a letter to his aunt Edith MacDonald on January 2nd 1936: "He who put us in this life does not abandon His work for any reason or default at the end of it. That is all I have come to learn out of my life. So there is no fear."
2. *Dayspring Mishandled* is the title of a late short story by Kipling in which one theme is a character's mishandling of the dawning of inspiration within him.

January 19

• Edgar Allan Poe born January 19th 1809 while his travelling-actor parents were on the road. Three years later he was orphaned
• Ex-performance poet George MacBeth born in Lanarkshire January 19th 1932

From The Triumph of Charis

Have you seen but a bright lily grow,
  Before rude hands have touched it?
Ha' you marked but the fall o' the snow
  Before the soil hath smutched it?
Ha' you felt the wool o' the beaver?
    Or swan's down ever?
Or have smelt o' the bud o' the brier?
    Or the nard[1] in the fire?
Or have tasted the bag o' the bee?
O so white, O so soft, O so sweet is she!

Ben Jonson
(probably June 11th 1572 – August 6th 1637)

On this day in 1619 Ben Jonson left the home of William Drummond of Hawthornden after some weeks with him, towards the end of his Scottish tour, which began in June 1618. Drummond's notes of their talks are a main source of biographical information on Jonson.

Also on this day, in 1623, Ben Jonson's piece *Time Vindicated to Himselfe and to his Honors* was performed.

Ben Jonson was born in Westminster and brought up by his stepfather, a bricklayer, as his own father, who had been a minister, died a month before the birth. Having fought for the Dutch against the Spanish, killing an enemy champion in single combat, Jonson became an actor, then a playwright, and was an admiring friend of Shakespeare's ("Sweet swan of Avon ... The applause, delight, the wonder of our stage").

Jonson killed an actor in a duel in 1598, escaping the gallows by pleading benefit of clergy. In 1605 he was imprisoned and in danger of having his nose and ears split for his share in a comedy that was derogatory to the Scots. In 1616 James I appointed him as in effect the first Poet Laureate, with the grant of a royal pension. Jonson became London's "literary dictator", with younger writers in his "tribe" calling themselves the "sons of Ben".

1. spikenard – an aromatic plant.

• *John Ruskin, author, art critic and poet, died January 20th 1900. His last regret, having founded a guild, school and college, was not having rid himself of all his wealth before his death*

From Love's Labour's Lost
Act V Scene ii

When icicles hang by the wall,
　And Dick the shepherd blows his nail[1],
And Tom bears logs into the hall,
　And milk comes frozen home in pail,
When blood is nipped and ways be foul,
Then nightly sings the staring owl,
　　　Tu-whit,
Tu-who! a merry note,
While greasy Joan doth keel the pot.

When all aloud the wind doth blow,
　And coughing drowns the parson's saw,
And bird sits brooding in the snow,
　And Marian's nose looks red and raw,
When roasted crabs hiss in the bowl,
Then nightly sings the staring owl,
　　　Tu-whit,
Tu-who! a merry note,
While greasy Joan doth keel the pot.

William Shakespeare
(April 23rd 1564 – April 23rd 1616)

Coming as it does at the very end of the play, this simple rustic song contrasts sharply with the cleverness and pedantry which permeate *Love's Labour's Lost*. Granville-Barker remarked: "The play finishes, as a play of merry-making should, with everyone ranged for our last look at them."

1. blowing on his nails to warm his hands, a phrase asssociated with enforced idleness during cold spells.

January 21

• Henry Howard, Earl of Surrey, executed at Tower Hill on January 21st 1547
• Richard P. Blackmur, American poet and Princeton professor, born January 21st 1904

Giving Up Smoking

There's not a Shakespeare sonnet
Or a Beethoven quartet
That's easier to like than you
Or harder to forget.

You think that sounds extravagant?
I haven't finished yet –
I like you more than I would like
To have a cigarette.

Wendy Cope
(July 21st 1945 –)

"I gave up smoking on 21st January 1985 and wrote this a couple of weeks later," Wendy Cope comments, adding: "People who have never been addicted to nicotine don't understand what an intense love poem it is."

28

- *Byron born in London January 22nd 1788*
- *On this day in 1805, William Blake offered his patron William Hayley to do engravings for the latter's Ballads: "I consider myself as only put in trust with this work, and that the copyright is for ever yours," he told Hayley. In the end it was agreed he should receive 20 guineas each for five plates*

The Divine Image

To Mercy, Pity, Peace, and Love
All pray in their distress;
And to these virtues of delight
Return their thankfulness.

For Mercy, Pity, Peace, and Love
Is God, our father dear,
And Mercy, Pity, Peace, and Love
Is Man, his child and care.

For Mercy has a human heart,
Pity a human face,
And Love, the human form divine,
And Peace, the human dress.

Then every man, of every clime,
That prays in his distress,
Prays to the human form divine,
Love, Mercy, Pity, Peace.

And all must love the human form,
In heathen, Turk, or Jew;
Where Mercy, Love, & Pity dwell
There God is dwelling too.

William Blake
(November 28th 1757 – August 12th 1827)

As a young man Blake was greatly influenced by the work of Emmanuel Swedenborg – though disillusionment crept in later on in life. A central tenet of Swedenborg's teaching argued that, created in God's image, humans are in their true nature divine. Blake accepted this as one of his fundamental beliefs.

Thanks to Isaac Watts, the Wesleys and others, the eighteenth century was the great age of the hymn. It was part of popular culture in a sense we have since lost. Blake, a skilled self-employed artisan, was part of that culture, although he was not himself a church-goer. 'The Divine Image' falls effortlessly into that mould. It is used in a certain church hymnary today with the last verse carefully excised! Blake also wrote its contrary as a 'Song of Experience', but it is so grim that it was never published in his own lifetime. The first two lines read:

> Cruelty has a Human Heart,
> And Jealousy a Human Face....

January 23

• Katharine Tynan born January 23rd 1861
• Walt Whitman left partially paralysed by a stroke on January
  23rd 1873, at Camden, New Jersey, 19 years before his death
• Poet Louis Zukofsky born in New York January 23rd 1904
• Poet and ex-boxer Vernon Scannell born in Lincolnshire January
  23rd 1922
• West Indian poet and playwright Derek Walcott born in St Lucia
  January 23rd 1930

An Irish Airman Forsees His Death

I know that I shall meet my fate
Somewhere among the clouds above;
Those that I fight I do not hate,
Those that I guard I do not love;
My country is Kiltartan Cross,
My countrymen Kiltartan's poor,
No likely end could bring them loss
Or leave them happier than before.
Nor law, nor duty bade me fight,
Nor public men, nor cheering crowds,
A lonely impulse of delight
Drove to this tumult in the clouds;
I balanced all, brought all to mind,
The years to come seemed waste of breath,
A waste of breath the years behind
In balance with this life, this death.

William Butler Yeats
(June 13th 1865 – January 28th 1939)

The Irish airman in this poem was Robert Gregory, who was killed in action in Italy on January 23rd 1918 and buried in the Pavoda main cemetery. He was the son of Sir William and Lady Gregory, and had designed the sets of early Abbey Theatre productions. Yeats thought of him as a Renaissance man: "painter, classical scholar, scholar in painting and in modern literature, boxer, horseman, airman"; and after Gregory's death he commented: "Major Gregory [said] ... that the months since he joined the Army had been the happiest of his life. I think this brought him peace of mind ... from his constant struggle to resist those other gifts that brought him ease and friendship. Leading his squadron in France or in Italy, mind and hand were at one, will and desire." Yeats wrote this poem in 1918.

• William Congreve, poet and plawright who wrote Love for Love,
  born in Bardsey near Leeds January 24th 1670
• Dylan Thomas' dramatic poem 'Under Milk Wood' broadcast
  19 weeks after his death, on January 24th 1954

Story of a Hotel Room

Thinking we were safe—insanity!
We went in to make love. All the same
Idiots to trust the little hotel bedroom.
Then in the gloom . . .
... And who does not know that pair of shutters
With the awkward hook on them
All screeching whispers? Very well then, in the gloom
We set about acquiring one another
Urgently! But on a temporary basis
Only as guests—just guests of one another's senses.

But idiots to feel so safe you hold back nothing
Because the bed of cold, electric linen
Happens to be illicit. . . .
To make love as well as that is ruinous.
Londoner, Parisian, someone should have warned us
That without permanent intentions
You have absolutely no protection
—If the act is clean, authentic, sumptuous,
The concurring deep love of the heart
Follows the naked work, profoundly moved by it.

Rosemary Tonks
(1932 –)

Rosemary Tonks has apparently ceased to publish since converting to Christianity in the 1970s. Her published work includes poetry volumes such as *Notes on Cafés and Bedrooms* (1963), novels such as *Businessmen as Lovers*, and writings for children such as *On Wooden Wings*. She was expelled from Wentworth School at 16 and married at 19.

January 25

• Donne was ordained by the Bishop of London in 1615, probably on January 25th
• Robert Burns born in Alloway, Ayrshire, January 25th 1759
• Dorothy, Wordsworth's sister and lifelong companion, died January 25th 1855, after many years of senility
• Poet and novelist Sasha Moorsom born January 25th 1931
• Poet and critic Tom Paulin born in Leeds January 25th 1949

My Love is Like a Red Red Rose

My love is like a red red rose
   That's newly sprung in June:
My love is like the melody
   That's sweetly play'd in tune.

As fair art thou, my bonnie lass,
   So deep in love am I:
And I will love thee still, my dear,
   Till a' the seas gang dry.

Till a' the seas gang dry, my dear,
   And the rocks melt wi' the sun:
And I will love thee still, my dear,
   While the sands o' life shall run.

And fare thee weel, my only love,
   And fare thee weel a while!
And I will come again, my love,
   Tho' it were ten thousand mile.

Robert Burns
(January 25th 1759 – July 21st 1796)

Maurice Lindsey commented: "And did ever lover, vowing human constancy in terms of eternity, swear more movingly than Burns, who apparently knew so little of the meaning of constancy where women's love was concerned." This song and 'Auld Lang Syne' are among the two hundred that Burns wrote or collected for The Scots Musical Museum. Burns is Scotland's national poet with Burns Night on January 25th celebrated by his fellow-countrymen around the world. In 1859, at a dinner to mark the centenary of Burns' birth, Ralph Waldo Emerson declared that "The Confession of Augsburg, The Declaration of Independence, the French Rights of Man, and the 'Marseillaise' are not more weighty documents in the history of freedom than the songs of Burns".

Burns was a labourer and ploughman (with a "ploughman's stoop") on his father's ailing farm, and later on unsuccessful farms of his own. "At the plough, scythe or reap hook, I feared no competitor," he wrote, "but I spent the evenings after my own heart ... To the sons and daughters of labour and poverty, the ardent hope, the stolen interview, the tender farewell, are the greatest and most delicious enjoyments."

Australia

Last sea-thing dredged by sailor Time from Space,
Are you a drift Sargasso, where the West
In halcyon calm rebuilds her fatal nest?
Or Delos of a coming Sun-God's race?
Are you for Light, and trimmed, with oil in place,
Or but a Will o' Wisp on marshy quest?
A new demesne for Mammon to infest?
Or lurks millennial Eden 'neath your face?

The cenotaphs of species dead elsewhere
That in your limits leap and swim and fly,
Or trail uncanny harp-strings from your trees,
Mix omens with the auguries that dare
To plant the Cross upon your forehead sky,
A virgin helpmate Ocean at your knees.

Bernard O'Dowd
(April 11th 1866 – September 1st 1953)

January 26th is Australia's National Day. On this day in 1788 Captain Arthur Phillip landed at Sydney Cove with a fleet of convict ships: "We ... had the satisfaction of finding the finest harbour in the world in which a thousand sail of the line may ride with the most perfect security."

The poet Bernard O'Dowd was born in Beaufort, Australia, the son of Ulster immigrants and he grew up in Ballarat, Victoria. He gained both arts and law degrees and ended up as a chief parliamentary legal draftsman. He married Eva Fryer in 1889 but left her for the socialist poet Marie E. J. Pitt. In his 1909 address *Poetry Militant*, he declared that the poet has a socialist obligation to further humanity's best interests.

This sonnet 'Australia' is from his first collection published in 1903, entitled *Dawnward?*, with the question mark perhaps indicating his doubts as to Australia's direction. In his poem 'The Bush', however, he envisages for Australia a future as glorious as that of ancient Greece and Rome. A later volume of poetry, *The Silent World* (1909), speculates about a mystic world beyond the physical world; and his *Alma Venus* (1921) is a poetic exploration of the mysteries of sex. He wrote almost no poetry after 1921.

• Lewis Carroll (the pseudonym of Charles Lutwidge Dodgson) was born January 27th 1832 in Daresbury, Cheshire, the third of eleven children. In 1855 he became a lecturer in mathematics at Christ Church, Oxford

Jabberwocky
(from *Through the Looking-Glass*)

'Twas brillig, and the slithy toves
  Did gyre and gimble in the wabe:
All mimsy were the borogoves,
  And the mome raths outgrabe.

'Beware the Jabberwock, my son!
  The jaws that bite, the claws that catch!
Beware the Jubjub bird, and shun
  The frumious Bandersnatch!'

He took his vorpal sword in hand:
  Long time the manxome foe he sought –
So rested he by the Tumtum tree,
  And stood awhile in thought.

And, as in uffish thought he stood,
  The Jabberwock, with eyes of flame,
Came whiffling through the tulgey wood,
  And burbled as it came!

One, two! One, two! And through and through
  The vorpal blade went snicker-snack!
He left it dead, and with its head
  He went galumphing back.

'And hast thou slain the Jabberwock?
  Come to my arms, my beamish boy!
O frabjous day! Callooh! Callay!'
  He chortled in his joy.

'Twas brillig, and the slithy toves
  Did gyre and gimble in the wabe:
All mimsy were the borogoves,
  And the mome raths outgrabe.

Lewis Carroll
(January 27th 1832 – January 14th 1898)

Some critics consider 'Jabberwocky', with its portmanteau words, to be a burlesque of Edmund Spenser's word-coinages. "Take care of the sounds," Carroll advised "and the sense will take care of itself." Some of the nonsense words in it, such as 'chortle' and 'burble', have since entered normal usage. The poem appeared in *Through the Looking-Glass*, published in 1871, a sequel to his *Alice's Adventures in Wonderland* of 1865.

- *Canadian doctor and poet John McCrae died of pneumonia whilst with the British Army in France, January 28th 1918*
- *W. B. Yeats died of myocarditis on January 28th 1939*
- *Patric Dickinson, poet, playwright and translator, died January 28th 1994*

Sailing to Byzantium

That is no country for old men. The young
In one another's arms, birds in the trees
—Those dying generations—at their song,
The salmon-falls, the mackerel-crowded seas,
Fish, flesh, or fowl, commend all summer long
Whatever is begotten, born, and dies.
Caught in that sensual music all neglect
Monuments of unageing intellect.

An aged man is but a paltry thing,
A tattered coat upon a stick, unless
Soul clap its hands and sing, and louder sing
For every tatter in its mortal dress,
Nor is there singing school but studying
Monuments of its own magnificence;
And therefore I have sailed the seas and come
To the holy city of Byzantium.

O sages standing in God's holy fire
As in the gold mosaic of a wall,
Come from the holy fire, perne in a gyre°,   *reel in spiral revolutions*
And be the singing-masters of my soul.
Consume my heart away; sick with desire
And fastened to a dying animal
It knows not what it is; and gather me
Into the artifice of eternity.

Once out of nature I shall never take
My bodily form from any natural thing,
But such a form as Grecian goldsmiths make
Of hammered gold and gold enamelling
To keep a drowsy Emperor awake;
Or set upon a golden bough to sing
To lords and ladies of Byzantium
Of what is past, or passing, or to come.

William Butler Yeats
(June 13th 1865 – January 28th 1939)

The typescript of this poem is dated September 26th 1926. For a BBC Belfast broadcast of his poems in 1931, Yeats wrote: "Now I am trying to write about the state of my soul, for it is right for an old man to make his soul, and some of my thoughts on that subject I have put into a poem called 'Sailing to Byzantium'. When Irishmen were illuminating the *Book of Kells* [8th/9th century] and making the jewelled croziers in the National Museum, Byzantium was the centre of European civilisation and the source of its spiritual philosophy, so I symbolise the search for the spiritual life by a journey to that city."

January 29

- *American poet and children's writer Susan Coolidge born January 29th 1835*
- *Edward Lear, who wrote and illustrated* A Book of Nonsense *for the grandchildren of the earl of Derby, died January 29th 1888*
- *Robert Frost died January 29th 1963*

Stopping by Woods on a Snowy Evening

Whose woods these are I think I know.
His house is in the village, though;
He will not see me stopping here
To watch his woods fill up with snow.

My little horse must think it queer
To stop without a farmhouse near
Between the woods and frozen lake
The darkest evening of the year.

He gives his harness bells a shake
To ask if there is some mistake.
The only other sound's the sweep
Of easy wind and downy flake.

The woods are lovely, dark, and deep,
But I have promises to keep,
And miles to go before I sleep,
And miles to go before I sleep.

Robert Frost
(March 26th 1874 – January 29th 1963)

This was Frost's favourite poem, he termed it "my best bid for remembrance". In John Ciardi's account, one night Frost "had sat down after supper to work at a long piece of blank verse. The piece never worked out, but Mr. Frost found himself so absorbed in it that, when next he looked up, dawn was at his window. He rose, crossed to the window, stood looking out for a few minutes, and then it was that 'Stopping by Woods' suddenly 'just came', so that all he had to do was cross the room and write it down." In fact, the poem required fine-tuning. For instance, Frost noted that "I wrote the third line of the last stanza of 'Stopping by Woods' in such a way as to call for another stanza when I didn't want another stanza and didn't have another stanza in me, but with great presence of mind and a sense of what a good boy I was I instantly struck the line out and made my exit with a repeat end."

- *William Savage Landor born January 30th 1775*
- *Arthur William Edgar O'Shaughnessy died January 30th 1881*
- *Yeats fell in love with Maud Gonne January 30th 1889*
- *Ezra Pound met Mussolini, January 30th 1935* [1]

Dance Figure
For the Marriage in Cana of Galilee

Dark eyed,
O woman of my dreams,
Ivory sandalled,
There is none like thee among the dancers,
None with swift feet.
I have not found thee in the tents,
In the broken darkness.
I have not found thee at the well-head
Among the women with pitchers.

Thine arms are as a young sapling under the bark;
Thy face as a river with lights.

White as an almond are thy shoulders;
As new almonds stripped from the husk.
They guard thee not with eunuchs;
Not with bars of copper.

Gilt turquoise and silver are in the place of thy rest.
A brown robe, with threads of gold woven in
    patterns, hast thou gathered about thee,
O Nathat-Ikanaie, 'Tree-at-the-river'.

As a rillet among the sedge are thy hands upon me;
Thy fingers a frosted stream.

Thy maidens are white like pebbles;
Their music about thee!

There is none like thee among the dancers;
None with swift feet.

Ezra Pound
(October 30th 1885 – November 1st 1972)

1. Pound recited some lines of his poetry to Mussolini before presenting him with a draft copy of the *Cantos*. Mussolini declared himself amused. In January 1941, Pound began broadcasting anti-Semitic and anti-American diatribes from Rome.

January 31

• Derek Jarman, filmmaker, painter and poet, born in Northwood, Middlesex, January 31st 1942

The Song of Wandering Aengus

I went out to the hazel wood,
Because a fire was in my head,
And cut and peeled a hazel wand,
And hooked a berry to a thread;
And when white moths were on the wing,
And moth-like stars were flickering out,
I dropped the berry in a stream
And caught a little silver trout.

When I had laid it on the floor
I went to blow the fire aflame,
But something rustled on the floor,
And some one called me by my name:
It had become a glimmering girl
With apple blossom in her hair
Who called me by my name and ran
And faded through the brightening air.

Though I am old with wandering
Through hollow lands and hilly lands,
I will find out where she has gone,
And kiss her lips and take her hands;
And walk among long dappled grass,
And pluck till time and times are done
The silver apples of the moon,
The golden apples of the sun.

William Butler Yeats
(June 13th 1865 – January 28th 1939)

This poem was written on January 31st (1893?). Yeats' note reads, in part: "An old man who was cutting a quickset hedge near Gort, in Galway, said, only the other day, 'One time I was cutting timber over in Inchy, and about eight o'clock one morning, when I got there, I saw a girl picking nuts, with her hair hanging down over her shoulders; brown hair; and she had a good clean face, and she was tall, and nothing on her head, and her dress no way gaudy, but simple. And when she felt me coming up, she gathered herself up, and was gone, as if the earth had swallowed her up. And I followed her, and looked for her, but I never could see her again from that day to this, never again.' "

• Sir John Suckling born into an old Norfolk family February 1st 1609
• Mary Shelley, author of Frankenstein and wife of the poet, died
  February 1st 1851
• Black poet, writer and playwright Langston Hughes born in Joplin,
  Missouri, February 1st 1902
• Galway Kinnell born in Providence, Rhode Island, February 1st 1927

February 1

Why so pale and wan?

Why so pale and wan, fond lover?
  Prithee, why so pale?
Will, when looking well can't move her,
  Looking ill prevail?
  Prithee, why so pale?

Why so dull and mute, young sinner?
  Prithee, why so mute?
Will, when speaking well can't win her,
  Saying nothing do 't?
  Prithee, why so mute?

Quit, quit for shame! This will not move;
  This cannot take her.
If of herself she will not love,
  Nothing can make her:
  The devil take her!

Sir John Suckling
(February 1st 1609 – c. 1642)

The poet was said by Aubrey to have invented the game of cribbage. He led the life of a rich man's son, at the age of 17 inheriting an enormous fortune from his father. Suckling immediately left Trinity College, Cambridge, and travelled on the Continent. At the age of 28, he insisted on lavish staging for his play *Aglaura* (from which the above is a song) – the actors had to wear real lace and embroideries of "pure gold and silver". In 1639 he raised a troop of one hundred mounted men for Charles I's Scottish expedition, clothing them in luxurious scarlet coats. In 1641, he failed in his conspiracy to rescue the Earl of Strafford from the Tower of London and fled to France. Some accounts say he committed suicide; others, that he was stabbed to death by a servant. He was 33.

February 2

• Shakespeare's company performed for the dying queen at
  Richmond, February 2nd 1603
• Adelaide Anne Procter, for whose volume of sentimental and
  morbid verse Dickens wrote a foreword, died February 2nd 1864
• Novelist James Joyce, author of Ulysses, who also wrote a volume
  of verse entitled 'Pomes Penyeach', was born February 2nd 1882
• American poet James Dickey born February 2nd 1923

Song

O blush not so! O blush not so!
  Or I shall think you knowing;
And if you smile the blushing while,
  Then maidenheads are going.

There's a blush for won't, and a blush for shan't,
  And a blush for having done it:
There's a blush for thought, and a blush for naught,
  And a blush for just begun it.

O sigh not so! O sigh not so!
  For it sounds of Eve's sweet pippin;
By those loosened lips you have tasted the pips
  And fought in an amorous nipping.

Will you play once more at nice-cut-core,
  For it only will last our youth out?
And we have the prime of the kissing time,
  We have not one sweet tooth out.

There's a sigh for yes, and a sigh for no,
  And a sigh for I can't bear it !
O what can be done, shall we stay or run?
  O, cut the sweet apple and share it!

John Keats
(October 31st 1795 – February 23rd 1821)

Keats' biographer Walter Jackson Bate describes how on the morning of January 31st 1818 Keats began an effervescent letter to John Hamilton Reynolds that turned almost entirely into verse. He made up a song of five stanzas (above), and then stopped, saying: "I proposed to write you a serious political letter." But he soon had had enough of being serious: "I cannot write in prose. It is a sun-shiny day" and proceeded to add further impromptu poetry to his letter.

• George Crabbe, who was Jane Austen's favourite poet, died February 3rd 1832. He had been rescued from poverty by Edmund Burke
• Stream-of-consciousness author Gertrude Stein ("I knew that nouns must go in poetry as they had gone in prose") born February 3rd 1874

The Scholars

Bald heads forgetful of their sins,
Old, learned, respectable bald heads
Edit and annotate the lines
That young men, tossing on their beds,
Rhymed out in love's despair
To flatter beauty's ignorant ear.

All shuffle there; all cough in ink;
All wear the carpet with their shoes;
All think what other people think;
All know the man their neighbour knows.
Lord, what would they say
Did their Catullus walk that way?

William Butler Yeats
(June 13th 1865 – January 28th 1939)

The manuscript of this poem is dated April 1915.

February 4

• Gavin Ewart was born in London February 4th 1916

To Margo

In life's rough-and-tumble
you're the crumble on my apple crumble
and the fairy on my Christmas tree!
In life's death-and-duty
you've the beauty of the Beast's own Beauty –
I feel humble as a bumble-bee!

In life's darkening duel
I'm the lighter, you're the lighter fuel –
and the tide that sways my inland sea!
In life's meet-and-muster
you've the lustre of a diamond cluster –
a blockbuster – just a duster, me!

Gavin Ewart
(February 4th 1916 – October 23rd 1995)

Gavin Ewart commented: "This is a birthday Poem for my wife (29th December)."

• *Marianne Moore, "the leading American woman poet", died February 5th 1972*

What are Years?

What is our innocence,
what is our guilt? All are
   naked, none is safe. And whence
is courage: the unanswered question,
the resolute doubt,—
dumbly calling, deafly listening—that
in misfortune, even death,
      encourages others
      and in its defeat, stirs

   the soul to be strong? He
sees deep and is glad, who
   accedes to mortality
and in his imprisonment rises
upon himself as
the sea in a chasm, struggling to be
free and unable to be,
      in its surrendering
      finds its continuing.

So he who strongly feels,
behaves. The very bird,
   grown taller as he sings, steels
his form straight up. Though he is captive,
his mighty singing
says, satisfaction is a lowly
thing, how pure a thing is joy.
      This is mortality,
      this is eternity.

Marianne Moore
(November 15th 1887 – February 5th 1972)

Characterised by her modesty, Marianne Moore once remarked: "I can see no reason for calling my work poetry except that there is no other category in which to put it. Anyone could do what I do; and I am, therefore, the more grateful that those whose judgment I trust should regard it as poetry."

February 6

The Passionate Shepherd to his Love

Come live with me, and be my love,
And we will all the pleasures prove,
That valleys, groves, hills, and fields,
Woods, or steepy mountain yields.

And we will sit upon the rocks,
Seeing the shepherds feed their flocks,
By shallow rivers to whose falls
Melodious birds sing madrigals.

And I will make thee beds of roses,
And a thousand fragrant posies,
A cap of flowers, and a kirtle°,   *gown or skirt*
Embroidered all with leaves of myrtle;

A gown made of the finest wool,
Which from our pretty lambs we pull;
Fair linèd slippers for the cold,
With buckles of the purest gold;

A belt of straw and ivy buds,
With coral clasps and amber studs:
And if these pleasures may thee move,
Come live with me, and be my love.

The shepherds' swains shall dance and sing
For thy delight each May morning.
If these delights thy mind may move,
Then live with me, and be my love.

Christopher Marlowe
(February 6th 1564 – May 30th 1593)

Marlowe was born in Canterbury, the son of a shoemaker. He graduated from Corpus Christi College, Cambridge, and wrote his four best-known plays – *Tamburlaine*, *Dr Faustus*, *The Jew of Malta* and *Edward II*, within a six year period. He was involved in a street fight where a man was killed, was deported from the Netherlands for trying to forge gold coins and was on the point of being arrested for spreading atheistic opinions when he too was killed in a brawl. It was a tavern argument with one Ingram Frizer about paying the bill; Marlowe attacked him and was himself then stabbed, dying instantly. His contemporary writers paid tribute to his work – he was Shakespeare's 'dead shepherd' in *As You Like It*.

The above poem was published in *The Passionate Pilgrim* in 1599 and a year later again, this time with a poem in response by Sir Walter Raleigh, beginning:

> If all the world and love were young,
> And truth in every shepherd's tongue,
> These pretty pleasures might me move,
> To live with thee and be thy love.

• On February 7th 1921 Thomas Hardy congratulated John
Galsworthy on his novel In Chancery and wished he could
see California without having to go there

From King Richard II
Act II Scene i

Gaunt. This royal throne of kings, this sceptered isle,
This earth of majesty, this seat of Mars,
This other Eden, demi-Paradise;
This fortress built by Nature for herself
Against infection and the hand of war;
This happy breed of men, this little world;
This precious stone set in the silver sea,
Which serves it in the office of a wall,
Or as a moat defensive to a house,
Against the envy of less happier lands;
This blessèd plot, this earth, this realm, this England,
This nurse, this teeming womb of royal kings,
Feared by their breed, and famous by their birth,
Renowned for their deeds as far from home,
For Christian service and true chivalry,
As is the sepulchre, in stubborn Jewry,
Of the world's ransom, blessed Mary's Son;
This land of such dear souls, this dear dear land,
Dear for her reputation through the world,
Is now leased out – I die pronouncing it –
Like to a tenement or pelting farm:
England, bound in with the triumphant sea,
Whose rocky shore beats back the envious siege
Of watery Neptune, is now bound in with shame,
With inky blots, and rotten parchment bonds:
That England, that was wont to conquer others,
Hath made a shameful conquest of itself.

William Shakespeare
(April 23rd 1564 – April 23rd 1616)

On this day in 1601, the day before the Earl of Essex's planned rebellion against Elizabeth I, Essex's agents bribed the Chamberlain's Men to put on a performance of *Richard II*, believing that the play's deposition scene (Act IV, Scene i, in which the unpopular monarch willingly abdicates his reign) would steel the rebels in their purpose. Essex was executed on February 25th 1603.

February 8

• *Samuel Butler, author of* Erewhon, *a Utopian satire, and of a poem with the refrain "O God! O Montreal!", was baptised February 8th 1612*
• *John Ruskin, author and art critic, who also wrote Byronesque verse, was born February 8th 1819*
• *Elizabeth Bishop born in Worcester, Mass., February 8th 1911*

One Art

The art of losing isn't hard to master;
so many things seem filled with the intent
to be lost that their loss is no disaster.

Lose something every day. Accept the fluster
of lost door keys, the hour badly spent.
The art of losing isn't hard to master.

Then practice losing farther, losing faster:
places, and names, and where it was you meant
to travel. None of these will bring disaster.

I lost my mother's watch. And look! my last, or
next-to-last, of three loved houses went.
The art of losing isn't hard to master.

I lost two cities, lovely ones. And, vaster,
some realms I owned, two rivers, a continent.
I miss them, but it wasn't a disaster.

—Even losing you (the joking voice, a gesture
I love) I shan't have lied. It's evident
the art of losing's not too hard to master
though it may look like (*Write* it!) like disaster.

Elizabeth Bishop
(February 8th 1911 – October 6th 1979)

Elizabeth Bishop's father died when she was 8 months old and she never saw her mother again once the latter was confined to a mental hospital. Her biographer Brett Miller attributes this poem to 1975, an alcoholic time in Elizabeth's life when she was barely functioning or even writing letters. The draft of this villanelle started out with the title 'How to Lose Things', and referred to her companion Alice Methfesell "an average-sized not exceptionally / beautiful or dazzlingly intelligent person" (who in fact later returned to her, and was invaluable as her secretary, chauffeur, travelling companion and nurse). Miller identifies the lost houses as in Key West, Petrópolis and Ouro Pêtro, one of the cities as Rio de Janeiro, and the continent as South America (lost to her since her friend Lota Soares' suicide). In addition to alcoholism, Elizabeth Bishop suffered from depression and physical ailments. She died of cerebral aneurysm. "Awful but cheerful" were the words she had wanted Alice to put on her tombstone.

- *The large cigar-smoking American Imagist poet, Amy Lowell, was born February 9th 1874*
- *Oscar Wilde's 'The Ballad of Reading Gaol' published February 9th 1898*

February 9

From The Jungle Books
Quiquern (chapter heading)

The People of the Eastern Ice, they are melting like the snow—
They beg for coffee and sugar; they go where the white men go.
The People of the Western Ice, they learn to steal and fight;
They sell their furs to the trading-post; they sell their souls to the white.
The People of the Southern Ice, they trade with the whaler's crew;
Their women have many ribbons, but their tents are torn and few.
But the People of the Elder Ice, beyond the white man's ken—
Their spears are made of the narwhal-horn, and they are the last of the Men!

Rudyard Kipling
(December 30th 1865 – January 18th 1936)

Rudyard Kipling was born in Bombay. He was separated from his parents at the age of six by being sent for five years to boarding schools in England, and it was perhaps the cruelties he experienced there that made him sensitive later in life to the sufferings of victimised natives and Tommies. His tales for children, the two *Jungle Books*, were published in 1894–5. He won the Nobel prize for literature in 1907.

February 10

- William Congreve, poet and playwright ("Hell hath no fury like a woman scorned"), baptised February 10th 1670
- Charles Lamb, who wrote 'The Old Familiar Faces', born February 10th 1775
- Alexander Pushkin died of wounds received "defending his wife's honour" in a duel, February 10th 1837
- Boris Pasternak, Russian lyric poet and author of Dr Zhivago, born February 10th 1890
- Playwright and poet Bertolt Brecht born February 10th 1898
- Fleur Adcock born in New Zealand February 10th 1934

Sonnet 116

Let me not to the marriage of true minds
Admit impediments. Love is not love
Which alters when it alteration finds,
Or bends with the remover to remove:
Oh no, it is an ever fixèd mark
That looks on tempests and is never shaken;
It is the star to every wandering bark,
Whose worth's[1] unknown, although his height[2] be taken.
Love's not Time's fool, though rosy lips and cheeks
Within his bending sickle's compass come;
Love alters not with his brief hours and weeks,
But bears it out even to the edge of doom.
   If this be error and upon me proved,
   I never writ, nor no man ever loved.

William Shakespeare
(April 23rd 1564 – April 23rd 1616)

On this day in 1616, Shakespeare's younger daughter Judith married his old friend Thomas Quiney, four years her junior, at the Stratford-on-Avon parish church.

Shakespeare's wording in this sonnet of course echoes that of the marriage service ("If any of you know cause, or just impediment, why these two persons should not be joined together in holy Matrimony, ye are to declare it").

1. Astral influence.
2. A height taken so as to calculate longitude.

48

• Roy Fuller, the lucid and sardonic poet who was an Oxford
  Professor of Poetry, was born February 11th 1912
• Sylvia Plath committed suicide February 11th 1963 [1]

Words

Axes
After whose stroke the wood rings,
And the echoes!
Echoes traveling
Off from the center like horses.

The sap
Wells like tears, like the
Water striving
To re-establish its mirror
Over the rock

That drops and turns,
A white skull,
Eaten by weedy greens.
Years later I
Encounter them on the road—

Words dry and riderless,
The indefatigable hoof-taps.
While
From the bottom of the pool, fixed stars
Govern a life.

Sylvia Plath
(October 27th 1932 – February 11th 1963)

---

1. Exactly three years earlier, Sylvia Plath had written to her mother and brother with new[
book of poems, *The Colossus*, being accepted by Heinemann. "Amaze of amaze," she

February 12

• *George Meredith, cerebral poet and novelist, born February 12th 1828*
• *Christopher Caudwell, Marxist poet and literary critic, killed in Spain February 12th 1937*

Warning

When I am an old woman I shall wear purple
With a red hat which doesn't go, and doesn't suit me.
And I shall spend my pension on brandy and summer gloves
And satin sandals, and say we've no money for butter.
I shall sit down on the pavement when I'm tired
And gobble up samples in shops and press alarm bells
And run my stick along the public railings
And make up for the sobriety of my youth.
I shall go out in my slippers in the rain
And pick the flowers in other people's gardens
And learn to spit.

You can wear terrible shirts and grow more fat
And eat three pounds of sausages at a go
Or only bread and pickle for a week
And hoard pens and pencils and beermats and things in boxes.

But now we must have clothes that keep us dry
And pay our rent and not swear in the street
And set a good example for the children.
We must have friends to dinner and read the papers.

But maybe I ought to practise a little now?
So people who know me are not too shocked and surprised .
When suddenly I am old, and start to wear purple.

Jenny Joseph
(May 7th 1932 –)

Jenny Joseph was born in Birmingham, and became a scholar at St Hilda's College, Oxford. She has worked as a reporter, a lecturer and a pub landlady. This poem comes from her collection *Rose in the Afternoon* published in 1974.

- *Burns' father died on February 13th 1784 and his son wrote the epitaph for the headstone*
- *On February 13th 1875, W. E. Henley received his first hospital visit from Robert Louis Stevenson, who wrote: "The poor fellow sat up in bed, with his hair and beard all tangled, and talked as cheerfully as if he had been in a King's Palace."*
- *Frances Horovitz was born in London February 13th 1938*

Rain – Birdoswald

I stand under a leafless tree
more still, in this mouse-pattering
    thrum of rain,
than cattle shifting in the field.
    It is more dark than light.
A Chinese painter's brush of deepening grey
    moves in a subtle tide.

    The beasts are darker islands now.
Wet-stained and silvered by the rain
    they suffer night,
marooned as still as stone or tree.
    We sense each other's quiet.

    Almost, death could come
inevitable, unstrange
    as is this dusk and rain,
and I should be no more
    myself, than raindrops
glimmering in last light
    on black ash buds

or night beasts in a winter field.

Frances Horovitz
(February 13th 1938 – October 2nd 1983)

Frances Horovitz began to write poetry after her marriage to the performance poet Michael Horovitz. In 1980, inspired by a commission on the theme of Hadrian's Wall, she lived in a farmhouse at Kiln Hill, near the Roman fort of Birdoswald in Cumbria. Many of her poems at that time took their inspiration from the Irthing Valley below Birdoswald.

She died at the age of 45 after a long struggle with cancer, and her *Collected Poems* were edited by her second husband, Roger Garfitt.

February 14

• On February 14th 1613, Shakespeare's The Tempest was
  probably performed at the wedding of "the Princes Highnes the
  Lady Elizabeth and the Prince Pallatyne Elector"
• Sir Cecil Spring-Rice, the British ambassador to the States, who
  wrote 'I vow to thee, my country', died February 14th 1918

Valentine

Not a red rose or a satin heart.

I give you an onion.
It is a moon wrapped in brown paper.
It promises light
like the careful undressing of love.

Here.
It will blind you with tears
like a lover.
It will make your reflection
a wobbling photo of grief.

I am trying to be truthful.

Not a cute card or a kissogram.

I give you an onion.
Its fierce kiss will stay on your lips,
possessive and faithful
as we are,
for as long as we are.

Take it.
Its platinum loops shrink to a wedding-ring,
if you like.
Lethal.
Its scent will cling to your fingers,
cling to your knife.

Carol Ann Duffy
(December 23rd 1955 –)

Carol Ann Duffy writes: "This was written for radio one February. There was a basket of onions on the kitchen table, where I was sitting with my notebook. A couple of years later, a reader sent me a lovely watercolour based on the poem. More recently, a proof copy from a publisher misprinted 'onion' throughout as 'opinion'. An improvement, perhaps."

Harp Song of the Dane Women

What is a woman that you forsake her,
And the hearth-fire and the home-acre,
To go with the old grey Widow-maker?

She has no house to lay a guest in
But one chill bed for all to rest in,
That the pale suns and the stray bergs nest in.

She has no strong white arms to fold you,
But the ten-times-fingering weed to hold you–
Out on the rocks where the tide has rolled you.

Yet, when the signs of summer thicken,
And the ice breaks, and the birch-buds quicken,
Yearly you turn from our side, and sicken–

Sicken again for the shouts and the slaughters.
You steal away to the lapping waters,
And look at your ship in her winter-quarters.

You forget our mirth, and talk at the tables,
The kine in the shed and the horse in the stables–
To pitch her sides and go over her cables.

Then you drive out where the storm-clouds swallow,
And the sound of your oar-blades, falling hollow,
Is all we have left through the months to follow.

Ah, what is Woman that you forsake her,
And the hearth-fire and the home-acre,
To go with the old grey Widow-maker?

Rudyard Kipling
(December 30th 1865 – January 18th 1936)

Embittered by a quarrel with his brother-in-law in America, and by the death of his daughter and the
loss of his son in the Great War, Kipling lived in relative seclusion in Burwash, Sussex, but continued
to venture forth on travels to South Africa and elsewhere.

February 16

• Gray's 'Elegy in a Country Churchyard' published February 16th 1751
• On February 16th 1821, Shelley sent his poem 'Epipsychidion' from Italy to his publisher Ollier in London, asking for 100 copies to be published anonymously. It contains his defence of free love, in which marriage is condemned as "the dreariest and longest journey" undertaken "With one chained friend, perhaps a jealous foe"

Love's Philosophy

The fountains mingle with the river
   And the rivers with the Ocean,
The winds of Heaven mix for ever
   With a sweet emotion;
Nothing in the world is single;
   All things by a law divine
In one spirit meet and mingle.
   Why not I with thine ?—

See the mountains kiss high Heaven
   And the waves clasp one another;
No sister-flower would be forgiven
   If it disdained its brother;
And the sunlight clasps the earth
   And the moonbeams kiss the sea:
What is all this sweet work worth
   If thou kiss not me ?

Percy Bysshe Shelley
(August 4th 1792 – July 8th 1822)

Shelley flirted with the young and attractive Sophia Stacey, a ward of one of his uncles, who came with her chaperone to visit Mary Shelley and him in Florence in December 1819. Mary commented that "the younger one was entousiasmée to see him – the elder said he was a very shocking man". Whilst Mary stayed at home looking after their child, Shelley would take Sophia and her chaperone out to galleries. Sophia, Mary admitted, "sings well for an english dilettante" and Shelley wrote her several love lyrics, including this one.

• James Macpherson, who tried to pass off his poem 'Fingal' as the translation of an ancient Gaelic epic, died February 17th 1796
• German poet Heinrich Heine, who called himself "the last Romantic", died February 17th 1856
• Andrew "Banjo" Paterson, the Australian poet who wrote the words of 'Waltzing Matilda', born February 17th 1864

Up-Hill

Does the road wind up-hill all the way?
   Yes, to the very end.
Will the day's journey take the whole long day?
   From morn to night, my friend.

But is there for the night a resting-place?
   A roof for when the slow dark hours begin.
May not the darkness hide it from my face?
   You cannot miss that inn.

Shall I meet other wayfarers at night?
   Those who have gone before.
Then must I knock, or call when just in sight?
   They will not keep you standing at that door.

Shall I find comfort, travel-sore and weak?
   Of labour you shall find the sum.
Will there be beds for me and all who seek?
   Yea, beds for all who come.

Christina Rossetti
(December 5th 1830 – December 29th 1894)

On this day in 1827, Christina's older sister, Maria Francesca Rossetti, was born. The most responsible and practical of the siblings, Maria, a Dante scholar, only felt herself free of family responsibilities at the age of 46. She entered an Anglican sisterhood, but her health soon failed and she died several years later in 1876.

Christina Rossetti was born in London, her father Italian and her mother half-Italian. The house was a magnet for literary refugees and she was educated at home, and lived there all her life, retiring from work as a governess as a result of ill-health. "Differing from her Bohemian brother, Dante Gabriel, and more like her older sister, she found the world evil. She repudiated pleasure: 'I cannot possibly use the word "happy" without meaning something beyond this present life' " (Louis Untermeyer).

February 18

- Michelangelo, Italian painter, sculptor, architect and poet, died February 18th 1564
- Eeva Kilpi, Finnish poet, born February 18th 1928
- Audre Geraldin Lorde, described on the jacket cover of her poetry as "black, lesbian, mother, cancer survivor, urban woman", born in New York February 18th 1934

Long-Legged Fly

That civilisation may not sink,
Its great battle lost,
Quiet the dog, tether the pony
To a distant post;
Our master Caesar is in the tent
Where the maps are spread,
His eyes fixed upon nothing,
A hand under his head.
Like a long-legged fly upon the stream
His mind moves upon silence.

That the topless towers be burnt
And men recall that face,
Move most gently if move you must
In this lonely place.
She thinks, part woman, three parts a child,
That nobody looks; her feet
Practise a tinker shuffle
Picked up on a street.
Like a long-legged fly upon the stream
Her mind moves upon silence.

That girls at puberty may find
The first Adam in their thought,
Shut the door of the Pope's chapel,
Keep those children out.
There on that scaffolding reclines
Michael Angelo.
With no more sound than the mice make
His hand moves to and fro.
Like a long-legged fly upon the stream
His mind moves upon silence.

William Butler Yeats
(June 13th 1865 – January 28th 1939)

Michelangelo does not recline on the scaffolding in his own poem 'On the Painting of the Sistine Chapel': "I've grown a goitre by dwelling in this den / ... crosswise I strain me like a Syrian bow: / ... foul I fare and painting is my shame" (see John Addington Symonds's version in *99 Poems in Translation*, edited by Pinter and others).

It was Helen's beauty that led to the burning of Troy's 'topless towers' (in the second stanza).

- On February 19th 1592 Shakespeare's company, Lord Strange's men, opened the Rose, a new theatre which Philip Henslowe had erected on the Bankside, Southwark
- Georg Büchner, German author of poetical drama Woyzeck, died February 19th 1937
- Poet Jeffrey Wainwright born in Stoke-on-Trent February 19th 1944
- Derek Jarman, filmmaker who also wrote poetry, died February 19th 1994

From Cymbeline
Act IV Scene ii

Gui Fear no more the heat o' the sun,
   Nor the furious winter's rages,
   Thou thy worldly task hast done,
   Home art gone, and ta'en thy wages.
   Golden lads, and girls all must,
   As chimney-sweepers come to dust.

Arv Fear no more the frown o' th' great,
   Thou art past the tyrant's stroke,
   Care no more to clothe and eat,
   To thee the reed is as the oak;
   The sceptre, learning, physic must
   All follow this, and come to dust.

Gui Fear no more the lightning flash,
Arv Nor th' all-dreaded thunderstone.
Gui Fear not slander, censure rash.
Arv Thou hast finish'd joy and moan.
Both All lovers young, all lovers must,
   Consign to thee and come to dust.

Gui No exorciser harm thee,
Arv Nor no witch-craft charm thee.
Gui Ghost unlaid forbear thee.
Arv Nothing ill come near thee.
Both Quiet consummation have,
   And renowned be thy grave.

William Shakespeare
(April 23rd 1564 – April 23rd 1616)

This dirge is spoken in turns by Guiderius and Arviragus, the two lost sons of Cymbeline, King of Britain, who live as the children of Bellarius in a cave in Wales. They have found Fidele, their page (actually their sister Imogen in disguise), apparently dead. She revives quickly enough once they leave her alone.

Dr Johnson found the play ridiculous: "To remark the folly of the fiction, the absurdity of the conduct, the confusion of the names and manners of different times, and the impossibility of the events in any system of life, were to waste criticism upon unresisting imbecility, upon faults too evident for detection, and too gross for aggravation." Tennyson, who was rather fonder of the play, died with a copy of it lying next to him on his bed.

February 20

• Henry James Pye, a much ridiculed Poet Laureate, born February 20th 1745

The Starlight Night

Look at the stars! look, look up at the skies!
　O look at all the fire-folk sitting in the air!
　The bright boroughs, the circle-citadels there!
Down in dim woods the diamond delves! the elves'-eyes!
The grey lawns cold where gold, where quickgold lies!
　Wind-beat whitebeam! airy abeles[1] set on a flare!
　Flake-doves sent floating forth at a farmyard scare!–
Ah well! it is all a purchase, all is a prize.

Buy then! bid then!–What?–Prayer, patience, alms, vows.
Look, look: a May-mess, like on orchard boughs!
　Look! March-bloom, like on mealed-with-yellow sallows[2]!
These are indeed the barn; withindoors house
The shocks[3]. This piece-bright paling[4] shuts the spouse
　Christ home, Christ and his mother and all his hallows.

Gerard Manley Hopkins
(July 28th 1844 – June 8th 1889)

A couple of years before he wrote 'The Starlight Night' Hopkins described a visit to Ugbrooke Park, the Devon home of a Catholic peer, Lord Clifford: "As we drove home the stars came out thick: I leant back to look at them and my heart opening more than usual praised our Lord, to and in whom all that beauty comes home."

Hopkins described this poem and 'God's Grandeur' to his mother (March 1st 1877) as "two sonnets I wrote in a freak the other day ... They are not so queer, but have a few metrical effects, mostly after Milton". And to Robert Bridges he added the note "to be read, both of them, slowly, strongly marking the rhythms and fetching out the syllables."

1. White poplars with waving (flaring) leaves.
2. Goat willows with yellow catkins.
3. Piles of sheaves.
4. Perhaps paling-boards of the barn with "pieces" of light shining through the gaps.

- St Robert Southwell hung, drawn and quartered for being a Jesuit priest February 21st 1595
- Thomas Flatman, poet and painter of miniatures, born in London February 21st 1635
- On this day in 1653 Milton recorded Marvell's appointment as his assistant in the secretaryship for foreign tongues
- W. H. Auden, the major 'Poet of the Thirties', who emigrated to the States in 1939, born February 21st 1907

February 21

From To His Coy Mistress

Had we but world enough, and time,
This coyness, Lady, were no crime.
We would sit down, and think which way
To walk, and pass our long love's day.
Thou by the Indian Ganges' side
Shouldst rubies find: I by the tide
Of Humber would complain. I would
Love you ten years before the Flood:
And you should, if you please, refuse
Till the conversion of the Jews.
My vegetable love should grow
Vaster than empires, and more slow.
An hundred years should go to praise
Thine eyes, and on thy forehead gaze.
Two hundred to adore each breast:
But thirty thousand to the rest.
An age at least to every part,
And the last age should show your heart.
For, Lady, you deserve this state;
Nor would I love at lower rate.
　But at my back I always hear
Time's wingèd chariot hurrying near:
And yonder all before us lie
Deserts of vast eternity.
Thy beauty shall no more be found;
Nor, in thy marble vault, shall sound
My echoing song: then worms shall try
That long preserved virginity:
And your quaint honour turn to dust;
And into ashes all my lust.
The grave's a fine and private place,
But none I think do there embrace.
　Now therefore, while the youthful hue
Sits on thy skin like morning dew,
And while thy willing soul transpires
At every pore with instant fires,
Now let us sport us while we may;
And now, like amorous birds of prey,
Rather at once our time devour,
Than languish in his slow-chapt power.
Let us roll all our strength, and all
Our sweetness, up into one ball:
And tear our pleasures with rough strife,
Through the iron gates of life.
Thus, though we cannot make our sun
Stand still, yet we will make him run.

Andrew Marvell
(March 31st 1621 – August 16th 1678)

February 22

• Abolitionist James Russell Lowell born February 22nd 1819
• Edna St Vincent Millay born in Rockland, Maine, February 22nd 1892
• Henry Reed, poet, radio dramatist and translator, born February 22nd 1914
• Poet Gerald Stern, author of Lucky Life, born in Pittsburg February 22nd 1925
• Spanish poet Antonio Machado died February 22nd 1939

First Fig

My candle burns at both ends;
    It will not last the night;
But ah, my foes, and oh, my friends
    It gives a lovely light!

Edna St Vincent Millay
(February 22nd 1892 – October 19th 1950)

Concerning the rewards and pitfalls of her profession, Edna St Vincent Millay once remarked : "A person who publishes a book wilfully appears before the populace with his pants down... If it is a good book nothing can hurt him. If it is a bad book, nothing can help him."

• *John Keats died February 23rd 1821. His epitaph read: "Here Lies One Whose Name was writ in Water"*
• *Ernest Dowson died, an alcoholic, February 23rd 1900*

February 23

From[1] Adonais[2]
An Elegy on the Death of John Keats, Author of Endymion, Hyperion, &c.

He is made one with Nature: there is heard
His voice in all her music, from the moan
Of thunder, to the song of night's sweet bird;
He is a presence to be felt and known
In darkness and in light, from herb and stone,
Spreading itself where'er that Power may move
Which has withdrawn his being to its own;
Which wields the world with never-wearied love,
Sustains it from beneath, and kindles it above.

He is a portion of the loveliness
Which once he made more lovely: he doth bear
His part, while the one Spirit's plastic stress[3]
Sweeps through the dull dense world, compelling there,
All new successions to the forms they wear;
Torturing th' unwilling dross that checks its flight
To its own likeness, as each mass may bear;
And bursting in its beauty and its might
From trees and beasts and men into the Heaven's light.

The splendours of the firmament of time
May be eclipsed, but are extinguished not;
Like stars to their appointed height they climb,
And death is a low mist which cannot blot
The brightness it may veil. When lofty thought
Lifts a young heart above its mortal lair,
And love and life contend in it, for what
Shall be its earthly doom, the dead live there
And move like winds of light on dark and stormy air.

Percy Bysshe Shelley
(August 4th 1792 – July 8th 1822)

'Adonais' was completed on June 16th 1821. Shelley wrote to John Gisborne: "It is a highly wrought piece of art, perhaps better in point of composition than anything I have written." In his preface, Shelley gives his highly partial version of Keats's death: "The savage criticism of his 'Endymion', which appeared in the *Quarterly Review*, produced the most violent effect on his susceptible mind; the agitation thus originated ended in the rupture of a blood-vessel in the lungs; a rapid consumption ensued, and the succeeding acknowledgements from more candid critics, of the true greatness of his powers, were ineffectual to heal the wound thus wantonly inflicted."

1. Stanzas 42 – 44.
2. The name derives from Adonis, the young hunter and god of beauty and fertility in Greek legend who was loved by Aphrodite and killed by a boar.
3. "Plastic stress" means roughly "shaping force".

February 24

• George Moore, Irish poet, novelist and journalist, born February 24th 1852
• August Derleth, Wisconsin poet and writer, born February 24th 1909

Spleen

I was not sorrowful, I could not weep,
And all my memories were put to sleep.

I watched the river grow more white and strange,
All day till evening I watched it change.

All day till evening I watched the rain
Beat wearily upon the window pane.

I was not sorrowful, but only tired
Of everything that ever I desired.

Her lips, her eyes, all day became to me
The shadow of a shadow utterly.

All day mine hunger for her heart became
Oblivion, until the evening came,

And left me sorrowful, inclined to weep,
With all my memories that could not sleep.

Ernest Dowson
(August 2nd 1867 – February 23rd 1900)

Born into an eminent family at Belmont Hill in Kent, Dowson left Queen's College, Oxford, without finishing his studies, and became part of Wilde's and Beardsley's set in London. He inherited a dry dock from his father, but, having become a heavy drinker, he lived there in squalor, later moving to France and converting to Roman Catholicism. He died at the age of 32.

- *Thomas Moore, Irish poet who was as popular in his lifetime as Byron, died February 25th 1852*
- *Robert Hayden, American poet who won the poetry prize at the 1966 World Festival of Negro Arts in Senegal, died February 25th 1980*

February 25

Those Winter Sundays

Sundays too my father got up early
and put his clothes on in the blueblack cold,
then with cracked hands that ached
from labor in the weekday weather made
banked fires blaze. No one ever thanked him.

I'd wake and hear the cold splintering, breaking.
When the rooms were warm, he'd call,
and slowly I would rise and dress,
fearing the chronic angers of that house,

Speaking indifferently to him,
who had driven out the cold
and polished my good shoes as well.
What did I know, what did I know
of love's austere and lonely offices?

Robert Hayden
(August 4th 1913 – February 25th 1980)

Robert Hayden was born in Detroit and educated at Wayne State University. His poetry books included *Heart-Shape in the Dust* (1940) and *Words in the Mourning Time* (1970). He was the editor of *Kaleidoscope – Poems by American Negro Poets* (1967). In this book, he warned against the black writer being consigned to "a kind of literary ghetto" where he would be "not considered as a writer but a species of race–relations man".

February 26

• *Victor Hugo, French Romantic poet and novelist, author of* Les Misérables, *born February 26th 1802*
• *John Keats buried in Rome February 23rd 1821*
• *George Barker born February 26th 1913*
• *Sylvia Plath first met Ted Hughes ("The one man in the room as big as his poems, huge...") at a party in Cambridge, February 26th 1956*

To My Mother

Most near, most dear, most loved and most far,
Under the window where I often found her
Sitting as huge as Asia, seismic with laughter,
Gin and chicken helpless in her Irish hand,
Irresistible as Rabelais, but most tender for
The lame dogs and hurt birds that surround her,—
She is a procession no one can follow after
But be like a little dog following a brass band.

She will not glance up at the bomber, or condescend
To drop her gin and scuttle to a cellar,
But lean on the mahogany table like a mountain
Whom only faith can move, and so I send
O all my faith, and all my love to tell her
That she will move from mourning into morning.

George Barker
(February 26th 1913 – October 27th 1991)

George Barker's mother was Irish but his father was English and he was born in Loughton, Essex. He was educated at the Regent Street Polytechnic and was always aware of poverty and deprivation ('It was hard cash I needed at my roots"). He described himself as an "Augustinian anarchist". He was a youthful prodigy, with a book of poems and a novel published at the age of 20. Yeats described him as "a lovely subtle mind", whose poetry showed "a rhythmical invention comparable to Gerard Hopkins". Faber refused to publish his long poem 'The True Confesssion of George Barker', written in his early thirties, and there were complaints in parliament at its obscenity after its broadcast on the BBC Third Programme.

- Henry Wadsworth Longfellow, American poet who wrote 'Hiawatha' and 'Paul Revere's Ride', was born February 27th 1807
- Sir Cecil Spring-Rice, who wrote 'I vow to thee, my country', born February 27th 1859
- Lawrence Durrell, poet and writer, born in India February 27th 1912 and brought up in Corfu
- Poet and innovator Kenneth Koch born in Ohio February 27th 1925
- Edward Lucie-Smith born in Kingston, Jamaica, February 27th 1933
- Philip Gross born in Delabole, Devon, February 27th 1952

The Lesson

'Your father's gone,' my bald headmaster said.
His shiny dome and brown tobacco jar
Splintered at once in tears. It wasn't grief.
I cried for knowledge which was bitterer
Than any grief. For there and then I knew
That grief has uses – that a father dead
Could bind the bully's fist a week or two;
And then I cried for shame, then for relief.

I was a month past ten when I learnt this:
I still remember how the noise was stilled
In school-assembly when my grief came in.
Some goldfish in a bowl quietly sculled
Around their shining prison on its shelf.
They were indifferent. All the other eyes
Were turned towards me. Somewhere in myself
Pride, like a goldfish, flashed a sudden fin.

Edward Lucie-Smith
(February 27th 1933 –)

Edward Lucie-Smith comments: "This is set in Jamaica, where I was brought up, during World War II. I was at a boys' prep school, where I was badly bullied. My father worked for the old colonial government, and died rather rapidly of lung cancer in 1943. I never saw him during his illness, and was in fact only rather remotely aware that something was wrong. In any case I had been largely brought up by servants before being sent to boarding school: I wasn't close to my parents and today have very few memories of my father as a result. The poem is essentially about the difference between what one is supposed to feel and what one actually does feel, when faced with some sort of 'shaping' event. I think I wrote the poem itself sometime in the 1950s, and it reflects my then interest in strict verse forms."

February 28

- *Arthur Symons, poet of the Decadent movement, born February 28th 1865*
- *Kipling in a New York hospital with pneumonia February 28th 1899. The German Kaiser and Henry James sent telegrams*
- *Irish poet John Montague, noted for poetry of precision and elegance, born February 28th 1929*
- *Louis Aragon married Elsa Triolet February 28th 1939*

The Soldier

If I should die, think only this of me:
    That there's some corner of a foreign field
That is for ever England. There shall be
    In that rich earth a richer dust concealed;
A dust whom England bore, shaped, made aware,
    Gave, once, her flowers to love, her ways to roam,
A body of England's, breathing English air,
    Washed by the rivers, blessed by suns of home.

And think, this heart, all evil shed away,
    A pulse in the eternal mind, no less
        Gives somewhere back the thoughts by England given;
Her sights and sounds; dreams happy as her day;
    And laughter, learnt of friends; and gentleness,
        In hearts at peace, under an English heaven.

Rupert Brooke
(August 3rd 1887 – April 23rd 1915)

On February 28th 1915, Brooke's naval ship sailed for the Dardanelles. On the way there, and weakened by sunstroke, he died of blood-poisoning at the Greek island of Skyros. Winston Churchill telegrammed that he should be buried there, and added: "We shall not see his like again." The grave is in an olive grove in the far south of Skyros, a Greek heaven with air and sun and sights and sounds to rival any English delights, although somewhat encroached on of late by Greek naval emplacements.

Rupert Brooke in his brief life showed enormous energy and enthusiasm. Before the war, he had written to a friend: "I want to walk a thousand miles, and write one thousand plays, and drink one thousand pots of beer, and kiss one thousand girls." Walter de la Mare remarked that "he flung himself into the world, as a wasp into a cake shop, Hotspur into the fighting".

Time is ...

I fear time's tumbril hurrying us
      – bare wee foetuses
hardly rubbed with God's pleasure –
      to the place of execution.
"Stay!" My beloved, Giacometti above,
      Renoir below,
spirit shining, horse to horse,
      leaps in the way.
An angel rapes a neuron in her brain:
"Celebrate! Our rescue remedy is
      the timeless now –
      her handmaids
commitment, compassion and conspiracy,
the breathing together of love.
      Life *is* delightful
from womb bliss to birth bliss,
from home bliss to death bliss
      and beyond
our lives ripple through eternity.
      Enjoy!"

Alan Beam
(Feb 29th 1948 –)

Alan Beam comments: "I was here imagining my wife sharing with me a sudden illumination as to how a belief in the timelessness of the present might offer some reassurance about life's fleetingness as we entered middle age."

Alan Beam was born on this day in St Albans in 1948 and is primarily a non-fiction writer and editor.

March 1

• Edward III paid £16 to ransom Geoffrey Chaucer, a soldier captured by the French during the seige of Rheims, March 1st 1360
• William Dean Howells, poet, novelist, critic and US consul in Venice, born in Martin's Ferry, Ohio, March 1st 1837
• Basil Bunting, author of 'Briggflatts', born March 1st 1900
• Robert Lowell, Jr, heavy drinking poet, conscientious objector to World War II and the Vietnam war, born March 1st 1917
• Richard Wilbur born March 1st 1921
• Gabriele D'Annunzio, Italian poet, writer and political adventurer, dictator of Fiume, died March 1st 1938

For K. R. on Her Sixtieth Birthday

Blow out the candles of your cake.
They will not leave you in the dark,
Who round with grace this dusky arc
Of the grand tour which souls must take.

You who have sounded William Blake,
And the still pool, to Plato's mark,
Blow out the candles of your cake.
They will not leave you in the dark.

Yet, for your friends' benighted sake,
Detain your upward-flying spark;
Get us that wish, though like the lark
You whet your wings till dawn shall break:
Blow out the candles of your cake.

Richard Wilbur
(March 1st 1921 –)

Richard Wilbur writes: "This poem, which fell into the form of a rondel, was written for Kathleen Raine, a scholar of Blake and of the Neo-Platonists, one of whose poems is entitled 'The Still Pool'. I used the word 'mark' in the nautical sense, as a measure of the depth of water."

- *The Russian-Jewish writer Sholem Aleichem, on whose stories the musical Fiddler on the Roof is based, was born March 2nd 1859*
- *Playwright, novelist and meditative poet James Merrill born in New York March 2nd 1926*
- *D. H. Lawrence died March 2nd 1930*

From The Ship of Death

5

Build then the ship of death, for you must take
the longest journey, to oblivion.

And die the death, the long and painful death
that lies between the old self and the new.

Already our bodies are fallen, bruised, badly bruised,
already our souls are oozing through the exit
of the cruel bruise.

Already the dark endless ocean of the end
is washing in through the breeches of our wounds,
already the flood is upon us.

O build your ship of death, your little ark
and furnish it with food, with little cakes, and wine
for the dark flight down oblivion.

D. H. Lawrence
(September 11th 1885 – March 2nd 1930)

Lawrence worked on this poem as he lay dying of tuberculosis in the South of France. In *Etruscan Places* he had described the tomb of an Etruscan prince: "The sacred treasures of the dead, the little bronze ship of death that should bear him over to the other world, the vases of jewels for his arraying, the vases of small dishes, the little bronze statuettes and tools, the armour."

"Do I fear the invisible dark hand of death," Lawrence had once asked, "plucking me into the darkness, gathering me blossom by blossom from the stem of life into the unknown of my afterwards? I fear it only in reverence and with strange satisfaction."

Kenneth Rexroth commented that "'The Ship of Death' [poem] would make a small book of meditations, a contemporary 'Holy Dying'. It is curious to think that once such a book would have been a favourite gift for the hopelessly ill. Today people die in hospitals, badgered by nurses, stupefied with barbiturates. This is not an age in which a 'good death' is a desired end in life ... In a world where death had become a nasty, pervasive secret like defecation or masturbation, Lawrence re-instated it in all its grandeur – the oldest and most powerful of the gods."

March 3

• *Edward Herbert (Lord Herbert of Cherbury), a deistical philosopher who wrote contorted poetry, born March 3rd 1583*
• *English MP and poet Edmund Waller, who wrote 'Panegyrics' to both Cromwell and Charles II, was born March 3rd 1606*
• *George Herbert died March 3rd 1633*
• *Childe Harold (Cantos 1 & 11) published March 3rd 1812. As Byron put it: "I awoke one morning and found myself famous"*
• *Edward Thomas, nature poet whom Robert Frost encouraged, and who was killed in action in 1917, was born March 3rd 1878*

Love

Love bade me welcome; yet my soul drew back,
   Guilty of dust and sin.
But quick-eyed Love, observing me grow slack
   From my first entrance in,
Drew nearer to me, sweetly questioning
   If I lack'd anything.

'A guest,' I answer'd, 'worthy to be here':
   Love said, 'You shall be he.'
'I, the unkind, ungrateful? Ah, my dear,
   I cannot look on Thee.'
Love took my hand and smiling did reply,
   'Who made the eyes but I?'

'Truth, Lord: but I have marr'd them: let my shame
   Go where it doth deserve.'
'And know you not,' says Love, 'Who bore the blame?'
   'My dear, then I will serve.'
'You must sit down,' says Love, 'and taste my meat.'
   So I did sit and eat.

George Herbert
(April 3rd 1593 – March 3rd 1633)

George Herbert, brother of Lord Herbert of Cherbury (see above), was born in Montgomery. He was elected a fellow at Trinity College, Cambridge in 1614, at the age of 22; he became an MP for Montgomery in 1624; and was ordained a priest in 1630.

Of the role of the country parson, Herbert wrote, "Love is his business and aime"; he himself was revered by his contemporaries as "holy George Herbert", a kindly, saintly man with a love of music. His first biographer Izaak Walton recounts how he died of consumption in his 39th year, on his deathbed composing "such hymns and anthems as the angels and he now sing in heaven". Realising he was dying, Herbert sent his poems to his friend Ferrar, telling him to publish them only if he thought they might "turn to the advantage of any dejected soul", otherwise to burn them. Of the 169 poems from this posthumous volume entitled *The Temple*, more than one hundred have their own individual metre, and many are arranged on the page in the shape of their subject matter, such as a bird's wing, a cross or an altar.

- On March 4th 1603 a warrant was issued signed by 13 magistrates for John Bunyan's arrest for unlicensed preaching
- Kipling's daughter Josephine died, chilled from waiting in a drafty New York customs hall, March 6th 1899. Kipling nearly died too
- Alan Sillitoe, son of a Nottingham labourer, poet, and author of Saturday Night and Sunday Morning, born March 4th 1928
- Irina Ratushinskaya born March 4th 1954
- William Carlos Williams, American poet, novelist and doctor, died March 4th 1963

No, I'm Not Afraid

No, I'm not afraid: after a year
Of breathing these prison nights
I will survive into the sadness
To name which is escape.

The cockerel will weep freedom for me
And here, knee-deep in mire —
My gardens shed their water
And the northern air blows in draughts.

And how am I to carry to an alien planet
What are almost tears, as though towards home . . .
It isn't true, I *am* afraid, my darling!
But make it look as though you haven't noticed.

Irina Ratushinskaya
(March 4th 1954 –)
translated by David McDuff

On March 4th 1983, her 29th birthday, Irina Ratushinskaya was sentenced to seven years in the Soviet 'strict regime' labour camp at Barashevo where she was beaten frequently, starved, frozen, force-fed and kept in solitary confinement. Her crime was the "manufacture and dissemination" of her poetry, coupled with "anti-Soviet agitation and propaganda". After world-wide campaigns on her behalf, Ratushinskaya was released from prison on October 9th 1986, and on December 18th 1986 she was allowed to leave the Soviet Union for Britain, accompanied by her husband, the human rights activist Igor Gerashchenko.

• *Russian poet Anna Akmatova, whose husband was shot as a counter-revolutionary, and who wrote the very moving cycle of poems* Requiem *when her son was arrested during the Stalin's purges, died March 5th 1966*

As Kingfishers Catch Fire

As kingfishers catch fire, dragonflies dráw fláme;
  As tumbled over rim in roundy wells
  Stones ring; like each tucked[1] string tells, each hung bell's
Bow[2] swung finds tongue to fling out broad its name;
Each mortal thing does one thing and the same:
  Deals out that being indoors each one dwells;
  Selves[3]–goes itself; *myself* it speaks and spells;
Crying *Whát I dó is me: for that I came.*

I say móre: the just man justices;
  Kéeps gráce: thát keeps all his goings graces;
Acts in God's eye what in God's eye he is–
  Chríst–for Christ plays in ten thousand places,
Lovely in limbs, and lovely in eyes not his
  To the Father through the features of men's faces.

Gerard Manley Hopkins
(July 28th 1844 – June 8th 1889)

This poem was probably composed in March or April of 1877. Hopkins wrote elsewhere that "every workman has a use for every object he makes. Much more has God ... The thunder speaks of his terror, the lion is like his strength, ... the honey like his sweetness, ... they tell of him, they give him glory." His justification as a Jesuit for loving the material world so intensely he derived from a medieval Franciscan theologian, Duns Scotus, who argued that the material world was necessary to make God available to the human senses. The discovery of Duns Scotus's work left Hopkins "flush with a new stroke of enthusiasm".

1. plucked, touched.
2. 'sound-bow', the part of the bell struck by the hammer.
3. realises its individuality.

- *Michelangelo (Buonarroti), Italian painter, sculptor, architect and poet, born March 6th 1475*
- *Elizabeth Barrett Browning born March 6th 1806*
- *Pastor Martin Niemöller, who spent seven years in concentration camps for his opposition to Hitler, died March 6th 1984*

How do I love thee? Let me count the ways

How do I love thee? Let me count the ways.
I love thee to the depth and breadth and height
My soul can reach, when feeling out of sight
For the ends of being and ideal grace.
I love thee to the level of every day's
Most quiet need, by sun and candlelight.
I love thee freely, as men strive for right;
I love thee purely, as they turn from praise.
I love thee with the passion put to use
In my old griefs, and with my childhood's faith.
I love thee with a love I seemed to lose
With my lost saints—I love thee with the breath,
Smiles, tears, of all my life!—and, if God choose,
I shall but love thee better after death.

> *Elizabeth Barrett Browning*
> *(March 6th 1806 – June 29th 1861)*

An invalid living in Wimpole Street under the possessive eye of her father, who refused to allow any of his children to marry, Elizabeth Barrett Browning was approaching her forties and seemed destined to the life of a recluse. On May 20th 1845, after a long exchange of letters, she allowed Robert Browning, who was six years her junior, to visit her. In his first letter he had written: "I love your verses with all my heart, dear Miss Barrett ... And I love you too." On September 12th 1846, she secretly married him, eventually settling in Florence, giving birth to a son in her 45th year.

This sonnet was the penultimate poem from the 43 'Sonnets from the Portuguese', written during the Brownings' courtship (Robert Browning called her "little Portuguese" because of her olive skin). The sonnets mark her passage from hesitation, through doubt and disbelief, to joy at their mutual love.

She kept the sonnets secret from Robert for the first three years of marriage. She chose to reveal them when the death of his mother precipitated a crisis of faith in him. It seems that her intention was to demonstrate the fluid, shape-changing, but eternal nature of love – love defying death.

She placed the sonnets hurriedly in his pocket, then turned and left the room. Robert wrote his sister an astonished letter saying that they now knew one another better than ever.

In the same year, Mrs Browning wrote to her sister: "Ours is a true marriage and not a conventional *match*. We live heart to heart all day long, and every day the same." She was to die in Robert's arms.

Virginia Woolf once snobbishly asserted that "the only place in the mansion of literature" for Mrs Browning was "downstairs in the servants' quarters in company with Mrs Hemans, Eliza Cook, Jean Inglelow ..."

March 7

• *Cambridge University begrudgingly gave a degree to Donne, James I's new chaplain, during James I's visit March 7th 1615*
• *Alessandro Manzoni, sacred lyric poet and the novelist who wrote I Promessi Sposi ('The Betrothed'), born March 7th 1785*
• *Stevie Smith died of a brain tumour at Ashburton College Hospital in Devon, March 7th 1971*

Not Waving But Drowning

Nobody heard him, the dead man,
But still he lay moaning:
I was much further out than you thought
And not waving but drowning.

Poor chap, he always loved larking
And now he's dead
It must have been too cold for him his heart gave way,
They said.

Oh, no no no, it was too cold always
(Still the dead one lay moaning)
I was much too far out all my life
And not waving but drowning.

Stevie Smith
(September 20th 1902 – March 7th 1971)

Stevie Smith was born in Hull, but lived most of her life with her aunt in Palmers Green, London. She is known for her witty, acerbic poetry, adorned with her drawings and doodling, that often have loneliness and death as their themes. In conversation with her friend, the novelist Kay Dick, Stevie Smith said: "I'm terribly pro old age really, because it's so relaxed, you know, oh so marvellous. You just go around and do exactly what you like, and somehow it's so delightful.

"I love death, I think it's the most exciting thing. As one gets older one gets into this – well it's like a race, before you get to the waterfall, when you feel the water slowly getting quicker and quicker, and you can't get out, and all you want to do is get to the waterfall and over the edge. How exciting it is! Why do people grumble about old age so much?"

Stevie Smith died at the relatively young age of 68. Her collection *Not Waving But Drowning* was published in 1957.

Little Elegy
for a child who skipped rope

Here lies resting, out of breath,
Out of turns, Elizabeth
Whose quicksilver toes not quite
Cleared the whirring edge of night.

Earth whose circles round us skim
Till they catch the lightest limb,
Shelter now Elizabeth
And for her sake trip up death.

X. J. Kennedy
(August 21st 1929 –)

X. J. Kennedy remarks, "This very early poem – it dates from about 1958 – owes whatever merit it may have to those brief elegies for children written by Herrick ('Here she lies, a pretty bud'), Ben Jonson (elegy for his son), and Wordsworth ('A Slumber Did My Spirit Seal'). Young poets learn by imitation."

X. J. Kennedy (the pseudonym for Joseph Charles Kennedy) was born in Dover, New Jersey, educated at Columbia University and the Sorbonne and served in the United States Navy for four years till 1955. In 1977 he gave up a tenured professorship to concentrate on writing and editing, and has edited the best-selling *An Introduction to Poetry*. His verse for children includes *Brats* (1986) and *Ghastlies, Goops, and Pincushions* (1989).

X. J. Kennedy once referred to himself as "one of an endangered species: people who still write in meter and rime". He published with his wife Dorothy the magazine *Counter/Measures*, in defence of traditional poetry.

March 9

- Burns wrote to 'Clarinda' telling him he was now married, March 9th 1789. Clarinda was indignant
- Vita Sackville-West was born in Knole House, Kent, March 9th 1892, the daughter of Baron Sackville. She married the homosexual diplomat Harold Nicholson and had affairs with Violet Trefusis and Virginia Woolf. She was a poet and novelist whose main passion was perhaps her estate and garden at Sissinghurst

The Greater Cats

The greater cats with golden eyes
Stare out between the bars.
Deserts are there, and different skies,
And night with different stars.
They prowl the aromatic hill,
And mate as fiercely as they kill,
And hold the freedom of their will
To roam, to live, to drink their fill;
But this beyond their wit know I:
Man loves a little, and for long shall die.

Their kind across the desert range
Where tulips spring from stones,
Not knowing they will suffer change
Or vultures pick their bones.
Their strength's eternal in their sight,
They rule the terror of the night,
They overtake the deer in flight,
And in their arrogance they smite;
But I am sage, if they are strong:
Man's love is transient as his death is long.

Yet oh what powers to deceive!
My wit is turned to faith,
And at this moment I believe
In love, and scout at death.
I came from nowhere, and shall be
Strong, steadfast, swift, eternally:
I am a lion, a stone, a tree,
And as the Polar star in me
Is fixed my constant heart on thee.
Ah, may I stay forever blind
With lions, tigers, leopards, and their kind.

Vita Sackville-West
(March 9th 1892 – June 2nd 1962)

• Sir John Denham, Irish poet and architect (who had Sir Christopher Wren as his deputy), was captured in the Civil War at Farnham Castle, became a Knight of the Bath at the Restoration, and died March 10th 1669
• Laurence Binyon, who wrote 'For the Fallen' (" ... They shall not grow old, as we that are left grow old ..."), died March 10th 1943

From The Princess

Ask me no more: the moon may draw the sea;
   The cloud may stoop from heaven and take the shape
   With fold to fold, of mountain or of cape;
But O too fond, when have I answer'd thee?
      Ask me no more.

Ask me no more: what answer should I give?
   I love not hollow cheek or faded eye:
   Yet, O my friend, I will not have thee die!
Ask me no more, lest I should bid thee live;
      Ask me no more.

Ask me no more: thy fate and mine are seal'd:
   I strove against the stream and all in vain:
   Let the great river take me to the main:
No more, dear love, for at a touch I yield;
      Ask me no more.

Alfred, Lord Tennyson
(August 6th 1809 – October 6th 1892)

On this day in 1843 Charles Dickens sent copies of his work to Tennyson in homage to the 'Truth and Beauty' of his works.

'Ask me no more' was one of the songs that Tennyson added as an afterthought to the third edition of *The Princess* in 1850, the year in which he was appointed Poet Laureate in succession to Wordsworth.

March 11

• Italian poet Torquato Tasso, who was locked up as mad for seven years by the Duke Alphonso II, was born March 11th 1544
• Shakespeare's brother Richard baptised March 11th 1574
• D. J. Enright, editor, novelist and poet who advocated "the poetry of civility, passion and order", born March 11th 1920

Say not the Struggle Nought Availeth

Say not the struggle nought availeth,
    The labour and the wounds are vain,
The enemy faints not, nor faileth,
    And as things have been, things remain.

If hopes were dupes, fears may be liars;
    It may be, in yon smoke concealed,
Your comrades chase e'en now the fliers,
    And, but for you, possess the field.

For while the tired waves, vainly breaking,
    Seem here no painful inch to gain,
Far back through creeks and inlets making
    Comes, silent, flooding in, the main,

And not by eastern windows only,
    When daylight comes, comes in the light,
In front the sun climbs slow, how slowly,
    But westward, look, the land is bright.

Arthur Hugh Clough
(January 1st 1819 – November 13th 1861)

Churchill quoted from this poem on several occasions in 1941 – the last line helped him to emphasise Britain's expectations of her ally in the West. On this day in 1941, the American Lend-Lease Act was passed which allowed President Roosevelt to provide equipment to Britain, whose reserves were almost totally exhausted.

In a speech broadcast from Chequers in the Spring of 1941, Churchill spoke of how the United States were "very closely bound up with us now" and he recited from Clough's poem, remarking how its sentiments were "apt and appropriate to our fortunes tonight" and would be so judged "wherever the English language is spoken or the flag of freedom flies".

• *Gabriele D'Annunzio, Italian poet and political leader who lost an eye in air combat in 1916, was born March 12th 1863*

March 12

To Daffodils

Fair daffodils, we weep to see
   You haste away so soon:
As yet the early-rising sun
   Has not attained his noon
     Stay, stay,
   Until the hasting day
     Has run
   But to the evensong;
And, having prayed together, we
   Will go with you along.

We have short time to stay as you;
   We have as short a spring;
As quick a growth to meet decay,
   As you or anything.
     We die,
   As your hours do, and dry
     Away
   Like to the summer's rain;
Or as the pearls of morning's dew,
   Ne'er to be found again.

Robert Herrick
(August 24th 1591 – October 15th 1674)

Herrick took up his position as vicar of Dean Prior with some reluctance, expecting to find himself surrounded by dull and uncultured country people. One Sunday he is supposed to have thrown his sermon at an inattentive congregation, cursing them from the pulpit in his frustration. Gradually, though, he came to develop a feeling for the Devonshire rural life, becoming fascinated by folk-custom and festivals, and learning to appreciate the land.

March 13

• Shelley left Dover and debts for permanent exile in Italy on March 13th 1817
• Gerard Manley Hopkins wrote 'Binsey Poplars' March 13th 1879

Binsey Poplars
felled 1879

My aspens dear, whose airy cages quelled,
Quelled or quenched in leaves the leaping sun,
All felled, felled, are all felled;
　　Of a fresh and following folded rank
　　　　Not spared, not one
　　　　That dandled a sandalled
　　Shadow that swam or sank
On meadow and river and wind-wandering
　weed-winding bank.

O if we but knew what we do
　　When we delve or hew—
　　Hack and rack the growing green!
　　　Since country is so tender
　To touch, her being só slender,
　That, like this sleek and seeing ball
　But a prick will make no eye at all,
　Where we, even where we mean
　　　To mend her we end her,
　　When we hew or delve:
After-comers cannot guess the beauty been.
　Ten or twelve, only ten or twelve
　　Strokes of havoc únselve
　　　The sweet especial scene,
　Rural scene, a rural scene,
　Sweet especial rural scene.

Gerard Manley Hopkins
(July 28th 1844 – June 8th 1889)

One of Hopkins's favourite walks took him from Oxford across Port Meadow and towards Binsey, passing a double row of aspens which hung over the towpath. Writing to his friend R. W. Dixon on this day in 1879, he added a postscript to the letter: "I have been up to Godstow this afternoon. I am sorry to say that the aspens that lined the river are everywhere felled." Irony piled on insult for Hopkins once he learned that the trees had been felled to make brake shoes for locomotives of the Great Western Railway, a company whose noisy, land-devouring works he considered responsible for the destruction of beautiful landscapes right across the region.

Ode (We are the Music Makers)

We are the music-makers,
And we are the dreamers of dreams,
Wandering by lone sea-breakers,
And sitting by desolate streams;
World-losers and world forsakers,
On whom the pale moon gleams:
Yet we are the movers and shakers
Of the world for ever, it seems.

With wonderful deathless ditties
We build up the world's great cities.
And out of a fabulous story
We fashion an empire's glory:
One man with a dream, at pleasure,
Shall go forth and conquer a crown;
And three with a new song's measure
Can trample an empire down.

We, in the ages lying
In the buried past of the earth,
Built Nineveh with our sighing,
And Babel itself with our mirth;
And o'erthrew them with prophesying
To the old of the new world's worth;
For each age is a dream that is dying,
Or one that is coming to birth.

Arthur William Edgar O'Shaughnessy
(March 14th 1844 – January 30th 1881)

The anthologist Palgrave improved this poem by cutting it down from nine stanzas to three, and it is for this shortened poem alone that O'Shaughnessy is nowadays remembered. He was born in London, and at the age of 19 started work in the British Museum, ending up in the zoological department, specialising in icthyology. This ode and other of his "Victorian escapist verse" appeared in his book *Music and Moonlight* published in 1874. He died of influenza in his 39th year.

March 15

• Thomas Hardy accepted an honorary degree of Doctor of Law from the University of St Andrews March 15th 1922

Sonnet 30

When to the sessions of sweet silent thought
I summon up remembrance of things past,
I sigh the lack of many a thing I sought,
And with old woes new wail my dear times' waste:
Then can I drown an eye, unus'd to flow,
For precious friends hid in death's dateless night,
And weep afresh love's long since cancell'd woe,
And moan the expense of many a vanish'd sight:
Then can I grieve at grievances foregone,
And heavily from woe to woe tell o'er
The sad account of fore-bemoaned moan,
Which I new pay as if not paid before.
  But if the while I think on thee, dear friend,
  All losses are restor'd and sorrows end.

William Shakespeare
(April 23rd 1564 – April 23rd 1616)

On this day in 1604, Shakespeare's company walked in the procession from Tower Bridge to Westminster that accompanied the new king, James I, on his formal entry into London. Ben Jonson and Thomas Dekker were amongst those who had penned a series of speeches for the day's entertainment.

- *Nobel-prize winning French poet René Prudhomme born March 16th 1839*
- *Belgian poet Émile Cammaerts, whose World War I poetry was translated into English by his wife, was born March 16th 1878*
- *H. E. Monro, poet and founder of the Poetry Bookshop in London, died March 16th 1932*

From Hamlet
Act III Scene i

Hamlet. To be, or not to be: that is the question:
Whether 'tis nobler in the mind to suffer
The slings and arrows of outrageous fortune,
Or to take arms against a sea of troubles,
And by opposing end them? To die: to sleep;
No more; and, by a sleep to say we end
The heart-ache and the thousand natural shocks
That flesh is heir to, 'tis a consummation
Devoutly to be wish'd. To die, to sleep;
To sleep: perchance to dream: ay, there's the rub;
For in that sleep of death what dreams may come
When we have shuffled off this mortal coil,
Must give us pause. There's the respect
That makes calamity of so long life;
For who would bear the whips and scorns of time,
The oppressor's wrong, the proud man's contumely,
The pangs of dispriz'd love, the law's delay,
The insolence of office, and the spurns
That patient merit of the unworthy takes,
When he himself might his quietus° make   *exit*
With a bare bodkin°? Who would fardels° bear,   *small dagger / burdens*
To grunt and sweat under a weary life,
But that the dread of something after death,
The undiscover'd country from whose bourn
No traveller returns, puzzles the will,
And makes us rather bear those ills we have
Than fly to others that we know not of?
Thus conscience does make cowards of us all;
And thus the native hue of resolution
Is sicklied o'er with the pale cast of thought,
And enterprises of great pitch and moment
With this regard their currents turn awry,
And lose the name of action.

William Shakespeare
(April 23rd 1564 – April 23rd 1616)

On this day in 1976 a performance of *Hamlet* with Albert Finney in the lead role opened the National Theatre in London, some 25 years after work on the building first started.

Charles Lamb wrote in his essay *On the Tragedies of Shakespeare*: "I confess myself utterly unable to appreciate that celebrated soliloquy ... 'To be or not to be', or to tell whether it be good, bad or indifferent, it has been so handled and pawed about by declamatory boys and men."

March 17

• *Ebenezer Elliot, who wrote simple, best-selling, satirical poetry attacking the Bread Tax, was born March 17th 1781*

Apollinaire Said

Apollinaire said
'Come to the edge'
'It is too high'
'Come to the edge'
'We might fall'
'Come to the edge'
And they came
And he pushed them
And they flew

Anonymous

On this day in 1918, the French poet Guillaume Apollinaire was wounded in the head by a shell splinter (subsequently dying in the influenza epidemic on November 9th 1918)

- *Tobias Smollett, author of* The Expedition of Humphry Clinker, *whose poems include 'The Tears of Scotland', born the son of a Scots laird March 18th 1721*
- *Stéphane Mallarmé, whose poem 'L'Après-midi d'un faune' was illustrated by Manet, was born March 18th 1842*
- *Wilfred Owen born March 18th 1893*

Futility

Move him into the sun—
Gently its touch awoke him once,
At home, whispering of fields unsown.
Always it woke him, even in France,
Until this morning and this snow.
If anything might rouse him now
The kind old sun will know.

Think how it wakes the seeds—
Woke, once, the clays of a cold star.
Are limbs, so dear-achieved, are sides,
Full-nerved—still warm—too hard to stir?
Was it for this the clay grew tall?
—O what made fatuous sunbeams toil
To break earth's sleep at all?

Wilfred Owen
(March 18th 1893 – November 4th 1918)

In his preface to the collection of his poems that included 'Futility', Wilfred Owen wrote:

"This book is not about heroes. English Poetry is not yet fit to speak of them.

Nor is it about deeds, or lands, nor anything about glory, honour, might, majesty, dominion, or power, except War.

Above all I am not concerned with Poetry.

My subject is War, and the pity of War.

The poetry is in the pity.

Yet these elegies are to this generation in no sense consolatory. They may be to the next. All a poet can do today is warn. That is why the true Poets must be truthful.

If I thought the letter of this book would last, I might have used proper names; but if the spirit of it survives – survives Prussia – my ambition and those names will have achieved themselves fresher fields than Flanders ..."

• *Sir Richard Francis Burton, the explorer who wrote 40 travel books and two poetry books and who translated* The Kama Sutra *and other erotic works, was born March 19th 1821*

From **Lessons of the War**

To Alan Mitchell
Viri duellis nupet idoneus
Et militavi non sine gloria [1]

Naming of Parts

Today we have naming of parts. Yesterday,
We had daily cleaning. And tomorrow morning,
We shall have what to do after firing. But today,
Today we have naming of parts. Japonica
Glistens like coral in all of the neighbouring gardens,
    And today we have naming of parts.

This is the lower sling swivel. And this
Is the upper sling swivel, whose use you will see,
When you are given your slings. And this is the piling swivel,
Which in your case you have not got. The branches
Hold in the gardens their silent, eloquent gestures,
    Which in our case we have not got.

This is the safety-catch, which is always released
With an easy flick of the thumb. And please do not let me
See anyone using his finger. You can do it quite easy
If you have any strength in your thumb. The blossoms
Are fragile and motionless, never letting anyone see
    Any of them using their finger.

And this you can see is the bolt. The purpose of this
Is to open the breech, as you see. We can slide it
Rapidly backwards and forwards: we call this
Easing the spring. And rapidly backwards and forwards
The early bees are assaulting and fumbling the flowers:
    They call it easing the Spring.

They call it easing the Spring: it is perfectly easy
If you have any strength in your thumb: like the bolt,
And the breech, and the cocking-piece, and the point of balance,
Which in our case we have not got; and the almond-blossom
Silent in all of the gardens and the bees going backwards and forwards,
    For today we have naming of parts.

Henry Reed
(February 22nd 1914 –)

On this day in 1941 several hundred people were killed in air raids on Glasgow and Clydeside.
1. 'Lately I have lived in the midst of battles, creditably enough, / And have soldiered, not without glory.'
Reed plays on the opening lines of a poem by Horace (III.26), substituting 'duellis' (war/battles) for Horace's word 'puellis' (girls).

- *Prolific Roman poet Ovid, whose poetry includes* Ars Amandi *and* Metamorphoses, *born 43 BC*
- *Norwegian dramatist Henrik Ibsen, author of* Peer Gynt, *but in his own view "more of a poet", born March 20th 1823*
- *Poet and novelist David Malouf born in Brisbane March 20th 1934*
- *Lord Alfred Bruce Douglas, poet and companion of Oscar Wilde, to whom Wilde addressed 'De Profundis' from prison, died March 20th 1944*

Spring

Nothing is so beautiful as spring—
   When weeds, in wheels, shoot long and lovely and lush;
   Thrush's eggs look little low heavens, and thrush
Through the echoing timber does so rinse and wring
The ear, it strikes like lightnings to hear him sing;
   The glassy peartree leaves and blooms, they brush
   The descending blue; that blue is all in a rush
With richness; the racing lambs too have fair their fling.

What is all this juice and all this joy?
   A strain of the earth's sweet being in the beginning
In Eden garden.—Have, get, before it cloy,
   Before it cloud, Christ, lord, and sour with sinning,
Innocent mind and Mayday in girl and boy,
   Most, O maid's child, thy choice and worthy the winning.

Gerard Manley Hopkins
(July 28th 1844 – June 8th 1889)

On this day in 1884, Coventry Patmore, a haughty Catholic poet to whom Hopkins had shown his poems, replied discouragingly: "... to the already sufficiently arduous character of such poetry you seem to me to have added the difficulty of following several entirely novel and simultaneous experiments in versification and construction, together with an altogether unprecedented system of alliteration and compound words;—any one of which novelties would be startling and productive of distraction from the poetic matter ..."

March 21

*Robert Southey died March 21st 1843

• *Robert Southey died March 21st 1843*
• *The American Pulitzer Prize-winning poet Phyllis McGinley, whose poems include 'Epithalamion (If Spenser Had Been on the Staff of The Bride's Magazine)', was born March 21st 1905*

The Old Man's Comforts
and how he gained them

You are old, Father William, the young man cried,
    The few locks which are left you are grey;
You are hale, Father William, a hearty old man,
    Now tell me the reason, I pray.

In the days of my youth, Father William replied,
    I remember'd that youth would fly fast,
And abused not my health and my vigour at first,
    That I never might need them at last.

You are old, Father William, the young man cried,
    And pleasures with youth pass away;
And yet you lament not the days that are gone,
    Now tell me the reason, I pray.

In the days of my youth, Father William replied,
    I remember'd that youth could not last;
I thought of the future, whatever I did,
    That I never might grieve for the past.

You are old, Father William, the young man cried,
    And life must be hastening away;
You are cheerful, and love to converse upon death,
    Now tell me the reason, I pray.

I am cheerful, young man, Father William replied,
    Let the cause thy attention engage;
In the days of my youth I remember'd my God!
    And He hath not forgotten my age.

Robert Southey
(August 12th 1774 – March 21st 1843)

Southey was born in Bristol and from the age of two to six he was handed by his draper father and mother to his mother's half-sister to bring up. As an adult he would "kiss and weep on his mother" in his dreams. He was thrown out of Westminster School for starting *The Flagellant* magazine and at Oxford almost persuaded Coleridge to migrate to America to set up a Pantisocrat commune utopia. In June 1798, he set up home independently for the first time in a rented former ale-house at Westbury-on-Trym in Gloucestershire, with his wife and his now widowed mother. He wrote 'Old Man's Comfort' at Westbury in the spring of 1799 at the age of 24, having undertaken to supply poems for the *Morning Post* at a guinea a week. "This was one of the happiest portions of my life," he wrote later, "I never before or since produced so much poetry in the same space of time."

He became very conservative in later life and was made Poet Laureate. At the age of 60 he wrote: "I have been parted from my wife by something worse than death. Forty years she has been the life of my life, and I have left her this day in a lunatic asylum." He remarried, but his own mind began to fail and he died at the age of 70.

• *Johann Wolfgang von Goethe, German court official, theatre director, novelist, scientist, poet and dramatist (author of the poetic drama* Faust*), died March 22nd 1832*
• *Francis William Bourdillon born March 22nd 1852*

Night

The night has a thousand eyes,
   And the day but one;
Yet the light of the bright world dies
   With the dying sun.

The mind has a thousand eyes,
   And the heart but one;
Yet the light of a whole life dies,
   When love is done.

Francis William Bourdillon
(March 22nd 1852 – January 30th 1921)

Bourdillon was the son of a priest. He was educated at Worcester College, Oxford, became the resident tutor to the two sons of the Prince and Princess Christian at Cumberland Lodge, and later took private pupils for the University of Eastbourne. He produced a number of books and translations, including *Early Editions of the Roman de la Rose* and *Preludes and Romances*. He lived in Buddington near Midhurst in Sussex with his wife Agnes and they had two sons and a daughter.

• *John Davidson committed suicide March 23rd 1909*
• *Poet and critic Jeremy Hooker, author of* Master of the Leaping Figures, *born in Warsash near Southampton March 23rd 1941*

Imagination

There is a dish to hold the sea,
    A brazier to contain the sun,
A compass for the galaxy,
    A voice to wake the dead and done!

That minister of ministers,
    Imagination, gathers up
The undiscovered Universe,
    Like jewels in a jasper cup.

Its flame can mingle north and south;
    Its accent with the thunder strive;
The ruddy sentence of its mouth
    Can make the ancient dead alive.

The mart of power, the fount of will,
    The form and mold of every star,
The source and bound of good and ill,
    The key of all the things that are,

Imagination, new and strange
    In every age, can turn the year;
Can shift the poles and lightly change
    The mood of men, the world's career

John Davidson
(April 11th 1857 – March 23rd 1909)

The Scottish playwright and poet John Davidson was born in Barrhead, Renfrewshire. His family background was somewhat unstable – he was the son of a minister from an extreme sect and had a brother who tried to kill his mother with a carving knife. At 13, he worked in a chemical works, and two years later became a pupil-teacher. Yeats described meeting him in the British Museum Reading Room in about 1894. "I am writing verse," Davidson told him. "I had been writing prose for a long time, and then one day I thought I might just as well write what I liked, as I must starve in any case. It was the luckiest thought I ever had, for my agent now gets me forty pounds for a ballad, and I made three hundred out of my last book of verse."

But a few months after this meeting, Yeats wrote, "Davidson had spent his inspiration. 'The fires are out', he said, 'and I must hammer the cold iron.' When I heard a few years ago that he had drowned himself [off Penzance], I knew that I had always expected some such end."

Nevertheless, Yeats spoke of his poetry as finding "new subject matter, new emotions"; and T. S. Eliot described Davidson's satiric Cockney monologue 'Thirty Bob A Week' as a "great poem for ever".

- *William Morris, poet, craftsman and socialist, born March 24th 1834*
- *Henry Wadsworth Longfellow ('Hiawatha') died March 24th 1882*
- *J. M. Synge, whom Yeats described as "Passionate and simple like his heart", died from Hodgkin's disease March 24th 1909*
- *Lawrence Ferlinghetti born March 24th 1919*
- *Hardy's favourite, Charlotte Mew ("the best woman poet of our day") committed suicide March 24th 1928*
- *Ian Hamilton, poet and editor, born in King's Lynn March 24th 1938*

Don't Let that Horse

Don't let that horse
                              eat that violin

        cried Chagall's mother

                              But he
            kept right on
                              painting

And became famous

And kept on painting
                              The Horse With Violin In Mouth
And when he finally finished it
he jumped up upon the horse
                              and rode away
            waving the violin

And then with a low bow gave it
to the first naked nude he ran across

And there were no strings
                              attached

Lawrence Ferlinghetti
(March 24th 1919 –)

Lawrence Ferlinghetti was born in Yonkers, New York, and educated at Columbia University and the Sorbonne. As the City Lights Book publisher of Allen Ginsberg's *Howl*, he is identified with the Beat movement. Apart from his best-selling *A Coney Island of the Mind* (1958), his poetry has included *Pictures of the Gone World* (1955) and *Open Eye, Open Heart* (1973). He has said that much of his work was written by talking into a tape recorder and was designed to be read aloud.

March 25

• *Shelley was expelled from University College, Oxford, after refusing to admit authorship of* The Necessity of Atheism, *March 25th 1811*
• *The youngest of the Brontë sisters, Anne Brontë, poet and novelist (pseudonym Acton Bell) was born March 25th 1820*
• *John Drinkwater, a prolific poet who founded a theatre company in Birmingham and wrote plays, died March 25th 1937*

The Destruction of Sennacherib

The Assyrian came down like a wolf on the fold,
And his cohorts were gleaming in purple and gold;
And the sheen of their spears was like stars on the sea,
When the blue wave rolls nightly on deep Galilee.

Like the leaves of the forest when Summer is green,
That host with their banners at sunset were seen;
Like the leaves of the forest when Autumn hath blown,
That host on the morrow lay withered and strown.

For the Angel of Death spread his wings on the blast,
And breathed in the face of the foe as he pass'd;
And the eyes of the sleepers wax'd deadly and chill,
And their hearts but once heaved, and for ever grew still!

And there lay the steed with his nostril all wide;
But through it there roll'd not the breath of his pride:
And the foam of his gasping lay white on the turf,
And cold as the spray of the rock-beating surf.

And there lay the rider, distorted and pale,
With the dew on his brow and the rust on his mail;
And the tents were all silent, the banners alone,
The lances uplifted, the trumpet unblown.

And the widows of Ashur are loud in their wail;
And the idols are broke in the temple of Baal;
And the might of the Gentile, unsmote by the sword,
Hath melted like snow in the glance of the Lord!

George Gordon, Lord Byron
(January 22nd 1788 – April 19th 1824)

On this day in 1812, Annabella Milbanke, a reserved and serious woman, saw Byron for the first time and recorded her impressions of this darling of fashionable society. "His mouth," she observed, "continually betrays the acrimony of his spirit." His pride and passion inflamed by her snubs, Byron launched a calculated courtship, posing as the hell-raising rake who longed to reform.

Once won round, Annabella quickly discovered that Byron's infatuation fell a long way short of love. Only hours after their wedding and still in the carriage which had brought them from the church, Byron taunted her: "Whatever induced you to marry me? What a dupe you have been to your imagination! How is it possible that a woman of your sense could form the wild hope of reforming me? It is enough for me that you are my wife for me to hate you! If you were the wife of any other man, I own you might have charm."

Exactly twelve months later she arranged a legal separation. Byron fought the action unsuccessfully, furious that she should have chosen to leave him.

- *A. E. Housman born March 26th 1859*
- *New England poet Robert Frost was born in San Francisco March 26th 1874*
- Leaves of Grass *poet, Walt Whitman, paralysed since 1873, died in Camden, New Jersey, March 26th 1892*
- *Beat Generation poet Gregory Corso (author of* Gasoline *and* Bomb*) born March 26th 1930*

From A Shropshire Lad
XXXII

From far, from eve and morning
  And yon twelve-winded sky,
The stuff of life to knit me
  Blew hither: here am I.

Now—for a breath I tarry
  Nor yet disperse apart—
Take my hand quick and tell me,
  What have you in your heart.

Speak now, and I will answer;
  How shall I help you, say;
Ere to the wind's twelve quarters
  I take my endless way.

A. E. Housman
(March 26th 1859 – April 30th 1936)

Housman formed a passionate friendship with Moses Jackson whilst at St John's College, Oxford. Soon after Jackson's marriage and emigration to India, Housman began writing poetry, and he published *A Shropshire Lad* privately in 1896. Its poems became very popular during the First World War. Housman himself withdrew from the world to become the stiff, aloof, austere man who admitted: "The emotional part of my life was over when I was thirty five years old."

March 27

• Louis Simpson born in Jamaica March 27th 1923. Of American poetry he writes: "Whatever it is, it must have / A stomach that can digest / Rubber, coal, uranium, moons, poems ..."

From Ode: Intimations of Immortality from Recollections of Early Childhood

There was a time when meadow, grove, and stream,
    The earth, and every common sight
      To me did seem
    Apparell'd in celestial light,
The glory and the freshness of a dream.
It is not now as it has been of yore;—
      Turn wheresoe'er I may,
      By night or day,
The things which I have seen I now can see no more!
    The rainbow comes and goes,
    And lovely is the rose;
    The moon doth with delight
Look round her when the heavens are bare;
    Waters on a starry night
    Are beautiful and fair;
    The sunshine is a glorious birth;
    But yet I know, where'er I go,
That there hath pass'd away a glory from the earth.

William Wordsworth
(April 7th 1770 – April 23rd 1850)

In her Grasmere Journal for March 27th 1802, Wordsworth's sister Dorothy wrote: "A divine morning. At breakfast Wm. wrote part of an ode [above]. Mr Oliff sent the dung and Wm. went to work in the garden. We sate all day in the orchard."

• *William Wycherley, playwright whose verses Alexander Pope revised, was born in Clive near Shrewsbury March 28th 1641. The fortune left him by his wife the Countess of Drogheda involved him in a lawsuit which left him penniless. He was sent to the Fleet prison for debt. Several years later, James II, who had seen his play* The Plain Dealer, *freed him and gave him a pension*

My Heart Leaps Up

My heart leaps up when I behold
    A rainbow in the sky:
So was it when my life began;
So is it now I am a man;
So be it when I shall grow old,
    Or let me die!
The Child is father of the Man;
And I could wish my days to be
Bound each to each by natural piety.

William Wordsworth
(April 7th 1770 – April 23rd 1850)

This poem was written on March 26th 1802, as is noted by Wordsworth's sister Dorothy in her journal's account of the day: "A beautiful morning. William wrote to Annette, then worked on 'The Cuckoo'. I was ill and in bad spirits – After dinner I sate 2 hours in the orchard. William and I walked together after tea, first to the top of White Moss, then to Mr Oliff's. I left Wm. and while he was absent wrote out poems. I grew alarmed and went to seek him – I met him at Mr. Cliff's. He has been trying, without success, to alter a passage – in 'Silver Hew' poem. He had written a conclusion just before he went out. While I was getting into bed, he wrote 'The Rainbow' [My heart leaps up]."

Their friend Coleridge considered this poem an expression of the truth that "men are ungrateful to others only when they have ceased to look back on their former selves with joy and tenderness. They exist in fragments."

March 29

Charles Wesley, writer of 5,000 hymns (including 'Hark, the Herald Angels sing'), died March 29th 1788
Welsh priest and poet of harsh pastoral themes, R. S. Thomas was born in Cardiff March 29th 1913

Thou art indeed just, Lord

*Justus quidem tu es, Domine, si disputem tecum: verumtamen
justa loquar ad te: Quare via impiorum prosperatur? &c.*[1]

Thou art indeed just, Lord, if I contend
With thee; but, sir, so what I plead is just.
Why do sinners' ways prosper? and why must
Disappointment all I endeavour end?
   Wert thou my enemy, O thou my friend,
How wouldst thou worse, I wonder, than thou dost
Defeat, thwart me? Oh, the sots and thralls of lust
Do in spare hours more thrive than I that spend,
Sir, life upon thy cause. See, banks and brakes[2]
Now, leavèd how thick! lacèd they are again
With fretty chervil[3], look, and fresh wind shakes
Them; birds build—but not I build; no, but strain,
Time's eunuch, and not breed one work that wakes.
Mine, O thou lord of life, send my roots rain.

*Gerard Manley Hopkins
(July 28th 1844 – June 8th 1889)*

On this day in 1883, Hopkins wrote from Dublin to his old university friend Alexander Baillie: "It is a great help to have someone ... that will answer my letters, and it supplies some sort of intellectual stimulus. I sadly need that and a general stimulus to being, so dull and yet harassed is my life."

Hopkins wrote this sonnet in the spring of 1889. Several months before he had felt a sense of despair whilst on a retreat at St Stanislaus's College, Tullamore: "What is my wretched life? Five wasted years almost have passed in Ireland. I am ashamed of the little I have done, of my waste of time, although my helplessness and weakness is such that I could scarcely do otherwise ... All my undertakings miscarry: I am like a straining eunuch. I wish then for death: yet if I died now I should die imperfect, no master of myself, and that is the worst failure of all. O my God, look down on me ..."

Hopkins commented on this sonnet to Robert Bridges: "Observe it must be read ... with great stress."

1. The Latin quotation comes from the Vulgate version of Chapter 12 of the Book of Jeremiah. The first three lines of the poem translate the Latin, while the "&c" suggests the relevance to the poem of the rest of the Chapter.
2. Thickets.
3. Cow-parsley, a herb with leaves like lace or fretwork.

- *French poet Paul Verlaine, who in 1873 shot Rimbaud in the wrist, was born in Metz, March 30th 1844*
- *Frances Cornford born March 30th 1886*
- *Julian Grenfell, who wrote 'Into Battle' and was killed at Ypres in 1915, was born March 30th 1888*

To a Fat Lady Seen from the Train
Triolet

O why do you walk through the fields in gloves,
   Missing so much and so much?
O fat white woman whom nobody loves,
Why do you walk through the fields in gloves,
When the grass is soft as the breast of doves
   And shivering-sweet to the touch?
O why do you walk through the fields in gloves,
   Missing so much and so much?

Frances Cornford
(March 30th 1886 – August 19th 1960)

Frances Cornford, the granddaughter of Charles Darwin, was born and lived in Cambridge. This is her best known poem. She married the philosopher, Francis M. Cornford. Their son John, a Communist at the LSE, was the first Englishman to enrol against Franco, and was killed in Spain in 1936.

March 31

• *Andrew Marvell born at Winestead in Yorkshire, the son of a clergyman, March 31st 1621*
• *John Donne died March 31st 1631*
• *Translator and poet Edward FitzGerald born March 31st 1809*
• *Charlotte Brontë, author of* Jane Eyre, *who published* Poems *jointly with her three sisters, died March 31st 1855*
• *Mexican poet and diplomat Octavio Paz born March 31st 1914*

Death, Be Not Proud

Death, be not proud, though some have called thee
Mighty and dreadful, for thou art not so:
For those whom thou think'st thou dost overthrow
Die not, poor Death; nor yet canst thou kill me.
From Rest and Sleep, which but thy pictures be,
Much pleasure, then from thee much more must flow;
And soonest our best men with thee do go –
Rest of their bones and souls' delivery.
Thou'rt slave to fate, chance, kings, and desperate men,
And dost with poison, war, and sickness dwell;
And poppy or charms can make us sleep as well
And better than thy stroke. Why swell'st thou then?
One short sleep past, we wake eternally,
And Death shall he no more: Death, thou shalt die.

John Donne
(c. June 1572 – March 31st 1631)

Donne wanted control of his own dying. He wrote a treatise entitled *Biathanatos* in defence of suicide in which he claimed that Jesus committed suicide. To a friend he wrote: "I would not that death should take me asleep. I would not have him merely seize me, and only declare me to be dead, but win me, and overcome me." He died dramatically, rising from his sick-bed to preach a last sermon, getting dressed in his shroud to have his portrait painted, and then, according to Izaak Walton, "he was so happy to have nothing to do but to die ... As ... his last breath departed from him, he closed his own eyes, and then disposed his hands and body into such a posture, as required not the least alteration by those that came to shroud him."

- *John Wilmot, Earl of Rochester, born April 1st 1647*
- *Wordsworth at first declined to become Poet Laureate as being too old to fulfil its duties, April 1st 1843*
- *French poet and dramatist Edmond Rostand, author of* Cyrano de Bergerac, *born April 1st 1868*
- *Emily Dickinson's beloved clergyman, Revd. Charles Wadsworth, died April 1st 1882. "Love has but one Date" for Emily thereafter*
- *Blunt and realistic war poet Isaac Rosenberg, the son of Russian Jewish émigrés, killed in battle near Arras April 1st 1918*

A Song of a Young Lady to Her Ancient Lover

Ancient person, for whom I
All the flattering youth defy,
Long be it ere thou grow old,
Aching, shaking, crazy, cold;
   But still continue as thou art,
   Ancient person of my heart.

On thy withered lips and dry,
Which like barren furrows lie,
Brooding kisses I will pour
Shall thy youthful heat restore
(Such kind showers in autumn fall,
And a second spring recall);
   Nor from thee will ever part,
   Ancient person of my heart.

Thy nobler part, which but to name
In our sex would be counted shame,
By age's frozen grasp possessed,
From his ice shall be released,
And soothed by my reviving hand,
In former warmth and vigor stand.
All a lover's wish can reach
For thy joy my love shall teach,
And for thy pleasure shall improve
All that art can add to love.
   Yet still I love thee without art,
   Ancient person of my heart.

John Wilmot, Earl of Rochester
(April 1st 1647 – July 26th 1680)

John Wilmot was born in Ditchley in Oxfordshire, with a Royalist father and a mother with a Parliamentarian background, who was nevertheless in the 1650s forced into exile with her children. John became Earl of Rochester at the age of 12 and lived a recklessly brave and dissolute, bisexual existence at the court of Charles II. He married the rich heiress he had previously forcibly abducted (and been sent to the Tower for so doing). He died, either of kidney stones or syphilis, at the age of 32, having made his peace with both his wife and his maker. In Samuel Johnson's view, Rochester had "blazed out his youth and his health in lavish voluptuousness".

April 2

- Danish poet and author of fairy tales (such as 'The Emperor's New Clothes'), Hans Christian Andersen was born the son of a poor shoemaker April 2nd 1805
- On April 2nd 1849, Tennyson read Palgrave songs for The Princess and poems on Hallam; "some exquisite," said Palgrave
- Kipling elected as youngest member of Athenaeum April 2nd 1897, his nomination seconded by Henry James
- Katharine Tynan died April 2nd 1931

Joining the Colours
(West Kents, Dublin, 1914)

There they go marching all in step so gay!
　Smooth-cheeked and golden, food for shells and guns.
Blithely they go as to a wedding day,
　　　The mothers' sons.

The drab street stares to see them row on row
　On the high tram-tops, singing like the lark.
Too careless-gay for courage, singing they go
　　　Into the dark.

With tin whistles, mouth-organs, any noise,
　They pipe the way to glory and the grave;
Foolish and young, the gay and golden boys
　　　Love cannot save.

High heart! High courage! The poor girls they kissed
　Run with them: they shall kiss no more, alas!
Out of the mist they stepped – into the mist
　　　Singing they pass.

Katharine Tynan
(January 23rd 1861 – April 2nd 1931)

Katharine Tynan was born into a Catholic farming family in County Dublin. She became a friend of Yeats – indeed he wondered at one point whether he ought to propose to her – and played her part in the Celtic literary revival. Her two sons served in the First World War.

- *George Herbert born April 3rd 1593*
- *Donne preached the first sermon that Charles I heard as new king on April 3rd 1625*
- *Donne buried at St Paul's Cathedral April 3rd 1631*

Virtue

Sweet day, so cool, so calm, so bright!
The bridal of the earth and sky—
The dew shall weep thy fall tonight;
    For thou must die.

Sweet rose, whose hue angry and brave
Bids the rash gazer wipe his eye,
Thy root is ever in its grave,
    And thou must die.

Sweet spring, full of sweet days and roses,
A box where sweets compacted lie,
My music shows ye have your closes,
    And all must die.

Only a sweet and virtuous soul,
Like season'd timber, never gives;
But though the whole world turn to coal,
    Then chiefly lives.

George Herbert
(April 3rd 1593 – March 3rd 1633)

Herbert was born in Montgomery into a distinguished Anglo-Welsh family. His mother, Lady Magdalen, was Donne's patron, to whom Donne addressed his *Holy Sonnets*. Donne seems to have helped influence Herbert away from political and court life towards the church, which he entered shortly after marriage to Jane Danvers, the rich and beautiful cousin of his stepfather.

As a young man, Herbert was criticised for placing too much value on his noble ancestry, but as a priest he was noted for his humility and popularity, befriending all his parishioners and encouraging them to read. He wrote, "The Countrey Parson preacheth constantly, the Pulpit is his joy and his throne."

He died of consumption, aged 40. Like Donne, he prepared for his death – his first biographer Izaak Walton describes him on his deathbed composing "such hymns and anthems as the angels and he now sing in heaven".

April 4

• Shakespeare's sister Ann buried April 4th 1579, aged seven
• As You Like It and Much Ado About Nothing placed on the Stationers Register in London, April 4th 1600
• Dissipated poet ('The Deserted Village'), novelist ('The Vicar of Wakefield') and playwright ('She Stoops to Conquer'), Oliver Goldsmith died aged 46 on April 4th 1774
• On April 4th 1843 Wordsworth accepted Poet Laureateship
• Maya Angelou born April 4th 1928

Still I Rise

You may write me down in history
With your bitter, twisted lies,
You may trod me in the very dirt
But still, like dust, I'll rise.

Does my sassiness upset you?
Why are you beset with gloom?
'Cause I walk like I've got oil wells
Pumping in my living room.

Just like moons and like suns,
With the certainty of tides,
Just like hopes springing high,
Still I'll rise.

Did you want to see me broken?
Bowed head and lowered eyes?
Shoulders falling down like teardrops,
Weakened by my soulful cries.

Does my haughtiness offend you?
Don't you take it awful hard
'Cause I laugh like I've got gold mines
Diggin' in my own back yard.

You may shoot me with your words,
You may cut me with your eyes,
You may kill me with your hatefulness,
But still, like air, I'll rise.

Does my sexiness upset you?
Does it come as a surprise
That I dance like I've got diamonds
At the meeting of my thighs?

Out of the huts of history's shame
I rise
Up from a past that's rooted in pain
I rise
I'm a black ocean, leaping and wide,
Welling and swelling I bear in the tide.

Leaving behind nights of terror and fear
I rise
Into a daybreak that's wondrously clear
I rise
Bringing the gifts that my ancestors gave,
I am the dream and the hope of the slave.
I rise
I rise
I rise.

Maya Angelou
(April 4th 1928 –)

Maya Angelou has a volume of verse with the title *And Still I Rise*. Her spirit and joie de vivre seem intact despite a difficult upbringing – her parents broke up, she was raped by her mother's boyfriend, became mute for five years and was for a time a prostitute. Her passionate stories of life as a singer, performer, dancer and Black activist unfold in her autobiographies, starting with *I Know Why the Caged Bird Sings*. More recently she wrote and recited a poem for Clinton's inauguration as President.

• *Algernon Charles Swinburne born April 5th 1837*
• *Richard Eberhart, who wrote the war poem 'The Fury of Aerial Bombardment', born in Austin, Minnesota, April 5th 1904*

Love and Sleep

Lying asleep between the strokes of night
   I saw my love lean over my sad bed,
   Pale as the duskiest lily's leaf or head,
Smooth-skinned and dark, with bare throat made to bite,
Too wan for blushing and too warm for white,
   But perfect-coloured without white or red.
And her lips opened amorously, and said –
I wist not what, saving one word – Delight.

And all her face was honey to my mouth,
   And all her body pasture to mine eyes;
      The long lithe arms and hotter hands than fire
The quivering flanks, hair smelling of the south,
   The bright light feet, the splendid supple thighs
      And glittering eyelids of my soul's desire.

Algernon Charles Swinburne
(April 5th 1837 – April 10th 1909)

Swinburne was born in London, the son of Admiral Charles Swinburne and Lady Jane Ashburnham. Beating and bullying received at Eton left him with a masochistic preoccupation with flagellation. He failed to graduate from Balliol College, Oxford. This was the man who, according to Edgell Rickword, "shattered the virginal reticence of Victoria's serenest years with a book of poems" – the uninhibited tone of Swinburne's *Poems and Ballads* of 1866 with their celebration of "the roses and raptures of vice" were a sensation at the time. But his constitution became too frail for his Bohemian lifestyle – Rossetti would have to pin Swinburne's address to his coat collar as the only way to ensure his safe return from drinking bouts. For the last forty years of his life he lodged with his friend Theodore Watts-Dunton at No. 2 The Pines, Putney. His friend weaned him from drink, but the exuberance and rebelliousness gradually faded from his writing.

April 6

From The General Prologue *to* The Canterbury Tales

Whan that Aprill with his shoures soote°   *sweet*
The droghte of March hath perced to the roote,
And bathed every veyne° in swich° licour°   *veins (ie. in plants); such; liquid*
Of which vertu° engendred is the flour;   *potency*
When Zephirus° eek° with his sweete breeth   *the west wind; also*
Inspired° hath in every holt and heeth°   *Quickened; woodland and heathland*
The tendre croppes°, and the yonge sonne   *shoots*
Hath in the Ram° his halve cours yronne,   *Aries*
And smale foweles° maken melodye,   *birds*
That slepen al the nyght with open ye°   *eye*
(So priketh° hem° nature in hir corages°);   *incites; them; hearts*
Thanne longen folk to goon on pilgrimages,
And palmeres° for to seken straunge strondes°,   *professional pilgrims; shores*
To ferne halwes°, kowthe° in sondry londes;   *far-off shrines; known*
And specially from every shires ende
Of Engelond to Caunterbury they wende°,   *go*
The hooly blisful° martir° for to seke,   *blessed; St Thomas à Beckett*
That hem hath holpen° whan that they were seeke°.   *helped; sick*

Geoffrey Chaucer
(ca. 1343 – October 25th 1400)

Many Latin and Italian works have introductory lines on Spring. These Mediterranean models may account for March being described as a dry month. It has been suggested on very slender evidence that Chaucer himself went on a pilgrimage to Canterbury in April 1387 or 1388, perhaps because his wife Philippa was ill.

From Intimations of Immortality from Recollections of Early Childhood

Our birth is but a sleep and a forgetting:
The Soul that rises with us, our life's Star,
    Hath had elsewhere its setting,
     And cometh from afar:
    Not in entire forgetfulness,
    And not in utter nakedness,
But trailing clouds of glory do we come
    From God, who is our home:
Heaven lies about us in our infancy!
Shades of the prison-house begin to close
    Upon the growing Boy,
But He beholds the light, and whence it flows,
    He sees it in his joy;
The Youth, who daily farther from the east
    Must travel, still is Nature's Priest,
    And by the vision splendid
    Is on his way attended;
At length the Man perceives it die away,
And fade into the light of common day.

William Wordsworth
(April 7th 1770 – April 23rd 1850)

Wordsworth in his dictated memoirs says: "I was born at Cockermouth, in Cumberland, on April 7th 1770, the second son of John Wordsworth, attorney-at-law ... The time of my infancy and early boyhood was passed partly at Cockermouth, and partly with my mother's parents at Penrith, where my mother, in the year 1778, died of a decline, brought on by a cold ... My father never recovered his usual cheerfulness of mind after this loss, and died when I was in my fourteenth year, a schoolboy ...[It was told me that I] was the only one of her five children about whose future ... [my mother] was anxious ... [that I would be] remarkable either for good or for evil. The cause of this was, that I was of a stiff, moody, and violent temper."

He described this poem's origins on his childhood's "sense of the indomitableness of the spirit within me".

April 8

From The Jungle Books
Mowgli's Brothers (chapter heading)

Now Chil the Kite brings home the night
    That Mang the Bat sets free—
The herds are shut in byre and hut,
    For loosed till dawn are we.
This is the hour of pride and power,
    Talon and tush and claw.
Oh, hear the call!—Good hunting all
    That keep the Jungle Law!

Rudyard Kipling
(December 30th 1865 – January 18th 1936)

On this day in 1891, Kipling wrote to Hallam Tennyson in gratitude for his father's kind words about Kipling's work. If there is any good in it, "he knows more than I," and he added that Tennyson's commendation was worth more than a decoration in the field to him.

The Jungle Books appeared in 1894 and 1895. *Mowgli's Brothers* was inspired in part by a scene from H. Rider Haggard's *Nada the Lily*. The immutable Law of the Jungle to which Kipling refers above is partly defined in *The Jungle Books* as follows:

As the creeper that girdles the tree trunk, the Law runneth forward and back –
For the strength of the Pack is the Wolf, and the strength of the Wolf is the Pack.
The jackal may follow the tiger, but, Cub, when thy whiskers are grown,
    Remember the wolf is a hunter – go forth and get food of thine own.
Keep peace with the Lords of the Jungle – the Tiger, the Panther, the Bear;
    And trouble not Hathi the Silent, and mock not the Bear in his lair.
Now these are the Laws of the Jungle, and many and mighty are they;
    But the head and the hoof of the Law and the haunch and the hump is –
Obey!

- *Charles Baudelaire, who was prosecuted for impropriety for his poems Les Fleurs du mal, was born April 9th 1821*
- *Adela Florence Nicolson (pseudonym 'Laurence Hope', author of Indian Love Lyrics) born April 9th 1865*
- *Susan Coolidge, poet from Ohio who also wrote stories for girls, died April 9th 1905*
- *E. J. Scovell born April 9th 1907*
- *Edward Thomas killed in the battle of Arras by a shell blast April 9th 1917*

Love's Immaturity

Not weaned yet, without comprehension loving,
We feed at breasts of love; like a still cat
That wears and loves the fire in peace, till moving
She slips off fire and love, to cross the mat

As new as birth; so by default denying
House-roof and human friends that come and go,
The landscape of life's dream. Antelopes flying
Over his wild earth serve the lion so.

We are blind children who answer with love
A warmth and sweetness. Those even we love most
We sleep within their lives like cats, and rove
Out in the night, and late return and coast

Their souls like furniture. Oh, life should give
Light till we understand they live, they live.

E. J. Scovell
(April 9th 1907 –)

E. J. Scovell comments: "In this poem (from the 1930s) a young woman at a very happy time of life is surprised by noticing the selfishness & flightiness in her love & wishes it away."

E(dith) J(oy) Scovell was born in Sheffield, received a degree from Somerville College, Oxford, worked as an ecological field assistant in Brazil and Panama, has two children and lives in Oxford. Her poems, published by Carcanet, have been described by Philip Hobsbaum as showing "attention to detail and an almost mystical sense of the process of life".

April 10

• On April 10th 1791, Burns' third son was born – a few days before his illegitimate daughter by Anne Park
• Coleridge discharged from army as 'insane' April 10th 1794
• John Keats dated his Preface to 'Endymion' April 10th 1818 [1]
• Algernon Charles Swinburne, reformed Bohemian, died from pneumonia at the home of Watts-Dunton, April 10th 1909
• Liverpool 'Pop Poet' Adrian Henri born April 10th 1932

From Endymion
Book I

A thing of beauty is a joy for ever:
Its loveliness increases, it will never
Pass into nothingness; but still will keep
A bower quiet for us, and a sleep
Full of sweet dreams, and health, and quiet breathing.
Therefore, on every morrow, are we wreathing
A flowery band to bind us to the earth,
Spite of despondence, of the inhuman dearth
Of noble natures, of the gloomy days,
Of all the unhealthy and o'er-darkened ways
Made of our searching; yes, in spite of all,
Some shape of beauty moves away the pall
From our dark spirits.

John Keats
(October 31st 1795 – February 23rd 1821)

1. In his Preface to 'Endymion' Keats warned readers that they "must soon perceive great inexperience, immaturity, and every error denoting a feverish attempt, rather than a deed accomplished" in the poetry that followed. Reviewing the work for *Blackwood's Magazine*, John Gibson Lockhart, no lover of what he called 'The Cockney School of Poetry', agreed and ventured the opinion that the poem was one of "calm, settled, imperturbable, drivelling idiocy".

- *Christopher Smart born April 11th 1722*
- *John Davidson, Scottish poet of "dingy urban images" (T. S. Eliot), born in Barrhead, Renfrewshire, April 11th 1857*
- *Australian poet Bernard O'Dowd born April 11th 1886*

From A Song to David

Strong is the horse upon his speed;
Strong in pursuit the rapid glede°,   *bird of prey*
　　Which makes at once his game:
Strong the tall ostrich on the ground;
Strong through the turbulent profound
　　Shoots Xiphias to his aim.

Strong is the lion – like a coal
His eyeball, – like a bastion's mole
　　His chest against the foes:
Strong the gier-eagle on his sail;
Strong against tide th' enormous whale
　　Emerges as he goes.

But stronger still, in earth and air,
And in the sea, the man of prayer,
　　And far beneath the tide:
And in the seat to faith assign'd,
Where ask is have, where seek is find,
　　Where knock is open wide.

Christopher Smart
(April 11th 1722 – May 21st 1771)

Christopher Smart was born in Shipbourne, near Tunbridge Wells. He was summed up by Odell Shepard as "a university wit and scholar, a translator of Horace and a Grub Street hack, a drunkard, a Bedlamite, and a radiantly happy Christian who died in a debtors' prison". At Cambridge he slept in class, and drank heavily in taverns. By the age of 25 he was deeply in debt and in fear of his creditors. At the age of 34 he was admitted to the Bedlam asylum. There he was visited by Samuel Johnson, who concluded that Smart's behaviour was "not noxious to society. He insisted on people praying with him – also falling on his knees and saying his prayers in the street – but I'd as lief pray with Kit Smart as anyone else".

Denied the use of paper and pen in Bedlam, it is said that Smart scratched out 'A Song to David' with a key on his room's wainscot. The poem was written in self-identification with David the psalmist and inspired poet-priest, "the great Author of the Book of Gratitude". His friend W. Mason, on reading 'A Song to David', declared Smart "as mad as ever". But Browning compared the poem to a great cathedral – Smart designed it to have a mathematical and mystical structure based on the grouping of the stanzas.

Smart ended up as a debtor in the King's Bench Prison, dying there at the age of 49.

in Just–
spring   when the world is mud-
luscious the little
lame balloonman

whistles   far   and wee

and eddieandbill come
running from marbles and
piracies and it's
spring

when the world is puddle-wonderful

the queer
old balloonman whistles
far   and   wee
and bettyandisbel come dancing

from hop-scotch and jump-rope and

it's
spring
and
    the

            goat-footed

balloonMan   whistles
far
and
wee

> *e. e. cummings*
> *(October 14th 1894 – September 3rd 1962)*

On this day in 1930, Cummings wrote an exuberant, freewheeling letter to John Dos Passos: "...Q; Whence the phrase 'virgin forest'? / A; Only God can make a tree .../ (From the Sanscrit) HATS off to thea orthodox bee, / who attempted to bugger a bee / but emerged from thea fray / in a familea way .../which is why wea do things so fee-blea".

The manuscript version of the 'in Just - / spring' poem has "ooze-suave" instead of "puddle-wonderful". The poem has been associated with Cummings' childhood memories of his backyard in West Cambridge, Massachusetts, a small island of greenery with a tree house.

- *Cervantes, the Spanish author of* Don Quixote, *died April 13th 1616*
- *Marvell admitted as a scholar to Trinity College, Cambridge April 13th 1638*
- *John Dryden appointed Poet Laureate April 13th 1668*
- *Seamus Heaney born April 13th 1939*

From Mossbawn: Two Poems In Dedication
For Mary Heaney
Sunlight

There was a sunlit absence.
The helmeted pump in the yard
heated its iron,
water honeyed

in the slung bucket
and the sun stood
like a griddle cooling
against the wall

of each long afternoon.
So, her hands scuffled
over the bakeboard,
the reddening stove

sent its plaque of heat
against her where she stood
in a floury apron
by the window.

Now she dusts the board
with a goose's wing,
now sits, broad-lapped,
with whitened nails

and measling shins:
here is a space
again, the scone rising
to the tick of two clocks.

And here is love
like a tinsmith's scoop
sunk past its gleam
in the meal-bin.

Seamus Heaney
(April 13th 1939 –)

Seamus Heaney was born in Mossbawn, County Derry, Northern Ireland, the eldest of 11 children, and the son of a Catholic farmer. He won a scholarship to St Columb's College, and in 1965 became a lecturer and married Mary Devlin. The next year saw the publication of his first book of poetry, *Death of a Naturalist*. Some of his recent poetry, *The Haw Lantern* (1987) and *Seeing Things* (1991), has been concerned with the death of his parents.

• On April 14th 1816, Byron told Lady Byron that they "can never meet again in this world – nor the next"
• Russian playwright and poet Vladimir Mayakovsky, an outspoken supporter of the Revolution, but a disillusioned outsider in its wake, committed suicide April 14th 1930

From Memories of President Lincoln
(in *Leaves of Grass*)
O Captain! My Captain!

O Captain! my Captain! our fearful trip is done,
The ship has weathered every rack, the prize we sought is won,
The port is near, the bells I hear, the people all exulting,
While follow eyes the steady keel, the vessel grim and daring;
    But O heart! heart! heart!
      O the bleeding drops of red!
        Where on the deck my Captain lies,
          Fallen cold and dead.

O Captain! my Captain! rise up and hear the bells;
Rise up–for you the flag is flung–for you the bugle trills,
For you bouquets and ribboned wreaths–for you the shores a–crowding,
For you they call, the swaying mass, their eager faces turning;
    Here, Captain! dear father!
      This arm beneath your head!
        It is some dream that on the deck
          You've fallen cold and dead.

My Captain does not answer, his lips are pale and still,
My father does not feel my arm, he has no pulse nor will;
The ship is anchored safe and sound, its voyage closed and done,
From fearful trip the victor ship comes in with object won;
    Exult, O shores! and ring, O bells!
      But I, with mournful tread,
        Walk the deck my Captain lies,
          Fallen cold and dead.

Walt Whitman
(May 31st 1819 – March 26th 1892)

President Lincoln was shot on Good Friday April 14th 1865 at Ford's Theatre in Washington by J. Wilkes Booth, an actor, and died next morning. Walt Whitman was at home with his mother and family in Brooklyn at the time: "Mother prepared breakfast – and other meals afterwards as usual; but not a mouthful was eaten all day by any of us. We each drank half a cup of coffee: that was all. Little was said. We got every newspaper morning and evening, and the frequent extras of that period, and pass'd them silently to each other."

• *William Oldys, poet and once librarian to the Earl of Oxford,*
released from the Fleet prison in 1755, died April 15th 1761
• *Matthew Arnold died of heart failure in Liverpool April 15th*
1888. He once wrote: "I have less poetical sentiment than
Tennyson, and less intellectual vigour than Browning; yet, because
I have perhaps more of a fusion of the two than either of them, I
am likely enough to have my turn"

Dover Beach

The sea is calm tonight.
The tide is full, the moon lies fair
Upon the straits; on the French coast the light
Gleams and is gone; the cliffs of England stand,
Glimmering and vast, out in the tranquil bay.
Come to the window, sweet is the night-air!
Only, from the long line of spray
Where the sea meets the moon-blanched land,
Listen! you hear the grating roar
Of pebbles which the waves draw back, and fling,
At their return, up the high strand,
Begin, and cease, and then again begin
With tremulous cadence slow, and bring
The eternal note of sadness in.

Sophocles long ago
Heard it on the Aegean, and it brought
Into his mind the turbid ebb and flow
Of human misery; we
Find also in the sound a thought,
Hearing it by this distant northern sea.

The Sea of Faith
Was once, too, at the full, and round earth's shore
Lay like the folds of a bright girdle furled.
But now I only hear
Its melancholy, long, withdrawing roar,
Retreating, to the breath
Of the night-wind, down the vast edges drear
And naked shingles of the world.

Ah, love, let us be true
To one another! for the world, which seems
To lie before us like a land of dreams,
So various, so beautiful, so new,
Hath really neither joy, nor love, nor light,
Nor certitude, nor peace, nor help for pain;
And we are here as on a darkling plain
Swept with confused alarms of struggle and flight,
Where ignorant armies clash by night.

Matthew Arnold
(December 24th 1822 – April 15th 1888)

April 16

• Poet and writer Aphra Behn, brought up in Surinam, a spy for
Charles II, a wit at court ("the Incomparable"), imprisoned for
debt, and Britain's first professional female author. She died April
16th 1689 and was buried in Westminster Abbey
• Novelist and poet Kingsley Amis born April 16th 1922

I wandered lonely as a cloud

I wandered lonely as a cloud
That floats on high o'er vales and hills,
When all at once I saw a crowd,
A host, of golden daffodils;
Beside the lake, beneath the trees,
Fluttering and dancing in the breeze.

Continuous as the stars that shine
And twinkle on the milky way,
They stretched in never-ending line
Along the margin of a bay:
Ten thousand saw I at a glance,
Tossing their heads in sprightly dance.

The waves beside them danced; but they
Out-did the sparkling waves in glee:
A poet could not but be gay,
In such a jocund company:
I gazed–and gazed–but little thought
What wealth the show to me had brought:

For oft, when on my couch I lie
In vacant or in pensive mood,
They flash upon that inward eye
Which is the bliss of solitude;
And then my heart with pleasure fills
And dances with the daffodils.

William Wordsworth
(April 7th 1770 – April 23rd 1850)

William's sister Dorothy described these daffodils by Ullswater in her Grasmere Journal for April 15th 1802: "We set off after dinner from Eusemere ... The wind was furious and we thought we must have returned ... The wind seized our breath, the Lake was rough ... When we were in the woods beyond Gowbarrow park we saw a few daffodils close to the water side. We fancied that the lake had floated the seeds ashore and that the little colony had so sprung up. But as we went along there were more and yet more and at last under the boughs of the trees, we saw that there was a long belt of them along the shore, about the breadth of a country turnpike road. I never saw daffodils so beautiful they grew among the mossy stones about and about them, some rested their heads upon these stones as on a pillow for weariness and the rest tossed and reeled and danced and seemed as if they verily laughed with the wind that blew upon them over the lake, they looked so gay ever glancing ever changing. This wind blew directly over the lake to them. There was here and there a little knot and a few stragglers a few yards higher up but they were so few as not to disturb the simplicity and unity and life of that one busy highway ... We put on dry clothes at Dobson's ... We had a glass of warm rum and water. We enjoyed ourselves and wished for Mary [Wordsworth's wife]." The poem was written two years after Dorothy's journal entry. Wordsworth noted that "the two best lines in it ['They flash upon that inward eye / Which is the bliss of solitude'] are by Mary."

- Henry Vaughan born in Newton-by-Usk, Powys, April 17th 1622
- The Greek poet Constantine Cavafy, whose verse was at times erotic and explicitly homosexual, was born April 17th 1863
- Basil Bunting, whose poetry Ezra Pound admired, died April 17th 1985. Bunting described himself as a "minor poet, not conspicuously dishonest"

From The Night[1]

Through that pure Virgin-shrine,
That sacred veil drawn o'er thy glorious noon
That men might look and live as Glow-worms shine,
And face the Moon:
Wise Nicodemus saw such light
As made him know his God by night.

Were all my loud, evil days
Calm and unhaunted as is thy dark Tent,
Whose peace but by some Angels wing or voice
Is seldom rent;
Then I in Heaven all the long year
Would keep, and never wander here.

But living where the Sun
Doth all things wake, and where all mix and tyre
Themselves and others, I consent and run
To ev'ry myre,
And by this world's ill-guiding light,
Err more then I can do by night.

There is in God (some say)
A deep, but dazzling darkness; as men here
Say it is late and dusky, because they
See not all clear;
O for that night! where I in him
Might live invisible and dim.

Henry Vaughan
(April 17th 1622 – April 23rd 1695)

Henry Vaughan termed himself a 'Silurist', a native of Brecon, the land of the ancient tribe of Silures. His twin brother was an alchemist whose interest in Hermeticism and magic Henry shared, although he himself was a country doctor. On the death of his wife Catherine, with whom he had four children, he married her younger sister Elizabeth and they had another four. His "profane" poetry was followed by a profoundly spiritual volume entitled *Silex Scintillans* in 1650. This new direction he attributed to a fellow poet, "the blessed man, Mr. George Herbert, whose holy life and verse gained many converts, of whom I am the least".

1. Stanzas 1, 7, 8 and 9 of this 9 stanza poem.

April 18

• Donne's 'Sermon of Valediction at my going into Germany' was preached at Lincoln's Inn April 18th 1619
• Dick Davis born April 18th 1945
• Ezra Pound adjudged sane and released by US Federal Court on April 18th 1958, 13 years after being taken into custody charged with treason. Diagnosed when first indicted as incurably insane and so unable to stand trial, Pound had been held in an asylum since 1945

6 A.M. Thoughts

As soon as you wake they come blundering in
    Like puppies or importunate children;
What was a landscape emerging from mist
    Becomes at once a disordered garden.

And the mess they trail with them! Embarrassments,
    Anger, lust, fear—in fact the whole pig-pen;
And who'll clean it up? No hope for sleep now—
    Just heave yourself out, make the tea, and give in.

Dick Davis
(April 18th 1945 –)

Dick Davis writes: "The occasion for this poem became hidden as the lines were written. It began as a poem about how children redirect a marriage from the romantic to the quotidian; that fact was represented by the rude awakenings toddlers can inflict (compared to the lying in bed together newly-weds can indulge in) and from there came the sour thoughts and self-disgust which finally turned into the subject of the poem, the toddlers being relegated to the status of metaphor."

Dick Davis was born in Portsmouth and graduated from King's College, Cambridge. He lived for eight years in Iran, working as a teacher, and now teaches Persian at Ohio State University, Columbus. He has edited a new edition of Edward FitzGerald's *Rubáiyát of Omar Khayyám* and his own poetry has been published in London under the title *Devices and Desires*. Thom Gunn commented on his work: "It is wonderful to find a poet (English) whose poetry lives through its metre. His handling of it is masterful, and you are never aware of effort."

• *Byron died of a malarial fever in Greece, April 19th 1824* [1]
• *Poet and 1st World War naval historian Sir Henry John Newbolt,*
  who wrote the sea song 'Drake's Drum', died April 19th 1938

So We'll Go No More A-roving

So we'll go no more a-roving
　　So late into the night,
Though the heart be still as loving,
　　And the moon be still as bright.

For the sword outwears its sheath,
　　And the soul wears out the breast,
And the heart must pause to breathe,
　　And Love itself have rest.

Though the night was made for loving,
　　And the day returns too soon,
Yet we'll go no more a-roving
　　By the light of the moon.

George Gordon, Lord Byron
(January 22nd 1788 – April 19th 1824)

On February 19th 1817, Byron wrote to Augusta Leigh from Venice: "The Carnival closed last night, and I have been up all night at the masked ball of the Fenice, and am rather tired or so ... There has been the same sort of thing every night these last six weeks ... I went out now and then, but was less dissipated than you would expect."

Writing to Thomas Moore some days later he reported that he had found " 'the sword wearing out the scabbard' though I have just turned the corner of twenty nine ... If I live ten years longer, you will see, however, that it is not over with me – I don't mean literature, for that is nothing; and it may seem odd enough to say, I do not think it my vocation. But you will see that I shall do something or other – the times and fortune permitting ... But I doubt whether my constitution will hold out. I have, at intervals, exercised it most devilishly."

1. Byron formed 'Byron's Brigade' and gave money to the Greeks fighting for their liberation from the Turkish Empire. He contracted the fever in a rainstorm at Missolonghi whilst with the insurgents. When he died, his heart and lungs were buried in Greece; his intestines were placed in four sealed jars. His body (contained in an alcohol-filled casket) was returned to England, where both St Paul's Cathedral and Westminster Abbey refused to have it.

Lady Caroline Lamb famously described Byron as "mad, bad, dangerous to know", a characterisation gilded by Shelley's explanation to Thomas Love Peacock, that Byron "is an exceedingly interesting person, and as such it is not to be regretted that he is slave to the vilest and most vulgar prejudices and as mad as a hatter".

April 20

- Pietro Aretino, whose salacious sonnets angered Pope Leo X, was born in Arezzo, Tuscany, April 20th 1492
- 'Macbeth' performed at the Globe April 20th 1611
- Tennyson's first child, a son, born April 20th 1851, but did not survive the birth
- W. H. Davies born April 20th 1871
- Archibald MacLeish, American expatriate poet in Paris of the 20s who later won three Pulitzer Prizes, died April 20th 1982

Leisure

What is this life if, full of care,
We have no time to stand and stare?

No time to stand beneath the boughs
And stare as long as sheep or cows.

No time to see, when woods we pass,
Where squirrels hide their nuts in grass.

No time to see, in broad daylight,
Streams full of stars, like skies at night.

No time to turn at Beauty's glance,
And watch her feet, how they can dance.

No time to wait till her mouth can
Enrich that smile her eyes began.

A poor life this if, full of care,
We have no time to stand and stare.

W. H. Davies
(April 20th 1871 – September 26th 1940)

Sir John Squire writes: "Mr. Davies was born in 1871 at Newport, Monmouthshire. He wandered, as a young man, across the Atlantic. He set out with a companion for Klondyke, travelling as a stowaway on trains, missed his footing, and lost a leg." Back in England he lived in doss-houses. According to G. B. Shaw, who encouraged Davies to write and provided an introduction to *The Autobiography of a Super-Tramp*, Davies began at the age of 34 to write poems, and tried selling them door-to-door to pay to have them published: "He did not sell a single copy, though he made a house-to-house visitation in the suburbs. Most of the people he called upon were poor. They looked at the poet in amazement when he offered them a printed sheet for threepence. One richer woman, with a servant, gave him a penny, but refused altogether to accept the poems in return. When he reached his doss-house again that evening, he burnt every copy."

- *2nd edition of Burns poems published April 21st 1787 with his preface "I was bred to the plough and am independent". He made £500*
- *Poet and novelist Charlotte Brontë, author of* Jane Eyre, *born in Thornton, Yorkshire, the daughter of a clergyman, April 21st 1816*
- *On April 21st 1846 Tennyson was godfather to Dickens' son*
- *Robert Bridges died April 21st 1930, having published a long philosophical poem, 'The Testament of Beauty', in his 85th year*

La Belle Dame sans Merci

O what can ail thee, knight-at-arms,
    Alone and palely loitering?
The sedge is wither'd from the lake,
    And no birds sing.

O what can ail thee, knight-at-arms,
    So haggard and so woe-begone?
The squirrel's granary is full,
    And the harvest's done.

I see a lily on thy brow
    With anguish moist and fever dew;
And on thy cheek a fading rose
    Fast withereth too.

"I met a lady in the meads,
    Full beautiful—a faery's child,
Her hair was long, her foot was light,
    And her eyes were wild.

"I made a garland for her head,
    And bracelets too, and fragrant zone;
She look'd at me as she did love,
    And made sweet moan.

"I set her on my pacing steed
    And nothing else saw all day long,
For sideways would she lean, and sing
    A faery's song.

"She found me roots of relish sweet,
    And honey wild and manna dew,
And sure in language strange she said,
    'I love thee true !'

"She took me to her elfin grot,
    And there she wept and sigh'd full sore,
And there I shut her wild, wild eyes
    With kisses four.

"And there she lullèd me asleep,
    And there I dream'd—Ah! woe betide!
The latest dream I ever dream'd
    On the cold hill's side.

"I saw pale kings and princes too,
    Pale warriors, death-pale were they all;
Who cried—'La belle Dame sans Merci
    Hath thee in thrall !'

"I saw their starved lips in the gloam
    With horrid warning gapèd wide,
And I awoke and found me here
    On the cold hill's side.

"And this is why I sojourn here
    Alone and palely loitering,
Though the sedge is wither'd from the lake,
    And no birds sing."

John Keats
(October 31st 1795 – February 23rd 1821)

This was composed on either April 21st or the 28th 1819. Of the kisses (in the eighth stanza) Keats wrote in a letter to his brother George: "Why four kisses – you will say – why four, because I wish to restrain the headlong impetuosity of my Muse – she would have fain said 'score' without hurting the rhyme – but we must temper the Imagination as the Critics say with Judgment." In the published version of this poem, "wretched wight" was substituted for "knight at arms" in the first line of Keats' manuscript.

April 22

• C. H. Sisson born April 22nd 1914
• Poet Louise Glück, author of The House on Marshland, born
  in New York April 22nd 1943

Money

I was led into captivity by the bitch business
Not in love but in what seemed a physical necessity
And now I cannot even watch the spring
The itch for subsistence having become responsibility.

Money the she-devil comes to us under many veils
Tactful at first, calling herself beauty
Tear away this disguise, she proposes paternal solicitude
Assuming the dishonest face of duty.

Suddenly you are in bed with a screeching tear-sheet
This is money at last without her night-dress
Clutching you against her fallen udders and sharp bones
In an unscrupulous and deserved embrace.

C. H. Sisson
(April 22nd 1914 –)

C. H. Sisson gave up writing verses "at 20 because I had a great respect for poetry and did not think I could write it. The war and exile produced a few hesitant verses, wrung from me, but I stopped again without really having begun. A more productive start was about 1950, when I was already on the declining side *del cammin di nostra vita*; no wonder therefore that my themes have often been age, decline and death, with the occasional desperate hopes of the receding man." In the war, C. H. Sisson served in the British Army Intelligence Corps in India. Subsequently he worked for the Ministry of Labour and the Department of Employment, but his critical attitude to the civil service is illustrated in the couplet "Here lies a civil servant. He was civil / To everyone, servant to the devil".

- *William Shakespeare, tradition has it, was born April 23rd 1564, and died April 23rd 1616*
- *Welsh religious poet Henry Vaughan died April 23rd 1695*
- *William Wordsworth died at Rydal Mount, Ambleside, April 23rd 1850. The Prelude was published posthumously*
- *Tennyson laid the foundation stone for his Aldworth home near Haslemere April 23rd 1868*
- *Rupert Brooke died April 23rd 1915 and was buried on Skyros island*
- *James Kirkup, whose poem 'The Love that dares speak its name' was prosecuted in 1977 for blasphemous libel, was born April 23rd 1923*

From As You Like It
Act II Scene vii

Jaques. All the world's a stage,
And all the men and women merely players:
They have their exits and their entrances;
And one man in his time plays many parts,
His acts being seven ages. At first the infant,
Mewling and puking in the nurse's arms.
And then the whining school-boy, with his satchel,
And shining morning face, creeping like snail
Unwillingly to school. And then the lover,
Sighing like furnace, with a woful ballad
Made to his mistress' eyebrow. Then a soldier,
Full of strange oaths, and bearded like the pard,
Jealous in honour, sudden and quick in quarrel,
Seeking the bubble reputation
Even in the cannon's mouth. And then the justice,
In fair round belly with good capon lin'd,
With eyes severe, and beard of formal cut,
Full of wise saws and modern instances;
And so he plays his part. The sixth age shifts
Into the lean and slipper'd pantaloon,
With spectacles on nose and pouch on side,
His youthful hose well sav'd, a world too wide
For his shrunk shank; and his big manly voice,
Turning again toward childish treble, pipes
And whistles in his sound. Last scene of all,
That ends this strange eventful history,
Is second childishness and mere oblivion,
Sans teeth, sans eyes, sans taste, sans everything.

William Shakespeare
(April 23rd 1564 – April 23rd 1616)

Shakespeare was buried inside Stratford church with over the grave the lines:
Good friend, for Jesus's sake forbeare
To dig the dust enclosed heare;
Blest lie the man that spares these stones,
And curst be he that moves my bones.

Of *As You Like It*, the nineteenth-century prose writer and critic William Hazlitt remarked, "Jaques is the only contemplative character in Shakespeare. He thinks, and does nothing."

April 24

• Arthur Christopher Benson, who wrote 'Land of Hope and Glory', born April 24th 1862
• Poet and writer Robert Penn Warren born in Guthrie, Kentucky, April 24th 1905
• Poet and novelist Willa Cather died April 24th 1947

O sweet spontaneous

O sweet spontaneous
earth how often have
the
doting

    fingers of
prurient philosophers pinched
and
poked

thee
, has the naughty thumb
of science prodded
thy

    beauty   .how
often have religions taken
thee upon their scraggy knees
squeezing and

buffeting thee that thou mightest conceive
gods
    (but
true

to the incomparable
couch of death thy
rhythmic
lover

    thou answerest

them only with

    spring)

e.e. cummings
(October 14th 1894 – September 3rd 1962)

On this day in 1919, Cummings wrote to his mother: "You may be glad to know that Gleizes – ... after Picasso best known among painters of his type – was ... 'taken *out of* his feet' by the two things of mine at the Independent ... He said later on that they were the 'best things in oil' that he had seen in America."

- *Torquato Tasso, Italian poet, died April 25th 1595*
- *John Keble, author of* The Christian Year, *a popular volume of sacred verse, was born April 25th 1792*
- *Poet and hymn-writer William Cowper died April 25th 1800*
- *Byron left England bound for exile in Europe, April 25th 1826. Armed friends accompanied him, afraid that he would be attacked by a mob aroused by the scandal which his appalling treatment of his wife, Annabella Milbanke, had occasioned*
- *Poet and author Walter de la Mare born in Kent April 25th 1873*
- *James Fenton born in Lincoln April 25th 1949*

Nothing

I take a jewel from a junk-shop tray
And wish I had a love to buy it for.
Nothing I choose will make you turn my way.
Nothing I give will make you love me more.

I know that I've embarrassed you too long
And I'm ashamed to linger at your door.
Whatever I embark on will be wrong.
Nothing I do will make you love me more.

I cannot work. I cannot read or write.
How can I frame a letter to implore.
Eloquence is a lie. The truth is trite.
Nothing I say will make you love me more.

So I replace the jewel in the tray
And laughingly pretend I'm far too poor.
Nothing I give, nothing I do or say,
Nothing I am will make you love me more.

James Fenton
(April 25th 1949 –)

Of this poem Edward Lucie-Smith wrote that it "seems to me the equal of Auden's best lyrics".

Fenton was born in Lincoln and educated at Repton School and Magdalen College, Oxford. His poetry includes *Terminal Moraine* (1972), *The Memory of War* (1982) and *Manila Envelope* (1989). His riches derive from his percentage on the profits from the musical *Les Misérables* for which he was one of the librettists.

April 26

• *Shakespeare baptised on April 26th 1564, according to the Stratford parish register*
• *The poet Thomas Lodge was admitted as a student at Lincoln's Inn April 26th 1578*
• *Trial of Oscar Wilde began April 26th 1895*
• *On this day in 1925, Hardy told the Duchess of Hamilton that all animal protection societies should campaign for public slaughterhouses*

Home-thoughts, from Abroad

O to be in England
Now that April's there,
And whoever wakes in England
Sees, some morning, unaware,
That the lowest boughs and the brushwood sheaf
Round the elm-tree bole are in tiny leaf,
While the chaffinch sings on the orchard bough
In England—now!

And after April, when May follows,
And the whitethroat builds, and all the swallows!
Hark, where my blossomed pear-tree in the hedge
Leans to the field and scatters on the clover
Blossoms and dewdrops—at the bent spray's edge—
That's the wise thrush; he sings each song twice over,
Lest you should think he never could recapture
The first fine careless rapture!
And though the fields look rough with hoary dew,
All will be gay when noontide wakes anew
The buttercups, the little children's dower
—Far brighter than this gaudy melon-flower!

Robert Browning
(May 7th 1812 – December 12th 1889)

This poem was probably written in England during April 1845 when Browning was recalling his second tour of Italy, and the year before he took Elizabeth Barrett there as his wife.

- *Ralph Waldo Emerson died April 27th 1882 and was buried in Sleepy Hollow Cemetery close to Thoreau and Hawthorne*
- *Cecil Day Lewis (aka Nicholas Blake) born in Ireland April 27th 1904*
- *Edwin George Morgan born in Glasgow April 27th 1920*
- *American alcoholic poet Hart Crane committed suicide by jumping from a ship en route from Mexico to the States, April 27th 1932*
- *Poet and translator Jean Valentine born in Chicago April 22nd 1934*

Brahma

If the red slayer think he slays,
　　Or if the slain think he is slain,
They know not well the subtle ways
　　I keep, and pass, and turn again.

Far or forgot to me is near;
　　Shadow and sunlight are the same;
The vanquished gods to me appear;
　　And one to me are shame and fame.

They reckon ill who leave me out;
　　When me they fly, I am the wings;
I am the doubter and the doubt
　　And I the hymn the Brahmin sings.

The strong gods pine for my abode,
　　And pine in vain the sacred Seven,
But thou, meek lover of the good!
　　Find me, and turn thy back on heaven.

Ralph Waldo Emerson
(May 25th 1803 – April 27th 1882)

Famed as the "God-intoxicated Yankee" with an unbending passion for independence (who still swam naked in Walden Pond daily at the age of 77), Emerson declared a credo of self-reliance: "Whoso would be a man must be a nonconformist ... A foolish consistency is the hobgoblin of little minds." He resigned as a Unitarian minister in 1832 and helped found a Transcendentalism movement, which drew on Hinduism and a sense of the mystical oneness of the individual, nature and God.

April 28

• Charles Cotton, poet who wrote love poems to his wife (and cousin) Isabella, born at Beresford, Staffs., April 28th 1630
• T. S. Eliot left his job at Lloyds Bank to take up a position at Faber and Faber, April 28th 1925

Quantum est quod desit[1]

'Twas a new feeling—something more
Than we had dar'd to own before,
   Which then we hid not;
We saw it in each other's eye,
And wish'd in every broken sigh
   To speak, but did not!

She felt my lips' impassion'd touch;
'Twas the first time I dar'd so much,
   And yet, she chid not;
But whisper'd o'er my burning brow,
'Oh! do you doubt I love you now?'
   Sweet soul! I did not!

Warmly I felt her bosom thrill,
I prest it closer, closer still,
   Though gently bid not;
Till—oh! the world hath seldom heard
Of lovers, who so nearly err'd,
   And yet who—did not!

Thomas Moore
(May 28th 1779 – February 25th 1852)

Thomas Moore has been described as "the national bard of Ireland" and his collection *Irish Melodies* was a bestseller – in his time only Byron's verse was more popular.

On this day in 1916, the Easter Rising in central Dublin was underway, led by the Irish Republican Brotherhood and Sinn Fein. The Rising was put down. 450 of the rebels died, 2,000 were injured and the leaders were executed.

1. Roughly: 'To the brink but no further'.

• Greek poet Constantine Cavafy, who lived in Alexandria,
  Egypt, died April 29th 1933
• Ezra Pound handed over to the American army by Italian
  partisans and held in solitary confinement in an outdoor cage
  at Pisa, April 29th 1945

Wild Nights – Wild Nights!

Wild Nights – Wild Nights!
Were I with thee
Wild Nights should be
Our luxury!

Futile – the Winds –
To a Heart in port –
Done with the Compass –
Done with the Chart!

Rowing in Eden –
Ah, the Sea!
Might I but moor – Tonight –
In Thee!

Emily Dickinson
(December 10th 1830 – May 15th 1886)

In the 'Presbyterian' for this day in 1882, there is an article by 'Calvin' about the Revd. Charles Wadsworth, "a prince among preachers... Dr Wadsworth was born a poet and could not cease to be one". Wadsworth has been conjectured to be the (platonically) loved one in Emily Dickinson's life who may have inspired the passion in these lines. She first met him in May 1854 when he was 40 and happily married and she was 23. Later in life she referred to him as "the beloved clergyman", "the shepherd from 'little girl'hood", "dearest earthly friend", "whom to know was life". On his deathbed Wadsworth requested that a copy of his published sermons be sent to her.

According to one critic, William H. Sinar, Emily Dickinson felt that she had undergone a form of marriage of the spirit to Wadsworth, with the lovers agreeing to a lifetime of painful separation and a subsequent marriage in heaven.

April 30

• Stein's secretary, Alice B. Toklas, born April 30th 1877
• John Crowe Ransom born in Tennessee April 30th 1888
• A. E. Housman, poet and Latin professor, died April 30th 1936
• Poet and translator Tony Harrison born in Leeds April 30th 1937

Byzantium

The unpurged images of day recede;
The Emperor's drunken soldiery are abed;
Night resonance recedes, night-walkers' song
After great cathedral gong;
A starlit or a moonlit dome disdains
All that man is,
All mere complexities,
The fury and the mire of human veins.

Before me floats an image, man or shade,
Shade more than man, more image than a shade;
For Hades' bobbin bound in mummy-cloth
May unwind the winding path;
A mouth that has no moisture and no breath
Breathless mouths may summon;
I hail the superhuman;
I call it death-in-life and life-in-death.

Miracle, bird or golden handiwork,
More miracle than bird or handiwork,
Planted on the starlit golden bough,
Can like the cocks of Hades crow,
Or, by the moon embittered, scorn aloud
In glory of changeless metal
Common bird or petal
And all complexities of mire or blood.

At midnight on the Emperor's pavement flit
Flames that no faggot feeds, nor steel has lit,
Nor storm disturbs, flames begotten of flame,
Where blood-begotten spirits come
And all complexities of fury leave,
Dying into a dance,
An agony of trance,
An agony of flame that cannot singe a sleeve.

Astraddle on the dolphin's mire and blood,
Spirit after spirit! The smithies break the flood.
The golden smithies of the Emperor!
Marbles of the dancing floor
Break bitter furies of complexity,
Those images that yet
Fresh images beget,
That dolphin-torn, that gong-tormented sea.

William Butler Yeats
(June 13th 1865 – January 28th 1939)

In the spring of 1930, Yeats was at a hotel at Portofina Vetta overlooking the bay of Genoa, recovering from a vicious bout of Malta fever which had made him ill enough to write three lines of a will witnessed by Ezra Pound and Basil Bunting. On April 30th, Yeats made a note in his diary under the heading 'Subject for a Poem': "Describe Byzantium as it is in the system [ie. in Yeats' book *A Vision*] towards the end of the first Christian millennium. A walking mummy. Flames at the street corners where the soul is purified, birds of hammered gold singing in the golden trees, in the harbour dolphins, offering their backs to the wailing dead that they may carry them to Paradise."

"I think that if I could be given a month of Antiquity and leave to spend it where I chose," Yeats wrote in *A Vision*, "I would spend it in Byzantium, a little before Justinian opened St Sophia and closed the Academy of Plato."

As for the "Hades' bobbin" that may "unwind the winding path" (in the second verse), Yeats speculated elsewhere that "the unpurified dead ... examine their past if undisturbed by our importunity, tracing events to their source, and as they take the form their thought suggests, seem to live backward through time."

- *Shakespeare bought 107 acres near Stratford for £320 May 1st 1602*
- *Joseph Addison, founder of The Spectator, born May 1st 1672*
- *John Dryden, poet, playwright and translator, died May 1st 1700*
- *Anglo-Irish poet Thomas William Rolleston born May 1st 1857*
- *Emily Dickinson's beloved Charles Wadsworth moved away from New York to California, May 1st 1862*
- *Paul Celan, born in Czernowitz (Romania). Both parents died in an extermination camp, and he drowned himself in the Seine May 1st 1970*
- *Novelist and poet Sylvia Townsend Warner died May 1st 1978*

Happy the Man

Happy the man, and happy he alone,
    He who can call today his own:
    He who, secure within, can say,
Tomorrow do thy worst, for I have lived today.
    Be fair or foul or rain or shine
The joys I have possessed, in spite of fate, are mine.
Not Heaven itself upon the past has power,
But what has been, has been, and I have had my hour.

John Dryden
(August 9th 1631 – May 1st 1700)
translating Horace (65 – 8 BC), Odes, Book III, xxix

Horace was taught in all English schools in the 17th century. Dryden was educated at Westminster School and Trinity College, Cambridge. He adapted himself to his turbulent times, with his 'Heroic Stanzas' on the death of Cromwell soon followed by 'Astrea Redux' in praise of the Restoration of Charles II. In 1682 he wrote a poem upholding Anglicanism, and three years later another defending his new Roman Catholicism. At the Revolution of 1688 he lost his court positions as Poet Laureate and Historiographer Royal, returning first to the writing of plays and later to translations of Horace, Homer, Virgil, Ovid, Boccaccio and others.

May 2

• Poet Ruth Fainlight born in New York May 2nd 1931. She married the novelist Alan Sillitoe in 1959

Body

What was so quiet a companion,
My dumb friend,
Now cries out, groans,
Swells up with noxious fluid
Clamouring for attention.
Did I neglect you,
Taking for granted
The ease with which you walked, breathed,
Ran for a bus?
We that were one, are two.
I bow before you.

Sasha Moorsom
(January 25th 1931 – June 22nd 1993)

Sasha's daughter, Sophie Young, was born on this day in 1961. Sophie nursed her mother during her last illness and remembers that "this poem was written towards the end of Sasha's illness, when her condition had deteriorated after a period of remission. She refused to let the pain and weakness of her body prevent her from writing poetry and she was still able to see the beauty in everything. The week before she died, she wrote these few lines in her diary:

Skin now soft and bloated can take
Any impression like the cliffs at Lyme Regis.
On the side of my knee a beautiful shell
Fans itself out like an ammonite. "

- *Shakespeare's brother Edmund was baptised May 3rd 1580*
- *On this day in 1787, Burns wrote to a friend his belief that his "meteor-like" success would only last whilst he remained a novelty*
- *Gaelic League poet Thomas MacDonagh, whose plays were performed at the Abbey, executed on May 3rd 1916 for his part in the Easter Rising*

To be a Slave of Intensity

Friend, hope for the Guest while you are alive.
Jump into experience while you are alive!
Think . . . and think . . . while you are alive.
What you call 'salvation' belongs to the time before death.

If you don't break your ropes while you're alive,
do you think
ghosts will do it after?

The idea that the soul will join with the ecstatic
just because the body is rotten—
that is all fantasy.
What is found now is found then.
If you find nothing now,
you will simply end up with an apartment in the City of Death.
If you make love with the divine now, in the next life you will
    have the face of satisfied desire.

So plunge into the truth, find out who the Teacher is,
    Believe in the Great Sound!

Kabir says this: When the Guest is being searched for, it is the
    intensity of the longing for the Guest that does all the work.
Look at me, and you will see a slave of that intensity.

Kabir
(c. 15th Century)
Translated by Robert Bly
(December 23rd 1926 –)

Kabir wrote in Hindi. Rabindranath Tagore and Evelyn Underhill translated him into Victorian English, themselves working from a Bengali translation. Robert Bly, working from the Tagore-Underhill book, has adapted the poems for today's reader. His *Kabir Book* was published by the Beacon Press in Boston in 1977.

Legend relates that Kabir was the son of a Brahman widow, by whom he was exposed, only to be found on a lotus in Lahar Talao, a pond near Benares, by a Musulman weaver named Ali. Kabir's brief mystical poems, the *Ramainis*, proclaim, writes Sir Charles Lyall, "the unity of the Godhead, the vanity of idols, the powerlessness of brahmans or mullahs to guide or help, and the divine origin of the human soul ... Life is a gift of God and must not be violated, the shedding of blood, whether of man or animals, is a heinous crime ... The followers of Kabir do not observe celibacy, and live quiet unostentatious lives. They have been compared to Quakers for their hatred of violence and unobtrusive piety." It is a religion of the inner life, for as Kabir asks, in Bly's translation: "Suppose you scrub your ethical skin until it shines, but inside there is no music, what then?"

May 4

• On May 4th 1597 Shakespeare bought for £60 the largest house in Stratford-on-Avon, a house known as New Place
• Poet Thomas Kinsella, author of Butcher's Dozen and editor of The New Oxford Book of Irish Verse, born in Dublin May 4th 1928
• Sir Osbert Sitwell, who wrote poetry, fiction and autobiography, died May 4th 1969

From Love's Labour's Lost
Act IV Scene iii

Berowne. A lover's eyes will gaze an eagle blind,
A lover's ear will hear the lowest sound,
When the suspicious head of theft is stopped.
Love's feeling is more soft and sensible
Than are the tender horns of cockled snails.
Love's tongue proves dainty Bacchus gross in taste.
For valour, is not Love a Hercules,
Still climbing trees in the Hesperides?
Subtle as Sphinx; as sweet and musical
As bright Apollo's lute, strung with his hair.
And when Love speaks, the voice of all the gods
Makes heaven drowsy with the harmony.
Never durst poet touch a pen to write
Until his ink were temp'red with Love's sighs;
O then his lines would ravish savage ears
And plant in tyrants mild humility,
From women's eyes this doctrine I derive.
They sparkle still the right Promethean fire;
They are the books, the arts, the academes,
That show, contain, and nourish all the world.

William Shakespeare
(April 23rd 1564 — April 23rd 1616)

Sir Walter Cope wrote to Robert Cecil in 1604: "I have sent and bene all thys morning huntyng for players Juglers and such kinde of creaturs, but finde them harde to finde, wherefore leavinge notes for them to seeke me, Burbage ys come, and sayes ther ys no new playe that the quene hath not seene, but they have reyved an olde one, Cawled Loves Labore Lost, which for wytt and mirthe he sayes will please her exceedingly."

She was a phantom of delight

She was a phantom of delight
When first she gleam'd upon my sight:
A lovely apparition, sent
To be a moment's ornament;
Her eyes as stars of twilight fair;
Like Twilight's, too, her dusky hair;
But all things else about her drawn
From May-time and the cheerful dawn;
A dancing shape, an image gay,
To haunt, to startle, and waylay.

I saw her upon nearer view,
A spirit, yet a woman too!
Her household motions light and free,
And steps of virgin-liberty;
A countenance in which did meet
Sweet records, promises as sweet;
A creature not too bright or good
For human nature's daily food,
For transient sorrows, simple wiles,
Praise, blame, love, kisses, tears, and smiles.

And now I see with eye serene
The very pulse of the machine;
A being breathing thoughtful breath,
A traveller between life and death:
The reason firm, the temperate will,
Endurance, foresight, strength, and skill;
A perfect woman, nobly plann'd
To warn, to comfort, and command;
And yet a Spirit still, and bright
With something of an angel-light.

William Wordsworth
(April 7th 1770 – April 23rd 1850)

On this day in 1805, Wordsworth told Sir George Beaumont that he had been trying to write a commemorative poem on the death of his brother John in a shipwreck, but had been too much agitated to remember what he wrote.

According to Justice Coleridge, Wordsworth said that 'Phantom of Delight' "was written on 'his dear wife', of whom he spoke in the sweetest manner; and a manner full of the warmest love and admiration, yet with delicacy and reserve," and Wordswoth noted: "It was written from my heart, as is sufficiently obvious."

May 6

• Donne was admitted at Lincoln's Inn May 6th 1592
• Bengali writer Rabindranath Tagore born May 6th 1861
• Henry David Thoreau, the Walden hermit, died May 6th 1862
• Rundull Jarrell, American poet and critic, born May 6th 1914
• Poet Chris Wallace-Crabbe born in Melbourne May 6th 1934

From Ode to a Nightingale[1]

My heart aches, and a drowsy numbness pains
   My sense, as though of hemlock I had drunk,
Or emptied some dull opiate to the drains
   One minute past, and Lethe-wards had sunk:
'Tis not through envy of thy happy lot,
   But being too happy in thy happiness –
     That thou, light-wingèd Dryad of the trees,
       In some melodious plot
Of beechen green, and shadows numberless,
     Singest of summer in full-throated ease.

I cannot see what flowers are at my feet,
   Nor what soft incense hangs upon the boughs,
But, in embalmèd darkness, guess each sweet
   Wherewith the seasonable month endows
The grass, the thicket, and the fruit-tree wild:
   White hawthorn, and the pastoral eglantine;
     Fast fading violets cover'd up in leaves;
       And mid-May's eldest child,
The coming musk-rose, full of dewy wine,
     The murmurous haunt of flies on summer eves.

Darkling I listen; and, for many a time
   I have been half in love with easeful death,
Called him soft names in many a musèd rhyme,
   To take into the air my quiet breath;
Now more than ever seems it rich to die,
   To cease upon the midnight with no pain,
     While thou art pouring forth thy soul abroad
       In such an ecstasy!
Still wouldst thou sing, and I have ears in vain–
   To thy high requiem become a sod.

John Keats
(October 31st 1795 – February 23rd 1821)

This Ode was written in May 1819. Charles Brown's perhaps unreliable version of the story is that "in the spring of 1819 a nightingale had built her nest near my house. Keats felt a tranquil and continual joy in her song; and one morning he took his chair from the breakfast-table to the grass-plot under a plum-tree, where he sat for two or three hours. When he came into the house, I perceived he had some scraps of paper in his hand, and those he was quietly thrusting behind the books. On inquiry, I found these scraps, four or five in number, contained his poetic feeling on the song of our nightingale."

1. Stanzas 1, 5 and 6 of this 8 stanza poem.

- *Robert Browning born in Camberwell, the only son of a Bank of England clerk, May 7th 1812*
- *American poet and librarian Archibald MacLeish born May 7th 1892*
- *Jenny Joseph born in Birmingham May 7th 1932*

The sun has burst the sky

The sun has burst the sky
Because I love you
And the river its banks.

The sea laps the great rocks
Because I love you
And takes no heed of the moon dragging it away
And saying coldly 'Constancy is not for you'.

The blackbird fills the air
Because I love you
With spring and lawns and shadows falling on lawns.

The people walk in the street and laugh
I love you
And far down the river ships sound their hooters
Crazy with joy because I love you.

Jenny Joseph
(May 7th 1932 –)

Jenny Joseph's writings include books for children, an experimental poem-novel *Persephone* (1985) and her *Selected Poems* (1992). She lives in Gloucestershire.

May 8

• J. Meade Falkner, antiquarian, poet and novelist, author of The
  Lost Stradivarius, born May 8th 1858
• Edmund Wilson, poet, author and critic, born in New Jersey May
  8th 1895. His third wife was the novelist Mary McCarthy
• American Zen primitivist poet Gary Snyder born May 8th 1930

An Epilogue

I have seen flowers come in stony places
And kind things done by men with ugly faces,
And the gold cup won by the worst horse at the races,
So I trust, too.

John Masefield
(June 1st 1878 – May 12th 1967)

On this day in 1930, John Masefield drafted a letter to the Lord Chamberlain concerning his forthcoming appointment as Poet Laureate. Other living poets championed for the vacancy included Housman, Kipling, Yeats and Walter de la Mare. But Masefield was then at the peak of his popularity. *The Times* commented that it was good to have as Poet Laureate a non-university man like Masefield who was used to manual work and could "touch to beauty the plain speech of everyday life".

- *Friedrich Schiller died May 9th 1805*
- *Austin Clarke born May 9th 1896*
- *Anti-war activist, Daniel Berrigan, author of* Prison Poems,
  born in Minnesota May 9th 1921
- *Poet Charles Simic, author of* The Book of Gods and Devils,
  born in Yugoslavia May 9th 1938

Time

'Established' is a good word, much used in garden books,
'The plant, when established' . . .
Oh, become established quickly, quickly, garden!
For I am fugitive, I am very fugitive –

Those that come after me will gather these roses,
And watch, as I do now, the white wistaria
Burst, in the sunshine, from its pale green sheath.

Planned. Planted. Established. Then neglected,
Till at last the loiterer by the gate will wonder
At the old, old cottage, the old wooden cottage,
And say, 'One might build here, the view is glorious;
This must have been a pretty garden once.'

Mary Ursula Bethell
(October 6th 1874 – January 15th 1945)

Mary Ursula Bethell was born in England but her parents soon returned to New Zealand. She herself became a social worker in Christchurch, New Zealand, and in London, returning permanently to New Zealand after the First World War. She built a house in the Cashmere Hills, with a fine view over Christchurch, and her first book of poems (in 1929) concerned her garden, where she would plant primroses to remind her of Spring in England. The poet D'Arcy Cresswell wrote: "New Zealand wasn't truly discovered ... until Ursula Bethell, 'very earnestly digging', raised her head to look at the mountains," and Peter Simpson wrote that "Ursual Bethell felt herself to be a transplanted English-woman for whom her garden ... was both a reminder of her exile and a compensation for it. To some degree, she stands for all New Zealanders, colonists all, gardening the antipodes. The garden was her pilgrimage, her way to God."

As a committed Anglican, her poetry became gradually more devotional in content and formal in style. She lived in her house with her long-term companion Effie Pollen. After Effie's death in 1934, she left the house that they had shared, and wrote little more, apart from the anguished poetry dedicated to Effie in *Six Memorials*.

May 10

• Having sent copies to Bridges, Hopkins burnt his poems, noting the event as "slaughter of the innocents", May 10th 1868

Two in the Campagna

I wonder do you feel to-day
  As I have felt, since, hand in hand
We sat down on the grass, to stray
  In spirit better through the land,
This morn of Rome and May?

For me, I touched a thought, I know,
  Has tantalised me many times,
(Like turns of thread the spiders throw
  Mocking across our path) for rhymes
To catch at and let go.

Help me to hold it: first it left
  The yellowing fennel, run to seed
There, branching from the brickwork's cleft
  Some old tomb's ruin: yonder weed
Took up the floating weft,

Where one small orange cup amassed
  Five beetles,—blind and green they grope
Among the honey-meal,—and last,
  Everywhere on the grassy slope
I traced it. Hold it fast!

The champaign with its endless fleece
  Of feathery grasses everywhere!
Silence and passion, joy and peace,
  An everlasting wash of air—
Rome's ghost since her decease.

Such life here, through such lengths of hours,
  Such miracles performed in play
Such primal naked forms of flowers,
  Such letting Nature have her way
While Heaven looks from its towers.

How say you? Let us, O my dove,
  Let us be unashamed of soul,
As earth lies bare to heaven above.
  How is it under our control
To love or not to love?

I would that you were all to me,
  You that are just so much, no more—
Nor yours nor mine,—nor slave nor free!
  Where does the fault lie? what the core
Of the wound, since wound must be?

I would I could adopt your will,
  See with your eyes, and set my heart
Beating by yours, and drink my fill
  At your soul's springs,—your part, my part
In life, for good and ill.

No. I yearn upward—touch you close,
  Then stand away. I kiss your cheek,
Catch your soul's warmth,—I pluck the rose
  And love it more than tongue can speak—
Then the good minute goes.

Already how am I so far
  Out of that minute? Must I go
Still like the thistle-ball, no bar,
  Onward, whenever light winds blow,
Fixed by no friendly star?

Just when I seemed about to learn!
  Where is the thread now? Off again!
The old trick! Only I discern—
  Infinite passion and the pain
Of finite hearts that yearn.

Robert Browning
(May 7th 1812 – December 12th 1889)

On May 10th 1854 Mrs Browning wrote: "The pleasantest days in Rome we have spent with the Kembles – the two sisters – who are charming and excellent both of them in different ways; and certainly they have given us some exquisite hours on the Campagna, upon picnic excursions, they and certain of their friends."

Love is Love

The lowest trees have tops, the ant her gall,
The fly her spleen, the little spark his heat:
The slender hairs cast shadows, though but small,
And bees have stings, although they be not great;
   Seas have their source, and so have shallow springs;
   And love is love, in beggars and in kings.

Where waters smoothest run, there deepest are the fords,
The dial stirs, yet none perceives it move;
The firmest faith is found in fewest words,
The turtles do not sing, and yet they love;
   True hearts have ears and eyes, no tongues to speak;
   They hear and see, and sigh, and then they break.

Sir Edward Dyer
(ca. 1543 – May 1607)

Sir Edward Dyer, poet and diplomat, was born in Sharpham Park, Somerset. He was educated at either Broadgates Hall or Balliol College, Oxford, and then introduced at court by the Earl of Leicester. He wrote an elegy to his friend Sir Philip Sidney but the most well-known poem attributed to him, 'My mind to me a kingdom is', is probably not by him. Betjeman spoke of his poetry as "easily among my favourites". In later life Dyer lived in quiet seclusion.

May 12

• Edward Lear born in London of Danish ancestry May 12th
  1812. He suffered from epilepsy and asthma from the age of six.
  A Book of Nonsense was published anonymously in 1846
• Poet and painter Dante Gabriel Rossetti born May 12th 1828
• On May 12th 1846, Browning met Tennyson, a "hazy kind of
  man, at least just after dinner"
• John Masefield, Poet Laureate who once served an uncompleted
  apprenticeship on a windjammer, died May 12th 1967

The Owl and the Pussy-Cat

The Owl and the Pussy-Cat went to sea
  In a beautiful pea-green boat.
They took some honey, and plenty of money,
  Wrapped up in a five-pound note.
The Owl looked up to the stars above,
  And sang to a small guitar,
'O lovely Pussy! O Pussy, my love,
  What a beautiful Pussy you are,
      You are,
      You are!
  What a beautiful Pussy you are!'

Pussy said to the Owl, 'You elegant fowl!
  How charmingly sweet you sing!
O let us be married! too long we have tarried:
  But what shall we do for a ring?'
They sailed away, for a year and a day,
  To the land where the Bong-Tree grows,
And there in a wood a Piggy-wig stood,
  With a ring at the end of his nose,
      His nose,
      His nose,
  With a ring at the end of his nose.

'Dear Pig, are you willing to sell for one shilling
  Your ring?' Said the Piggy, 'I will.'
So they took it away, and were married next day
  By the Turkey who lives on the hill.
They dinèd on mince, and slices of quince,
  Which they ate with a runcible spoon;
And hand in hand, on the edge of the sand,
  They danced by the light of the moon,
      The moon,
      The moon,
  They danced by the light of the moon.

Edward Lear
(May 12th 1812 – January 29th 1888)

• Canadian poet and writer Earle Birney born May 13th 1904
• At a ceremony at Terlington, May 13th 1922, Kipling sees a
  memorial to "Gunga-Din stretcher bearer" among the graves
• Osip Mandelstam arrested by Cheka May 13th 1934
• Bruce Chatwin, author of The Songlines, born May 13th 1940
• Poet A. S. J. Tessimond died May 13th 1962
• Kathleen Jamie born May 13th 1962

The way we live

Pass the tambourine, let me bash out praises
to the Lord God of movement, to Absolute
non-friction, flight, and the scarey side:
death by avalanche, birth by failed contraception.
Of chicken tandoori and reggae, loud, from tenements,
commitment, driving fast and unswerving
friendship. Of tee-shirts on pulleys, giros and Bombay,
barmen, dreaming waitresses with many fake-gold
bangles. Of airports, impulse, and waking to uncertainty,
to strip-lights, motorways, or that pantheon –
the mountains. To overdrafts and grafting

and the fit slow pulse of wipers as you're
creeping over Rannoch, while the God of moorland
walks abroad with his entourage of freezing fog,
his bodyguard of snow.
Of endless gloaming in the North, of Asiatic swelter,
to launderettes, anecdotes, passions and exhaustion,
Final Demands and dead men, the skeletal grip
of government. To misery and elation; mixed,
the sod and caprice of landlords.
To the way it fits, the way it is, the way it seems
to be: let me bash out praises – pass the tambourine.

Kathleen Jamie
(May 13th 1962 –)

Kathleen Jamie's travels, mainly in the East, are reflected in her collections *The Way We Live* (1987) and
The Autonomous Region (1993) and in her travel book *The Golden Peak* (1992).
Jamie was born in Renfrewshire and now lives in Fife. Her collection *The Queen of Sheba* was published
in 1994.

May 14

- *Dante Alighieri, author of the Divina Commedia, born in Florence, the son of a lawyer, May 14th 1265*
- *On this day in 1786, Burns exchanged bibles as a symbol of betrothment with Mary Campbell, who agreed to sail with him to Jamaica. On the same day in 1792 he wrote her the poem 'Highland Mary'*
- *Dylan Thomas' first public reading of 'Under Milk Wood', May 14th 1953*

Psalm 23
A Psalm of David

The Lord is my shepherd; I shall not want.
He maketh me to lie down in green pastures;
He leadeth me beside the still waters.
He restoreth my soul;
He leadeth me in the paths of righteousness for his name's sake.
Yea, though I walk through the valley of the shadow of death,
I will fear no evil: for thou art with me;
Thy rod and thy staff they comfort me.
Thou preparest a table before me in the presence of mine enemies.
Thou anointest my head with oil; my cup runneth over.
Surely goodness and mercy shall follow me all the days of my life.
And I will dwell in the house of the Lord forever.

King David
(Died c. 990 BC)

On this day in 1948, David Ben-Gurion announced the creation of the state of Israel, following the partition of Palestine and the ending of the British Mandate.

Of the Psalms, Donne wrote: "The songs are these, which Heaven's high Holy Muse / Whisper'd to David, David to the Jewes" and Disraeli called King David "the most popular poet in England ... the sweet singer of Israel". Psalm 23 was written about two and a half thousand years ago, and is one of the 73 psalms (out of the 150) that have been attributed by scholars to King David himself. On Saul's death, David ruled over Judah from about 1010 BC to 990 BC, annexing Jerusalem in the process, where he built a palace on Mount Zion and installed there the Ark of the Covenant. His kingdom ranged from the Euphrates to Egypt, although his later years were troubled by civil wars in which two of his sons were involved.

The early Christians went to their death with Psalm 23 on their lips – St Augustine chose this psalm as the Hymn of the Martyrs. E. C. D. Stanford wrote that its popularity has endured: "George Herbert paraphrased it: Ruskin learned to say it for his mother. In our day it is sung at the wedding of Queen and commoner."

Kathleen Strange associates the psalms's green pastures with the fertile Wadi Fara in Jordan, and the Valley of Death with the terrifying passage among the mountains between Jerusalem and the Dead Sea.

• *Emily Dickinson died of nephritis May 15th 1886. She had not left her home since 1865*
• *Scottish poet Edwin Muir born in Deerness May 15th 1887*

Because I could not stop for Death

Because I could not stop for Death –
He kindly stopped for me –
The Carriage held but just Ourselves –
And Immortality.

We slowly drove – He knew no haste
And I had put away
My labor and my leisure too,
For His Civility –

We passed the School, where Children strove
At Recess – in the Ring –
We passed the Fields of Gazing Grain –
We passed the Setting Sun –

Or rather – He passed Us –
The Dews drew quivering and chill –
For only Gossamer, my Gown –
My Tippet[1] – only Tulle –

We paused before a House that seemed
A Swelling of the Ground –
The Roof was scarcely visible –
The Cornice – in the Ground –

Since then – 'tis Centuries – and yet
Feels shorter than the Day
I first surmised the Horses' Heads
Were toward Eternity –

Emily Dickinson
(December 10th 1830 – May 15th 1886)

By her forties, Dickinson had completed her retreat from the outside world, refusing to leave the house. Only seven of her 1,800 poems were published in her lifetime. Discouraged the one time she actively sought publication, she appears to have accepted her "Barefoot-Rank" status. Some of her verses circulated privately in Amherst, Massachusetts, to a largely condescending group who pitied her eccentricity.

1. A tulle tippet is a neck and shoulder scarf made of fine netting

May 16

• Mrs Felicia Dorothea Hemans, who wrote the original
'Casabianca' poem ('The boy stood on the burning deck ...'),
died May 16th 1835
• Feminist poet and critic Adrienne Rich, who wrote the polemical
poem 'The Phenomenology of Anger', was born in Baltimore
May 16th 1929

Casabianca

Love's the boy stood on the burning deck
trying to recite 'The boy stood on
the burning deck.' Love's the son
    stood stammering elocution
      while the poor ship in flames went down.

Love's the obstinate boy, the ship,
even the swimming sailors, who
would like a schoolroom platform, too,
    or an excuse to stay
      on deck. And love's the burning boy.

Elizabeth Bishop
(February 8th 1911 – October 6th 1979)

The publication of this poem in the August 1936 issue of *New Democracy* brought Elizabeth Bishop to an international audience. Brett C. Midler believes that the boy's love and fear in this poem stand for "Elizabeth's black conviction that love, especially parental love, is a non-negotiable trap ... It was a long time before she could write about ... any kind of love without screens of rhetorical statement."

• *Byron entrusted his Memoirs to Thomas Moore as a close friend.*
After Byron's death it became a question of what to do with them.
On this day in 1824, Thomas Moore induced Murray, to whom
he had sold the Memoirs for 2,000 guineas the previous
November, to return them to him, and at once burnt them,
having to borrow to repay Murray the money with interest

Oft in the Stilly Night

Oft in the stilly night
  Ere Slumber's chain has bound me,
Fond Memory brings the light
  Of other days around me;
    The smiles, the tears,
    Of boyhood's years,
  The words of love then spoken;
    The eyes that shone,
    Now dimmed and gone,
  The cheerful hearts now broken!
Thus, in the stilly night,
  Ere Slumber's chain has bound me,
Sad Memory brings the light
  Of other days around me.

When I remember all
  The friends so linked together,
I've seen around me fall,
  Like leaves in wintry weather:
    I feel like one
    Who treads alone
  Some banquet-hall deserted,
    Whose lights are fled,
    Whose garland's dead,
  And all but he departed!
Thus in the stilly night,
  Ere Slumber's chain has bound me,
Fond Memory brings the light
  Of other days around me.

Thomas Moore
(May 28th 1779 – February 25th 1852)

Thomas Moore was born in Dublin, the son of a Catholic grocer. His *Poems* of 1801 and his talent as a singer were his entrée into high society. He married Bessy Dyke, an actress, and they lived in Wiltshire. His *Irish Melodies* brought him an income of £500 a year. But his deputy registrar at the Admiralty Court in Bermuda defaulted with £6,000, and in 1819 Moore had to flee to the Continent to avoid arrest for this debt, returning three years later. In 1830 he published a life of Byron, despite having previously burnt Byron's Memoirs.

May 18

• Persian poet, mathematician and astronomer Omar Khayyám born
in Níshápur May 18th 1048. His 'Rubáiyát' or quatrains were
adapted and translated by Edward FitzGerald in 1859
• Novelist and cerebral poet George Meredith died May 18th 1909

The Eagle

He clasps the crag with crookèd hands;
Close to the sun in lonely lands,
Ring'd with the azure world, he stands.

The wrinkled sea beneath him crawls;
He watches from his mountain walls,
And like a thunderbolt he falls.

Alfred, Lord Tennyson
(August 6th 1809 – October 6th 1892)

On this day in 1866, Tennyson told his wife that when he heard of the death of Byron, he carved Byron's name into the rectory wall at Somersby. He added that he thought Byron was popular because he wrote vulgarly and that he himself was popular because he was Poet Laureate – "something like being a Lord". Tennyson wrote 'The Eagle' into the album of Dora Wordsworth when in the Lake District in the summer of 1850.

- Shakespeare's King's Company given a royal licence May 19th 1603
- World War I poet Charles Hamilton Sorley ("When you see millions of the mouthless dead") born May 19th 1895
- Oscar Wilde released from Pentonville Prison May 19th 1896
- Ogden Nash ("I would live all my life in nonchalance and insouciance / Were it not for making a living, which is rather a nousiance") died May 19th 1971
- Sir John Betjeman, "poet and hack" (his phrase), died May 19th 1984

Slough

Come, friendly bombs, and fall on Slough
It isn't fit for humans now,
There isn't grass to graze a cow
   Swarm over, Death!

Come, bombs, and blow to smithereens
Those air-conditioned, bright canteens,
Tinned fruit, tinned meat, tinned milk, tinned beans
   Tinned minds, tinned breath.

Mess up the mess they call a town—
A house for ninety-seven down
And once a week a half-a-crown
   For twenty years,

And get that man with double chin
Who'll always cheat and always win,
Who washed his repulsive skin
   in women's tears,

And smash his desk of polished oak
And smash his hands so used to stroke
And stop his boring dirty joke
   And make him yell.

But spare the bald young clerks who add
The profits of the stinking cad;
It's not their fault that they are mad,
   They've tasted Hell.

It's not their fault they do not know
The birdsong from the radio,
It's not their fault they often go
   To Maidenhead

And talk of sports and makes of cars
In various bogus Tudor bars
And daren't look up and see the stars
   But belch instead.

In labour-saving homes, with care
Their wives frizz out peroxide hair
And dry it in synthetic air
   And paint their nails.

Come, friendly bombs, and fall on Slough
To get it ready for the plough.
The cabbages are coming now;
   The earth exhales.

John Betjeman
(August 28th 1906 – May 19th 1984)

John Betjeman was born in Highgate, the son of a Dutch-descended manufacturer of household objects. He was educated at Marlborough, which he disliked, and Oxford, which he left without a degree. He was a contemporary there of Louis MacNeice and W. H. Auden, who admired his verse. His range of interests as a poet, broadcaster and writer are indicated by the following sample titles: *Ghastly Good Taste: or, A Depressing Story of the Rise and Fall of English Architecture* (1933), *Continual Dew: A Little Book of Bourgeois Verse* (1937), *English Churches* (1964) and *London's Historic Railway Stations* (1972). He was the founder of the Victorian Society. As William Plomer put it: "His lifelong love-affair with Edwardian England (in many ways the last period of Victorian England) has included old churches, old railways, old gaslit streets, old country-towns, old dons, and old invalids; it has also given him a distaste for much of what is supposed to represent progress." Betjeman was named as Poet Laureate in 1972.

May 20

• Robert Browning first visited Elizabeth Barrett at her home, May
  20th 1845; the following autumn they eloped and married
• John Clare, the poet son of a labourer, died in Northampton
  General Asylum on May 20th 1864
• Half-French poet and novelist Michèle Roberts born on May 20th
  1949. Winner of the W. H. Smith Literary Award in 1993
• Poet and electro-plater Alison Brackenbury born May 20th 1953

Magnificat
for Sian, after thirteen years

oh this man
what a meal he made of me
how he chewed and gobbled and sucked

in the end he spat me all out

you arrived on the dot, in the nick
of time, with your red curls flying
I was about to slip down the sink like grease
I nearly collapsed, I almost
wiped myself out like a stain
I called for you, and you came, you voyaged
fierce as a small archangel with swords and breasts
you declared the birth of a new life
in my kitchen there was an annunciation
and I was still, awed by your hair's glory

you commanded me to sing of my redemption

oh my friend, how
you were mother for me, and how
I could let myself lean on you
comfortable as an old cloth, familiar as enamel saucepans
I was a child again, pyjamaed
in winceyette, my hair plaited, and you
listened, you soothed me like cakes and milk
you listened to me for three days, and I poured
it out, I flowed all over you
like wine, like oil, you touched the place where it hurt
at night we slept together in my big bed
your shoulder eased me towards dreams

when we met, I tell you
it was a birthday party, a funeral
it was a holy communion
between women, a Visitation

it was two old she-goats butting
and nuzzling each other in the smelly fold

Michèle Roberts
(May 20th 1949 –)

- *Satirical poet Alexander Pope born the son of a linen merchant May 21st 1688. At 12, his growth was stunted by Pott's disease*
- *Christopher Smart died in a debtors' prison, May 21st 1771*
- *American Black Mountain College poet Robert Creeley born May 21st 1926. He once commented that "I write to realize the world as one has come to live in it, thus to give testament. I write to move in* words, *a human delight"*

The Way

My love's manners in bed
are not to be discussed by me,
as mine by her
I would not credit comment upon gracefully.

Yet I ride by the margin of that lake in
the wood, the castle,
and the excitement of strongholds,
and have a small boy's notion of doing good.

Oh well, I will say here,
knowing each man,
let you find a good wife too,
and love her as hard as you can.

Robert Creeley
(May 21st 1926 –)

Robert Creeley writes: "The burden of this poem seems to remain true despite I wrote it forty or more years ago. In fact, the older one gets, the more insistent what's said here becomes. Onward!"

May 22

• Poet, novelist and dramatist Victor Hugo, exiled to Guernsey by
  Napoleon III, in 1876 became a French senator, and died May
  22nd 1885
• Playwright Lady Augusta Gregory, Yeats' associate, died May
  22nd 1932
• Black poet, song-writer and short-story writer Langston Hughes
  died May 22nd 1967
• Cecil Day Lewis, Irish poet, critic and detective story-writer (as
  'Nicholas Blake') died May 22nd 1972

Jazzonia

Oh, silver tree!
Oh, shining rivers of the soul.

In a Harlem cabaret
Six long-headed jazzers play.
A dancing girl whose eyes are bold
Lifts high a dress of silken gold.

Oh, singing tree!
Oh, shining rivers of the soul!

Were Eve's eyes
In the first garden
Just a bit too bold?

Was Cleopatra gorgeous
In a gown of gold?

Oh, shining tree!
Oh, silver rivers of the soul!

In a whirling cabaret
Six long-headed jazzers play.

Langston Hughes
(February 1st 1902 – May 22nd 1967)

Langston Hughes was born in Joplin, Missouri, the son of a lawyer. He earned a degree from Lincoln
University, and his career as a prolific writer got underway with encouragement from his mentor and
fellow poet Vachel Lindsay. Many of his poems have been set to music. His autobiographical works are
The Big Sea and *I Wonder as I Wander*.

• *Humorous and satirical poet Thomas Hood ("I remember, I remember ..."), born May 23rd 1799. His poem 'Song of the Shirt' had as theme the wretched conditions of London workers*

The Tables Turned

Up, up! my Friend, and quit your books;
　　Or surely you'll grow double:
Up, up! my Friend, and clear your looks
　　Why all this toil and trouble?

The sun, above the mountain's head,
　　A freshening lustre mellow
Through all the long green fields has spread,
　　His first sweet evening yellow.

Books! 'tis a dull and endless strife:
　　Come, hear the woodland linnet,
How sweet his music! on my life,
　　There's more of wisdom in it.

And hark! how blithe the throstle sings!
　　He, too, is no mean preacher:
Come forth into the light of things,
　　Let Nature be your teacher.

She has a world of ready wealth,
　　Our minds and hearts to bless—
Spontaneous wisdom breathed by health,
　　Truth breathed by cheerfulness.

One impulse from a vernal wood
　　May teach you more of man,
Of moral evil and of good,
　　Than all the sages can.

Sweet is the lore which Nature brings;
　　Our meddling intellect
Mis-shapes the beauteous forms of things:—
　　We murder to dissect.

Enough of Science and of Art;
　　Close up those barren leaves;
Come forth and bring with you a heart
　　That watches and receives.

William Wordsworth
(April 7th 1770 – April 23rd 1850)

Composed about May 23rd 1798. At the time, the Wordsworths were bringing up Basil Montagu. "We teach him nothing at present," explained Dorothy Wordsworth, "but what he learns from the evidence of his senses. He has his own insatiable curiosity which we are always careful to satisfy to the best of our ability. It is directed to everything he sees, the sky, the fields, trees, shrubs, corn, the making of tools, etc. ..."

May 24

• Joseph Brodsky born in Leningrad to Russian-Jewish parents May 24th 1940. Sentenced to five years in Siberia and expelled from the Soviet Union in 1972
• Singer and song-writer Bob Dylan born as Robert Allen Zimmerman in Duluth, Minnesota, May 24th 1941

From The Song of Solomon

I am come into my garden, my sister, my spouse: I have gathered my myrrh with my spice; I have eaten my honeycomb with my honey; I have drunk my wine with my milk: eat, O friends; drink, yea, drink abundantly, O beloved.

I sleep, but my heart waketh: it is the voice of my beloved that knocketh, saying, Open to me, my sister, my love, my dove, my undefiled: for my head is filled with dew, and my locks with the drops of the night.

Behold, thou art fair, my love; behold thou art fair; thou hast doves' eyes within thy locks: thy hair is as a flock of goats, that appear from mount Gilead.

Thy teeth are like a flock of sheep that are even shorn, which came up from the washing; whereof every one bear twins, and none is barren among them.

Thy lips are like a thread of scarlet, and thy speech is comely: thy temples are like a piece of pomegranate within thy locks.

My beloved is white and ruddy, the chiefest among ten thousand.

His head is as the most fine gold, his locks are bushy and black as a raven.

His eyes are as the eyes of doves by the rivers of waters, washed with milk, and fitly set.

Thy neck is like the tower of David builded for an armoury, whereon there hang a thousand bucklers, all shields of mighty men.

Thy two breasts are like two young roes that are twins, which feed among the lilies.

Until the day break, and the shadows flee away, I will get me to the mountain of myrrh, and to the hill of frankincense.

Thou art all fair, my love; there is no spot in thee.

His cheeks are as a bed of spices, as sweet flowers: his lips like lilies, dropping sweet smelling myrrh.

His hands are as gold rings set with the beryl: his belly is as bright ivory overlaid with sapphires.

His legs are as pillars of marble, set upon sockets of fine gold: his countenance is as Lebanon, excellent as the cedars.

Come with me from Lebanon, my spouse, with me from Lebanon: look from the top

[Continued]

of Amana, from the top of Shenir and Hermon, from the lions' den, from the mountains of the leopards.

Thou hast ravished my heart, my sister, my spouse: thou hast ravished my heart with one of thine eyes, with one chain of thy neck.

How fair is thy love, my sister, my spouse! how much better is thy love than wine! and the smell of thine ointments than all spices!

Thy lips, O my spouse, drop as the honeycomb: honey and milk are under thy tongue; and the smell of thy garments is like the smell of Lebanon.

A garden inclosed is my sister, my spouse; a spring shut up, a fountain sealed.

His mouth is most sweet: yea, he is altogether lovely. This is my beloved, and this is my friend, O daughters of Jerusalem.

The highly erotic Song of Solomon survived in the bible under disguise as an allegory. Where the Song has, for instance, "my beloved put in his hand by the hole of the door, and my bowels were moved for him", the commentary reads "the church having a taste of Christ's love is sick of love". The Song of Solomon (at one time attributed to Solomon, but now thought to be from a later date, perhaps the 4th or 3rd century BC) is an anthology of Hebrew love poems, with two different voices – the man and the woman's voice in the version here printed represents a conflation of Chapters 4 and 5 (and was read as a dialogue by bride and groom at a recent wedding).

Rabbi Akibu wrote that "The whole world is not worth the day on which the Song of Songs was given to Israel; for all the scriptures are holy, but the Song of Songs is the Holy of Holies." How so, if it is merely sensual love poetry? Robert Davidson tells the story of a Jewish tailor talking to a Christian friend: "The real difference between a Jew and a Christian is that we Jews believe in sex".

May 25

• Ralph Waldo Emerson born in Boston, May 25th 1803 of
ministerial stock. He resigned his own Unitarian ministry in 1833
• Oscar Wilde sentenced to two years for sodomy May 25th 1895
• Theodore Roethke born in Saginaw, Michigan, May 25th 1908
• Poet and short-story writer Raymond Carver born May 25th 1938

From Hamatreya

Ah! the hot owner sees not Death, who adds
Him to his land, a lump of mould the more.
Hear what the Earth says:

Earth-Song

'Mine and yours;
Mine, not yours.
Earth endures;
Stars abide –
Shine down in the old sea;
Old are the shores;
But where are old men?
I who have seen much,
Such have I never seen.

'The lawyer's deed
Ran sure,
In tail,
To them, and to their heirs
Who shall succeed,
Without fail,
Forevermore.

'Here is the land,
Shaggy with wood,
With its old valley,
Mound and flood.
But the heritors?
Fled like the flood's foam. –
The lawyer, and the laws,
And the kingdom,
Clean swept herefrom.

'They called me theirs,
Who so controlled me;
Yet every one
Wished to stay, and is gone,
How am I theirs,
If they cannot hold me,
But I hold them?'

When I heard the Earth-song
I was no longer brave;
My avarice cooled
Like lust in the chill of the grave.

Ralph Waldo Emerson
(May 25th 1803 – April 27th 1882)

"We have listened too long to the courtly muses of Europe," Emerson wrote. "The spirit of the
American free man is already suspected to be timid, imitative, tame. Not so, brothers and friends, please
God, ours shall be not so. We will walk on our own feet; we will work with our own hands; we will
speak with our own minds."

- *Shakespeare's first daughter Susanna was baptised at Stratford parish church May 26th 1583*
- *Julian Grenfell, who wrote the poem 'Into Battle', was killed on the Western front at Ypres, May 26th 1915*
- *Simon Armitage born May 26th 1963*

Poem

And if it snowed and snow covered the drive
he took a spade and tossed it to one side.
And always tucked his daughter up at night.
And slippered her the one time that she lied.

And every week he tipped up half his wage.
And what he didn't spend each week he saved.
And praised his wife for every meal she made.
And once, for laughing, punched her in the face.

And for his mum he hired a private nurse.
And every Sunday taxied her to church.
And he blubbed when she went from bad to worse.
And twice he lifted ten quid from her purse.

Here's how they rated him when they looked back:
sometimes he did this, sometimes he did that.

Simon Armitage
(May 26th 1963 –)

Simon Armitage was born in Huddersfield, West Yorkshire, and studied geography at Portsmouth Polytechnic and social work at Manchester University. He is a probation officer and lives in Marsden near Huddersfield, which has been described as Britain's "alternative poetry capital". His poetry includes *Zoom* (1989) and *Kid* (1992).

The Battle Hymn of the Republic

Mine eyes have seen the glory of the coming of the Lord:
He is trampling out the vintage where the grapes of wrath are stored;
He hath loosed the fatal lightning of His terrible swift sword:
    His truth is marching on.

I have seen Him in the watch-fires of a hundred circling camps,
They have builded Him an altar in the evening dews and damps;
I can read His righteous sentence by the dim and flaring lamps:
    His day is marching on.

I have read a fiery gospel writ in burnished rows of steel:
'As ye deal with my contemners, so with you my grace shall deal;
Let the Hero, born of woman, crush the serpent with his heel,
    Since God is marching on.'

He has sounded forth the trumpet that shall never call retreat;
He is sifting out the hearts of men before His judgement seat:
Oh, be swift, my soul, to answer Him! Be jubilant, my feet!
    Our God is marching on.

In the beauty of the lilies Christ was born across the sea,
With a glory in his bosom that transfigures you and me:
As he died to make men holy, let us die to make men free,
    While God is marching on.

Julia Ward Howe
(May 27th 1819 – October 17th 1910)

Julia Ward Howe, a wealthy banker's daughter, was born in New York and became in due course a suffragette and anti-slavery activist. On visiting the Union Army of the Potomac, she was asked to write dignified patriotic words to the tune of 'John Brown's Body' for use as a marching song, and this 'Battle Hymn of the Republic' was the result, first published in 1862. She later edited *Woman's Journal* and wrote the book *Sex and Education*.

• *Thomas Moore born in Dublin May 28th 1779. In his lifetime his poetry was as popular as that of his friend Byron*
• *Anne Brontë, the youngest of the three sisters, died in Scarborough May 28th 1849. Only two volumes of the joint Brontë Poems were sold*

Do Not Go Gentle Into That Good Night

Do not go gentle into that good night,
Old age should burn and rave at close of day;
Rage, rage against the dying of the light.

Though wise men at their end know dark is right,
Because their words had forked no lightning they
Do not go gentle into that good night.

Good men, the last wave by, crying how bright
Their frail deeds might have danced in a green bay,
Rage, rage against the dying of the light.

Wild men who caught and sang the sun in flight,
And learn, too late, they grieved it on its way,
Do not go gentle into that good night.

Grave men, near death, who see with blinding sight
Blind eyes could blaze like meteors and be gay,
Rage, rage against the dying of the light.

And you, my father, there on the sad height,
Curse, bless, me now with your fierce tears, I pray.
Do not go gentle into that good night.
Rage, rage against the dying of the light.

Dylan Thomas
(October 27th 1914 – November 9th 1953)

'Do Not Go Gentle Into That Good Night' was completed by Dylan Thomas on this day in 1951. It was written for his agnostic father who had cancer of the throat. "The only person," wrote Dylan, "I can't show the ... poem to who doesn't know he's dying." A jotting on the manuscript adds: "Pain made him skin and bone and spirit."

His father died on December 16th 1952 – Dylan survived him by a mere ten months.

May 29

• Frederick Locker-Lampson, author of London Lyrics, born May 29th 1821
• W. S. Gilbert died May 29th 1911 [1]
• Juan Ramon Jiménez, whose Spanish poem 'Platero y Yo' is the story of a poet and his donkey, died May 29th 1958

To the Terrestrial Globe
By a Miserable Wretch

Roll on, thou ball, roll on!
Through pathless realms of Space
   Roll on!
What though I'm in a sorry case?
What though I cannot meet my bills?
What though I suffer toothache's ills?
What though I swallow countless pills?
   Never *you* mind!
   Roll on!

Roll on, thou ball, roll on!
Through seas of inky air
   Roll on!
It's true I've got no shirts to wear;
It's true my butcher's bill is due;
It's true my prospects all look blue—
But don't let that unsettle you!
   Never *you* mind!
   Roll on!

             [It rolls on.]

W. S. Gilbert
(November 18th 1836 – May 29th 1911)

1. Gilbert's death seems to have resulted from an attempt to help a young friend who had got out of her depth while swimming near his home. Hearing her cries, Gilbert dived in to rescue her, but at 74 years old the exertion proved too great for him. He died of heart failure.

- Christopher Marlowe killed in a tavern brawl May 30th 1593
- Alexander Pope died May 30th 1744, leaving his property to Martha Blount, his childhood friend and caretaker.
- Alfred Austin, the Poet Laureate who dismissed the work of Tennyson, Browning, Swinburne, Hugo and Wordsworth as inferior to his own, born May 30th 1834
- Boris Pasternak, author of Dr Zhivago, died May 30th 1960

From An Essay on Man, Epistle II.
Of the Nature and State of Man With Respect
to Himself, as an Individual

Know then thyself, presume not God to scan;
The proper study of mankind is Man.
Placed on this isthmus of a middle state,
A being darkly wise, and rudely great:
With too much knowledge for the skeptic side,
With too much weakness for the Stoic's pride,
He hangs between; in doubt to act, or rest,
In doubt to deem himself a god, or beast;
In doubt his mind or body to prefer,
Born but to die, and reasoning but to err;
Alike in ignorance, his reason such,
Whether he thinks too little, or too much:
Chaos of thought and passion, all confused;
Still by himself abused, or disabused;
Created half to rise, and half to fall;
Great lord of all things, yet a prey to all;
Sole judge of truth, in endless error hurled:
The glory, jest, and riddle of the world!

Alexander Pope
(May 21st 1688 – May 30th 1744)

The largely self-educated son of a linen draper, Pope was a precocious poet, producing publishable work by the age of 12, the age at which a tubercular infection of his spine crippled his growth. He achieved financial independence through his translations of Homer, buying a villa in Twickenham where he lived with his mother. Many of his poems were immensely popular, ranging from his *Rape of the Lock*, a mock epic on the stealing of a lock of hair from the head of a society lady, to his mock-heroic satire *The Dunciad*. His *Essay on Man* was published in 1733-34. Louis Kronenberger concludes that Pope "was at bottom a man of sensibility, and the age was hard; of vanity, and the age was cruel; of sensibility, and the age was coarse. Hence the deformed, disabled poet with his biting tongue fell in with the practices of the day, and in settling private scores became the most formidable of satirists."

May 31

• *Walt Whitman born May 31st 1819*
• *French poet St-John Perse (Alexis Saint-Léger Léger), whose 'Anabase' was translated by Eliot, was born on a coral island off Guadeloupe, his nurse a Shiva priestess, May 31st 1887*
• *Judith Wright born in Armidale, New South Wales, May 31st 1915*

From Memories of President Lincoln (in *Leaves of Grass*) *From the section* When Lilacs Last in the Dooryard Bloom'd[1]

Come, lovely and soothing Death,
Undulate round the world, serenely arriving, arriving,
In the day, in the night, to all, to each,
Sooner or later, delicate Death.

Praised be the fathomless universe
For life and joy, and for objects and knowledge curious;
And for love, sweet love—But praise! O praise and praise
For the sure-enwinding arms of cool-enfolding Death.

Dark Mother, always gliding near, with soft feet,
Have none chanted for thee a chant of fullest welcome?
Then I chant it for thee—I glorify thee above all;
I bring thee a song, that, when thou must indeed come, thou come unfalteringly.

Approach, encompassing Death—strong deliveress!
When it is so—when thou hast taken them, I joyously sing the dead
Lost in the loving, floating ocean of thee,
Laved in the flood of thy bliss, O Death.

Walt Whitman
(May 31st 1819 – March 26th 1892)

Walt Whitman was born in West Hills, near Huntington, Long Island (USA) – "well-begotten, and rais'd by a perfect mother," as he put it. His most passionate subsequent relationships were with younger men. He became in turn a printer, teacher, newspaper editor and freelance writer. The first edition of *Leaves of Grass* was published when he was 36.

President Lincoln, whom these verses commemorate, was shot in 1865 (see also April 14th in this anthology). Whitman himself was permanently disabled by a stroke, probably brought on by his untiring work giving emotional support to the young men hospitalised during the civil war. He died in Camden, New Jersey, conscious to the end, with Horace Traubel, his Boswell, holding his hand.

1. Lines 135 to 150 of this 206 line section.

- Henry Francis Lyte, the clergyman who wrote the hymn
  'Abide with me', was born June 1st 1793
- Publication of Tennyson's In Memoriam June 1st 1850
- John Masefield born in Ledbury, Herefordshire, June 1st 1878
- John Drinkwater, the poet and playwright who founded
  the company which became the Birmingham Repertory
  Company, was born June 1st 1882
- Theatre director (and poet) John McGrath born June 1st 1935

Cargoes

Quinquireme of Nineveh from distant Ophir
Rowing home to haven in sunny Palestine,
With a cargo of ivory,
And apes and peacocks,
Sandalwood, cedarwood, and sweet white wine.

Stately Spanish galleon coming from the Isthmus,
Dipping through the Tropics by the palm-green shores,
With a cargo of diamonds,
Emeralds, amethysts,
Topazes, and cinnamon, and gold moidores.

Dirty British coaster with a salt-caked smoke stack
Butting through the Channel in the mad March days,
With a cargo of Tyne coal,
Road-rail, pig-lead,
Firewood, iron-ware, and cheap tin trays.

John Masefield
(June 1st 1878 – May 12th 1967)

This poem was written in 1902 and published in Masefield's *Ballads and Poems* in 1910. To an Eton schoolboy who wrote to the poet to point out that the quinquireme would have had trouble rowing home to haven in Nineveh, as Nineveh was 200 miles inland, Masefield replied: "I can only suggest that a Ninevian syndicate must have chartered the ship; even so it was odd."

As a child, Masefield learnt poetry by heart before he could read, and said that the first poems to move him were Tennyson's 'The Dying Swan' and Hood's 'I remember, I remember' which he learnt so as to recite to his mother. His mother died when he was six, his father had a mental breakdown and died soon after, and the aunt who looked after him was not enamoured of his literary aspirations. At 13 he was sent to the naval training ship HMS Conway. They sailed for Chile, but Masefield suffered from sea-sickness, had what seems to have been a breakdown and was returned home. At 17 he deserted his second ship and wandered through America, taking odd jobs.

He became Poet Laureate in 1930.

June 2

• Thomas Hardy born June 2nd 1840
• John Lehmann, poet, writer and publisher, born in Bourne End, Bucks, June 2nd 1907
• Vita Sackville-West, the model for Virginia Woolf's Orlando, died June 2nd 1962

A Thunderstorm In Town

She wore a new 'terra-cotta' dress,
And we stayed, because of the pelting storm,
Within the hansom's dry recess,
Though the horse had stopped; yea, motionless
    We sat on, snug and warm.

Then the downpour ceased, to my sharp sad pain
And the glass that had screened our forms before
Flew up, and out she sprang to her door:
I should have kissed her if the rain
    Had lasted a minute more.

Thomas Hardy
(June 2nd 1840 – January 11th 1928)

Hardy was born in Upper Bockhampton, near Dorchester in Dorset, the son of a stonemason. Trained as an architect, he began writing novels. He only turned his attention to poetry in his late fifties, cured of concern for the critical opinion of others by what he called the "shrill crescendo of invective" launched at his later novels. He tried to write poetry in a colloquial language that avoided "the jewelled line".

In a less than flattering tribute to his forerunner, W. H. Auden commented: "Hardy was a good poet, perhaps a great one, but not *too* good. Much as I loved him, even I could see that his diction was often clumsy and forced and that a lot of his poems were plain bad. This gave me hope, where a flawless poet might have made me despair."

• *Allen Ginsberg, author of 'Howl' ("the pent up rage and frustrations of the inner being" – Kerouac), born in Newark, New Jersey, June 3rd 1926. His father was a poet and his mother a Russian émigré*

June 3

From As You Like It
Act V Scene iii

It was a lover, and his lass,
With a hey, and a ho, and a hey nonino,
That o'er the green corn field did pass,
   In the spring time, the only pretty ring time,
   When birds do sing, hey ding a ding, ding.
   Sweet lovers love the spring.

Between the acres of the rye,
With a hey, and a ho, and a hey nonino,
Those pretty country folks would lie,
   In spring time, the only pretty ring time,
   When birds do sing, hey ding a ding, ding.
   Sweet lovers love the spring.

This carol they began that hour,
With a hey, and a ho, and a hey nonino:
How that a life was but a flower,
   In spring time, the only pretty ring time,
   When birds do sing, hey ding a ding, ding.
   Sweet lovers love the spring.

And therefore take the present time.
With a hey, and a ho, and a hey nonino,
For love is crowned with the prime.
   In spring time, the only pretty ring time,
   When birds do sing, hey ding a ding, ding.
   Sveet lovers love the spring.

William Shakespeare
(April 23rd 1564 – April 23rd 1616)

Thomas Morley, who is thought to have collaborated with Shakespeare in writing this song, said of himself that he was "no professor, but like a blind man groping for my way". The song is sung by the clown Touchstone to Audrey. 'Ring time' is a time for exchanging rings and a time for dancing in rings.

June 4

* On this day in 1805 Blake pleaded with his patron Hayley to
allow him to do an engraving: "I write to entreat that you would
contrive so as that my plate may come into the work, as its
omission would be to me a loss that I could not now sustain, as it
would cut off ten guineas ... which sum I am in absolute want of"

The Garden of Love

I went to the Garden of Love,
And saw what I never had seen:
A Chapel was built in the midst,
Where I used to play on the green.

And the gates of this Chapel were shut,
And 'Thou shalt not' writ over the door;
So I turn'd to the Garden of Love
That so many sweet flowers bore;

And I saw it was filled with graves,
And tomb-stones where flowers should be;
And Priests in black gowns were walking their rounds,
And binding with briars my joys & desires.

William Blake
(November 28th 1757 – August 12th 1827)

For Blake, Love is innocence, spirituality released from materialism. Churches and Chapels belong to
The Beast, the State and their coercive order (see E. P. Thompson's *Witness Against the Beast*).
Alexander Gilchrist, Blake's first biographer, tells the possibly apocryphal story of a visitor finding Blake
and his wife naked in their garden summer house. "Come in!" said Blake, "it's only Adam and Eve you
know!"

- *Shakespeare's eldest surviving daughter Susanna married John Hall, a Puritan physician, June 5th in 1607*
- *On June 5th 1867 Tennyson visited the high Blackdown site for his new home, with his mother carried up in a basket-carriage*
- *Federico García Lorca born June 5th 1898*

The Faithless Wife

So I took her to the river
believing she was a maiden,
but she already had a husband.
It was on Saint James's night
and almost as if I was obliged to.
The lanterns went out
and the crickets lighted up.
In the farthest street corners
I touched her sleeping breasts,
and they opened to me suddenly
like spikes of hyacinth.
The starch of her petticoat
sounded in my ears
like a piece of silk
rent by ten knives.
Without silver light on their foliage
the trees had grown larger
and a horizon of dogs
barked very far from the river.

Past the blackberries,
the reeds and the hawthorn,
underneath her cluster of hair
I made a hollow in the earth.
I took off my tie.
She took off her dress.
I my belt with the revolver.
She her four bodices.
Nor nard nor mother-o'-pearl
have skin so fine,
nor does glass with silver
shine with such brilliance.
Her thighs slipped away from me
like startled fish,
half full of fire,
half full of cold.
That night I ran
on the best of roads
mounted on a nacre mare
without bridle or stirrups.
As a man, I won't repeat
the things she said to me.
The light of understanding
has made me most discreet.
Smeared with sand and kisses
I took her away from the river.
The swords of the lilies
battled with the air.

I behaved like what I am.
Like a proper gypsy.
I gave her a large sewing basket,
of straw-coloured satin,
and I did not fall in love
for although she had a husband
she told me she was a maiden
when I took her to the river.

Federico García Lorca
(June 5th 1898 – August 19th 1936)
translated by Stephen Spender
and J. L. Gili

Lorca was born in Fuente Vaqueros in Andalusia, later reacting against his label of "poet of the gypsies". A friend of Salvador Dali, he was a painter in his own right, but also a musician and playwright. He was assassinated in the Spanish Civil War, and his body was never found.

June 6

- *Pierre Corneille, author of 'Le Cid' ("O rage! ô désespoir! ô viellesse ennemie! ..."), born June 6th 1606*
- *Russia's greatest poet, Alexander Pushkin, author of* Eugene Onegin *and* Boris Godunov, *born in Moscow June 6th 1799*
- *Sir Henry Newbolt, who wrote 'Drake's Drum' and other nautical ballads, was born June 6th 1862*

Duet

1. Is it the wind of the dawn that I hear
   in the pine overhead?
2. No; but the voice of the deep as it hollows
   the cliffs of the land.
1. Is there a voice coming up with the
   voice of the deep from the strand,
   One coming up with a Song in the
   flush of the glimmering red?
2. Love that is born of the deep coming
   up with the sun from the sea.
1. Love that can shape or can shatter a
   life till the life shall have fled?
2. Nay, let us welcome him, Love that
   can lift up a life from the dead.
1. Keep him away from the lone little isle.
   Let us be, let us be.
2. Nay, let him make it his own, let him
   reign in it—he, it is he,
   Love that is born of the deep coming
   up with the sun from the sea.

Alfred, Lord Tennyson
(August 6th 1809 – October 6th 1892)

On June 6th 1829, Tennyson, who was 19, was announced winner of the Chancellor's Medal at Cambridge University for his poem on the set subject of Timbuctoo.

'Duet' comes from Act 2, scene 1, of Tennyson's third play, *Beckett*, which was written in 1876-9, but only published in 1884. The actor-manager Henry Irving had been certain that the play would be a disaster theatrically and would cost £135 a night to stage. He suggested to Tennyson a shorter work in a more modern idiom.

- *Shelley's favourite child, William, died in Rome, aged four, on June 7th 1819*
- *On June 7th 1855 Tennyson thanked Lear for sending him his Book of Nonsense which his son Hallam would enjoy*
- *Dorothy Parker, whose surname came from her first husband, died alone in her Manhattan apartment June 7th 1967*

She rose to His Requirement – dropt

She rose to His Requirement – dropt
The Playthings of Her Life
To take the honorable Work
Of Woman, and of Wife –

If aught She missed in Her new Day,
Of Amplitude, or Awe –
Or first Prospective – Or the Gold
In using, wear away,

It lay unmentioned – as the Sea
Develop Pearl, and Weed,
But only to Himself – be known
The Fathoms they abide –

Emily Dickinson
(December 10th 1830 – May 15th 1886)

On this day in 1862, Emily Dickinson wrote to Thomas Wentworth Higginson that "my dying tutor [Benjamin Newton] told me he would like to live till I had been a poet". She was, however, to remain virtually unpublished in her lifetime. Earlier in Spring of the same year Higginson had received a letter from Emily Dickinson containing four of her poems. He told a friend that her verses were "remarkable, though odd ... too *delicate* – not strong enough to be published." In a third letter to him, Emily Dickinson consented to his verdict:

"I smile when you suggest that I delay 'to publish' – that being foreign to my thought, as Firmament to Fin.

If fame belonged to me, I could not escape her – if she did not, the longest day would pass me on the chase – and the approbation of my Dog, would forsake me – then. My Barefoot-Rank is better.

You think my gait 'spasmodic'. I am in danger, Sir.

You think me 'uncontrolled'. I have no Tribunal.

The Sailor cannot see the North, but knows the Needle arm."

Emily Dickinson remained unmarried herself. Once, turning down a request for a photo, she wrote: "I have no picture, but am small, like the wren; my hair is bold, like the chestnut burr; and my eyes, like the sherry in the glass that the guest leaves."

June 8

- On this day in 1812, Wordsworth told his brother Christopher that he had found more poetry in Blake and Burns than in Scott and Byron – the latter's Childe Harold being the talk of the hour
- Gerard Manley Hopkins died June 8th 1889 [1]
- Poet Gillian Clarke, author of Letter from a Far Country, born in Cardiff June 8th 1937

God's Grandeur

The world is charged with the grandeur of God.
  It will flame out, like shining from shook foil[2];
  It gathers to a greatness, like the ooze of oil
Crushed. Why do men then now not reck his rod?
Generations have trod, have trod, have trod;
  And all is seared with trade; bleared, smeared with toil;
  And wears man's smudge and shares man's smell: the soil
Is bare now, nor can foot feel, being shod.

And for all this, nature is never spent;
  There lives the dearest freshness deep down things;
And though the last lights off the black West went
  Oh, morning, at the brown brink eastward, springs—
Because the Holy Ghost over the bent
  World broods with warm breast and with ah! bright wings.

Gerard Manley Hopkins
(July 28th 1844 – June 8th 1889)

This sonnet was written whilst studying theology at St Beuno's in the valley of the Elwy in North Wales. H. N. Fairlight suggests that Hopkins' nature poems "might not too rashly be interpreted as a deliberate campaign to Christianise the romantic cult of nature. 'God's Grandeur' may well be a direct answer to [Wordsworth's] 'The World is Too Much with Us' ".

1. Jesuits at the time lived twenty years less than other men on average. Hopkins was ill with a "sort of typhoid" for six weeks before his death in Ireland. His parents were summoned from London to visit him on his deathbed. He was heard to say "I am so happy, I am so happy" and died peacefully.
2. In a letter to Robert Bridges written January 4th 1883, Hopkins explained: "I mean foil in its sense of leaf or tinsel, and no other word whatever will give the effect I want. Shaken goldfoil gives off broad glares like sheet lightning and also, and this is true of nothing else, owing to its zigzag dints and crossings and network of small many cornered facets, a sort of fork lightning too."

• Shelley's illegitimate baby Elena Adelaide Shelley, died in Naples on
June 9th 1820. In July, around the time the news reached Shelley, "it
was a beautiful summer evening," wrote Mary Shelley; "while wandering
along the lanes … we heard the carolling of the skylark."
• Keith Douglas ("Simplify me when I'm dead") killed in Normandy on
June 9th 1944

From To a Skylark[1]

Hail to thee, blithe Spirit!
  Bird thou never wert,
That from Heaven, or near it,
  Pourest thy full heart
In profuse strains of unpremeditated art.

Higher still and higher
  From the earth thou springest
Like a cloud of fire;
  The blue deep thou wingest,
And singing still dost soar, and soaring ever singest.

In the golden lightning
  Of the sunken sun,
O'er which clouds are bright'ning,
  Thou dost float and run;
Like an unbodied joy whose race is just begun.

The pale purple even
  Melts around thy flight;
Like a star of Heaven,
  In the broad daylight
Thou art unseen, but yet I hear thy shrill delight,

Keen as are the arrows
  Of that silver sphere,
Whose intense lamp narrows
  In the white dawn clear
Until we hardly see—we feel that it is there.

All the earth and air
  With thy voice is loud,
As, when night is bare,
  From one lonely cloud
The moon rains out her beams, and Heaven is overflowed.

What thou art we know not;
  What is most like thee?
From rainbow clouds there flow not
  Drops so bright to see
As from thy presence showers a rain of melody.

Percy Bysshe Shelley
(August 4th 1792 – July 8th 1822)

1. Stanzas 1 to 7 of this 21 stanza poem.

June 10

* James Joyce and Nora Barnacle first met in Dublin on June 10th 1904

From Alice's Adventures in Wonderland

'Will you walk a little faster?' said a whiting to a snail,
'There's a porpoise close behind us, and he's treading on my tail.
See how eagerly the lobsters and the turtles all advance!
They are waiting on the shingle—will you come and join the dance?
　Will you, wo'n't you, will you, wo'n't you, will you join the dance?
　Will you, wo'n't you, will you, wo'n't you, wo'n't you join the dance?

'You can really have no notion how delightful it will be
'When they take us up and throw us, with the lobsters, out to sea!'
But the snail replied 'Too far, too far!' and gave a look askance—
Said he thanked the whiting kindly, but he would not join the dance.
　Would not, could not, would not, could not, would not join the dance.
　Would not, could not, would not, could not, could not join the dance.

'What matters it how far we go?' his scaly friend replied.
'There is another shore, you know, upon the other side.
The further off from England the nearer is to France—
Then turn not pale, beloved snail, but come and join the dance.
　Will you, wo'n't you, will you, wo'n't you, will you join the dance?
　Will you, wo'n't you, will you, wo'n't you, wo'n't you join the dance?'

Lewis Carroll
(January 27th 1832 – January 14th 1898)

On this day in 1864, Lewis Carroll wrote to Tom Taylor: "I should be very glad if you could help me in fixing on a name for my fairy-tale ... Here are the ... names I have thought of:
　Alice among the elves / goblins
　Alice's hours / doings / activities
　Alice in elfland / wonderland."

Alice's Adventures in Wonderland, as the fairy-tale came to be entitled, was inspired by a boat trip Lewis Carroll made with Alice Liddell, the daughter of the dean of his college, and her two sisters, Lorina and Edith, "all in the golden afternoon" of July 4th 1862. He enjoyed the friendship of young girls and liked to take their photos.

Lewis Carroll was the pseudonym for Charles Dodgson, who for 26 years lectured on mathematics at Oxford. It is said that when Queen Victoria expressed an interest in more works from the hand of the author of *Alice in Wonderland*, he sent her *An Elementary Treatise on Determinants*.

• *Poet and dramatist Ben Jonson, author of* Volpone, *who once killed a fellow actor in a duel, was born in Westminster June 11th 1572*
• *Poet W. E. Henley, befriended in hospital by Stevenson, and the inspiration for the latter's Long John Silver, died June 11th 1903*

Conception

Death did not come to my mother
Like an old friend.
She was a mother, and she must
Conceive him.

Up and down the bed she fought crying
Help me, but death
Was a slow child
Heavy. He

Waited. When he was born
We took and tired him, now he is ready
To do his good in the world.

He has my mother's features.
He can go among strangers
To save lives.

Josephine Miles
(June 11th 1911 –)

Josephine Miles, poet, critic and English professor, crippled by arthritis since childhood, was born in Chicago on this day in 1911. Her *Collected Poems* were published in 1983.

June 12

• On this day in 1786 Burns spoke of loving Jean Armour to distraction (despite his recent betrothal to Mary Campbell)
• Byron composed 'She Walks in Beauty' June 12th 1814
• Djuna Barnes, novelist, illustrator and poet, author of 'The Antiphon', born in Cornwall-on-Hudson June 12th 1892

She Walks in Beauty

She walks in beauty, like the night
  Of cloudless climes and starry skies;
And all that's best of dark and bright
  Meet in her aspect and her eyes:
Thus mellowed to that tender light
  Which heaven to gaudy day denies.

One shade the more, one ray the less,
  Had half impaired the nameless grace
Which waves in every raven tress,
  Or softly lightens o'er her face;
Where thoughts serenely sweet express
  How pure, how dear their dwelling-place.

And on that cheek, and o'er that brow,
  So soft, so calm, yet eloquent,
The smiles that win, the tints that glow,
  But tell of days in goodness spent,
A mind at peace with all below,
  A heart whose love is innocent!

George Gordon, Lord Byron
(January 22nd 1788 – April 19th 1824)

On June 11th 1814, James Webster dragged Byron against his will to a party at Lady Sitwell's in Seymour Road in London. Webster recounts that "he there for the first time saw his cousin, the beautiful Mrs Wilmot [who had appeared in mourning with numerous spangles on her dress]. When we returned to ... the Albany, he ... desired Fletcher to give him a tumbler of Brandy, which he drank at once to Mrs Wilmot's health ... The next day he wrote those charming lines upon her."

• On this day in 1789 Burns comes to his new farm at Ellisland
  ("a poet's choice, not a farmer's" said Allan Cunninghan)
• Tennyson finally married Emily Sellwood June 13th 1850
• W. B. Yeats born of Irish Protestant origins June 13th 1865, the
  eldest son of a painter who was married to a shipowner's daughter
• Mark Van Doren, whose Collected Poems won the Pulitzer
  prize in 1940, was born in Hope, Illinois, June 13th 1894

The Lake Isle Of Innisfree

I will arise and go now, and go to Innisfree,
And a small cabin build there, of clay and wattles made:
Nine bean-rows will I have there, a hive for the honey-bee,
And live alone in the bee-loud glade.

And I shall have some peace there, for peace comes dropping slow,
Dropping from the veils of the morning to where the cricket sings;
There midnight's all a-glimmer, and noon a purple glow[1],
And evening full of the linnet's wings.

I will arise and go now, for always night and day
I hear lake water lapping with low sounds by the shore;
While I stand on the roadway, or on the pavements grey,
I hear it in the deep heart's core.

William Butler Yeats
(June 13th 1865 – January 28th 1939)

This early poem of Yeats' was written in 1890. "I had still the ambition," he wrote, "formed in Sligo in my teens, of living in imitation of Thoreau on Innisfree, a little island in Lough Gill, and when walking through Fleet Street very homesick I heard a little trickle of water and saw a fountain in a shop window which balanced a little ball upon its jet, and began to remember lake water. From the sudden remembrance came my poem 'Innisfree', my first lyric with anything in its rhythm of my own music." In later life, he wrote to Miss Ruth Watt, a very young admirer of his poems: "Please don't think 'The Lake Isle of Innisfree' is better than all the rest, for I don't." Another admirer of this poem was Robert Louis Stevenson, who wrote to Yeats from Samoa to say that it had laid him under a spell, "it is so quaint and airy, simple and artful, and eloquent to the heart."

1. Yeats explained in a radio broadcast that this referred to the reflection of heather in the water. 'Innisfree' means 'Heather Island'.

June 14

• Scholar and poet Edward FitzGerald died June 14th 1883
• Kathleen Raine, neo-Blakean poet, born June 14th 1908
• Blind Argentinian writer Jorge Luis Borges died June 14th 1986

From[1] The Rubáiyát[2] of Omar Khayyám[3] of Naishápúr

I sent my Soul through the Invisible,
Some letter of that Afterlife to spell:
   And by and by my Soul returned to me,
And answered 'I Myself am Heav'n and Hell:'

Heav'n but the Vision of fulfilled Desire,
And Hell the Shadow from a Soul on fire,
   Cast on the Darkness into which Ourselves,
So late emerged from, shall so soon expire.

We are no other than a moving row
Of Magic Shadow-shapes that come and go
   Round with the Sun-illumined Lantern held
In Midnight by the Master of the Show;

But helpless Pieces of the Game He plays
Upon his Checkerboard of Nights and Days;
   Hither and thither moves, and checks, and slays,
And one by one back in the Closet lays.

The Ball no question makes of Ayes and Noes,
But Here or There as strikes the Player goes;
   And He that tossed you down into the Field,
He knows about it all—HE knows—**HE** knows!

The Moving Finger writes; and, having writ,
Moves on: nor all your Piety nor Wit
   Shall lure it back to cancel half a Line,
Nor all your Tears wash out a Word of it.

And that inverted Bowl they call the Sky,
Whereunder crawling cooped we live and die
   Lift not your hands to *It* for help—for It
As impotently moves as you or I.

With Earth's first Clay They did the Last Man knead,
And there of the Last Harvest sowed the Seed:
   And the first Morning of Creation wrote
What the Last Dawn of Reckoning shall read.

YESTERDAY *This* Day's Madness did prepare;
TOMORROW's Silence, Triumph, or Despair:
   Drink! for you know not whence you came, nor why:
Drink! for you know not why you go, nor where.

Edward FitzGerald
(March 31st 1809 – June 14th 1883)

1. Stanzas 66 to 74 from the 97 stanza fourth edition.
2. Plural of 'ruba'i', meaning quatrain in Arabic.
3. Persian astronomer-poet, lived in Naishápúr in the eleventh century. In his translation of *The Rubáiyát*, FitzGerald made substantial alterations to the original.

• *Poet and dramatist (author of* Hey for Honesty*) Thomas Randolph, friend of Ben Jonson, born June 15th 1605*
• *Thomas Campbell, poet and writer of war-songs ('Ye Mariners of England'), died June 15th 1844, in Boulogne, having given a farewell party to his friends in London the previous year*
• *Poet Amy Clampitt born in Iowa June 15th 1920. Her debut volume* The Kingfisher *was published when she was 63*

The Promised Garden
for Suzanne

There is a garden where our hearts converse,
At ease beside clear water, dreaming
A whole and perfect future for yourself,
Myself, our children and our friends.

And if we must rise and leave,
Put on identity and fight,
Each day more desperate than the last
And further from our future, that
Is no more than honour and respect shown
To all blocked from the garden that we own.

There is a garden at the heart of things,
Our oldest memory guards it with her strong will.
Those who by love and work attain there
Bathe in her living waters, lift up their hearts and
Turn again to share the steep privations of the hill;
They walk in the market but their feet are still.

There is a garden where our hearts converse,
At ease beside clear water, dreaming
A whole and perfect future for yourself,
Myself, our children and our friends.

Theo Dorgan
(September 21st 1953 –)

Theo Dorgan writes: "In the Gaelic tradition, 'Gáirdín Phárthais' or the Paradise Garden is a recurrent image derived not only from the Garden of Eden but also from Oriental ideas of the magical garden of transformations, an idea which finds its point of pure expression in the Sufi idea of the Garden as a place of human perfection. Such gardens are often attained in the first flush of love, and as often lost if the lovers do not acknowledge that this garden, to endure, must be in the world, not out of it. I had in mind, perhaps, the need to acknowledge the privileges of love as well as the responsibilities of sharing the human, everyday world. I had certainly in mind the magical lines from Osip Mandelstam 'I am garden, and gardener too / And un-alone in this vast dungeon'."

June 16

• *Sylvia Plath and Ted Hughes married June 16th 1956*

This is just to say

I have eaten
the plums
that were in
the icebox

and which
you were probably
saving
for breakfast

Forgive me
they were delicious
so sweet
and so cold

William Carlos Williams
(September 17th 1883 – March 4th 1963)

William Carlos Williams' poetry books include *Al Que Quiere!* (1917) and *Journey to Love* (1953). His concerns come across in several of his remarks, such as: "All art begins in the local" and "Rigour of beauty is the quest."

As a medical student at the University of Pennsylvania, Williams began a lifelong friendship with Pound who was a special student there. Williams became head paediatrician at the General Hospital in Paterson, and his *Autobiography* (1951) relates his poetry to his medical experiences treating his largely working-class patients.

- *Politician and essayist Joseph Addison died June 17th 1719*
- *Poet and editor Allen Curnow, author of* Continuum, *born in New Zealand June 17th 1911*
- *Black poet Gwendolyn Brooks born in Topeka June 17th 1917*
- *Christopher Benson, who wrote 'Land of Hope and Glory', died June 17th 1925*
- *Poet and novelist John Cowper Powys died June 17th 1963*

From In a Gondola

The moth's kiss first!
Kiss me as if you made believe
You were not sure, this eve,
How my face, your flower, had pursed
Its petals up; so, here and there
You brush it, till I grow aware
Who wants me, and wide ope I burst.

The bee's kiss, now!
Kiss me as if you entered gay
My heart at some noonday,
A bud that dares not disallow
The claim, so all is rendered up,
And passively its shattered cup
Over your head to sleep I bow.

Robert Browning
(May 7th 1812 – December 12th 1889)

Robert Browning never went to school, his education coming from the 6,000 volumes in his father's library and the occasional tutor. He dropped out of London University in his second term and began travelling – "Italy was my university". His poem *Sordello,* published when he was 28, was widely ridiculed for its obscurity. Tennyson said that of its 5,800 lines there were just two he could comprehend, the first "Who will may hear Sordello's story told" and the last "Who would has heard Sordello's story told" – and that both these lines were lies.

At the age of 33, Browning began a romance with Elizabeth Barrett, who inspired his love poems. Among his most popular poetry in his lifetime were *Men and Women* and *The Ring and the Book.* His last poems, *Asolando,* were published on the day of his death. He was buried on December 31st 1889 in Westminster Abbey.

June 18

• Poet Geoffrey Hill, author of The Mystery of the Charity of Charles Péguy, was born in Bromsgrove June 18th 1932

To Jane: The Keen Stars Were Twinkling

The keen stars were twinkling,
And the fair moon was rising among them,
   Dear Jane!
  The guitar was tinkling,
But the notes were not sweet till you sung them
   Again.

As the moon's soft splendour
O'er the faint cold starlight of Heaven
   Is thrown,
  So your voice most tender
To the strings without soul had then given
   Its own.

The stars will awaken,
Though the moon sleep a full hour later,
   Tonight;
  No leaf will be shaken
Whilst the dews of your melody scatter
   Delight.

Though the sound overpowers,
Sing again, with your dear voice revealing
   A tone
  Of some world far from ours,
Where music and moonlight and feeling
   Are one.

Percy Bysshe Shelley
(August 4th 1792 – July 8th 1822)

This poem was written for Jane Williams, with whom Shelley became increasingly infatuated. She and her husband lived with Shelley and his wife Mary in Italy at the Casa Magni in Lerici in the summer of 1822. Shelley was unable to borrow 70 to 80 guineas to buy Jane a harp from Paris, and gave her a guitar instead. On this day in 1822, three weeks before his death by drowning, Shelley wrote to John Gisborne: "I like Jane more and more, and I find Williams the most amiable of companions. She has a taste for music, and an elegance of form and motions that compensates in some degree for the lack of literary refinement ... I listen the whole evening on our terrace to the simple melodies with excessive delight. I have a boat here ... Williams is captain, and we drive along this delightful bay in the evening wind, under the summer moon, until earth appears another world. Jane brings her guitar, and if the past and future could be obliterated, the present would content me so well that I could say with Faust to the passing moment 'Remain, thou, thou art so beautiful.' "

This particular poem Shelley left in Jane's room with a note: "I commend [it] to your secrecy and your mercy, and will try to do better another time."

From The Brook

I come from haunts of coot[1] and hern°,   *heron*
   I make a sudden sally
And sparkle out among the fern,
    To bicker° down a valley.   *to flow noisily*

By thirty hills I hurry down,
   Or slip between the ridges,
By twenty thorps°, a little town,   *hamlets*
   And half a hundred bridges.

Till last by Philip's farm I flow
   To join the brimming river,
For men may come and men may go,
   But I go on for ever.

I chatter over stony ways,
   In little sharps and trebles,
I bubble into eddying bays,
   I babble on the pebbles.

With many a curve my banks I fret
   By many a field and fallow,
And many a fairy foreland set
   With willow-weed and mallow.

I chatter, chatter, as I flow
   To join the brimming river,
For men may come and men may go
   But I go on for ever.

Alfred, Lord Tennyson
(August 6th 1809 – October 6th 1892)

A map in Bag Enderby church in Lincolnshire (near to Somersby where Tennyson was born) claims to show places referred to in this poem, but, according to Peter Levi, Tennyson in his old age denied that there were these links.

1. A water-fowl with a distinctive white spot on its forehead, an extension of the beak, suggesting baldness and giving us the phrase 'bald as a coot'.

June 20

• Poet Paul Muldoon, author of Quoof, born in Portadown,
County Armagh, June 20th 1951
• Vikram Seth born June 20th 1952

All You Who Sleep Tonight

All you who sleep tonight
Far from the ones you love,
No hand to left or right,
And emptiness above –

Know that you aren't alone.
The whole world shares your tears,
Some for two nights or one,
And some for all their years.

Vikram Seth
(June 20th 1952 –)

Vikram Seth was born in Calcutta and educated at Oxford, Stanford and Nanjing universities, training as an economist.

This poem comes from *All You Who Sleep Tonight*, a slim collection of his short poems from the previous seven years that was published in 1990. His other work includes *The Golden Gate*, a novel in verse published in 1986, and *A Suitable Boy* (1993), a novel (in prose) of 1,349 pages, that was judged by Lord Gowrie to be too long to deserve the Booker prize.

• *Poet John Skelton, suspended as rector of Diss, probably for having children with his concubine, attacked the church in 'Colyn Cloute' ("My name is Colyn Clout ... / though my rhyme be ragged,/ Tattered and jagged,/ Rudely rain-beaten,/ Rusty and moth-eaten,/ If ye take well therewith / It hath in it some pith."). He took refuge from Cardinal Wolsey in Westminster Abbey and died there June 21st 1529*

From The Tempest
Act V Scene i

Ariel. Where the bee sucks, there suck I:
In a cowslip's bell I lie;
There I couch when owls do cry;
On the bat's back I do fly
After summer merrily:
Merrily, merrily shall I live now
Under the blossom that hangs on the bough.

William Shakespeare
(April 23rd 1564 – April 23rd 1616)

Ariel's song is placed here in celebration of the summer solstice, June 21st.

Hazlitt observes that "there is a peculiar charm in the songs introduced in Shakespeare, which, without conveying any distinct images, seem to recall all the feelings connected with them, like snatches of half-gotten music heard indistinctly and at intervals. This is the effect produced by Ariel's songs, which seem to sound in the air, and as if the person playing them were invisible."

It has been pointed out that if Shakespeare is implying here that bats migrate, they do not, but Elizabethans thought that they did.

June 22

• Shakespeare's will proved June 22nd 1616, with his wife receiving his second best bed
• American poet Alan Seeger, who was killed in action in 1916, was born in New York City June 22nd 1888
• Walter De La Mare, poet and novelist for both children and adults, who retired on a state pension in 1908 to take up full-time writing, died June 22nd 1956 in Twickenham. His ashes are in the crypt of St Paul's where there is a memorial plaque to him
• Sasha Moorsom died June 22nd 1993

The Company of the Birds

Ah the company of the birds
I loved and cherished on earth
Now, freed of flesh we fly
Together, a flock of beating wings,
I am as light, as feathery,
As gone from gravity we soar
In endless circles.

Sasha Moorsom
(January 25th 1931 – June 22nd 1993)

Sasha's daughter, Sophie Young, writes: "Sasha loved birds. They seemed to represent the freedom of spirit that soared in her own heart. She would delight in watching them from the kitchen window, splashing in the bird-bath she had sculpted, and always making sure they had enough food in the winter. This poem was read at the end of Sasha's funeral, a sad but beautiful reminder of immortality. As she said herself not long before she died, 'My spirit is strong, it's just the body that's collapsing.' "

• Poet Anna Akhmatova, author of the banned 'Requiem', born in
  Odessa, the daughter of a naval officer, June 23rd 1889
• Poet and critic Anthony Thwaite born in Chester June 23rd 1930

From The Voyage
for T. S. Eliot

We imitate, oh horror! tops and bowls
in their eternal waltzing marathon;
even in sleep, our fever whips and rolls –
like a black angel flogging the brute sun.

Strange sport! where destination has no place
or name, and may be anywhere we choose –
where man, committed to his endless race,
runs like a madman diving for repose!

Our soul is a three-master seeking port:
a voice from starboard shouts, 'We're at the dock!'
Another, more elated, cries from port,
'Here's dancing, gin and girls!' Balls! it's a rock!

The islands sighted by the lookout seem
the El Dorados promised us last night;
imagination wakes from its drugged dream,
sees only ledges in the morning light.

Robert Lowell
(March 1st 1917 – September 12th 1977)
based on a French poem by Charles Baudelaire
(April 9th 1821 – August 31st 1867)

A ceaseless innovator, Lowell collected his translations in the volume *Imitations*, containing many purposeful inaccuracies. The adaptations thus produced give many clues to the way Lowell approached poetic sources.

"I belong to no 'school' of poetry," he claimed, "but various living or once-living poets have fascinated me – W. C. Williams, Pound, Tate, Ransom, Eliot, and Yeats. And many, many others, though perhaps I've tried to be a chameleon in vain."

His first marriage, through which he became an ardent convert to Roman Catholicism, was fraught with violence and mental instability, often brought on by bouts of heavy drinking. He married twice more, never throwing off the agonising bouts of mania which could reduce his life to chaos. Instead he made this private disorder the subject of a personal, highly confessional and often tortured poetry.

Lowell was imprisoned as a conscientious objector during 1944 for six months; in the late 1960s his opposition to the Vietnam War brought him broad public attention.

June 24

• Poet and Cambridge lecturer J. H. Prynne, author of The White Stones, born June 24th 1936

Different

Not to say what everyone else was saying
not to believe what everyone else believed
not to do what everybody did,
then to refute what everyone else was saying
then to disprove what everyone else believed
then to deprecate what everybody did,

was his way to come by understanding

how everyone else was saying the same as he was saying
believing what he believed
and did what doing.

Clere Parsons
(1908 – 1931)

Clere Parsons died at the age of 23 from pneumonia and a severe form of diabetes. Louis MacNeice thought of Clere Parsons as different from the norm, describing him from his Oxford days as "a bleached frail little man, who brought special bread with him to lunch because he had diabetes" and who had "an invalid's fanaticism" in politics, though sensitive to the "melody of words". Grigson described him as "young, thin, tall, white face under pale hair". At Oxford, he helped found a poetry society by involving MacNeice, Stephen Spender and others.

He was born in India, where his father worked in the Indian Civil Service.

• *On June 25th 1794 Robert Burns tells Mrs Dunlop that a "flying gout" is likely to punish him for the foibles of his youth*

John Anderson My Jo

John Anderson my jo°, John,   *darling*
    When we were first acquent;
Your locks were like the raven,
    Your bony brow was brent[1];
But now your brow is bald, John,
    Your locks are like the snaw;
But blessings on your frosty pow°,   *head*
    John Anderson my Jo.

John Anderson my jo, John,
    We clamb the hill the gither°;   *together*
And mony a canty° day, John,   *merry*
    We've had wi' ane anither:
Now we maun totter down, John,
    And hand in hand we'll go;
And sleep the gither at the foot,
    John Anderson my Jo.

Robert Burns
(January 25th 1759 – July 21st 1796)

Burns has here metamorphosed a bawdy version of this song. In the original (he was not above writing bawdy verses himself, and this version has been attributed to him in some collections): "When first that ye began / Ye had as good a tail-tree / As any ither man; / But now its waxen wan, John, / And wrinkles to and fro; / I've twa gae-ups for one gae-down, / John Anderson, my jo ..."

Burns himself did not live to an old age, dying of rheumatic heart disease in his 37th year. Ten thousand people followed his coffin to the grave.

1. High and straight (because of a thick head of hair).

June 26

• Laurie Lee born June 26th 1914
• Poet and novelist Ford Madox Ford, co-founder of the Transatlantic Review, died June 26th 1939

Home From Abroad

Far-fetched with tales of other worlds and ways,
My skin well-oiled with wines of the Levant,
I set my face into a filial smile
To greet the pale, domestic kiss of Kent.

But shall I never learn? That gawky girl,
Recalled so primly in my foreign thoughts,
Becomes again the green-haired queen of love
Whose wanton form dilates as it delights.

Her rolling tidal landscape floods the eye
And drowns Chianti in a dusky stream;
The flower-flecked grasses swim with simple horses,
The hedges choke with roses fat as cream.

So do I breathe the hayblown airs of home,
And watch the sea-green elms drip birds and shadows,
And as the twilight nets the plunging sun
My heart's keel slides to rest among the meadows.

Laurie Lee
(June 26th 1914 –)

Laurie Lee described his childhood in *Cider with Rosie* (1959) which has now sold over two million copies. He was born in Stroud, Gloucestershire, and educated at Slad village school and at Stroud Central School. In June 1934, at the age of 19, he left home and walked to London where he worked as a labourer. His travels through Spain in 1935 and 1936 are recounted in *As I Walked Out One Midsummer Morning* (1969). In 1936, "June came in full blast, with the heat bouncing off the sea as from a buckled sheet of tin"; he witnessed the first stirrings of the Spanish Civil War in Castillo: a Falangist boy of about twenty had been shot through the head and his body left sprawled on the river bank.

Laurie Lee married Catherine Francesca Polge in 1950 and they have a daughter. His *Selected Poems* were published in 1983.

• *On this day in 1924 Hardy agreed to sign a letter to* The Times
*proposing a memorial to Byron in Westminster Abbey. When the dean
turned this down, he wrote the poem 'A Refusal'*

June 27

Adlestrop

Yes. I remember Adlestrop—
The name, because one afternoon
Of heat the express-train drew up there
Unwontedly. It was late June.

The steam hissed. Someone cleared his throat.
No one left and no one came
On the bare platform. What I saw
Was Adlestrop—only the name

And willows, willow-herb, and grass,
And meadowsweet, and haycocks dry,
No whit less still and lonely fair
Than the high cloudlets in the sky.

And for that minute a blackbird sang
Close by, and round him, mistier,
Farther and farther, all the birds
Of Oxfordshire and Gloucestershire.

Edward Thomas
(March 3rd 1878 – April 9th 1917)

Edward Thomas only started to write poetry at the age of 36, encouraged by Robert Frost, and with a sense of urgency brought on by the start of the First World War. Up until then, he had been struggling to support a family by churning out books, anthologies and reviews. He had become depressed and at times suicidal, "so confoundedly busy I feel as if the back of my head would come out". He was killed at Aras in 1917, having written his 143rd poem, but before his first collection was published.

Walter de la Mare, in the foreword to Thomas' *Collected Poems*, wrote that with his death "a mirror of England was shattered of so pure and true a crystal that a clearer and tenderer reflection of it can be found no other where than in these poems ... England's roads and heaths and woods, its secret haunts and solitudes, its houses, its people ... were to him 'lovelier than any mysteries' ".

June 28

• On June 28th 1816, whilst travelling in Switzerland with Lord
  Byron (and despite feeling inhibited in Byron's company), Shelley
  began to draft his poem 'Hymn to Intellectual Beauty'
• Alfred Noyes, anti-Modernist poet, anthologist, playwright and
  novelist, died June 28th 1958

Bermudas

Where the remote Bermudas ride
In th' ocean's bosom unespied,
From a small boat, that rowed along,
The list'ning winds received this song.

   "What should we do but sing His praise
That led us through the wat'ry maze,
Unto an isle so long unknown,
And yet far kinder than our own?
Where he the huge sea–monsters wracks°,   *wrecks*
That lift the deep upon their backs.
He lands us on a grassy stage,
Safe from the storms' and prelates' rage;
He gave us this eternal Spring
Which here enamels every thing,
And sends the fowls to us in care,
On daily visits through the air;
He hangs in shades the orange bright,
Like golden lamps in a green night,
And does in the pomegranates close
Jewels more rich than Ormus° shows;   *Hormuz (diamond market)*
He makes the figs our mouths to meet,
And throws the melons at our feet,
But apples° plants of such a price,   *pineapples*
No tree could ever bear them twice;
With cedars, chosen by his hand,
From Lebanon, he stores the land;
And makes the hollow seas, that roar,
Proclaim the ambergris on shore;
He cast (of which we rather boast)
The Gospel's pearl upon our coast,
And in these rocks for us did frame
A temple, where to sound His name.
Oh, let our voice his praise exalt
Till it arrive at Heaven's vault,
Which thence (perhaps) rebounding, may
Echo beyond the Mexique Bay."

   Thus sung they, in the English boat,
An holy and a cheerful note,
And all the way, to guide their chime,
With falling oars they kept the time.

Andrew Marvell
(March 31st 1621 – August 16th or 18th 1678)

- *Elizabeth Barrett Browning died in her husband Robert's arms on June 29th 1861, 15 years of happy marriage since her escape from her father and Wimpole Street*
- *French airman and writer, Antoine de Saint-Exupéry, whose books such as Le Petit Prince are poetic in style, was born in Lyon June 29th 1900*
- *Poet James K. Baxter born in Dunedin, New Zealand, June 29th 1926. He began to write verse aged seven and lived towards the end of his life in a Maori settlement, dying at the age of 46*

One Flesh

Lying apart now, each in a separate bed,
He with a book, keeping the light on late,
She like a girl dreaming of childhood,
All men elsewhere — it is as if they wait
Some new event: the book he holds unread,
Her eyes fixed on the shadows overhead.

Tossed up like flotsam from a former passion,
How cool they lie. They hardly ever touch,
Or if they do it is like a confession
Of having little feeling — or too much.
Chastity faces them, a destination
For which their whole lives were a preparation.

Strangely apart, yet strangely together,
Silence between them like a thread to hold
And not wind in. And time itself's a feather
Touching them gently. Do they know they're old,
These two who are my father and my mother
Whose fire, from which I came, has now grown cold?

Elizabeth Jennings
(July 18th 1926 –)

Elizabeth Jennings was born in Boston, Lincolnshire, and educated at Oxford High School and St Anne's College, Oxford. She once wrote that "for me, poetry is always a search for order. I started writing at the age of thirteen ... My Roman Catholic religion and my poems are the most important things in my life".

Her collections *Recoveries* (1964) and *The Mind has Mountains* (1966) include poems about illness, hospital and the tensions of family life. Her *Collected Poems* were published in 1967 and *Times and Seasons* in 1992.

June 30

• John Gay, who made £1,000 through publishing his poems by
subscription, and who wrote The Beggar's Opera, was born in
Barnstaple June 30th 1685
• Polish writer and poet Czeslaw Milosz, winner of the 1980
Nobel Prize for literature, was born June 30th 1911

Song

And when our streets are green again
When metalled roads are green
And girls walk barefoot through the weeds
Of Regent Street, Saint Martin's Lane

And children hide in factories
Where burdock blooms and vetch and rust,
And elms and oaks and chestnut trees
Are tall again and hope is lost

When up the Strand the foxes glide
And hedgehogs sniff and wildcats yell
And golden orioles come back
To flash through Barnes and Clerkenwell

When governments and industries
Lie choked by weeds in fertile rain
For sure the few who stay alive
Will laugh and grow to love again

John McGrath
(June 1st 1935 –)

John McGrath was the founder-director of the radical popular theatre company 7:84, taking theatre
to working class audiences. His *A Good Night Out* is a statement of the aims of the counter-theatre
movement, and his plays include *Events While Guarding the Bofors Gun* and *Yobbo Nowt*.

Angry at the "cultural terrorism" of the Thatcher years, he dedicated his book *The Bone Won't Break*
to "The Resistance, to those who have had their lives distorted or destroyed so others could consume;
to those who insist that co-operation rather than individual possessiveness is the better principle for the
future happiness of humanity; may they survive, and that principle bring more joy to the lives of more
people".

• *Alun Lewis who wrote the poem 'All Day it has Rained', and who was killed in Burma in 1944, was born in a Welsh mining village July 1st 1915*

From Holy Sonnets
14

Batter my heart, three-person'd God; for, you
As yet but knock, breathe, shine, and seek to mend;
That I may rise, and stand, o'erthrow me, and bend
Your force, to break, blow, burn and make me new.
I, like an usurp'd town, to another due,
Labour to admit you, but Oh, to no end,
Reason your viceroy in me, me should defend,
But is captiv'd, and proves weak or untrue.
Yet dearly I love you, and would be loved fain,
But am betroth'd unto your enemy:
Divorce me, untie, or break that knot again,
Take me to you, imprison me, for I
Except you enthral me, never shall be free,
Nor ever chaste, except you ravish me.

John Donne
(c. June 1572 – March 31st 1631)

On this day in 1627, Donne gave a sermon at the funeral of Lady Danvers, George Herbert's mother. It was to Lady Danvers that Donne had sent his *Divine Poems* twenty years before.

Donne was brought up a Catholic and thus was debarred from taking a university degree. His brother Henry died in prison having harboured a Catholic suspected of being a priest (the latter was hanged, cut down and disembowelled). John Donne about that time renounced his Catholicism.

This sonnet reflects the Protestant belief that faith is entirely in God's gift, and that man as a fallen creature is incapable of good works.

John Carey writes that Donne's "love poems display, in their obsession with woman's inconstancy, a profound anxiety about his own ability to attract or merit stable affection. His fear of damnation and of exclusion from God's love in the 'Holy Sonnets' reflects the same anxiety, transposed to the religious sphere."

July 2

• Ernest Hemingway, whose works include Three Stories and Ten Poems (1923) and For Whom the Bell Tolls (1940), shot himself in the mouth in Ketchum, Idaho, dying July 2nd 1961
' Russian novelist and poet Vladimir Nabokov, author of Lolita, died in Montreux July 2nd 1977

my love

my love
thy hair is one kingdom
   the king whereof is darkness
thy forehead is a flight of flowers

thy head is a quick forest
   filled with sleeping birds
thy breasts are swarms of white bees
   upon the bough of thy body
thy body to me is April
in whose armpits is the approach of spring

thy thighs are white horses yoked to a chariot
   of kings
they are the striking of a good minstrel
between them is always a pleasant song

my love
thy head is a casket
   of the cool jewel of thy mind
the hair of thy head is one warrior
   innocent of defeat
thy hair upon thy shoulders is an army
   with victory and with trumpets

thy legs are the trees of dreaming
whose fruit is the very eatage of forgetfulness

thy lips are satraps in scarlet
   in whose kiss is the combining of kings
thy wrists
are holy
   which are the keepers of the keys of thy blood
thy feet upon thy ankles are flowers in vases
   of silver

in thy beauty is the dilemma of flutes

   thy eyes are the betrayal
of bells comprehended through incense

e.e. cummings
(October 14th 1894 – September 3rd 1962)

On this day in 1917, Cummings wrote to his mother that Paris had "the finest girls God ever allowed to pasture in this fresh earth". A virgin at 22, he became attached to Marie Louise Lallemand, a Parisian whore, who is thought to be associated with his poem "goodby Betty, don't remember me".

• *Tennessee-born poet and critic John Crowe Ransom, who described himself as "in manners, aristocratic; in religion, ritualistic; in art, traditional", died July 3rd 1974*

Absence

I visited the place where we last met.
Nothing was changed, the gardens were well-tended,
The fountains sprayed their usual steady jet;
There was no sign that anything had ended
And nothing to instruct me to forget.

The thoughtless birds that shook out of the trees,
Singing an ecstasy I could not share,
Played cunning in my thoughts. Surely in these
Pleasures there could not be a pain to bear
Or any discord shake the level breeze.

It was because the place was just the same
That made your absence seem a savage force,
For under all the gentleness there came
An earthquake tremor: fountain, birds and grass
Were shaken by my thinking of your name.

Elizabeth Jennings
(July 18th 1926 –)

This poem first appeared in *A Way of Looking* (1955). In the preface to her *Collected Poetry*, Elizabeth Jennings writes: "When I re-read my past work I can see a development; to such an effect, indeed, that some of them no longer seem to be any part of me. But of course, once a poem is published it ceases to have much to do with oneself. Art is not self-expression while, for me, 'confessional poetry' is almost a contradiction in terms."

July 4

• *Lewis Carroll's* Alice's Adventures in Wonderland *stemmed from a boat trip which Carroll made with the three daughters of the dean of his college "all in the golden afternoon" of July 4th 1862*
• *Alan Seeger killed in action July 4th 1916*
• *American poet Ted Berrigan, author of* The Sonnets (1964), *died from a perforated ulcer July 4th 1983*

Rendezvous

I have a rendezvous with Death
At some disputed barricade,
When Spring comes back with rustling shade
And apple-blossoms fill the air –
I have a rendezvous with Death
When Spring brings back blue days and fair.

It may be he shall take my hand
And lead me into his dark land
And close my eyes and quench my breath –
It may be I shall pass him still.
I have a rendezvous with Death
On some scarred slope of battered hill,
When Spring comes round again this year
And the first meadow-flowers appear.

God knows 'twere better to be deep
Pillowed in silk and scented down,
Where love throbs out in blissful sleep,
Pulse nigh to pulse, and breath to breath,
Where hushed awakenings are dear . . .
But I've a rendezvous with Death
At midnight in some flaming town,
When Spring trips north again this year,
And I to my pledged word am true,
I shall not fail that rendezvous.

Alan Seeger
(June 22nd 1888 – July 4th 1916)

Alan Seeger was born in New York, educated at Harvard, and lived in the Latin Quarter of Paris. In World War I he enlisted in the French Foreign Legion. On this day in 1916, his company went into attack near Belloy-en-Santerre, and, though wounded, he continued urging his men on. His body was found in a shell hole the next day. He was awarded the Croix de Guerre posthumously.

• *Jean Cocteau, French poet, film director, playwright and opium eater, born July 5th 1889*

The Clod and the Pebble

'Love seeketh not Itself to please,
'Nor for itself hath any care,
'But for another gives its ease,
'And builds a Heaven in Hell's despair.'

So sung a little Clod of Clay
Trodden with the cattle's feet,
But a Pebble of the brook
Warbled out these metres meet:

'Love seeketh only Self to please,
'To bind another to Its delight,
'Joys in another's loss of ease,
'And builds a Hell in Heaven's despite.'

William Blake
(November 28th 1757 – August 12th 1827)

On this day in 1826 Blake wrote to Mr Linnell: "I thank you for the receipt of five pounds this morning, and compliment you on the receipt of another fine boy ... I am getting better every hour. My plan is diet only; but if the machine is capable of it, shall make an old man yet ... These paroxysms ... I now believe will never more return."

For Blake in this poem, the Clod of Clay represents unselfish love and innocence. The hard Pebble is materialism. These are the contraries we live with. To transcend them calls for "the annihilation of selfhood" and the release of the poetic genius.

• *The first edition of* Leaves of Grass *by Walt Whitman was on sale by July 6th 1855*

From Song of Myself (in *Leaves of Grass*)

5

I believe in you my soul, the other I am must not abase itself to you,
And you must not be abased to the other.

Loafe with me on the grass, loose the stop from your throat,
Not words, not music or rhyme I want, not custom or lecture, not even the
    best,
Only the lull I like, the hum of your valvèd voice.

I mind how once we lay such a transparent summer morning,
How you settled your head athwart my hips and gently turn'd over upon me,
And parted the shirt from my bosom-bone, and plunged your tongue to my
    bare-stript heart,
And reach'd till you felt my beard, and reach'd till you held my feet.

Swiftly arose and spread around me the peace and knowledge that pass all the
    argument of the earth,
And I know that the hand of God is the promise of my own,
And I know that the spirit of God is the brother of my own,
And that all the men ever born are also my brothers, and the women my
    sisters and lovers,
And that a kelson[1] of the creation is love,
And limitless are leaves stiff or drooping in the fields,
And brown ants in the little wells beneath them,
And mossy scabs of the worm fence, heap'd stones, elder, mullein[2] and
    poke-weed[3].

Walt Whitman
(May 31st 1819 – March 26th 1892)

Whitman was renowned as a 'loafer'. "What was Adam, I should like to know, but a loafer?" he asked. "Of all human beings, none equals your genuine, inbred, unvarying loafer." He finished the first edition of his *Leaves of Grass* at the age of 36. His aim was for a "Divine Style": "Make no quotations and no references to any other writers. Lumber the writing with nothing—let it go as lightly as a bird flies in the air, or a fish swims in the sea ... Clearness, simplicity, no twistified or foggy sentences at all—the most translucid clearness without variation."

Expanded editions of *Leaves of Grass* were published throughout Whitman's lifetime, with the last in the year of his death. He had hoped to produce an edition with one poem for every day of the year, a scripture of everyday life, "the latest construction of the New Bible ... this main life work—the three hundred and sixty five".

1. In shipbuilding, a beam used to stiffen and strengthen the keel structure.
2. Erect plant with sharp yellow flowers.
3. Plant with poisonous, deep red or black berries – also known as Virginian poke or poke-berry.

My own Heart let me more have Pity on

My own heart let me more have pity on; let
Me live to my sad self hereafter kind,
Charitable; not live this tormented mind
With this tormented mind tormenting yet.
  I cast for comfort I can no more get
By groping round my comfortless, than blind
Eyes in their dark can day or thirst can find
Thirst's all-in-all in all a world of wet.

Soul, self; come, poor Jackself[1], I do advise
You, jaded, let be; call off thoughts awhile
Elsewhere; leave comfort root-room; let joy size
At God knows when to God knows what; whose smile
's not wrung, see you; unforeseen times rather—as skies
Betweenpie[2] mountains   lights a lovely mile.

Gerard Manley Hopkins
(July 28th 1844 – June 8th 1889)

This was probably one of the sonnets to which Hopkins referred in his letter to Robert Bridges of September 1st 1885: "I shall shortly have some sonnets to send you, five or more. Four of these came like inspirations unbidden and against my will. And in the life I lead now, which is one of a continually jaded and harassed mind, if in any leisure I try to do anything I make no way – nor with my work, alas! but so it must be." At the time he was Professor of Greek at University College, Dublin, overworked and ill.

1. Workaday, humble self.
2. Verb coined from 'pied': chequers, dapples.

July 8

- *The French poet Jean de La Fontaine, who wrote* Fables, *and whose patrons were aristocratic women, was born July 8th 1621*
- *Percy Bysshe Shelley drowned, July 8th 1822, when his sailing boat sank in the Bay of Spezia* [1]
- *Poet and novelist Richard Aldington, author of a World War I novel* Death of a Hero, *was born in Hampshire July 8th 1892*
- *Oscar Wilde began 'Ballad of Reading Gaol' July 8th 1897*

Ozymandias

I met a traveller from an antique land
Who said: Two vast and trunkless legs of stone
Stand in the desert. Near them, on the sand,
Half sunk, a shattered visage lies, whose frown,
And wrinkled lip, and sneer of cold command,
Tell that its sculptor well those passions read
Which yet survive, stamped on these lifeless things,
The hand that mocked them, and the heart that fed:
And on the pedestal these words appear:
'My name is Ozymandias, king of kings:
Look on my works, ye Mighty, and despair!'
Nothing beside remains. Round the decay
Of that colossal wreck, boundless and bare
The lone and level sands stretch far away.

Percy Bysshe Shelley
(August 4th 1792 – July 8th 1822)

Shelley visited the British Museum in 1817 with a fellow-poet Horace Smith and suggested that they should both produce a sonnet on the subject of the recent Egyptian finds. Shelley's sonnet, 'Ozymandias', reflects his lifelong hatred of tyranny. In a book by the ancient Greek historian Diodorus, Shelley had read an inscription to an Egyptian monarch's monument similar to that quoted here. The sonnet was first published on January 11th 1818 attributed to 'Glirastes' (from the Latin for dormouse, Mary Shelley's pet-name for her husband).

1. Shelley and Edward Williams had been keen to get home to their wives – Mary Shelley was still very weak at their boathouse in Lerici from a miscarriage on June 16th (Shelley had prevented his wife from haemorrhaging to death by placing her in a bath of icy water). Shelley found the time to write a love-note to Edward Williams' wife, Jane, also staying at the boathouse: "How soon those hours past, and how slowly they return to pass so soon again, and perhaps for ever, in which we have lived together so intimately so happily."

On July 8th, the weather was unsettled, but Shelley, Edward Williams and Charles Vian, their boat-boy, set off from Livorno in their 18ft sailing boat, the *Don Juan*. A storm came up rapidly and a local fishing boat claims to have offered to take them on board: "If you will not come on board, for God's sake reef your sails or you are lost." The *Don Juan* went down in the Gulf of Spezia under full sail. Shelley's body was recovered ten days later, with the face and arms eaten away. To comply with the quarantine laws, his body was buried with quicklime on the beach. Later, his body was dug up and burnt on the beach in the presence of Lord Byron, Leigh Hunt and others, and the ashes were buried in the Protestant Cemetery at Rome.

- *Money was left to Shakespeare's future bride in her father Richard Hathaway's will, which was proved July 9th 1582. It left 6p 13s 4d to Agnes [Anne] Hathaway "to be paid on the day of her marriage"*
- *John Heath-Stubbs, editor, critic and poet, was born in Oxford July 9th 1918*

From The Tempest
Act III Scene ii

Caliban. Be not afeard: the isle is full of noises,
Sounds and sweet airs, that give delight, and hurt not.
Sometimes a thousand twangling instruments
Will hum about mine ears; and sometime voices,
That, if I then had wak'd after a long sleep,
Will make me sleep again: and then, in dreaming,
The clouds methought would open and show riches
Ready to drop upon me; that, when I wak'd
I cried to dream again.

William Shakespeare
(April 23rd 1564 – April 23rd 1616)

Of this speech, Hazlitt wrote in 1817: "This is not more beautiful than it is true. The poet here shows us the savage with the simplicity of a child, and makes the strange monster amiable. Shakespeare had to paint the human animal rude and without choice in its pleasures, but not without the sense of pleasure or some germ of the affections."

July 10

• Poet and novelist Marcel Proust, author of A la recherche du temps perdu, born in Auteuil, Paris, July 10th 1871
• On this day in 1953 Walter de la Mare received the Order of Merit from Queen Elizabeth II. He commented: "H. M. is quite a marvel and I worship her – to such a barbarous degree that I quite forgot not to talk too much"

Good-bye

The last of last words spoken is, Good-bye—
The last dismantled flower in the weed-grown hedge,
The last thin rumour of a feeble bell far ringing,
The last blind rat to spurn the mildewed rye.

A hardening darkness glasses the haunted eye,
Shines into nothing the watcher's burnt-out candle,
Wreathes into scentless nothing the wasting incense,
Faints in the outer silence the hunting-cry.

Love of its muted music breathes no sigh,
Thought in her ivory tower gropes in her spinning,
Toss on in vain the whispering trees of Eden,
Last of all last words spoken is, Good-bye.

Walter De la Mare
(April 25th 1873 – June 22nd 1956)

De la Mare approached death with great serenity. "My days are getting shorter," he told Joyce Grenfell. "But there is more and more magic. More than in all poetry. Everything is increasingly wonderful and beautiful." On June 20th 1956 he wrote to a friend about the midsummer leaf and blossom: "One looks at it partly with amazed delight and partly with anticipatory regret at its transitoriness." He had a coronary thrombosis that same day. The next night, at 2am, the nurse asked if he was comfortable. "Yes, I'm perfectly all right," he replied – then he caught his breath, gasped and died.

Code Poem for the French Resistance

The life that I have is all that I have,
And the life that I have is yours.
The love that I have of the life that I have
Is yours and yours and yours.

A sleep I shall have
Λ rest I shall have,
Yet death will be but a pause,
For the peace of my years in the long green grass
Will be yours and yours and yours.

Leo Marks
(1920 –)

On this day in 1940, Marshal Pétain, at the spa town of Vichy, became head of a collaborationist 'French State', despite General de Gaulle's appeal to the French people the previous month. Pétain was sentenced to death for treason after the war, a sentence commuted to imprisonment on the Ile d'Yeu, where he subsequently died.

July 12

Henry David Thoreau born in Concord, Mass., July 12th 1817

Poet Pablo Neruda born in Parral, Chile, July 12th 1904

• D. H. Lawrence married Frieda Weekley, the wife of his old professor at Nottingham and cousin of the German war ace Baron Manfred von Richthofen, on July 13th 1914

Protocols

What can I say to you? How can I now retract
   All that that fool, my voice, has spoken –
Now that the facts are plain, the placid surface cracked,
   The protocols of friendship broken?

I cannot walk by day as now I walk at dawn
   Past the still house where you lie sleeping.
May the sun burn away these footprints on the lawn
   And hold you in its warmth and keeping.

Vikram Seth
(June 20th 1952 –)

This poem comes from Vikram Seth's collection *All You Who Sleep Tonight*, published in 1990. Seth has homes in both California and New Delhi and is the author of the best-selling novel *A Suitable Boy*.

- *John Clare born the son of a poor labourer, in Helpstone, near Peterborough, July 13th 1793*
- *Wordsworth finished his poem 'Tintern Abbey' July 13th 1798*
- *Siegfried Sassoon MC, pacifist, protester and poet, wounded in the head in France July 13th 1918*
- *Wole Soyinka, poet, dramatist and novelist, author of* Madmen and Specialists, *born in Western Nigeria July 13th 1934*

I Am

I am: yet what I am none cares or knows,
　　My friends forsake me like a memory lost;
I am the self-consumer of my woes,
　　They rise and vanish in oblivious host,
Like shades in love and death's oblivion lost;
And yet I am, and live with shadows tost

Into the nothingness of scorn and noise,
　　Into the living sea of waking dreams,
Where there is neither sense of life nor joys,
　　But the vast shipwreck of my life's esteems;
And een the dearest—that I loved the best—
Are strange—nay, rather stranger than the rest.

I long for scenes where man has never trod;
　　A place where woman never smiled or wept;
There to abide with my Creator, GOD,
　　And sleep as I in childhood sweetly slept:
Untroubling and untroubled where I lie;
The grass below—above the vaulted sky.

John Clare
(July 13th 1793 – May 20th 1864)

"If life had a second edition," wrote Clare, "how I would correct the proofs." He spent the last 22 years of his life in a lunatic asylum in Northampton, forsaken by his former friends and family. He had wished to be buried at his birth place in Helpstone, and despite the refusal of his former patron to supply the necessary money, enough was raised to enable Clare's wish to be fulfilled. He was buried there on May 25th 1864.

July 14

On a Fly Drinking Out of His Cup

Busy, curious, thirsty fly!
Drink with me and drink as I:
Freely welcome to my cup,
Couldst thou sip and sip it up:
Make the most of life you may,
Life is short and wears away.

Both alike are mine and thine
Hastening quick to their decline:
Thine's a summer, mine's no more,
Though repeated to threescore.
Threescore summers, when they're gone,
Will appear as short as one!

William Oldys
(July 14th 1696 – April 15th 1761)

William Oldys was the illegitimate son of the chancellor of Lincoln. He collected rare books and manuscripts, and sold his collection to the Earl of Oxford, who made him his librarian. He wrote a *Life of Sir Walter Raleigh*. Being appointed Norroy king-at-arms for the last six years of his life saved him from poverty and the Fleet prison.

This poem was first published in 1732.

• Poet, editor and historian Robert Conquest, author of Arias from
a Love Opera, born in Great Malvern July 15th 1917

The Song of a Man Who Has Come Through

Not I, not I, but the wind that blows through me!
A fine wind is blowing the new direction of Time.
If only I let it bear me, carry me, if only it carry me!
If only I am sensitive, subtle, oh, delicate, a winged gift!
If only, most lovely of all, I yield myself and am borrowed
By the fine, fine wind that takes its course through the chaos of the world
Like a fine, an exquisite chisel, a wedge-blade inserted;
If only I am keen and hard like the sheer tip of a wedge
Driven by invisible blows,
The rock will split, we shall come at the wonder, we shall find the Hesperides[1].

Oh, for the wonder that bubbles into my soul,
I would be a good fountain, a good well-head,
Would blur no whisper, spoil no expression.

What is the knocking?
What is the knocking at the door in the night?
It is somebody wants to do us harm.

No, no, it is the three strange angels[2].
Admit them, admit them.

D. H. Lawrence
(September 11th 1885   March 2nd 1930)

Lawrence's wife Frieda gave her book about their relationship the same title as this poem. The poem was written on or shortly after the day of their marriage, July 13th 1914. "Lawrence felt that his marriage was an ark in which he and Frieda might be saved, while Europe rushed towards the abyss of the First World War" (Keith Sagar).

1. The sisters who guarded the garden where the golden apples of Hera, queen of the gods, grew. Also the delightful garden itself, a place of fulfilment.

2. Possibly the three angels who appeared to Abraham in Genesis 18 to announce that Abraham and Sarah had been chosen to bear the seed of the future.

July 16

• *Ludovico Ariosto, author of* Orlando Furioso, *died July 16th 1533. His monument is in San Benedetto church in Ferrara*
• *On this day in 1828 Blake told his supporter John Linnell that he did not want John's son to be named William in his honour: "It very much troubles Me, as a Crime in which I shall be The Principal."*
• *Hilaire Belloc died, July 16th 1953, from burns he sustained falling into a fireplace*

From Milton

And did those feet in ancient time
Walk upon England's mountains green?
And was the holy lamb of God
On England's pleasant pastures seen?

And did the countenance divine
Shine forth upon our clouded hills?
And was Jerusalem builded here
Among those dark satanic mills?

Bring me my bow of burning gold:
Bring me my arrows of desire:
Bring me my spear: O clouds unfold!
Bring me my chariot of fire.

I will not cease from mental fight,
Nor shall my sword sleep in my hand
Till we have built Jerusalem
In England's green and pleasant land.

William Blake
(November 28th 1757 – August 12th 1827)

Blake gave this poem no name. His prose *Introduction to Milton* concludes with this poem, now best known as a hymn. There was a popular eighteenth century belief that Joseph of Arimethea brought the boy Jesus to Britain – thus the first verse. The dark satanic mills refer first and foremost to Oxford and Cambridge and the rigidity of classics and mathematics. The third verse treats of the poetic genius, humanity's bottom line and the foundation of all religions. 'Jerusalem' is the name of his greatest epic poem, engraved on a hundred copper plates, of which he finished only a single copy. He wrote of this magnum opus: "I may praise it since I dare not pretend to be any other than the secretary; the authors are in Eternity. I consider it as the grandest poem that the world contains."

- *William Somerville, who wrote 'The Chase', a poem in praise of hunting, died July 17th 1742. "He writes very well for a gentleman," commented Dr Johnson in* Lives of the English Poets
- *G. M. Hopkins converted to Roman Catholicism July 17th 1886*
- *Critic and poet Donald Davie born in Barnsley July 17th 1922*

From Much Ado About Nothing
Act II Scene iii

Sigh no more, ladies, sigh no more,
　　Men were deceivers ever,
One foot in sea and one on shore,
　　To one thing constant never:
Then sigh not so, but let them go,
　　And be you blithe and bonny,
Converting all your sounds of woe
　　Into Hey nonny, nonny.

Sing no more ditties, sing no more,
　　Of dumps so dull and heavy;
The fraud of men was ever so,
　　Since summer first was leafy:
Then sigh not so, but let them go,
　　And be you blithe and bonny,
Converting all your sounds of woe
　　Into Hey nonny, nonny.

William Shakespeare
(April 23rd 1564 – April 23rd 1616)

In Shakespeare's time, pronunciation of the word "nothing" is thought to have been more like "noting". The play abounds in puns on notes and noting. Deception and disguise are major themes.

July 18

• Novelist William Makepeace Thackeray, author of Vanity Fair,
  also wrote ballads. He was born July 18th 1811
• Elizabeth Jennings born in Boston, Lincolnshire, July 18th 1926
• Yevgeny Yevtushenko born in Zima in Sibena July 18th 1933

A Chorus

Over the surging tides and the mountain kingdoms,
Over the pastoral valleys and the meadows,
Over the cities with their factory darkness,
Over the lands where peace is still a power,
Over all these and all this planet carries
A power broods, invisible monarch, a stranger
To some, but by many trusted. Man's a believer
Until corrupted. This huge trusted power
Is spirit. He moves in the muscle of the world,
In continual creation. He burns the tides, he shines
From the matchless skies. He is the day's surrender.
Recognize him in the eye of the angry tiger,
In the sign of a child stepping at last into sleep,
In whatever touches, graces and confesses,
In hopes fulfilled or forgotten, in promises

Kept, in the resignation of old men –
This spirit, this power, this holder together of space
Is about, is aware, is working in your breathing.
But most he is the need that shows in hunger
And in the tears shed in the lonely fastness.
And in sorrow after anger.

Elizabeth Jennings
(July 18th 1926 –)

Peter Levi once wrote that Elizabeth Jennings "may be the last poet of what used to be called the soul".
Her book on mystical poetry, *Every Changing Shape*, was published in 1961.

• *Italian lyric poet Petrarch died July 19th 1374*
• *A. S. J. Tessimond born July 19th 1902*

Not Love Perhaps

This is not Love perhaps – Love that lays down
Its life, that many waters cannot quench, nor the floods drown –
But something written in lighter ink, said in a lower tone:
Something perhaps especially our own:
A need at times to be together and talk –
And then the finding we can walk
More firmly through dark narrow places
And meet more easily nightmare faces:
A need to reach out sometimes hand to hand –
And then find Earth less like an alien land:
A need for alliance to defeat
The whisperers at the corner of the street:
A need for inns on roads, islands in seas, halts for discoveries to be shared,
Maps checked and notes compared:
A need at times of each for each
Direct as the need of throat and tongue for speech.

A. S. J. Tessimond
(July 19th 1902 – May 13th 1962)

Arthur Seymour John Tessimond was born in Birkenhead, the only child of a bank inspector. He felt warmth in his childhood from an aunt, but felt unloved by his parents. His literary executor Hubert Nicholson writes in the introduction to *The Collected Poems of A. S. J. Tessimond* (1985) that "It was to his feeling of being starved of maternal affection that psychiatrists later attributed his sexual difficulties, a diagnosis that did nothing to effect a cure." At 16 he ran away from Charterhouse School (for a fortnight) to London. In 1925, he sent his poems to Ezra Pound, who wrote back biliously: "Can't see that yr. work has any marked individuality, or as yet any character to distinguish it from anyone elses. England has gone to hell, and if you are determined you had better go somewhere else, as you will get nothing but carion and pus from your surroundings." "Not hopeless," Pound added as an afterthought on the envelope, "if you are less than 21." He was 23.

Hubert Nicholson remembers him as "an elegant, fair, mannerly figure, at large with rolled umbrella in the big city streets, keen-eyed but uncynical", with a continually expressed desire for an "unperplexed, unvexed time".

This poem 'Not Love Perhaps' first appeared in his *Voices in a Giant City* (1947). "As a man," wrote Nicholson, "he was forever falling in love afresh: a long succession of never wholly consummated passions, the last psychological barrier never passed. He died a bachelor, without offspring, but he wrote touchingly and not always blindly about the girls he adored."

Tessimond spent half his £4,000 inheritance from his father on nightclub girls and striptease hostesses, and the other half on psychoanalysis. As a manic depressive, he had electric shock therapy at ever shorter intervals in middle age. At 59 he was found dead in his flat from a brain haemorrhage. He had been dead for two days.

July 20

- *Petrarch, whose Rime Sparse include a series in praise of Laura, was born at Arezzo July 20th 1304*
- *Thomas Lovell Beddoes, wandering doctor and poet, who committed suicide, was born in Clifton July 20th 1803*
- *Poet Caroline Anne Bowles who nursed Robert Southey in his last years, died July 20th 1854*
- *Oscar Wilde finished 'Ballad of Reading Gaol' July 20th 1897*

Whoso List To Hunt

Whoso list° to hunt, I know where is an hind°, *wishes; female deer*
But as for me, helas°, I may no more.   *alas*
The vain travail hath wearied me so sore,
I am of them that farthest cometh behind.
Yet may I by no means my wearied mind
Draw from the deer, but as she fleeth afore
Fainting I follow. I leave off therefore
Since in a net I seek to hold the wind.
Who list her hunt, I put him out of doubt,
As well as I may spend his time in vain.
And graven with diamonds in letters plain
There is written her fair neck round about:
"*Noli me tangere*° for Caesar's I am,   *Touch me not*
And wild for to hold though I seem tame."

Sir Thomas Wyatt
(1503 – October 11th 1542)
based on a sonnet by Petrarch
(July 20th 1304 – July 19th 1374)

This sonnet has echoes of Wyatt's relationship with Anne Boleyn in about 1527. Antonio Bonvisi claims that Wyatt went to King Henry VIII to warn him against marrying Anne Boleyn: "She is not meet to be copled with your grace, her conversation hath been so loose and base; which thing I know not so much by hear-say as by my own experience as one that have had my carnal pleasure with her."

Anne Gainsforth, one of Anne Boleyn's maids, gave this account of Wyatt's falling in love: "The knight in the beginning coming to be holden and surprised somewhat with the sight thereof, after much more with her witty and graceful speech, his ear also had him charmed unto her, so as finally his heart seemed to say, 'I could gladly yield to be tied for ever with the knot of her love.' "

Anne Boleyn's other lovers were executed. Wyatt was merely imprisoned in the Tower of London for a time, later returning to favour as ambassador to the court of Charles V in Spain.

- *Poet and secret agent Matthew Prior, who helped bring about the Treaty of Utrecht and wrote 'Alma' in jail, born in Wimborne July 21st 1664*
- *Robert Burns died in his 37th year July 21st 1796*
- *Poet and novelist Vladimir Nabokov, a precocious child, was born into a wealthy St Petersburg family July 21st 1870*
- *Poet Hart Crane, a "pederastic alcoholic" who later drowned himself by jumping off a steamboat, was born in Garrettsville, Ohio, July 21st 1899*
- *Poet and editor Maurice Lindsay, who wrote A Net to Catch the Winds, born in Glasgow July 21st 1918*
- *Wendy Cope born in Kent July 21st 1945*

From From June to December
Summer Villanelle

You know exactly what to do –
Your kiss, your fingers on my thigh –
I think of little else but you.

It's bliss to have a lover who,
Touching one shoulder, makes me sigh –
You know exactly what to do.

You make me happy through and through,
The way the sun lights up the sky –
I think of little else but you.

I hardly sleep – an hour or two;
I can't eat much and this is why –
You know exactly what to do.

The movie in my mind is blue –
As June runs into warm July
I think of little else but you.

But is it love? And is it true?
Who cares? This much I can't deny:
You know exactly what to do;
I think of little else but you.

Wendy Cope
(July 21st 1945 –)

Wendy Cope recalls: "I wrote this one hot Saturday morning in 1984 when I had been planning to go to Sainsburys. I felt guilty about lazing around writing a poem instead."

July 22

● *Alfred Percival Graves, a leader of the Irish literary renaissance, father of Robert Graves, born July 22nd 1846*
● *James Whitcomb Riley, American known as the 'Hoosier poet', who wrote in homely dialect ('Little Orfant Annie'), died July 22nd 1916*
● *Chicago-born poet and writer Carl Sandburg died July 22nd 1967*

From A Dialogue of Self and Soul[1]

I am content to follow to its source
Every event in action or in thought;
Measure the lot; forgive myself the lot!
When such as I cast out remorse
So great a sweetness flows into the breast
We must laugh and we must sing,
We are blest by everything,
Everything we look upon is blest.

William Butler Yeats
(June 13th 1865 – January 28th 1939)

On this day in 1921 the President of Sinn Fein, Eamon De Valera, agreed a truce with the British Government. Yeats had been impressed by a saying attributed to De Valera after the failed Easter Rising of 1916: "If the people had only come out with knives and forks."

'A Dialogue of Self and Soul' was written in 1928, Yeats notes, "during a long illness and indeed finished the day before a Cannes doctor told me to stop writing".

Yeats commented in an essay that "there is in the creative joy an acceptance of what life brings, because we have understood the beauty of what it brings, or a hatred of death for what it takes away, which arouses within us, through some sympathy perhaps with all other men, an energy so noble, so powerful, that we laugh aloud and mock, in the terror or the sweetness of our exultation, at death and oblivion."

1. The final stanza of section II, spoken by 'My Self'.

Woodniche

The dragonflies were here before us, friend:
Cupboard of branch and bramble, woodniche
Where the sun tumbles, foxgloves are gorgeous.
Children tore their knees among these thorns,

Fleshed their pullovers with raspberries.
Orange peel made ripples in the brown water,
Pebbles explored beyond our peering. I
Chewed dandelions and the sun brothered me.
Huge as policemen, sombre as soutanes,

The kind trees whispered in the long watch
And I used wonder in tremendous shadow
And be afraid of where the wonder led.

Summer was wealthy with a daze of suntraps,
Daffodil-spitting, sumptuous. Everywhere
Ours for the taking. Whoever has said
It is time to go home is an adult.

Aidan Carl Mathews
(January 16th 1956 –)

Aidan Carl Mathews was educated at Gonzaga College, University College, Dublin, Trinity College, Dublin, and Stanford University in California. He is the winner of several poetry prizes among them the Irish Times Award for 1974 and the Patrick Kavanagh Award for 1976. His collections of poems include *Windfalls* (1977) and *Minding Ruth* (Gallery Books, Dublin, 1983). He is married and lives in Dublin.

July 24

• *Robert Graves born July 24th 1895. On July 24th 1916, his 21st birthday, he read his obituary in* The Times, *having supposedly been killed in action*

Not to Sleep

Not to sleep all the night long, for pure joy,
Counting no sheep and careless of chimes
Welcoming the dawn confabulation
Of birds, her children, who discuss idly
Fanciful details of the promised coming –
Will she be wearing red, or russet, or blue,
Or pure white? – whatever she wears, glorious:
Not to sleep all the night long, for pure joy,
This is given to few but at last to me,
So that when I laugh and stretch and leap from bed
I shall glide downstairs, my feet brushing the carpet
In courtesy to civilized progression,
Though, did I wish, I could soar through the open window
And perch on a branch above, acceptable ally
Of the birds still alert, grumbling gently together.

Robert Graves
(July 24th 1895 – December 7th 1985)

Robert Graves was born in London, and educated at Charterhouse and St Johns College, Oxford (he studied English and left without taking a degree). The horrors of the First World War colour his autobiography *Goodbye to all that*. His first wife had to put up with his stormy relationship with the demanding Laura Riding, and after the Second World War he returned to Majorca with his second wife, Beryl Hodge.

On May 2nd 1963, Robert Graves wrote to James Reeves: "As a matter of record, I have never been so happy in my life as now: all the unhappiness of three years has peeled away. I wrote a poem two days ago beginning 'Not to sleep all the night gone, for pure joy ...' which is one of the few poems of utter happiness ever written ... this is mine, and may it excuse all the dark ones."

"Poets remain in love for the rest of their lives," Graves contended in an introduction to his *Poems About Love*, "watching the world with a detachment unknown to lawyers, politicians, financiers, and all other ministers of that blind and irresponsible successor to matriarch and patriarchy—the mechanarchy ... Poets look forward to a final reign of love-innocence when the so-called impracticable will once more become the inevitable, when miracles are accepted without surprise or question, and when the patently illogical machine has at last performed its *reductio ad absurdum*, by disintegrating."

- Burns' posthumous son Maxwell born during Burns' funeral service, July 25th 1796
- Poet André Chénier, who supported the Revolution but offended Robespierre with his pamphlets, was guillotined July 25th 1794
- Samuel Taylor Coleridge, who admitted his opium addiction in 1813, rarely left Dr Gillman's home for the last 18 years of his life and died July 25th 1834
- American Surrealist poet Frank O'Hara, whose poems were often in letters to friends, killed by a beach-buggy July 25th 1966

From The Tempest
Act I Scene ii

Ariel. Full fathom five thy father lies;
    Of his bones are coral made:
Those are pearls that were his eyes:
    Nothing of him that doth fade,
But doth suffer a sea-change
Into something rich and strange.
Sea-nymphs hourly ring his knell:
                    [*Burden*[1]: ding-dong.
Hark! now I hear them,—ding-dong, bell.

William Shakespeare
(April 23rd 1564 – April 23rd 1616)

Shakespeare is thought to have derived some of the inspiration for *The Tempest* from a shipwreck that began on this day in 1609, as described by Silvester Jourdan in *A Discovery of the Barmudas, Otherwise called the Ile of Divels*, published in 1610: 'I being in ship called the Sea-venture, with Sir Thomas Gates ... bound for Virginia ... we were taken with a most sharpe and cruell storme upon the five and twentieth day of July, Anno 1609, which did separate us from the residue of our fleete ... It pleased God to send her within halfe an English mile of ... the llandes of the Barmudas, ... ever esteemed, and reputed, a most prodigious and inchanted place ... Yet did we finde there the ayre so temperate and the Country so abundantly fruitful of all fit necessaries ... that we were there for the space of nine moneths ... well refreshed."

1. Refrain.

July 26

• "Hamlet, as it was lately acted by the Lord Chamberlain his
Servants", entered on the Stationer's Register July 26th 1602
• John Wilmot, Earl of Rochester, who gave away his health to the
"only important businesses of the age: Women, Politics and
Drinking", died aged 33 on July 26th 1680
• Spanish poet Antonio Machado born July 26th 1875

The Wind, One Brilliant Day

The wind, one brilliant day, called
to my soul with an odor of jasmine.

'In return for the odor of my jasmine,
I'd like all the odor of your roses.'

'I have no roses; all the flowers
in my garden are dead.'

'Well then, I'll take the withered petals
and the yellow leaves and the waters of the fountain.'

The wind left. And I wept. And I said to myself:
'What have you done with the garden that was entrusted to you?'

Antonio Machado
(July 26th 1875 – February 22nd 1939)
translated by Robert Bly
(December 23rd 1926 –)

Antonio Machado was born in Seville and wrote books of spirited if often melancholic poetry, such as
Campos de Castilla, and collaborated on plays with his brother.

Robert Bly includes Machado's work in his collection of 'poems for men', *The Rag and Bone Shop of
the Heart* (published by Harper Perennial).

• Poet and journalist Thomas Campbell born in Glasgow July 27th 1777
• Hilaire Belloc born in St Cloud near Paris, the son of a French barrister,
  July 27th 1870. He did French military service, became an English
  Liberal MP, was an outspoken Catholic and a close friend of G. K.
  Chesterton. His book The Servile State advocated a return to the
  medieval guilds

Tarantella

Do you remember an Inn,
Miranda?
Do you remember an Inn?
And the tedding and the spreading
Of the straw for a bedding,
And the fleas that tease in the High Pyrenees,
And the wine that tasted of the tar?
And the cheers and the jeers of the young muleteers
(Under the vine of the dark verandah)?
Do you remember an Inn, Miranda,
Do you remember an Inn?
And the cheers and the jeers of the young muleteers
Who hadn't got a penny,
And who weren't paying any,
And the hammer at the doors and the Din?
And the Hip! Hop! Hap!
Of the clap
Of the hands to the twirl and the swirl
Of the girl gone chancing,
Glancing,
Dancing,
Backing and advancing,
Snapping of a clapper to the spin
Out and in –
And the Ting, Tong, Tang of the Guitar!
Do you remember an Inn,
Miranda?
Do you remember an Inn?

Never more;
Miranda,
Never more.
Only the high peaks hoar:
And Aragon a torrent at the door.
No sound
In the walls of the Halls where falls
The tread
Of the feet of the dead to the ground
No sound:
But the boom
Of the far Waterfall like Doom.

Hilaire Belloc
(July 27th 1870 – July 16th 1953)

July 28

• *Precocious Royalist poet Abraham Cowley died July 28th 1667*
• *Gerard Manley Hopkins born in Stratford, London, the son of a marine insurance agent, July 28th 1844. He was educated at Highgate School and Balliol College, Oxford*
• *Malcolm Lowry, poet and novelist, author of* Under the Volcano, *born in Cheshire July 28th 1909*
• *Poet and playwright John Ashberry, author of* Self-Portrait in a Convex Mirror, *born in Rochester, New York, July 28th 1927*

The Windhover[1]
To Christ our Lord

I caught this morning morning's minion[2], king-
    dom of daylight's dauphin, dapple-dawn-drawn Falcon, in his riding
    Of the rolling level underneath him steady air, and striding
High there, how he rung upon the rein of a wimpling[3] wing
In his ecstasy! then off, off forth on swing,
    As a skate's heel sweeps smooth on a bow-bend: the hurl and gliding
    Rebuffed the big wind. My heart in hiding
Stirred for a bird, – the achieve of, the mastery of the thing!

Brute beauty and valour and act, oh, air, pride, plume, here
    Buckle! AND the fire that breaks from thee then, a billion
Times told lovelier, more dangerous, O my chevalier[4]!

No wonder of it: shéer plód makes plough down sillion[5]
Shine, and blue-bleak embers, ah my dear,
    Fall, gall themselves, and gash gold-vermilion.

Gerard Manley Hopkins
(July 28th 1844 – June 8th 1889)

Hopkins composed this sonnet on May 30th 1877. On June 22nd 1879 he wrote to Robert Bridges that this poem was "the best thing I ever wrote". In the last part of the poem Hopkins the Jesuit may be associating the "fire" that shines from the bird with the fire that comes from Christ, his "chevalier" – a fire that is hardly surprising, he says, given that even a mere plough can make the earth shine, and that embers when they break open, glow golden within.

1. "A name for the kestrel, from its habit of hovering or hanging with its head to the wind" (O. E. D.).
2. favourite.
3. rippling.
4. knight/champion.
5. furrow.

• *U(rsula) A(skham) Fanthorpe was born in London July 29th 1929.*
One of her recent poetry collections is Neck-Verse. *She lives in*
Gloucestershire

Milkmaid

The girl's far treble, muted to the heat,
calls like a fainting bird across the fields
to where her flock lies panting for her voice,
their black horns buried deep in marigolds.

They climb awake, like drowsy butterflies,
and press their red flanks through the tall branched grass,
and as they go their wandering tongues embrace
the vacant summer mirrored in their eyes.

Led to the limestone shadows of a barn
they snuff their past embalmed in the hay,
while her cool hand, cupped to the udder's fount,
distils the brimming harvest of their day.

Look what a cloudy cream the earth gives out,
fat juice of buttercups and meadow-rye;
the girl dreams milk within her body's field
and hears, far off, her muted children cry.

Laurie Lee
(June 26th 1914 –)

At about this time of year in 1936, Laurie Lee was 'rescued' from Spain and the Spanish Civil War by a British destroyer sent from Gibraltar to pick up marooned British subjects. He describes the scene in *As I Walked Out One Midsummer Morning:* " 'Hurry!' cried [Emilia]. 'Leaving everything–you are saved! Your king has sent you a ship. They are waiting for you on the beach and have come to take you home. Before God, who more fortunate than you?' "

July 30

• Thomas Gray died July 30th 1771 and was buried at Stoke
  Poges in Buckinghamshire, the village which inspired his 'Elegy'
• Emily Brontë born in Thornton, Yorkshire, July 30th 1818
• Poet Anne Ridler born in Rugby July 30th 1912

Elegy Written in a Country Churchyard

The curfew tolls the knell of parting day,
　The lowing herd wind slowly o'er the lea,
The plowman homeward plods his weary way,
　And leaves the world to darkness and to me.

Now fades the glimmering landscape on the sight,
　And all the air a solemn stillness holds,
Save where the beetle wheels his droning flight,
　And drowsy tinklings lull the distant folds;

Save that from yonder ivy-mantled tower
　The moping owl does to the moon complain
Of such as, wand'ring near her secret bower,
　Molest her ancient solitary reign.

Beneath those rugged elms, that yew-tree's shade,
　Where heaves the turf in many a mould'ring heap,
Each in his narrow cell for ever laid,
　The rude forefathers of the hamlet sleep.

The breezy call of incense-breathing morn,
　The swallow twitt'ring from the straw-built shed,
The cock's shrill clarion, or the echoing horn,
　No more shall rouse them from their lowly bed.

For them no more the blazing hearth shall burn,
　Or busy housewife ply her evening care:
No children run to lisp their sire's return,
　Or climb his knees the envied kiss to share.

Oft did the harvest to their sickle yield,
　Their furrow oft the stubborn glebe has broke:
How jocund did they drive their team afield!
　How bowed the woods beneath their sturdy stroke!

Let not Ambition mock their useful toil,
　Their homely joys, and destiny obscure;
Nor Grandeur hear with a disdainful smile
　The short and simple annals of the poor.

The boast of heraldry, the pomp of power,
　And all that beauty, all that wealth e'er gave,
Awaits alike th' inevitable hour:
　The paths of glory lead but to the grave.

Nor you, ye proud, impute to These the fault,
　If Memory o'er their tomb no trophies raise,
Where through the long-drawn aisle and fretted vault
　The pealing anthem swells the note of praise.

Can storied urn or animated bust
　Back to its mansion call the fleeting breath?

[Continued]

Can Honour's voice provoke the silent dust,
  Or Flatt'ry soothe the dull cold ear of death?

Perhaps in this neglected spot is laid
  Some heart once pregnant with celestial fire;
Hands, that the rod of empire might have swayed,
  Or waked to ecstasy the living lyre.

But Knowledge to their eyes her ample page
  Rich with the spoils of time did ne'er unroll;
Chill Penury repressed their noble rage,
  And froze the genial current of the soul.

Full many a gem of purest ray serene
  The dark unfathomed caves of ocean bear:
Full many a flower is born to blush unseen,
  And waste its sweetness on the desert air.

Some village Hampden that with dauntless breast
  The little tyrant of his fields withstood,
Some mute inglorious Milton here may rest,
  Some Cromwell guiltless of his country's blood.

Th' applause of list'ning senates to command,
  The threats of pain and ruin to despise,
To scatter plenty o'er a smiling land,
  And read their history in a nation's eyes,

Their lot forbade: nor circumscribed alone
  Their growing virtues, but their crimes confined;
Forbade to wade through slaughter to a throne.
  And shut the gates of mercy on mankind,

The struggling pangs of conscious truth to hide,
  To quench the blushes of ingenuous shame,
Or heap the shrine of Luxury and Pride
  With incense kindled at the Muse's flame.

Far from the madding crowd's ignoble strife
  Their sober wishes never learned to stray;
Along the cool sequestered vale of life
  They kept the noiseless tenor of their way.

Yet ev'n these bones from insult to protect
  Some frail memorial still erected nigh,
With uncouth rhymes and shapeless sculpture decked,
  Implores the passing tribute of a sigh.

Their name, their years, spelt by th' unlettered Muse,
  The place of fame and elegy supply:
And many a holy text around she strews,
  That teach the rustic moralist to die.

For who, to dumb Forgetfulness a prey,
  This pleasing anxious being e'er resigned,

[Continued]

Left the warm precincts of the cheerful day,
 Nor cast one longing ling'ring look behind?

On some fond breast the parting soul relies,
 Some pious drops the closing eye requires;
E'en from the tomb the voice of Nature cries,
 E'en in our Ashes live their wonted fires.

For thee, who, mindful of th' unhonoured dead,
 Dost in these lines their artless tale relate;
If chance, by lonely contemplation led,
 Some kindred spirit shall inquire thy fate,

Haply some hoary-headed Swain may say,
 'Oft have we seen him at the peep of dawn
Brushing with hasty steps the dews away
 To meet the sun upon the upland lawn.

'There at the foot of yonder nodding beech
 That wreathes its old fantastic roots so high,
His listless length at noontide would he stretch,
 And pore upon the brook that babbles by.

'Hard by yon wood, now smiling as in scorn,
 Mutt'ring his wayward fancies he would rove,
Now drooping, woeful wan, like one forlorn,
 Or crazed with care, or crossed in hopeless love.

'One morn I missed him on the customed hill,
 Along the heath and near his fav'rite tree;
Another came; nor yet beside the rill,
 Nor up the lawn, nor at the wood was he;

'The next with dirges due in sad array
 Slow through the church-way path we saw him borne.
Approach and read (for thou canst read) the lay
 Graved on the stone beneath yon aged thorn:'

The Epitaph

Here rests his head upon the lap of Earth
 A Youth to Fortune and to Fame unknown.
Fair Science frowned not on his humble birth,
 And Melancholy marked him for her own.

Large was his bounty, and his soul sincere,
 Heaven did a recompense as largely send:
He gave to Mis'ry all he had, a tear,
 He gained from Heaven ('twas all he wished) a friend.

No further seek his merits to disclose,
 Or draw his frailties from their dread abode,
(There they alike in trembling hope repose,)
 The bosom of his Father and his God.

Thomas Gray
(December 26th 1716 – July 30th 1771)

- *On this day in 1805, John Johnson, William Cowper's cousin, recorded Lady Hesketh's fears concerning Blake's rages and supposed madness: "I don't doubt," she told Johnson, that Blake "will poison [his patron Hayley] ... in his Turret or set fire to all his papers"*
- *Austrian poet and novelist Peter Rosegger born of peasant parents near Krieglach, Styria, July 31st 1843*

A Poison Tree

I was angry with my friend:
I told my wrath, my wrath did end.
I was angry with my foe:
I told it not, my wrath did grow.

And I water'd it in fears,
Night & morning with my tears;
And I sunned it with smiles,
And with soft deceitful wiles.

And it grew both day and night,
Till it bore an apple bright;
And my foe beheld it shine,
And he knew that it was mine,

And into my garden stole
When the night had veil'd the pole:
In the morning glad I see
My foe outstretch'd beneath the tree.

William Blake
(November 28th 1757 – August 12th 1827)

Blake's notebook from 1793 comments on the Poison Tree: "There is just such a tree at Java Found." The tree is the *upas*, which legend has endowed with the power to kill creatures for many miles around; its native name means 'poison'.

The theme of the poem is the nature of violence seen in terms of its origins. The last verse is utterly realistic. People do exult in the defeat of their enemies, but this is written not in exultation but as a warning. To Blake "Mutual forgiveness of each vice / Such are the gates of Paradise." This mutuality is new to Christian doctrine.

August 1

• W. R. Rodgers, whose poems include 'The Net' and 'Lent', born in Belfast August 1st 1909
• Theodore Roethke died of a heart attack whilst swimming August 1st 1963

The Waking

I wake to sleep, and take my waking slow.
I feel my fate in what I cannot fear.
I learn by going where I have to go.

We think by feeling. What is there to know?
I hear my being dance from ear to ear.
I wake to sleep, and take my waking slow.

Of those so close beside me, which are you?
God bless the Ground! I shall walk softly there,
And learn by going where I have to go.

Light takes the Tree; but who can tell us how?
The lowly worm climbs up a winding stair;
I wake to sleep, and take my waking slow.

Great Nature has another thing to do
To you and me; so take the lively air,
And, lovely, learn by going where to go.

This shaking keeps me steady. I should know.
What falls away is always. And is near.
I wake to sleep, and take my waking slow.
I learn by going where I have to go.

Theodore Roethke
(May 25th 1908 – August 1st 1963)

Roethke was born in Saginaw, Michigan. His father was of Prussian extraction and owned a large greenhouse. Roethke wrote about his youth among the greenhouse flowers in his collection *The Lost Son* (1948). He taught creative writing at Lafayette College and elsewhere, before becoming poet-in-residence at the University of Washington in Seattle. In 1953, he married Beatrice Heath O'Connell, a student at Bennington College from the time he taught there. In that year too, several of Roethke's more autobiographical poems appeared in his collection *The Waking*.

Jay Parini describes Roethke as "a latter-day transcendentalist, finding spiritual correspondences in physical things".

Roethke was institutionalised on several occasions for brief periods and liked "to identify himself with 'mad' poets of the past such as William Blake and Christopher Smart". When Roethke writes (last verse above) "This shaking keeps me steady", the words are in keeping with his view of his breakdowns as in essence spiritual crises.

There is an echo of this poem 'The Waking' in his poem 'Words for the Wind' where he writes "What falls away will fall; / All things bring me love."

- On August 2nd 1787 Robert Burns wrote an autobiographical letter to Dr Moore which is the main source of information on his early life
- Ernest Dowson, poet of the 'decadent' school, born August 2nd 1867
- American poet Wallace Stevens died August 2nd 1955
- Raymond Carver died August 2nd 1988

Late Fragment

And did you get what
you wanted from this life, even so?
I did.
And what did you want?
To call myself beloved, to feel myself
beloved on the earth.

Raymond Carver
(May 25th 1938   August 2nd 1988)

Raymond Carver, poet and short-story writer ("the American Chekhov") died aged 50 from cancer. This poem is the last in the book of poems *A New Path to the Waterfall*, published by The Atlantic Monthly Press. He prepared them whilst facing his death, with the help of his long-term partner Tess Gallagher, whom he married in June 1988. In her introduction she comments about this poem that "for a recovering alcoholic, this self-recognition and more generalized feeling of love he was allowing himself was no small accomplishment. Ray knew he had been graced and blessed and that his writing had enabled him to reach far beyond the often mean circumstances from which he and those he wrote about had come, and also that through his writing those working-class lives had become part of literature. On a piece of scrap paper near his typewriter he had written: 'Forgive me if I'm thrilled with the idea, but just now I thought that every poem I write ought to be called Happiness.' "

August 3

• Burns legally married to Jean Armour August 3rd 1788
• Rupert Brooke was born at Rugby School on August 3rd 1887, where his father was an assistant master and where he was educated. In 1909 he settled in Grantchester
• Poet and critic Diane Wakoski, author of The Motorcycle Betrayal Poems, born in California August 3rd 1937

From The Old Vicarage, Grantchester
(Café des Westens, Berlin, May 1912)

Ah God! to see the branches stir
Across the moon at Grantchester!
To smell the thrilling-sweet and rotten
Unforgettable, unforgotten
River-smell and hear the breeze
Sobbing in the little trees.
Say, do the elm-clumps greatly stand
Still guardians of that holy land?
The chestnut shade, in reverend dream,
The yet unacademic stream?
Is dawn a secret shy and cold
Anadyomene[1], silver-gold?
And sunset still a golden sea
From Haslingfield to Madingley?
And after, ere the night is born,
Do hares come out about the corn?
Oh, is the water sweet and cool,
Gentle and brown, above the pool?
And laughs the immortal river still
Under the mill, under the mill?
Say, is there Beauty yet to find?
And Certainty? and Quiet kind?
Deep meadows yet, for to forget
The lies, and truths, and pain? . . . Oh! yet
Stands the Church clock at ten to three?
And is there honey still for tea?

Rupert Brooke
(August 3rd 1887 – April 23rd 1915)

On April 25th 1912, Brooke wrote to Ka Cox: "I'm just passing through Potsdam. I've a fancy you may be, just now, in Grantchester. I envy you frightfully. That river and the chestnuts – come back to me a lot. Tea on the lawn. Just wire to me and we'll spend the summer there; with Eddie to tea every Saturday and a fancy dress ball on Midsummer night." In the first draft, the clock stood at half past three (the actual time it had been stuck during most of 1911); the poem was entitled 'Home' – and in the next draft 'The Sentimental Exile'. He sent his editor a telegram : "A masterpiece on its way"; but to Mrs Cornford he merely wrote that he had "scrawled in a café a very long poem about Grantchester, that seemed to me to have pleasant silly passages".

1. A painting of Venus rising from the sea and wringing her hair which adorned the sanctuary of Aesculapius.

- On August 4th 1601 Elizabeth I complained that Shakespeare's *rebellion-fomenting* Richard II *had been played "forty times in open streets and houses"*
- *Shelley born in Field Place, near Horsham, August 4th 1792*
- *The Danish story-teller Hans Christian Anderson poet and author of fairy tales, died August 4th 1873*
- *American poet and novelist Conrad Aiken born August 4th 1889*
- *Black American poet Robert Hayden born August 4th 1913*

From Prometheus Unbound

To suffer woes which Hope thinks infinite;
To forgive wrongs darker than death or nights;
To defy Power, which seems omnipotent;
To love, and bear; to Hope till Hope creates
From its own wreck the thing it contemplates;
Neither to change, nor falter, nor repent;
This, like thy glory, Titan, is to be
Good, great and joyous, beautiful and free;
This is alone Life, Joy, Empire, and Victory.

Percy Bysshe Shelley
(August 4th 1792 – July 8th 1822)

As a child Shelley was idolised by his younger sisters, hated the bullying at his boarding schools (Syon House and Eton), and was expelled from Oxford for refusing to acknowledge having published a pamphlet entitled *The Necessity of Atheism*. Shelley eloped with 16 year old Harriet Westbrook and was expelled from Field Place, the family seat, by his father Sir Timothy Shelley, so that he would not corrupt his sisters, and was cut off from his inheritance. Eventually, Sir Timothy and Harriet's father felt obliged to give Shelley an annuity of £400 a year, to prevent him "cheating strangers" and leaving a trail of unpaid debts behind him – which Shelley did, nevertheless, escaping to Italy and being a total of some £25,000 in debt by the time of his death.

In Rome, on May 25th 1819, Shelley gave his second wife Mary the completed manuscript of his long poem 'Prometheus Unbound' to read. In his preface he commented: "This poem was chiefly written upon the mountainous ruins of the Baths of Caracalla [Roman baths built to accommodate 1,500 and in use until the Goths cut the aqueducts in the 6th century] among the flowery glades, and the thickets of odoriferous blossoming trees, which are extended in ever winding labyrinths upon its immense platforms and dizzy arches suspended in the air. The bright blue sky of Rome, and the effect of the vigorous awakening spring in that divinest climate, and the new life with which it drenches the spirits even to intoxication, were the inspiration of this drama." Of Prometheus, the fire bringer and liberator of mankind, he wrote: "The only imaginary being resembling in any degree Prometheus, is Satan; and Prometheus is, in my judgement, a more poetical character than Satan, because, in addition to courage, and majesty, and firm and patient opposition to omnipotent force, he is susceptible of being described as exempt from the taints of ambition, envy, revenge and a desire for personal aggrandisement ... [he] is, as it were, the type of the highest perfection of moral and intellectual nature."

August 5

- *Anne Finch, Countess of Winchelsea, melancholic poet, friend of Pope, Gay and Swift, died August 5th 1720*
- *Shelley arrived to visit Byron at Ravenna on August 5th 1821, and found inside Byron's "Circean Palace", the home of his lover Countess Guiccioli, three monkeys, five cats, eight dogs, an eagle, a crow, a falcon, five peacocks, two guinea hens and an Egyptian crane. "I wonder who all these animals were," Shelley wrote, "before they were changed into these shapes"*
- *Wendell Berry born on a Kentucky farm August 5th 1934*

Memory

One had a lovely face,
And two or three had charm,
But charm and face were in vain
Because the mountain grass
Cannot but keep the form
Where the mountain hare has lain.

William Butler Yeats
(June 13th 1865 – January 28th 1939)

Editors have associated the "lovely face" of the first line with Olivia Shakespear ("the centre of my life in London," wrote Yeats, "when first I met her, she was in her late twenties but in looks a lovely young girl"). The association for the "mountain hare" is with Iseult Gonne (who refused Yeats marriage, as her mother Maud Gonne had before her).

- *Shakespeare's widow died aged 67 August 6th 1623*
- *Ben Jonson died August 6th 1637*
- *Alfred Lord Tennyson born August 6th 1809. His memorial beacon on the summit of High Down above Freshwater on the Isle of Wight, was unveiled August 6th 1897*
- *French poet and playwright Paul Claudel born August 6th 1868*
- *Irish poet Richard Murphy, author of* The Battle of Aughrim, *born August 6th 1927*

Song: To Celia

Drink to me, only, with thine eyes,
 And I will pledge with mine;
Or leave a kiss but in the cup,
 And I'll not look for wine.
The thirst, that from the soul doth rise,
 Doth ask a drink divine:
But might I of Jove's nectar sup,
 I would not change for thine.

I sent thee, late, a rosy wreath,
 Not so much honouring thee,
As giving it a hope, that there
 It could not withered be.
But thou thereon did'st only breathe,
 And sent'st it back to me:
Since when it grows, and smells, I swear,
 Not of itself, but thee.

Ben Jonson
(June 11th 1572 – August 6th 1637)

The end of Jonson's life was marked by poverty. The story goes that Jonson arranged with the Dean of Westminster to be buried upright, as he could not afford the six feet of earth necessary for being buried lying down. The famous inscription on his tomb, "O Rare Ben Jonson", was carved by a mason who had been paid eighteen pence to inscribe the unmarked grave by a passer-by at Jonson's funeral.

August 7

• On August 7th 1904, Adela Florence Nicolson, the writer of love lyrics who adopted the pseudonym Laurence Hope, killed herself with poison after the death of her husband Colonel Nicolson of the Bengal army
• Indian poet and philosopher Rabindranath Tagore died August 7th 1941

Parting in Wartime

How long ago Hector took off his plume,
Not wanting that his little son should cry,
Then kissed his sad Andromache goodbye –
And now we three in Euston waiting-room.

Frances Cornford
(March 30th 1886 – August 19th 1960)

On this day in 1914, the first units of the British Expeditionary Force were sent across to France to reinforce the left wing of the French army.
Frances Cornford's son, the poet John Cornford, was killed in the Spanish Civil War.

• *Sara Teasdale born in St Louis, Missouri, August 8th 1884. She moved from love poetry to poems about death, and became reclusive, subsequently committing suicide*

The Dead at Clonmacnois

In a quiet water'd land, a land of roses,
    Stands Saint Kieran's city fair;
And the Warriors of Erin in their famous generations
    Slumber there.

There beneath the dewy hillside sleep the noblest
    Of the clan of Conn,
Each below his stone with name in branching Ogham
    And the sacred knot thereon.

There they laid to rest the seven Kings of Tara,
    There the sons of Cairbrè sleep—
Battle-banners of the Gael that in Kieran's plain of crosses
    Now their final hosting keep.

And in Clonmacnois they laid the men of Teffia,
    And right many a lord of Breagh;
Deep the sod above Clan Creidè and Clan Conaill,
    Kind in hall and fierce in fray.

Many and many a son of Conn the Hundred-Fighter
    In the red earth lies at rest;
Many a blue eye of Clan Colman the turf covers,
    Many a swan-white breast.

Thomas William Rolleston
(May 1st 1857 – December 5th 1920)
based on an original poem in Irish by Angus O'Gillan

Rolleston's son, C. H. Rolleston, wrote that "these lovely lines first appeared in *Poems and Ballads of Young Ireland* in 1888. Clonmacnois, on the bank of the Shannon in King's Country, was the burial place of the ancient Kings of Ireland – a spot as sacred to the Irish people as the Holy Hill of Tara itself."

T. W. Rolleston was the co-founder with Yeats and Ernest Rhys of the Rhymers' Club that met at the Cheshire Cheese in London during the early 1890s – Ernest Dowson was a member too. Rolleston was also the founder of the Irish Literary Society of London and author of *Myths and Legends of the Celtic Race*. One of his friends was the Irish poet George Russell. In his diary for this day in 1898, Rolleston wrote:

"George Russell came in to dine. And he talked – opalescently, about his spiritualistic experiences, his visions, dreams, and phantasms. Everything he saw was either opalescent or iridescent, and I wished at times he would opalesce himself into an iridescent vision. At last I could stand it no longer, and I went to bed, and read his poetry."

August 9

• English poet John Dryden born at a vicarage in Northamptonshire
  August 9th 1631
• Poet and social innovator Michael Young born August 9th 1915
• Philip Larkin born August 9th 1922
• Antoine de Saint-Exupéry reported missing on a flight over
  France, August 9th 1944

Days

What are days for?
Days are where we live.
They come, they wake us
Time and time over.

They are to be happy in:
Where can we live but days?

Ah, solving that question
Brings the priest and the doctor
In their long coats
Running over the fields.

Philip Larkin
(August 9th 1922 – December 2nd 1985)

Larkin was born at 2 Poultney Road, Radford, in the suburbs of Coventry, and was named Philip after the Renaissance poet Sir Philip Sydney. In Andrew Motion's account of his life, Larkin is represented ◀ as having been indulged in his childhood, although for him it became a "forgotten boredom". He stammered badly from the age of four. His father, "a Conservative [neo-fascist] Anarchist", "worked all day and shut himself away reading in the evening, or else gardening."

As for his mother, "the monotonous whining monologue she treated my father to before breakfast, and all of us at mealtimes, resentful, self-pitying, full of bunk and suspicion, must have remained in my mind as something I musn't *under any circumstances* risk encountering again ..."

Their marriage left him with two convictions, that people shouldn't live together, and that children should be taken from their parents "at an early age".

• Laurence Binyon, who wrote the war poem 'For the Fallen' ("They shall grow not old, as we that are left grow old ..."), was born August 10th 1869
• Witter Bynner, literary hoaxer and translator from the Chinese, born August 10th 1881

Ars Poetica

A poem should be palpable and mute
As a globed fruit

Dumb
As old medallions to the thumb

Silent as the sleeve-worn stone
Of casement ledges where the moss has grown –

A poem should be wordless
As the flight of birds

A poem should be motionless in time
As the moon climbs

Leaving, as the moon releases
Twig by twig the night-entangled trees,

Leaving, as the moon behind the winter leaves,
Memory by memory the mind –

A poem should be motionless in time
As the moon climbs

A poem should be equal to:
Not true

For all the history of grief
An empty doorway and a maple leaf

For love
The leaning grasses and two lights above the sea –

A poem should not mean
But be.

Archibald MacLeish
(May 7th 1892 – April 20th 1982)

MacLeish was born in Illinois, the son of a Chicago merchant born in Scotland. At 24 he married, at 25 he joined a hospital ship, went to France, transferred to an artillery unit, and was a captain by the end of the First World War. At 31, he gave up his job as a lawyer, to focus on his poetry, travelling abroad with his wife and two children. During World War II he was one of President Roosevelt's advisers.

August 11

• *Shakespeare buried his only son Hamnet in Stratford-on-Avon parish church August 11th 1596. The boy was 11 years old*
• *Tennyson's son, named Hallam after his childhood friend, was born August 11th 1852*
• *Hugh MacDiarmid born in Langholm August 11th 1892*
• *Poet and critic Louise Bogan born in Maine August 11th 1897*

Sonnet 18

Shall I compare thee to a summer's day?
Thou art more lovely and more temperate:
Rough winds do shake the darling buds of May,
And summer's lease hath all too short a date:
Sometime too hot the eye of heaven shines,
And often is his gold complexion dimm'd:
And every fair from fair sometime declines,
By chance, or nature's changing course untrimm'd;
But thy eternal summer shall not fade,
Nor lose possession of that fair thou ow'st,
Nor shall death brag thou wander'st in his shade,
When in eternal lines to time thou grow'st;
  So long as men can breathe, or eyes can see,
  So long lives this, and this gives life to thee.

William Shakespeare
(April 23rd 1564 – April 23rd 1616)

The first 17 poems in Shakespeare's much–disputed sonnet sequence urge the youth to whom they are addressed to marry and have children. Sonnet 18 changes tack, and describes the youth's surpassing beauty. These sonnets are addressed to a Mr W. H. whose identity, although speculated about, is unknown.

- Poet Laureate Robert Southey born August 12th 1774
- On August 12th 1803 Blake manhandled a soldier out of his garden and down the road, and was taken to court for assault and sedition (he was acquitted)
- William Blake died August 12th 1827 [1]
- Poet Donald Justice born in Miami August 12th 1925
- Poet Medbh McGuckian born in Belfast August 12th 1950

London

I wander through each chartered street,
Near where the chartered Thames does flow,
And mark in every face I meet
Marks of weakness, marks of woe.

In every cry of every man,
In every infant's cry of fear,
In every voice, in every ban,
The mind-forged manacles I hear.

How the chimney-sweeper's cry
Every blackening church appals;
And the hapless soldier's sigh
Runs in blood down palace walls.

But most through midnight streets I hear
How the youthful harlot's curse
Blasts the new-born infant's tear,
And blights with plagues the marriage hearse.

William Blake
(November 28th 1757 – August 12th 1827)

Blake loved pre-industrial London and its rural hinterland. He left it only once – for Felpham on the south coast, from 1800 to 1803, and soon regretted doing so. But also in London he found the things he hated: poverty, tyranny, violence and manacles in the mind. He indicted every degradation of the human spirit.

1. Blake's attitude to death is captured in his comment on the death of his friend Flaxman: "I cannot think of death as more than going out of one room into another". Two days before his own death, Blake was sketched in bed wearing a black skull-cap by John Linnell. Blake died on the Sunday evening. Earlier in the day, so the story goes, he told his wife: "Kate, you have been a good Wife. I will draw your portrait." He sketched her at the bedside, then threw the paper down and sang "Hallelujahs & songs of Joy & Triumph ... He sang loudly & with true exstatic energy and seemed, too, happy that he had finished his course, that he had ran his race, & that he was shortly to arrive at the Goal."

August 13

Creation Myth Haiku

After the First Night
the Sun kissed the Moon
'Darling, you were wonderful!'

Haiku: After the Orgies

All the Maenads had
terrible hangovers and
unwanted babies.

Haiku: The Season of Celebrity

With summer comes the
bluebottle; with pleasant fame
comes the Journalist.

North American Haiku

Hail, tribes of Outer
Alcoholia – the Rednose
and Goutfoot Indians!

Gavin Ewart
(February 4th 1916 – October 23rd 1995)

Gavin Ewart once wrote that "Good light verse is better than bad heavy verse / any day of the week" and he is the editor of the *Penguin Book of Light Verse* (1980) and *Other People's Clerihews* (1983). His poems were first published when he was still a 17 year old pupil at Wellington College.

• Augustus Montague Toplady, Calvinist vicar who wrote the hymn
'Rock of Ages', died August 14th 1778
• German poet and playwright Bertolt Brecht died August 14th 1956

Non sum qualis eram bonae sub regno Cynarae[1]

Last night, ah, yesternight, betwixt her lips and mine
There fell thy shadow, Cynara! thy breath was shed
Upon my soul between the kisses and the wine;
And I was desolate and sick of an old passion,
   Yea, I was desolate and bowed my head:
I have been faithful to thee, Cynara! in my fashion.

All night upon mine heart I felt her warm heart beat,
Night-long within mine arms in love and sleep she lay;
Surely the kisses of her bought red mouth were sweet;
But I was desolate and sick of an old passion,
   When I awoke and found the dawn was gray:
I have been faithful to thee, Cynara! in my fashion.

I have forgot much, Cynara! gone with the wind,
Flung roses, roses riotously with the throng,
Dancing, to put thy pale, lost lilies out of mind;
But I was desolate and sick of an old passion,
   Yea, all the time, because the dance was long:
I have been faithful to thee, Cynara! in my fashion.

I cried for madder music and for stronger wine,
But when the feast is finished and the lamps expire,
Then falls thy shadow, Cynara! the night is thine;
And I am desolate and sick of an old passion,
   Yea hungry for the lips of my desire:
I have been faithful to thee, Cynara! in my fashion.

Ernest Dowson
(August 2nd 1867 – February 23rd 1900)

After the death of his father and the suicide of his mother, Dowson lived an intemperate life in France, England and Ireland. In his world-weariness he remembered nostalgically the innocent Adelaide Foltinowicz (Millie), who was a girl of twelve when he met her in 1891.

1. "I am not as I was under the reign of the good Cynara" (from Horace, *Odes*, IV. i. The poet asks Venus to excuse him from further efforts in her service).

August 15

• *Donne's wife died in childbirth August 15th 1617, at the age of 37. In 16 years, they had 12 children. Only seven survived her*
• *Walter Scott, novelist and poet, born in Edinburgh August 15th 1771*

From Macbeth
Act V Scene v

Macbeth. Tomorrow, and tomorrow, and tomorrow,
Creeps in this petty pace from day to day,
To the last syllable of recorded time;
And all our yesterdays have lighted fools
The way to dusty death. Out, out, brief candle!
Life's but a walking shadow, a poor player
That struts and frets his hour upon the stage
And then is heard no more: it is a tale
Told by an idiot, full of sound and fury,
Signifying nothing.

William Shakespeare
(April 23rd 1564 – April 23rd 1616)

On August 15th 1057, Macbeth was killed by Malcolm at Lumphanan in Mar. He was buried on Iona.

- *Andrew Marvell died August 16th (or perhaps 18th) 1678*
- *Baroness Carolina Nairne, the Jacobite songwriter ("Will ye no come back again?"), was born August 16th 1766*
- *LA-based poet and writer Charles Bukowski born in Germany August 16th 1920*

From Thoughts in a Garden[1]

What wondrous life is this I lead!
Ripe apples drop about my head;
The luscious clusters of the vine
Upon my mouth do crush their wine;
The nectarine and curious peach
Into my hands themselves do reach;
Stumbling on melons, as I pass,
Ensnared with flowers, I fall on grass.

Meanwhile the mind from pleasure less
Withdraws into its happiness;
The mind, that Ocean where each kind
Does straight its own resemblance find;
Yet it creates, transcending these,
Far other worlds, and other seas;
Annihilating all that's made
To a green thought in a green shade.

Andrew Marvell
(March 31st 1621 – August 16th or 18th 1678)

Marvell's editors comment that "like Adam, the poet is placed ... in a paradise of delights, and like him he has a duty to contemplate them". Elsewhere in this poem Marvell contrasts the garden to the artificial life of courts and towns.

1. Stanzas 5 and 6 of this 9 stanza poem.

August 17

• Ted Hughes born in Mytholmroyd in Yorkshire, August 17th
1930. His father was a carpenter, one of only 30 men in his
regiment to survive Gallipoli
• Georgia-born poet and author Conrad Potter Aiken died August
17th 1973. He was 11 when his father shot his mother and then
himself

Thistles

Against the rubber tongues of cows and the hoeing hands of men
Thistles spike the summer air
And crackle open under a blue-black pressure.

Every one a revengeful burst
Of resurrection, a grasped fistful
Of splintered weapons and Icelandic frost thrust up

From the underground stain of a decayed Viking.
They are like pale hair and the gutterals of dialects.
Every one manages a plume of blood.

Then they grow grey like men.
Mown down, it is a feud. Their sons appear
Stiff with weapons, fighting back over the same ground.

Ted Hughes
(August 17th 1930 –)

Looking back, Ted Hughes writes: "In 1961 I was living in London, close to Primrose Hill. I had a season ticket for the zoo, and most mornings I would take my baby daughter to see the owls, lions and the rest. This meant passing the SE corner of Primrose Hill itself. As that year developed, so did a clump of thistles – just inside the railings there, on that corner. I watched them, day by day. It seems to me now that they became a focus, of a kind, for what I was thinking about certain things – about that ideal possibility, a durable, undating poetic language, for instance. An essential sort of language – not linked too closely to what changes with every decade and century, everliving yet solid with living stuff, like the pattern of lines on the human hand. At least, that is what I see behind these verses now – that preoccupation. At the time, I was aware of using those thistles, behind the railings there, in that dusty corner by the traffic lights, to prompt a little poem about my liking for thistles in general."

- *Andrew Marvell died August 18th 1678 or on the 16th, the exact date is uncertain*
- *William Blake married Catherine Boucher August 18th 1782* [1]
- *Robert Burns' child by Jean Armour born August 18th 1789*
- *On August 18th 1803, Wordsworth and Coleridge, the latter unwell, visited the Dumfries churchyard where Burns is buried*

From Auguries of Innocence

To see a World in a grain of sand,
And a Heaven in a wild flower,
Hold Infinity in the palm of your hand,
And Eternity in an hour.

A robin redbreast in a cage
Puts all Heaven in a rage.
A dove-house filled with doves and pigeons
Shudders Hell thro' all its regions.
A dog starved at his master's gate
Predicts the ruin of the State.
A horse misused upon the road
Calls to Heaven for human blood.

Each outcry of the hunted hare
A fibre from the brain does tear.
A skylark wounded in the wing,
A cherubim does cease to sing.

William Blake
(November 28th 1757 – August 12th 1827)

All 128 lines of this poem constitute a great manifesto of eco-philosophy two hundred years ahead of its time. Central to 'Auguries' is Blake's life-long struggle against both Platonic and Cartesian dualism, the artificial division between the head and the heart, the sciences and the arts.

1. Aged 25 and recovering from being jilted, William Blake met Catherine Boucher, age 21. Their initial courtship was exceptionally brief: he asked her "Do you pity me?" She replied "Indeed I do," and he declared "Then I love you". One year later they were married. Of their time spent together she was to explain, "I have very little of Mr Blake's company. He is always in Paradise."

August 19

• Ogden Nash born in Rye, New York, August 19th 1902
• Federico García Lorca shot by Franco sympathisers, after being forced to dig his own grave, on about August 19th 1936
• Cambridge-based poet Frances Cornford died August 19th 1960

To My Valentine

More than a catbird hates a cat,
Or a criminal hates a clue,
Or the Axis hates the United States,
That's how much I love you.

I love you more than a duck can swim,
And more than a grapefruit squirts,
I love you more than gin rummy is a bore,
And more than a toothache hurts.

As a shipwrecked sailor hates the sea,
Or a juggler hates a shove,
As a hostess detests unexpected guests,
That's how much you I love.

I love you more than a wasp can sting,
And more than the subway jerks,
I love you as much as a beggar needs a crutch,
And more than a hangnail irks.

I swear to you by the stars above,
And below, if such there be,
As the High Court loathes perjurious oaths,
That's how you're loved by me.

Ogden Nash
(August 19th 1902 – May 19th 1971)

Ogden Nash, failed Harvard student, failed bond salesman, failed 'serious' poet, immensely successful comic "wersifier" (his own self-description), married Frances Rider Leonard in 1931. They had two daughters, who, as Linell Smith and Isabel Eberstadt, have published a section of his verse entitled *Candy is Dandy: The Best of Ogden Nash* (1985).

• Edward Herbert (Lord Herbert of Cherbury), statesman, philosopher and poet, died August 20th 1648
• Poet, playwright and debauched courtier Sir Charles Sedley died August 20th 1701
• Emily Brontë christened August 20th 1818
• Edgar A. Guest born in England August 20th 1881. His homely doggerel verse was syndicated in American newspapers

Last Lines

No coward soul is mine,
No trembler in the world's storm-troubled sphere!
I see Heaven's glories shine,
And Faith shines equal, arming me from Fear.

O God within my breast,
Almighty ever-present Deity!
Life, that in me hast rest
As I, undying Life, have power in thee!

Vain are the thousand creeds
That move men's hearts, unutterably vain;
Worthless as withered weeds,
Or idlest froth, amid the boundless main

To waken doubt in one
Holding so fast by thy infinity,
So surely anchored on
The steadfast rock of Immortality.

With wide-embracing love
Thy spirit animates eternal years,
Pervades and broods above,
Changes, sustains, dissolves, creates and rears.

Though earth and moon were gone,
And suns and universes ceased to be,
And thou were left alone,
Every Existence would exist in thee.

There is not room for Death,
Nor atom that his might could render void,
Since thou art Being and Breath,
And what thou art may never be destroyed.

Emily Brontë
(July 30th 1818 – December 19th 1848)

Emily Brontë was christened on this day in St James' church, Thornton, Yorkshire, in 1818. She died aged 30 at her family home in Haworth, having refused all medical care and believing doctors "poisonous". Her life was, in the words of her poem 'The Death of A.G.A.', "stormy and brief".

August 21

• X. J. Kennedy born August 21st 1929
• Poet Denis Devlin, Irish ambassador to Italy, died August 21st
  1959

Nude Descending a Staircase

Toe upon toe, a snowing flesh,
A gold of lemon, root and rind,
She sifts in sunlight down the stairs
With nothing on. Nor on her mind.

We spy beneath the banister
A constant thresh of thigh on thigh –
Her lips imprint the swinging air
That parts to let her parts go by.

One-woman waterfall, she wears
Her slow descent like a long cape
And pausing, on the final stair
Collects her motions into shape.

X. J. Kennedy
(August 21st 1929 –)

X. J. Kennedy comments: "To have this particular poem assigned to my birthday seems fitting. Like most of us, I descended into this world quite as nude as a jaybird. The poem was inspired by Marcel Duchamp's painting of the same title, but describes that work only with very rough fidelity."

X. J. Kennedy was born in Dover, New Jersey. He was raised as a Roman Catholic, although his poetry expresses an often irreverent view of religion. His first volume of poetry *Nude Descending a Staircase*, won the 1961 Lamont Award. Of late, Kennedy has written mostly verse for children.

• Dorothy Parker born in West End, New Jersey, the daughter of a cloth salesman, August 22nd 1893. Her mother died when she was five

August 22

One Perfect Rose

A single flow'r he sent me, since we met.
    All tenderly his messenger he chose;
Deep-hearted, pure, with scented dew still wet –
    One perfect rose.

I knew the language of the floweret;
    'My fragile leaves', it said, 'his heart enclose'.
Love long has taken for his amulet
    One perfect rose.

Why is it no one ever sent me yet
    One perfect limousine, do you suppose?
Ah no, it's always just my luck to get
    One perfect rose.

Dorothy Parker
(August 22nd 1893 – June 7th 1967)

Of her poetic influences Dorothy Parker once remarked: "I was following in the exquisite footsteps of Miss Edna St Vincent Millay, unhappily in my own horrible sneakers." Renowned for the acerbity with which she commented on the vanity and foolishness of others, she could turn her wit on herself almost as easily. At her 70th birthday party she remarked: "If I had any decency, I'd be dead. Most of my friends are."

August 23

Madam Life's a piece in bloom

Madam Life's a piece in bloom
  Death goes dogging everywhere:
She's the tenant of the room,
  He's the ruffian on the stair.

You shall see her as a friend,
  You shall bilk him once or twice;
But he'll trap you in the end,
  And he'll stick you for her price.

With his kneebones at your chest,
  And his knuckles in your throat,
You would reason – plead – protest!
  Clutching at her petticoat;

But she's heard it all before,
  Well she knows you've had your fun,
Gingerly she gains the door,
  And your little job is done.

W. E. Henley
(August 23rd 1849 – June 11th 1903)

W. E. Henley was born in Gloucester and educated at the Crypt Grammar School, Gloucester. He was crippled by tubercular arthritis as a boy, had a foot amputated and was in pain most of his life. In hospital for two years (1873 to 1875), he met R. L. Stevenson, who became a close friend and described him later as burly, boisterous and piratic. Stevenson used him as his inspiration for his Long John Silver character in *Treasure Island*.

- *Robert Herrick born in London August 24th 1591*
- *Thomas Chatterton, who wrote poems purporting to be those of a 15th-century monk, killed himself with arsenic, aged 17, on August 24th 1770*
- *Jorge Luis Borges born in Buenos Aires August 24th 1899*
- *Poet Charles Causley born August 24th 1917 in Launceston, Cornwall. He still lives in Launceston*

The Bracelet: To Julia

Why I tie about thy wrist,
Julia, this silken twist;
For what other reason is't
But to show thee how, in part,
Thou my pretty captive art?
But thy bond-slave is my heart:
'Tis but silk that bindeth thee,
Knap the thread and thou art free;
But 'tis otherwise with me:
—I am bound and fast bound, so
That from thee I cannot go;
If I could, I would not so.

Robert Herrick
(August 24th 1591 – October 15th 1674)

Born into a prosperous family of jewellers, Robert Herrick was sixteen months old when his father died falling from a fourth-floor window in his London home. In due course Robert was apprenticed into the family firm under the (frequently neglectful) eye of his uncle, before going on to St John's College, Cambridge. Back in London he became one of Ben Jonson's circle and trained as a minister.

Age 38, Herrick was made vicar of Dean Prior in Devon. Though later he became attached to the place, at first he pined from his rural living for the delights of the city. For a time he left without permission from his bishop to live in London with Tomasin Parsons, who was 27 years younger than him.

As a Royalist, he was deprived of his living at Dean Prior by Parliament in 1647. He swore he would re-visit the place only when "Rocks turn to rivers, rivers turn to men", but in the event spent the last twelve years of his life there following the Restoration.

August 25

• English poet, pamphleteer and playwright Thomas Dekker died August 25th 1632
• Poet and writer Mary Coleridge, great-great-niece of Samuel Taylor Coleridge, died August 25th 1907
• Poet Charles Wright born in Pickwick Dam, Tennessee, on August 25th 1935

Sweet Content

Art thou poor, yet hast thou golden slumbers,
　　O sweet content!
Art thou rich, yet is thy mind perplexed?
　　O punishment!
Dost thou laugh to see how fools are vexed
To add to golden numbers, golden numbers?
O sweet content! O sweet, O sweet content!
　Work apace, apace, apace, apace;
　Honest labour bears a lovely face;
Then hey nonny nonny, hey nonny nonny!

Canst drink the waters of the crispèd spring?
　　O sweet content!
Swimm'st thou in wealth, yet sink'st in thine own tears?
　　O punishment!
Then he that patiently want's burden bears
No burden bears, but is a king, a king!
O sweet content! O sweet, O sweet content!
　Work apace, apace, apace, apace;
　Honest labour bears a lovely face;
Then hey nonny nonny, hey nonny nonny!

Thomas Dekker
(?1570 – August 25th 1632)

Thomas Dekker could have done with some "golden numbers", since he went to prison for debt on two occasions, the second time for nearly seven years (from 1612). Nevertheless he is said to have retained a sunny disposition and to have developed a strong sympathy for oppressed people and animals. 'Sweet Content', composed some time after his first spell in prison, is the basket maker's song from his play *Patient Grissill* (1603) which was written in collaboration with Chettle and Haughton. In the same year he published a graphic description of the plague in London, *The Wonderful Year*. Low life in London was his recurring subject matter, from whores and vagabonds to hen-pecked husbands and town gallants.

The Ninth Secret Poem

I worship your fleece which is the perfect triangle
  Of the Goddess
I am the lumberjack of the only virgin forest
  O my Eldorado
I am the only fish in your voluptuous ocean
  You my lovely Siren
I am the climber on your snowy mountains
  O my whitest Alp
I am the heavenly archer of your beautiful mouth
  O my darling quiver
I am the hauler of your midnight hair
  O lovely ship on the canal of my kisses
And the lilies of your arms are beckoning me
  O my summer garden
The fruits of your breast are ripening their honey for me
  O my sweet-smelling orchard
And I am raising you O Madeleine O my beauty above the earth
  Like the torch of all light

Guillaume Apollinaire
(August 26th 1880 – November 9th 1918)
translated by Oliver Bernard

Apollinaire was the illegitimate son of Angelica Kostrowitzky and a Swiss Italian nobleman, Francesco Flugi D'Aspermont, who disappeared very early on from Apollinaire's life. His mother tended to disappear too, once leaving him for the holidays at a hotel in the Ardennes with his younger brother, and at the end of the holidays sending them the rail fare so that they could abscond to Paris without paying the hotel bill.

In Paris Apollinaire became friendly with painters such as Picasso and Braque, brought out a selection of erotic literature and spent a period in jail on suspicion of having stolen statuettes from the Louvre. His poetry collection *Alcools* came out in 1913, and the next year he joined the army at Nîmes, where he had an affair with Louise de Coligny. One time, returning on the train from leave spent with her, he met a young woman teacher from Oran, and became engaged to her in August 1915. He was wounded in the head by a shell splinter in March 1916 and died in the 1918 influenza epidemic.

August 27

• James Thompson, Scottish poet who probably wrote 'Rule Britannia', died August 27th 1748

from The Princess

Now sleeps the crimson petal, now the white;
Nor waves the cypress in the palace walk;
Nor winks the gold fin in the porphyry font:
The fire-fly wakens: waken thou with me.

Now droops the milkwhite peacock like a ghost,
And like a ghost she glimmers on to me.

Now lies the Earth all Danae to the stars,
And all thy heart lies open unto me.

Now slides the silent meteor on, and leaves
A shining furrow, as thy thoughts in me.

Now folds the lily all her sweetness up,
And slips into the bosom of the lake:
So fold thyself, my dearest, thou, and slip
Into my bosom and be lost in me.

Alfred, Lord Tennyson
(August 6th 1809 – October 6th 1892)

Tennyson was fond of declaiming his poetry to a receptive audience. Montague Eliot told how Tennyson used to visit their house in Cornwall. He reckoned it put him off poetry for life – he and the younger children would be sat in the front row for Tennyson's recitals, and they would dread the occurrence of words with 'p's or 'b's in them, because then "we children were regaled with a shower of spittle".

• *Johann Wolfgang von Goethe born in Frankfurt August 28th 1749*
• *Poet and editor Leigh Hunt died August 28th 1859*
• *War poet Ivor Gurney born in Gloucester August 28th 1890*
• *John Betjeman born in Highgate August 28th 1906*

August 28

A Subaltern's Love-song

Miss J. Hunter Dunn, Miss J. Hunter Dunn,
Furnish'd and burnish'd by Aldershot sun,
What strenuous singles we played after tea,
We in the tournament – you against me!

Love-thirty, love-forty, oh! weakness of joy,
The speed of a swallow, the grace of a boy,
With carefullest carelessness, gaily you won,
I am weak from your loveliness, Joan Hunter Dunn.

Miss Joan Hunter Dunn, Miss Joan Hunter Dunn
How mad I am, sad I am, glad that you won.
The warm-handled racket is back in its press,
But my shock-headed victor, she loves me no less.

Her father's euonymus° shines as we walk,   *Spindle-tree shrub*
And swing past the summer-house, buried in talk
And cool the verandah that welcomes us in
To the six-o'clock news and a limejuice and gin.

The scent of the conifers, sound of the bath,
The view from my bedroom of moss-dappled path,
As I struggle with double-end evening tie,
For we dance at the Golf Club, my victor and I.

On the floor of her bedroom lie blazer and shorts
And the cream-coloured walls are be-trophied with sports,
And westering, questioning settles the sun
On your low-leaded window, Miss Joan Hunter Dunn.

The Hillman is waiting, the light's in the hall,
The pictures of Egypt are bright on the wall,
My sweet, I am standing beside the oak stair
And there on the landing's the light on your hair.

By roads 'not adopted', by woodlanded ways,
She drove to the club in the late summer haze,
Into nine-o'clock Camberley, heavy with bells
And mushroomy, pine-woody, evergreen smells.

Miss Joan Hunter Dunn, Miss Joan Hunter Dunn,
I can hear from the car-park the dance has begun.
Oh! full Surrey twilight! importunate band!
Oh! strongly adorable tennis-girl's hand!

Around us are Rovers and Austins afar,
Above us, the intimate roof of the car,
And here on my right is the girl of my choice,
With the tilt of her nose and the chime of her voice,

And the scent of her wrap, and the words never said,
And the ominous, ominous dancing ahead.
We sat in the car park till twenty to one
And now I'm engaged to Miss Joan Hunter Dunn.

Sir John Betjeman
(August 28th 1906 – May 19th 1984)

August 29

• *The Belgian poetic dramatist Maurice Maeterlink, who wrote
'Pelléas et Mélisande', was born August 29th 1862*
• *Thom Gunn born August 29th 1929*

Tamer and Hawk

I thought I was so tough,
But gentled at your hands
Cannot be quick enough
To fly for you and show
That when I go I go
At your commands.

Even in flight above
I am no longer free:
You seeled me with your love,
I am blind to other birds—
The habit of your words
Has hooded me.

As formerly, I wheel
I hover and I twist,
But only want the feel,
In my possessive thought,
Of catcher and of caught
Upon your wrist.

You but half-civilize,
Taming me in this way.
Through having only eyes
For you I fear to lose,
I lose to keep, and choose
Tamer as prey.

Thom Gunn
(August 29th 1929 –)

Thom Gunn was born in Gravesend and raised in Hampstead. After two years National Service, Gunn in 1950 went to Trinity College, Cambridge.

Timothy Steele comments that Donne and Shakespeare "contributed to the formation of his early style, which is exemplified in 'Tamer and Hawk' ".

Thom Gunn settled in San Francisco in 1961, and his poetry since has covered themes from psychedelic drugs (in *Moly*, 1971) to AIDS (in *The Man with Night Sweats*, 1992).

• *Mary Shelley, author of* Frankenstein *and wife of the poet, born August 30th 1797, the daughter of William Godwin and Mary Wollstonecraft*

Recension Day

Unburn the boat, rebuild the bridge,
Reconsecrate the sacrilege,
Unspill the milk, decry the tears,
Turn back the clock, relive the years
Replace the smoke inside the fire,
Unite fulfilment with desire,
Undo the done, gainsay the said,
Revitalise the buried dead,
Revoke the penalty and clause,
Reconstitute unwritten laws,
Repair the heart, untie the tongue,
Change faithless old to hopeful young,
Inure the body to disease
And help me to forget you please.

Duncan Forbes
(September 17th 1947 –)

Duncan Forbes read English at Corpus Christi College, Oxford, and has worked as a teacher. He is married with a son and daughter. His poetry collections include *August Autumn* (1984), *Public Confidential* (1989) and *Taking Liberties* (1993).

Gavin Ewart has commended him as a poet: "Duncan Forbes has a good sense of reality, and of what Thomas Hardy called 'life's little ironies'". U. A. Fanthorpe considers his poems "densely written and disturbing"; and in Anthony Thwaite's assessment Forbes is "a poet of many moods, hedonistic, flippant, caustic, comically fanciful and wistfully puzzled".

August 31

• *John Bunyan died August 31st 1688*
• *French Symbolist poet Charles Baudelaire died August 31st 1867*
• *Poet Charles Reznikoff, who walked five or six miles in New York City every day, born in Brooklyn August 31st 1894*
• *Russian poet Marina Tsvetayeva hanged herself August 31st 1941*

Valiant-for-Truth's Song

Who would true Valour see
Let him come hither;
One here will Constant be,
Come Wind, come Weather.
There's no Discouragement
Shall make him once Relent,
His first avow'd Intent,
To be a Pilgrim.

Who so beset him round,
With dismal Stories,
Do but themselves Confound;
His Strength the more is.
No Lyon can him fright,
He'll with a Giant Fight,
But he will have a right,
To be a Pilgrim.

Hobgoblin, nor foul Fiend,
Can daunt his Spirit:
He knows, he at the end,
Shall Life Inherit.
Then Fancies fly away,
He'll fear not what men say,
He'll labour Night and Day,
To be a Pilgrim.

John Bunyan
(Baptised November 30th 1628 –
August 31st 1688)

John Bunyan was born in Elstow, near Bedford, the son of a tinker. He was drafted into the parliamentary army in 1644, and about 1649 married his first wife, a poor woman who brought with her two religious books that had belonged to her father. These books, and Bunyan's own religious experiences, led him in due course to start preaching without a licence in the villages around Bedford. He was arrested in November 1660 and spent most of the next twelve years completing the writing of more than nine books in jail. He also began to write *The Pilgrim's Progress*. He was released after the Declaration of Indulgence in 1672, under which he became a licensed preacher, but was rearrested in 1673 when this Declaration was cancelled. The first part of *The Pilgrim's Progress* was finished during this renewed period of imprisonment. Bunyan died after riding through the rain from Reading to London, and was buried in Bunhill Fields.

- Gerard Manley Hopkins wrote 'Hurrahing in Harvest' in the Vale of Clwyd in Wales September 1st 1877
- Australian poet Bernard O'Dowd died September 1st 1953
- Writer and poet Siegfried Sassoon died September 1st 1967

Hurrahing in Harvest

Summer ends now; now, barbarous in beauty, the stooks arise
    Around; up above, what wind-walks! what lovely behaviour
    Of silk-sack clouds! has wilder, wilful-wavier
Meal-drift moulded ever and melted across skies?

I walk, I lift up, I lift up heart, eyes,
    Down all that glory in the heavens to glean our Saviour[1];
    And, éyes, heárt, what looks, what lips yet gave you a
Rapturous love's greeting of realer, of rounder replies?

And the azurous hung hills are his world-wielding shoulder
    Majestic—as a stallion stalwart, very-violet-sweet!—
These things, these things were here and but the beholder
    Wanting; which two when they once meet,
The heart réars wíngs bold and bolder
    And hurls for him, O half hurls earth for him off under his feet.

Gerard Manley Hopkins
(July 28th 1844 – June 8th 1889)

Hopkins noted that "The Hurrahing sonnet was the outcome of half an hour of extreme enthusiasm as I walked home alone one day from fishing in the Elwy."

1. To gather knowledge of Christ as gleaners gather corn during the harvest.

At Parting

Since we through war awhile must part
Sweetheart, and learn to lose
Daily use
Of all that satisfied our heart:
Lay up those secrets and those powers
Wherewith you pleased and cherished me these two years.

Now we must draw, as plants would,
On tubers stored in a better season,
Our honey and heaven;
Only our love can store such food.
Is this to make a god of absence?
A new-born monster to steal our sustenance?

We cannot quite cast out lack and pain.
Let him remain – what he may devour
We can well spare:
He never can tap this, the true vein.
I have no words to tell you what you were,
But when you are sad, think, Heaven could give no more.

Anne Ridler
(July 30th 1912 –)

On this day in 1939, the day after Britain demanded that Germany halt its invasion of Poland, all places of entertainment in London were closed in case of bombing.

Anne Ridler writes: "The parting was not to be a final one, for we have lived to celebrate our Golden Wedding. But it was hard enough to bear: we had only been married two years, and our first child was on the way. My husband was posted to the RAF base in Scapa Flow, Orkney, and I was able to join him there for a few months before he was sent to West Africa."

Her *Collected Poems* are published by Carcanet Press, Manchester (October 1994).

- *Shakespeare's rival dramatist Robert Greene died September 3rd 1592, on his deathbed writing to beware of this "upstart Crow, beautified with our feathers ... in his own conceit the only Shake-scene in a countrie"*
- *William Wordsworth completed the sonnet 'Composed upon Westminster Bridge' September 3rd 1802*
- *American poet e. e. cummings died September 3rd 1962*
- *Irish poet Louis MacNeice died September 3rd 1963*

Composed upon Westminster Bridge
September 3, 1802

Earth has not anything to show more fair:
Dull would he be of soul who could pass by
A sight so touching in its majesty:
This city now doth, like a garment, wear
The beauty of the morning; silent, bare,
Ships, towers, domes, theatres, and temples lie
Open unto the fields, and to the sky;
All bright and glittering in the smokeless air.
Never did sun more beautifully steep
In his first splendour, valley, rock, or hill;
Ne'er saw I, never felt, a calm so deep!
The river glideth at his own sweet will:
Dear God! the very houses seem asleep;
And all that mighty heart is lying still!

William Wordsworth
(April 7th 1770 – April 23rd 1850)

William's sister Dorothy wrote in her Grasmere Journal for 1802: "After various troubles and disasters we left London at half past 5 or 6 (I have forgot which). We mounted the Dover coach at Charing Cross. It was a beautiful morning. The City, St Paul's, with the River and a multitude of little Boats, made a beautiful sight as we crossed Westminster Bridge. The houses were not overhung by their cloud of smoke and they were spread out endlessly, yet the sun shone so brightly with such a pure light that there was even something like the purity of one of nature's own good spectacles."

September 4

• On September 4th 1786 a letter from Blacklock, delighted with Burns' poems, persuaded the latter not to sail off to the West Indies

The Fascination of What's Difficult

The fascination of what's difficult
Has dried the sap out of my veins, and rent
Spontaneous joy and natural content
Out of my heart. There's something ails our colt
That must, as if it had not holy blood
Nor on Olympus leaped from cloud to cloud,
Shiver under the lash, strain, sweat and jolt
As though it dragged road-metal. My curse on plays
That have to be set up in fifty ways,
On the day's war with every knave and dolt,
Theatre business, management of men.
I swear before the dawn comes round again
I'll find the stable and pull out the bolt.

William Butler Yeats
(June 13th 1865 – January 28th 1939)

In September 1909, Yeats wrote an outline of this poem in his diary: "Subject. To complain at the fascination of what's difficult. It spoils spontaneity and pleasure, and wastes time." Daniel Albright believes that this poem "anticipates Yeats' surrender, eight years later, to his wife's trances of automatic writing, and other strategies of self-liberation".

• Poet Robert Fergusson born in Edinburgh September 5th 1750. Later in life he became depressed following a religious experience, was declared insane after a fall downstairs and died in an asylum
• Poet Jorie Graham, whose collections include Erosion and The End of Beauty, born September 5th 1951. She teaches at the University of Iowa

From As You Like It
Act II Scene v

Amiens. Under the greenwood tree,
   Who loves to lie with me,
   And turn his merry note
   Unto the sweet bird's throat,
Come hither, come hither, come hither:
   Here shall he see
   No enemy
But winter and rough weather.

Amiens, Jaques and others.
   Who doth ambition shun,
   And loves to live i' the sun,
   Seeking the food he eats,
   And pleased with what he gets,
Come hither, come hither, come hither:
   Here shall he see
   No enemy
But winter and rough weather.

William Shakespeare
(April 23rd 1564 – April 23rd 1616)

On this day in 1571, Shakespeare's father John was appointed chief alderman for Stratford.

'Greenwood tree' songs were a familiar genre in Shakespeare's time. It has been suggested that it is used here partly to suggest scenery where perhaps there was none. (Thomas Hardy's novel *Under the Greeenwood Tree* came out in 1872.)

September 6

* On September 6th 1863 Hopkins wrote to Alexander Baillie (who was at Balliol with him): "The most inveterate fault of critics is the tendency to cramp and hedge in by rules the free movements of genius"

Walking Away
for Sean

It is eighteen years ago, almost to the day –
A sunny day with the leaves just turning,
The touch-lines new-ruled – since I watched you play
Your first game of football, then, like a satellite
Wrenched from its orbit, go drifting away

Behind a scatter of boys. I can see
You walking away from me towards the school
With the pathos of a half-fledged thing set free
Into a wilderness, the gait of one
Who finds no path where the path should be.

That hesitant figure, eddying away
Like a winged seed loosened from its parent stem
Has something I never quite grasp to convey
About nature's give-and-take – the small, the scorching
Ordeals which fire one's irresolute clay.

I have had worse partings, but none that so
Gnaws at my mind still. Perhaps it is roughly
Saying what God alone could perfectly show –
How selfhood begins with a walking away,
And love is proved in the letting go.

C. Day Lewis
(April 27th 1904 – May 22nd 1972)

Sean Day-Lewis, to whom this poem was dedicated, was the elder son of Cecil Day Lewis's first marriage; in 1980 he published a questioning biography of his father.

Cecil Day Lewis was born in Ballintogher, County Sligo, but moved with his family from Ireland to England the next year. At Oxford he edited *Oxford Poetry* (1927) with Auden, becoming a socialist and later a Communist, though he wrote more conservative poetry in later years. He was Professor of Poetry at Oxford from 1951 to 1956 and became Poet Laureate in 1968. He wrote a number of subtle detective novels under the pseudonym Nicholas Blake.

• *Hopkins became a Jesuit novice at Roehampton, September 7th 1868*
• *Edith Sitwell born in Scarborough September 7th 1887*
• *American abolitionist Quaker poet John Greenleaf Whittier died September 7th 1892*
• *Louise Bennett born in Jamaica September 7th 1919*
• *Fred E. Weatherly, English songwriter ('Roses of Picardy') died September 7th 1929*

Sir Beelzebub

When
Sir
Beelzebub called for his syllabub in the hotel in Hell
       Where Proserpine first fell,
Blue as the gendarmerie were the waves of the sea,
      (Rocking and shocking the barmaid).

Nobody comes to give him his rum but the
Rim of the sky hippopotamus-glum
Enhances the chances to bless with a benison
Alfred Lord Tennyson crossing the bar laid
With cold vegetation from pale deputations
Of temperance workers (all signed In Memoriam)
Hoping with glory to trip up the Laureate's feet,
      (Moving in classical metres) . . .

Like Balaclava, the lava came down from the
Roof, and the sea's blue wooden gendarmerie
Took them in charge while Beelzebub roared for his rum.
    . . . None of them come!

Edith Sitwell
(September 7th 1887 – December 9th 1964)

Edith Sitwell was still very young when, as she put it, she first "took an intense dislike to simplicity, morris-dancing, and every kind of sport except reviewer-baiting".

She first attracted notice with her editorship of *Wheels*, an anthology of new poetry which attacked the genteel quietism of Georgian verse. The reputation she acquired for eccentricity and controversy once led her to suggest: "I am like an unpopular electric eel in a pond full of flatfish." Always interested in innovation, her later poetry often develops from the rhythms of dance music, and particularly jazz.

September 8

• The Italian poet Ludovico Ariosto, who wrote 'Orlando Furioso', born September 8th 1474
• Frédéric Mistral, leader of the Félibrige literary movement to revive Provençal writing, born September 8th 1830
• French absurdist Alfred Jarry born in Laval September 8th 1873
• Siegfried Sassoon born September 8th 1886

Everyone Sang

Everyone suddenly burst out singing;
And I was filled with such delight
As prisoned birds must find in freedom,
Winging wildly across the white
Orchards and dark-green fields; on – on – and out of sight.

Everyone's voice was suddenly lifted;
And beauty came like the setting sun:
My heart was shaken with tears; and horror
Drifted away . . . O, but Everyone
Was a bird; and the song was wordless; the singing will never
    be done.

Siegfried Sassoon
(September 8th 1886 – September 1st 1967)

Siegfried Sassoon was born in Kent into a privileged, artistic family of Persian-Jewish origin. His parents divorced, his father died early, he was sickly as a child and he failed to take a degree at Clare College, Cambridge. He volunteered on the first day of the Great War, won the MC for bringing back a wounded lance-corporal under heavy fire, and was recommended, unsuccessfully, for a VC, after capturing a German trench single-handed. Agonised by the horrors of the trenches, he threw his MC into the Mersey, and his letter protesting the war was read out in the House of Commons. He attempted to have himself court-martialled for desertion, but was rescued by his friend Robert Graves who wangled him a place in the hospital at Craiglockhart under a diagnosis of shell-shock. Here he met Wilfred Owen, who greeted him "as a man; as a friend and a poet":

"Know that since mid-September, when you still regarded me as a tiresome little knocker on your door, I hold you as Keats + Christ + Elijah + my Colonel + my father-confessor + Amenophis IV in profile."

Sasson was discharged and eventually rejoined his former battalion in France. He was wounded in the head on July 13th 1918, and spent the remainder of the war on sick-leave.

In 1957 he became a Roman Catholic. Some of his devotional poems remain unpublished. He himself preferred his later poetry to his war poems, which were, he claimed, "improvised by an impulsive, intolerant, immature young creature under the extreme stress of experience" – ingredients which could be deemed, however, to constitute a near-perfect recipe for interesting and unusual poetry.

• Poet and writer Cesare Pavese born in Piedmont September 9th 1908
• Scottish poet Hugh MacDiarmid died September 9th 1978

Gunga Din

You may talk o' gin and beer
When you're quartered safe out 'ere,
An' you're sent to penny-fights an' Aldershot it;
But when it comes to slaughter
You will do your work on water,
An' you'll lick the bloomin' boots of 'im that's got it.
Now in Injia's sunny clime,
Where I used to spend my time
A-servin' of 'Er Majesty the Queen,
Of all them blackfaced crew
The finest man I knew
Was our regimental *bhisti*, Gunga Din.
   He was 'Din! Din! Din!
 You limpin' lump o' brick-dust, Gunga Din!
   Hi! Slippy *hitherao!*
   Water, get it! *Panee lao,*
 You squidgy-nosed old idol, Gunga Din.'

The uniform 'e wore
Was nothin' much before,
An' rather less than 'arf o' that be'ind,
For a piece o' twisty rag
An' a goatskin water-bag
Was all the field-equipment 'e could find.
When the sweatin' troop-train lay
In a sidin' through the day,
Where the 'eat would make your bloomin' eyebrows crawl,
We shouted 'Harry By!'
Till our throats were bricky-dry,
Then we wopped 'im 'cause 'e couldn't serve us all.
   It was 'Din! Din! Din!
 You 'eathen, where the mischief 'ave you been?
   You put some juldee in it
   Or I'll marrow you this minute
 If you don't fill up my helmet, Gunga Din!'

'E would dot an' carry one
Till the longest day was done;
An' 'e didn't seem to know the use o' fear.
If we charged or broke or cut,
You could bet your bloomin' nut,
'E'd be waitin' fifty paces right flank rear.
With 'is *mussick* on 'is back,
'E would skip with our attack,

[Continued]

An' watch us till the bugles made 'Retire',
An' for all 'is dirty 'ide
'E was white, clear white, inside
When 'e went to tend the wounded under fire!
    It was 'Din! Din! Din!'
  With the bullets kickin' dust-spots on the green.
    When the cartridges ran out,
    You could hear the front-ranks shout,
  'Hi! ammunition-mules an' Gunga Din!'

I shan't forgit the night
When I dropped be'ind the fight
With a bullet where my belt-plate should'a' been.
I was chokin' mad with thirst,
An' the man that spied me first
Was our good old grinnin', gruntin' Gunga Din.
'E lifted up my 'ead,
  An' he plugged me where I bled,
  An' 'e guv me 'arf-a-pint o' water green.
It was crawlin' and it stunk,
But of all the drinks I've drunk,
I'm gratefullest to one from Gunga Din.
    It was 'Din! Din! Din!
  'Ere's a beggar with a bullet through 'is spleen;
    'E's chawin' up the ground,
    An' 'e's kickin' all around:
  For Gawd's sake git the water, Gunga Din!'

'E carried me away
To where a *dooli* lay,
An' a bullet come an' drilled the beggar clean.
'E put me safe inside,
An' just before 'e died,
'I 'ope you liked your drink,' sez Gunga Din.
So I'll meet 'im later on
At the place where 'e is gone—
Where it's always double drill and no canteen.
'E'll be squattin' on the coals
Givin' drink to poor damned souls
An' I'll get a swig in hell from Gunga Din!
    Yes, Din! Din! Din!
  You Lazarushian-leather Gunga Din!
    Though I've belted you and flayed you,
    By the livin' Gawd that made you,
  You're a better man than I am, Gunga Din!

Rudyard Kipling
(December 30th 1865 – January 18th 1936)

• *American imagist poet Hilda Doolittle (H. D.) born in Bethlehem, Pennsylvania, September 10th 1886*
• *Austrian novelist, poet and playwright Franz Werfel born in Prague September 10th 1890*

Pied[1] Beauty

Glory be to God for dappled things –
   For skies of couple-colour as a brinded[2] cow;
     For rose-moles all in stipple upon trout that swim;
Fresh fire-coal chestnut-falls; finches' wings;
   Landscape plotted and pieced – fold, fallow, and plough;
     And áll trádes, their gear and tackle and trim.

All things counter, original, spare, strange;
   Whatever is fickle, freckled (who knows how?)
     With swift, slow; sweet, sour; adazzle, dim;
He fathers-forth whose beauty is past change:
              Praise him.

Gerard Manley Hopkins
(July 28th 1844 – June 8th 1889)

On this day in 1864, Hopkins in a letter to A. W. M. Baillie derided Tennyson's Parnassian style – the way the poet saw and described things "without further effort of inspiration".

1. Of various colours, often in patches or blotches.
2. Streaked.

September 11

• Pierre de Ronsard born in the Château de la Possonnière in Vendôme, September 11th 1524
• The Scottish poet James Thompson, who probably wrote 'Rule Britannia', was born September 11th 1700
• Poet and novelist D. H. Lawrence born in Eastwood, Notts, September 11th 1885

Piano

Softly, in the dusk, a woman is singing to me;
Taking me back down the vista of years, till I see
A child sitting under the piano, in the boom of the tingling strings
And pressing the small, poised feet of a mother who smiles as she sings.

In spite of myself, the insidious mastery of song
Betrays me back, till the heart of me weeps to belong
To the old Sunday evenings at home, with winter outside
And hymns in the cozy parlour, the tinkling piano our guide.

So now it is vain for the singer to burst into clamour
With the great black piano appassionato. The glamour
Of childish days is upon me, my manhood is cast
Down in the flood of remembrance, I weep like a child for the past.

D. H. Lawrence
(September 11th 1885 – March 2nd 1930)

Lawrence, whose early universe was passionately centered on his mother, remembered asking himself as a child, "why God was a man, not a woman. In heaven, God was the fount of right and wrong, and on earth, woman. Woman knows best. Man didn't care. God knows best of all – That was my childish argument of the moral scheme." Lawrence was the son of a Nottingham miner, who drank and bullied him, and his mother encouraged the boy to escape the mines through an education. When he was 26, his mother died and he became seriously ill, but recovered sufficiently to elope with Frieda Weekley, a mother of three children and six years his senior.

• *The British bombardment of Fort McHenry on this day in 1814
  inspired Francis Scott Key to write 'The Star Spangled Banner'*
• *Louis MacNeice born in Belfast September 12th 1907*
• *American poet Robert Lowell died September 12th 1977*

A Fanfare for the Makers

A cloud of witnesses. To whom? To what?
To the small fire that never leaves the sky.
To the great fire that boils the daily pot.

To all the things we are not remembered by,
Which we remember and bless. To all the things
That will not even notice when we die,

Yet lend the passing moment words and wings.

So Fanfare for the Makers: who compose
A book of words or deeds who runs may write
As many do who run, as a family grows

At times like sunflowers turning towards the light,
As sometimes in the blackout and the raids
One joke composed an island in the night,

As sometimes one man's kindliness pervades
A room or house or village, as sometimes
Merely to tighten screws or sharpen blades

Can catch a meaning, as to hear the chimes
At midnight means to share them, as one man
In old age plants an avenue of limes

And before they bloom can smell them, before they span
The road can walk beneath the perfected arch,
The merest greenprint when the lives began

Of those who walk there with him, as in default
Of coffee men grind acorns, as in despite
Of all assaults conscripts counterassault,

As mothers sit up late night after night
Moulding a life, as miners day by day
Descend blind shafts, as a boy may flaunt his kite

In an empty nonchalant sky, as anglers play
Their fish, as workers work and can take pride
In spending sweat before they draw their pay,

As horsemen fashion horses while they ride,
As climbers climb a peak because it is there,
As life can be confirmed even in suicide:

To make is such. Let us make. And set the weather fair.

Louis MacNeice
(September 12th 1907 – September 3rd 1963)

• *F.T. Prince, who wrote the poem 'Soldiers Bathing', born in South Africa September 13th 1912*

The Solitary Reaper

Behold her, single in the field,
Yon solitary Highland lass,
Reaping and singing by herself,
Stop here, or gently pass.
Alone she cuts and binds the grain,
And sings a melancholy strain;
O listen, for the vale profound
Is overflowing with the sound.

No Nightingale did ever chaunt
More welcome notes to weary bands
Of travellers in some shady haunt,
Among Arabian sands;
A voice so thrilling ne'er was heard
In spring-time from the Cuckoo-bird,
Breaking the silence of the seas
Among the farthest Hebrides.

Will no one tell me what she sings?—
Perhaps the plaintive numbers flow
For old unhappy far-off things
And battles long ago;
Or is it some more humble lay,
Familiar matter of to-day?
Some natural sorrow, loss or pain,
That has been and may be again?

Whate'er the theme, the Maiden sang
As if her song could have no ending;
I saw her singing at her work,
And o'er the sickle bending;—
I listened, motionless and still;
And, as I mounted up the hill,
The music in my heart I bore,
Long after it was heard no more.

William Wordsworth
(April 7th 1770 – April 23rd 1850)

Dorothy Wordsworth wrote in her journal for September 13th 1803 (during a tour that she and her brother made in Scotland): "It was harvest-time and the fields were quietly (might I be allowed to say passively?) enlivened by small companies of reapers. It is not uncommon in the more lonely parts of the Highlands to see a *single* person so employed." William Wordsworth wrote the poem on November 5th 1805.

- *Dante Alighieri died in Ravenna September 14th 1321*
- *On September 14th 1800 Blake wrote a delighted lyric in praise of his new cottage in Felpham ("The Bread of sweet Thought & the Wine of Delight / Feeds the Village of Felpham by day & by night"). But in the event he hated living there*

The Sick Rose

O rose, thou art sick!
The invisible worm
That flies in the night,
In the howling storm,

Has found out thy bed
Of crimson joy:
And his dark secret love
Does thy life destroy.

William Blake
(November 28th 1757 – August 12th 1827)

Blake's design for this poem has a rose drooping around the text, with a caterpillar eating one of its leaves, and a spirit expelled from the flower's closed centre.

The theme is erotic love. The merely sensuous worm enters the rose and drives out the spirit of joy, of authentic love. The caterpillar is the Church, with its sick preoccupation with sex as sin, eating away a life-giving leaf. Blake's pictures are not just visual representations of his text. They tell different parts of the story in visual counterpoint.

September 15

• *Writers must remember, said Thomas Hardy on September 15th 1913, "that a story must be worth the telling, that a good deal of life is not worth any such thing"*

From In Memoriam A. H. H.
XXVII

I envy not in any moods
    The captive void of noble rage,
    The linnet born within the cage,
That never knew the summer woods:

I envy not the beast that takes
    His license in the field of time,
    Unfetter'd by the sense of crime,
To whom a conscience never wakes;

Nor, what may count itself as blest,
    The heart that never plighted troth
    But stagnates in the weeds of sloth,
Nor any want-begotten rest.

I hold it true, whate'er befall;
    I feel it when I sorrow most;
    'Tis better to have loved and lost
Than never to have loved at all.

Alfred, Lord Tennyson
(August 6th 1809 – October 6th 1892)

Tennyson started writing this poem in 1833, and dedicated it to the memory of Arthur Henry Hallam who died in Vienna on September 15th 1833, whilst travelling with his father – "a blood vessel near the brain had suddenly burst," Tennyson was told. Hallam had been Tennyson's close friend at Cambridge, and the previous year, with both still in their early twenties, they had travelled together on the Continent. Tennyson said of *In Memoriam* that 'it must be remembered that this is a poem, *not* an actual biography. It is founded on our friendship, on the engagement of Arthur Hallam to my sister, on his sudden death at Vienna, just before the time fixed for their marriage, and on his burial at Clevedon Church." Elsewhere he said: "It's a very impersonal poem as well as personal ... It's too hopeful, this Poem ... more than I am myself."

- *Anne Bradstreet, first English poet of America, died September 16th 1672*
- *John Gay, who wrote* The Beggar's Opera, *born in Barnstaple September 16th 1685*
- *Alfred Noyes, who wrote 'The Highwayman', born September 16th 1880*
- *T.E. Hulme born September 16th 1883*
- *The aboriginal poet Oodgeroo of the Noonuccal, formerly Kath Walker, died September 16th 1993*

The Embankment
(The Fantasia of a Fallen Gentleman on a Cold, Bitter Night)

Once, in finesse of fiddles found I ecstasy,
In a flash of gold heels on the hard pavement.
Now see I
That warmth's the very stuff of poesy.
Oh, God, make small
The old star-eaten blanket of the sky,
That I may fold it round me and in comfort lie.

T. E. Hulme
(September 16th 1883 – September 28th 1917)

T. E. Hulme is yet another poet to have been killed in World War I – serving with the Royal Marine Artillery. His *Complete Poetical Works* (five poems, the longest being of nine lines) were printed in admiration by Ezra Pound as an addendum to the latter's *Ripostes* (1912). Eliot said of Hulme that he was "classical, reactionary and revolutionary ... the antipodes of the eccentric, tolerant and democratic mind of the end of the century".

Hulme was born in Endon, Staffordshire, and was expelled from St John's College, Cambridge, possibly for brawling (he is said to have carried a knuckle-duster around with him). In 1908, whilst living in London, he joined the 'experimental' Poets' Club.

September 17

• Poet and novelist Tobias Smollett died in Livorno, Italy,
September 17th 1771
• William Carlos Williams born September 17th 1883

Danse Russe

If when my wife is sleeping
and the baby and Kathleen
are sleeping
and the sun is a flame-white disc
in silken mists
above shining trees,—
if I in my north room
dance naked, grotesquely
before my mirror
waving my shirt round my head
and singing softly to myself:
'I am lonely, lonely.
I was born to be lonely,
I am best so!'
If I admire my arms, my face,
my shoulders, flanks, buttocks
against the yellow drawn shades,—

Who shall say I am not
the happy genius of my household?

William Carlos Williams
(September 17th 1883 – March 4th 1963)

In 1912 William Carlos Williams married Florence Herman ("Floss" in his poems). He worked as a doctor, and they settled in Rutherford, New Jersey, his home town, where they had two sons. Williams' approach to life is perhaps best encapsulated in his lines: "If a man die / it is because death / has first / possessed his imagination."

• Polymath (and poet) Samuel Johnson born in Lichfield September 18th 1709
• Poet Michael Hartnett born on a farm in County Limerick September 18th 1941. A Necklace of Wrens is in Irish with his own translations into English

No Worst, there is None

No worst, there is none. Pitched past pitch of grief,
More pangs will, schooled at forepangs, wilder wring.
Comforter, where, where is your comforting?
Mary, mother of us, where is your relief?
My cries heave, herds-long; huddle in a main, a chief
Woe, world-sorrow; on an age-old anvil wince and sing—
Then lull, then leave off. Fury had shrieked 'No ling-
ering! Let me be fell: force I must be brief'.

O the mind, mind has mountains; cliffs of fall
Frightful, sheer, no-man-fathomed. Hold them cheap
May who ne'er hung there. Nor does long our small
Durance deal with that steep or deep. Here! creep,
Wretch, under a comfort serves in a whirlwind: all
Life death does end and each day dies with sleep.

Gerard Manley Hopkins
(July 28th 1844 – June 8th 1889)

On this day in 1873 Hopkins wrote: "I had a nightmare last night. I thought something or someone leapt on me and held me quite fast: this I think woke me ... so that I could speak, whispering at first, then louder ... thinking I could recover myself if I could move my finger ... and then the arm and so the whole body. The feeling is terrible ... I cried on the holy name and by degrees recovered myself ... It made me think that this was how the souls in hell would be imprisoned in their bodies."

This sonnet was probably one of the ones Hopkins referred to in his letter of September 1st 1885 to Robert Bridges in which he wrote, "Four of these [sonnets] came like inspiration unbidden and against my will." Previously he had written to Bridges: "I think that my fits of sadness, though they do not affect my judgment, resemble madness ... I must absolutely have encouragement as much as crops rain."

September 19

• John Keats wrote 'To Autumn' September 19th 1819

To Autumn

Season of mists and mellow fruitfulness,
  Close bosom-friend of the maturing sun;
Conspiring with him how to load and bless
  With fruit the vines that round the thatch-eaves run;
To bend with apples the mossed cottage-trees,
  And fill all fruit with ripeness to the core;
    To swell the gourd, and plump the hazel shells
With a sweet kernel; to set budding more,
And still more, later flowers for the bees,
Until they think warm days will never cease,
    For Summer has o'er-brimmed their clammy cells.

Who hath not seen thee oft amid thy store?
  Sometimes whoever seeks abroad may find
Thee sitting careless on a granary floor,
  Thy hair soft-lifted by the winnowing wind;
Or on a half-reaped furrow sound asleep,
  Drowsed with the fume of poppies, while thy hook°   *sickle*
    Spares the next swath and all its twinèd flowers:
And sometimes like a gleaner° thou dost keep   *corn gatherer*
  Steady thy laden head across a brook;
  Or by a cider-press, with patient look,
    Thou watchest the last oozings hours by hours.

Where are the songs of Spring? Aye, where are they?
  Think not of them, thou hast thy music too—
While barrèd clouds bloom the soft-dying day,
  And touch the stubble-plains with rosy hue;
Then in a wailful choir the small gnats mourn
  Among the river sallows°, borne aloft   *willows*
    Or sinking as the light wind lives or dies;
And full-grown lambs loud bleat from hilly bourn;
  Hedge crickets sing; and now with treble soft
  The redbreast whistles from a garden-croft;
    And gathering swallows twitter in the skies.

John Keats
(October 31st 1795 – February 23rd 1821)

In September 1819 Keats wrote: "I 'kepen in solitariness' for Brown has gone a-visiting. I am surprised myself at the pleasure I live alone in. How beautiful the season is now – how fine the air. A temperate sharpness about it – I never liked stubble fields so much as now – Aye better than the chilly green of the Spring. Somehow a stubble field looks warm – in the same way that some pictures look warm. This struck me so much on my Sunday's walk that I composed upon it ... Oh how I admire the middlesized delicate Devonshire girls of about fifteen. There was one at the inn door holding a quatern of brandy – the very thought of her kept me warm a whole stage – and a 16 miler too."

The Heavenly City

I sigh for the heavenly country,
Where the heavenly people pass,
And the sea is as quiet as a mirror
Of beautiful, beautiful glass.

I walk in the heavenly field,
With lilies and poppies bright,
I am dressed in a heavenly coat
Of polished white.

When I walk in the heavenly parkland
My feet on the pastures are bare,
Tall waves the grass, but no harmful
Creature is there.

At night I fly over the housetops,
And stand on the bright moony beams;
Gold are all heaven's rivers,
And silver her streams.

Stevie Smith
(September 20th 1902 – March 7th 1971)

"I can't make up my mind," Stevie Smith once wrote, "if God is good, impotent or unkind."
In this untypically positive poem she could be Blake reincarnated as Emily Dickinson.

September 21

- Roman poet Virgil died September 21st 19 BC
- Scottish novelist and poet Sir Walter Scott died at Abbotsford September 21st 1832
- Leonard Cohen born in Montreal September 21st 1934
- Irish poet Theo Dorgan born September 21st 1953

Suzanne Takes You Down

Suzanne takes you down
to her place near the river,
you can hear the boats go by
you can stay the night beside her.
And you know that she's half crazy
but that's why you want to be there
and she feeds you tea and oranges
that come all the way from China.
Just when you mean to tell her
that you have no gifts to give her,
she gets you on her wave-length
and she lets the river answer
that you've always been her lover.

And you want to travel with her,
you want to travel blind
and you know that she can trust you
because you've touched her perfect body
with your mind.

Jesus was a sailor
when he walked upon the water
and he spent a long time watching
from a lonely wooden tower
and when he knew for certain
only drowning men could see him
he said All men will be sailors then
until the sea shall free them,
but he himself was broken
long before the sky would open,
forsaken, almost human,
he sank beneath your wisdom like a stone.

And you want to travel with him,
you want to travel blind
and you think maybe you'll trust him
because he touched your perfect body
with his mind.

Suzanne takes your hand,
and she leads you to the river,
she is wearing rags and feathers
from Salvation Army counters.
The sun pours down like honey
on our lady of the harbor
as she shows you where to look
among the garbage and the flowers,
there are heroes in the seaweed
there are children in the morning,
they are leaning out for love
they will lean that way forever
while Suzanne she holds the mirror.

And you want to travel with her
and you want to travel blind
and you're sure that she can find you
because she's touched her perfect body
with her mind.

Leonard Cohen
(September 21st 1934 –)

Over two decades since the composition of this song, Cohen, on tour as the dark guru of the disaffected and despondent, is as popular as ever. Of his gifts as a poet, D. D. C. Chambers has written: "The figures in Leonard Cohen's poems rise like figures in Chagall, transformed from the ordinary, surprised into a world of visionary experience. Out of the junk of the everyday – 'the garbage and the flowers' – the magical world of the imaginative is created. There is a strong sense in which his poetry is a prodigious search of experience for the exit from the ordinary."

- *Sir Philip Sidney mortally wounded at the battle of Zutphen September 22nd 1586*
- *Thomas Lodge's first volume of verse,* Romance Rosa, *licensed for the press September 22nd 1589.* Rosalynde *("in tedious prose enlivened by lyrics") was written on his voyage to the Canaries and published 1590*
- *Ben Jonson killed a fellow actor in a duel September 22nd 1598 and escaped the gallows by claiming benefit of clergy*

Rosalynde's Madrigal

Love in my bosome like a Bee
    doth sucke his sweete:
Now with his wings he playes with me,
    now with his feete.
  Within mine eyes he makes his nest,
  His bed amidst my tender breast,
  My kisses are his daily feast;
  And yet he robs me of my rest.
    Ah wanton, will ye?

And if I sleepe, then pearcheth he
    with prettie flight,
And makes his pillow of my knee
    the livelong night.
  Strike I my lute, he tunes the string;
  He musicke playes if so I sing,
  He lends me everie lovelie thing,
  Yet cruell he my heart doth sting.
    Whist wanton, still ye.

Else I with roses everie day
    will whip you hence;
And binde you when you long to play,
    for your offence.
  Ile shut mine eyes to keepe you in,
  Ile make you fast it for your sinne,
  Ile count your power not worth a pinne;
  Alas what hereby shall I winne
    If he gainsay me?

What if I beate the wanton boy
    with manie a rod?
He will repay me with annoy,
    because a God.
  Then sit thou safely on my knee,
  Then let thy bowre my bosome be:
  Lurke in mine eyes I like of thee;
  Oh Cupid so thou pitie me.
    Spare not but play thee.

Thomas Lodge
(ca. 1556 – September 1625)

September 23

• Mary Coleridge born September 23rd 1861
• Chilean poet Pablo Neruda died September 23rd 1973

Egypt's Might is Tumbled Down

Egypt's might is tumbled down
  Down a-down the deeps of thought;
Greece is fallen and Troy town,
Glorious Rome hath lost her crown,
  Venice' pride is nought.

But the dreams their children dreamed
  Fleeting, unsubstantial, vain.
Shadowy as the shadows seemed
Airy nothing, as they deemed,
  These remain.

Mary Coleridge
(September 23rd 1861 – August 25th 1907)

Mary Coleridge was born in London and educated at home. She was the great-great grandaughter of Samuel Taylor Coleridge's elder brother. Her family were on visiting terms with Browning, Tennyson, Millais and Robert Bridges, and it was the latter who encouraged her to publish her first poetry collection, *Fanny's Following*, in 1896.

After the death of her mother in 1898, she stayed at home to help her sister look after their father, publishing novels, essays and further poetry.

• *Horace Walpole, man of letters and poet, born in London*
September 24th 1717

From[1] Jubilate Agno[2]

For I will consider my Cat Jeoffry.

For he is the servant of the Living God duly and daily serving him.

For at the first glance of the glory of God in the East he worships in his way.

For is this done by wreathing his body seven times round with elegant
        quickness.

For then he leaps up to catch the musk, which is the blessing of God upon his
        prayer.

For he rolls upon prank to work it in.

For having done duty and received blessing he begins to consider himself.

For this he performs in ten degrees.

For first he looks upon his fore-paws to see if they are clean.

For secondly he kicks up behind to clear away there.

For thirdly he works it upon stretch with the fore paws extended.

For fourthly he sharpens his paws by wood.

For fifthly he washes himself.

For Sixthly he rolls upon wash.

For Seventhly he fleas himself, that he may not be interrupted upon the beat.

For Eighthly he rubs himself against a post.

For Ninthly he looks up for his instructions.

For Tenthly he goes in quest of food.

For having consider'd God and himself he will consider his neighbour.

For if he meets another cat he will kiss her in kindness.

For when he takes his prey he plays with it to give it a chance.

For one mouse in seven escapes by his dallying.

For when his day's work is done his business more properly begins.

For he keeps the Lord's watch in the night against the adversary.

For he counteracts the powers of darkness by his electrical skin & glaring eyes.

For he counteracts the Devil, who is death, by brisking about the life.

For in his morning orisons he loves the sun and the sun loves him.

For he is of the tribe of Tiger.

For the Cherub Cat is a term of the Angel Tiger.

For he has the subtlety and hissing of a serpent, which in goodness he
        suppresses.

For he will not do destruction if he is well-fed, neither will he spit without
        provocation.

For he purrs in thankfulness, when God tells him he's a good Cat.

For he is an instrument for the children to learn benevolence upon.

For every house is incompleat without him & a blessing is lacking in the spirit.

For the Lord commanded Moses concerning the cats at the departure of the
        Children of Israel from Egypt.

For every family had one cat at least in the bag.

For the English Cats are the best in Europe.

For he is the cleanest in the use of his fore-paws of any quadrupede.

[Continued]

For the dexterity of his defence is an instance of the love of God to him
    exceedingly.
For he is the quickest to his mark of any creature.
For he is tenacious of his point.
For he is a mixture of gravity and waggery.
For he knows that God is his Saviour.
For there is nothing sweeter than his peace when at rest.
For there is nothing brisker than his life when in motion.
For he is of the Lord's poor and so indeed is he called by benevolence
    perpetually—Poor Jeoffry! poor Jeoffry! the rat has bit thy throat.
For I bless the name of the Lord Jesus that Jeoffry is better.
For the divine spirit comes about his body to sustain it in compleat cat.
For his tongue is exceeding pure so that it has in purity what it wants in
    musick.
For he is docile and can learn certain things.
For he can set up with gravity which is patience upon approbation.
For he can fetch and carry, which is patience in employment.
For he can jump over a stick which is patience upon proof positive.
For he can spraggle upon waggle at the word of command.
For he can jump from an eminence into his master's bosom.
For he can catch the cork and toss it again.
For he is hated by the hypocrite and miser.
For the former is afraid of detection.
For the latter refuses the charge.
For he camels his back to bear the first notion of business.
For he is good to think on, if a man would express himself neatly.
For he made a great figure in Egypt for his signal services.
For he killed the Icneumon-rat very pernicious by land.
For his ears are so acute that they sting again.
For from this proceeds the passing quickness of his attention.
For by stroaking of him I have found out electricity.
For I have perceived God's light about him both wax and fire.
For the Electrical fire is the spiritual substance, which God sends from heaven
    to sustain the bodies both of man and beast.
For God has blessed him in the variety of his movements.
For, tho he cannot fly, he is an excellent clamberer.
For his motions upon the face of the earth are more than any other
    quadrupede.
For he can tread to all the measures upon the musick.
For he can swim for life.
For he can creep.

Christopher Smart
(April 11th 1722 – May 21st 1771)

1. Lines 697 to 770. Half a dozen fragments of the poem survive, 1,575 lines in total.
2. 'Rejoice in the Lamb' (Jesus, the Lamb of God). Smart wrote 'Jubilate Agno' while he was confined in an asylum for the insane. He described it as "my Magnificat" but it was not published until 1939.

- Samuel Butler, who wrote 'Hudibras', a satirical poem attacking puritanism, died in poverty September 25th 1680
- Felicia Dorothea Hemans, who wrote "The boy stood on the burning deck …", was born September 25th 1793
- Yeats completed his poem 'Easter' on September 25th 1916

Anthem for Doomed Youth

What passing-bells for these who die as cattle?
   Only the monstrous anger of the guns.
   Only the stuttering rifles' rapid rattle
Can patter out their hasty orisons.
No mockeries for them from prayers or bells,
   Nor any voice of mourning save the choirs,—
The shrill, demented choirs of wailing shells;
   And bugles calling for them from sad shires.

What candles may be held to speed them all?
Not in the hands of boys, but in their eyes
Shall shine the holy glimmers of good-byes.
   The pallor of girls' brows shall be their pall;
Their flowers the tenderness of silent minds,
And each slow dusk a drawing-down of blinds.

Wilfred Owen
(March 18th 1893 – November 4th 1918)

Owen sent this poem to his mother on September 25th 1917 from the Craiglockhart War Hospital in Edinburgh where he was recovering from shell-shock. Here he met the poet Siegfried Sassoon, an army officer and war protester whom the authorities preferred to treat as shell-shocked. The poem was provoked by remarks in *Poems of Today* about a poet who had supposedly gone "singing to lay down his life for his country's cause". The poem's first draft was largely unrhymed. Sassoon suggested 'Anthem for Dead Youth' as a title, which Owen changed to 'Doomed Youth'. On reading the fifth and final draft, Sassoon realised "that my little friend was much more than the promising minor poet I had hitherto acknowledged him to be. I now realised that his verse, with its sumptuous epithets and large-scale imagery, its noble naturalness and the depth of meaning, had impressive affinities with Keats, whom he took as his supreme exemplar. This new sonnet was a revelation … It confronted me with classic and imaginative serenity."

September 26

- *T. S. Eliot born in St Louis September 26th 1888*
- *Marina Tsvetayeva born September 26th 1892*
- *American poet and critic Harriet Monroe died September 26th 1936*
- *W. H. Davies, tramp, author and poet, died September 26th 1940*

From Yesterday he still looked in my eyes[1]

Yesterday he still looked in my eyes, yet
   today   his looks are bent aside.   Yesterday
he sat here until the birds began, but
   today,   all those larks are   ravens.

Yesterday he lay at my feet. He even
   compared me with the Chinese Empire! Then
suddenly he let his hands fall open, and
   my life fell out like   a rusty kopek.

I know everything, don't argue with me!
   I can see now, I'm a lover no longer.
And now I know wherever love holds power
   Death approaches soon   like a gardener.

It is almost like shaking a tree, in time
   some ripe apple comes falling down. So
for everything, for everything   forgive me,
   —my love   whatever it was I did to you.

Marina Tsvetayeva
(September 26th 1892 – 31st August 1941)
translated by Elaine Feinstein
(October 24th 1930 –)

Marina Tsvetayeva was born in Moscow, her father a Professor of Fine Arts. Her mother, a gifted pianist, died of tuberculosis when Marina was 14, enabling Marina to give up music for poetry. At the age of 18, she gained a reputation as poet with her first volume *Evening Album*. The poet Osip Mandelstam was in love with her for a time and she felt part of a worldwide community of like-minded poets. Later in life she corresponded with Rilke and also with Pasternak who was "overcome by the immense lyrical power of her poetic form".

In 1912 she married Sergei Efron, an orphan; they had two daughters and lived happily until the war. Sergei became an officer in the Tsarist Army, later joining the White Army. In the tumult of the Civil War period, they were separated for five years. During the Moscow famine, Marina was forced to put her younger daughter in an orphanage, where she died of hunger in 1919. Two years later, Marina heard that Sergei was alive in Prague and joined him in exile in Europe. On the orders of the Soviet Secret Police, Sergei assassinated a defector and fled back to Russia. Marina unwisely followed him. In 1939 her daughter Ariadna was arrested and shot, and her husband was arrested. During the war Marina was evacuated to Elabuga in the Tatar Autonomous Republic, where she hanged herself.

Even her love life had been unhappy: "Her marriage and her many passionate love-affairs," writes Elaine Feinstein, "were largely ill-fated."

1. Stanzas 1, 5, 9 and 10 of a 10 stanza poem(see *Selected Poems of Marina Tsvetayeva*, OUP). The first two lines above and the penultimate line rephrase a prayer that is sung in the Orthodox Church.

• English poet and critic Sir William Empson born in Howden, Yorkshire, September 27th 1906
• English poet and novelist Roy Fuller died September 27th 1991

September 27

My Boy Jack

'Have you news of my boy Jack?'
    Not this tide.
'When d'you think that he'll come back?'
    Not with this wind blowing, and this tide.

'Has anyone else had word of him?'
    Not this tide.
For what is sunk will hardly swim,
    Not with this wind blowing and this tide.

'Oh, dear, what comfort can I find?'
    None this tide,
    Nor any tide,
Except he did not shame his kind —
    Not even with that wind blowing, and that tide.

Then hold your head up all the more,
    This tide,
    And every tide;
Because he was the son you bore,
    And gave to that wind blowing and that tide!

        Rudyard Kipling
    (December 30th 1865 – January 18th 1936)

Kipling's son John was killed in the Battle of Loos on September 27th 1915. John's commanding officer wrote to the father that "we were under machine-guns and casualties were getting numerous ... Two of my men saw your son limping ... and I am very hopeful that he is a prisoner ... Your son behaved with great gallantry and coolness and handled his men splendidly. I trust that your great anxiety may be allayed by definite news of his safety soon. Please accept my most heartfelt sympathy. I had a great affection for him." Kipling conducted a two year search in vain for news of his son. His grief may be reflected not only in this poem but in this couplet from a poem with many voices:

My son died laughing at some jest, I would I knew
What it were, and it might serve me at a time when jests are few.

Kipling paid a gardener employed by the War Graves Commission to sound the Last Post at the Menin Gate every night in remembrance of his son, and this ceremony continued until the Germans invaded France in 1940.

September 28

- *Francis Turner Palgrave, poet and anthologist, born September 28th 1824*
- *G. M. Hopkins wrote 'Inversnaid' September 28th 1881*
- *Poet and novelist Herman Melville died September 28th 1891*
- *Poet Stephen Spender born in London September 28th 1909*
- *T.E. Hulme killed in action at Nieuwpoort September 28th 1917*

Inversnaid

This darksome burn°, horseback brown,   *stream*
His rollrock highroad roaring down,
In coop° and in comb° the fleece of his foam   *hollow; crest*
Flutes and low to the lake falls home.

A windpuff-bonnet of fáwn-fróth
Turns and twindles over the broth
Of a pool so pitchblack, féll-frówning,
It rounds and rounds Despair to drowning.

Degged° with dew, dappled with dew   *sprinkled*
Are the groins of the braes° that the brook treads through,   *steep banks*
Wiry heathpacks°, flitches of fern,   *heather*
And the beadbonny ash that sits over the burn.

What would the world be, once bereft
Of wet and of wildness? Let them be left,
O let them be left, wildness and wet;
Long live the weeds and the wilderness yet.

Gerard Manley Hopkins
(July 28th 1844 – June 8th 1889)

Never a town lover, Hopkins's patience had been greatly tried in the summer of 1881 when an unexpected extension of his work at St Joseph's in Glasgow left him without the regenerative holiday he needed before taking up his next post near London. Instead he was given "two days to see something of the Highlands", time which, he commented, would afford him nothing more than "a glimpse of their skirts". On September 28th he headed for Inversnaid on Loch Lomond: "The day was dark and partly hid the lake, yet it did not altogether disfigure it but gave it a pensive or solemn beauty which left a deep impression on me." The poem travels the course of the stream, Arklet Water, in reverse, taking us back to its source in Loch Arklet. Inversnaid is also the scene of Wordsworth's poem 'To a Highland Girl'.

• *Miguel de Cervantes Saavedra, the Spanish novelist and poet, probably born September 29th 1547*
• *William McGonagall, "the world's worst poet", who recited in Edinburgh pubs, died September 29th 1902*
• *W. H. Auden died September 29th 1973*

From Twelve Songs
IX

Stop all the clocks, cut off the telephone,
Prevent the dog from barking with a juicy bone,
Silence the pianos and with muffled drum
Bring out the coffin, let the mourners come.

Let aeroplanes circle moaning overhead
Scribbling on the sky the message He Is Dead,
Put the crêpe bows round the white necks of the public doves,
Let the traffic policemen wear black cotton gloves.

He was my North, my South, my East and West,
My working week and my Sundays rest,
My noon, my midnight, my talk, my song;
I thought that love would last for ever: I was wrong.

The stars are not wanted now: put out every one;
Pack up the moon and dismantle the sun;
Pour away the ocean and sweep up the wood.
For nothing now can ever come to any good.

W. H. Auden
(February 21st 1907 – September 29th 1973)

According to James Fenton, the first two stanzas were used initially in Auden and Isherwood's play *The Ascent of F6*, as a pastiche blues satirising the love of a population for a political leader. The sky-writing planes were for a dead Franco or Mussolini, not for a lover. In 1936, however, whilst working with Benjamin Britten, Auden decided to use these two verses as the start of this love song.

Auden died suddenly of a heart attack on this day in 1973, in Vienna, on his way back to London from a summer spent in Austria (his life there with his companion Chester Kallman is recollected in his *About the House*, 1966). His last collection of poems, *Thank You Fog*, was published posthumously in 1974.

September 30

• Sir Fulke Greville, poet and courtier, friend of Sir Philip Sidney, and a favourite of Queen Elizabeth, was murdered by an old retainer September 30th 1628

The Road Not Taken

Two roads diverged in a yellow wood,
And sorry I could not travel both
And be one traveler, long I stood
And looked down one as far as I could
To where it bent in the undergrowth;

Then took the other, as just as fair,
And having perhaps the better claim,
Because it was grassy and wanted wear;
Though as for that, the passing there
Had worn them really about the same,

And both that morning equally lay
In leaves no step had trodden black.
Oh, I kept the first for another day!
Yet knowing how way leads on to way,
I doubted if I should ever come back.

I shall be telling this with a sigh
Somewhere ages and ages hence:
Two roads diverged in a wood, and I —
I took the one less traveled by,
And that has made all the difference.

Robert Frost
(March 26th 1874 – January 29th 1963)

'The Road Not Taken' was inspired by Frost's friend, the poet Edward Thomas, and was intended to be gently ironic of the habit of regret. Frost said of Thomas, "He more than anyone else was accessory to what I had done and was doing."

• Pierre Corneille, French dramatist, author of 'Le Cid', died October 1st
  1684
• Louis Untermeyer, anthologist, editor of A Treasury of Great Poems,
  and poet who wrote parodies, born in New York, October 1st 1885

The Metronomic Moon

In other years I would say, how pretty they are,
The cherries outside our house.
This autumn I see the first leaves
Writhe from the green into the yellow and
From the yellow into what seems a frantic red
Before they corkscrew to their conclusion
When the morning wipers scrape them from the windscreens
To drop them in the dog shit on the pavement.
Their beauty has not brought them mercy.

The cherry flaunting first and shedding fastest
Flies a few prayer flags in tatters.
When the time is ripe (soon now)
The metronomic moon on cue will let slip
The north wind to bite the branches bare and
Lay out the bony tree against the back-lit tombgrey sky.
In other years I would say, how lucky we are,
The people inside our house.
But the luck has not brought us mercy.

Michael Young
(August 9th 1915 –)

This poem was occasioned by the illness of Michael Young's second wife, Sasha Moorsom, who died
in 1994. Their poems are published by Carcanet. A social innovator, Michael Young has helped found
the Consumers' Association and *Which?* magazine, the Open University, the Institute of Community
Studies in Bethnal Green, the College of Health, the Family Covenant Association and many other
organisations. He is the author of a number of books, of which perhaps the best known are *Family and
Kinship in East London* and *The Rise of the Meritocracy*. He was created a life peer in 1973.

• *Wallace Stevens born in Reading, Pennsylvania, October 2nd 1879*
• *South African poet and journalist Roy Campbell, who fought on Franco's side in the Spanish Civil War, born October 2nd 1901*
• *Frances Horovitz died from cancer in Herefordshire October 2nd 1983*

Tea at the Palaz of Hoon

Not less because in purple I descended
The western day through what you called
The loneliest air, not less was I myself.

What was the ointment sprinkled on my beard?
What were the hymns that buzzed beside my ears?
What was the sea whose tide swept through me there?

Out of my mind the golden ointment rained,
And my ears made the blowing hymns they heard.
I was myself the compass of that sea:

I was the world in which I walked, and what I saw
Or heard or felt came not but from myself;
And there I found myself more truly and more strange.

Wallace Stevens
(October 2nd 1879 – August 2nd 1955)

A reticent man, a lawyer and businessman as well as a poet, Stevens found peace in finely-structured and oblique poetry – in what he called "venerable complication". "Poetry," he said, "is my way of making the world palatable. It's the way of making one's experience, almost wholly inexplicable, acceptable."

• *Poet and courtier Sir Fulke Greville born in Beauchamp Court, Warwickshire, October 3rd 1554*
• *Surrealist poet and writer Louis Aragon born in Paris October 3rd 1897*
• *Sir Arnold Bax (pseudonym Dermot O'Byrne), poet and composer of Celtic music, died October 3rd 1953*

Last Poems
XL

Tell me not here, it needs not saying,
   What tune the enchantress plays
In aftermaths of soft September
   Or under blanching mays,
For she and I were long acquainted
   And I knew all her ways.

On russet floors, by waters idle,
   The pine lets fall its cone;
The cuckoo shouts all day at nothing
   In leafy dells alone;
And traveller's joy beguiles in autumn
   Hearts that have lost their own.

On acres of the seeded grasses
   The changing burnish heaves;
Or marshalled under moons of harvest
   Stand still all night the sheaves;
Or beeches strip in storms for winter
   And stain the wind with leaves.

Possess, as I possessed a season,
   The countries I resign,
Where over elmy plains the highway
   Would mount the hills and shine,
And full of shade the pillared forest
   Would murmur and be mine.

For nature, heartless, witless nature,
   Will neither care nor know
What stranger's feet may find the meadow
   And trespass there and go,
Nor ask amid the dews of morning
   If they are mine or no.

A. E. Housman
(March 26th 1859 – April 30th 1936)

"I am not a poet by trade; I am a professor of Latin." There was a 36 year gap between Housman's first and second collections (*Last Poems* were this second, and, in the event, penultimate, volume). "In barrenness," Housman admitted, "I hold a high place among English poets, excelling even Gray."

October 4

• Fred E. Weatherly, who wrote the song 'Roses of Picardy', was
born October 4th 1848
• Anne Sexton committed suicide October 4th 1974
• Wordsworth married Mary Hutchinson October 4th 1802

For My Lover, Returning to his Wife

She has always been there, my darling.
She is, in fact, exquisite.
Fireworks in the dull middle of February
and as real as a cast-iron pot.

Let's face it, I have been momentary.
A luxury. A bright red sloop in the harbor.
My hair rising like smoke from the car window.
Littleneck clams out of season.

She is more than that. She is your have to have,
has grown you your practical, your tropical growth.
This is not an experiment. She is all harmony.
She sees to oars and oarlocks for the dinghy,

I give you back your heart.
I give you permission –

She is so naked and singular.
She is the sum of yourself and your dream.
Climb her like a monument, step after step.
She is solid.

As for me, I am a watercolor.
I wash off.

Anne Sexton
(November 9th 1928 – October 4th 1974)

Anne Sexton once commented that "it is said of myself that I am part of the so-called 'confessional school'. I prefer to think of myself as an imagist who deals with reality and its hard facts. I write stories about life as I see it. As one critic put it I am 'metaphor-mad' ." She was born in Newton, Massachusetts; at 20 she eloped to get married (divorcing 26 years later) and was for two years a fashion model in Boston. She started writing poetry and was a fellow student with Sylvia Plath in a Robert Lowell workshop. After the birth of her first child in 1953, she suffered a mental breakdown and was hospitalised in 1962 and in 1973, committing suicide in 1974: "the death I wanted so badly and so long".

Amongst her poetry collections were *To Bedlam and Part Way Back* (1960), *Love poems* (1969), *The Death Notebooks* (1974) and *The Awful Rowing Towards God* (1975). The biography by Diana Middlebrook (1991) includes tapes made during Sexton's psychiatric sessions.

• Critic, translator and poet John Addington Symonds born in Bristol
  October 5th 1840
• Jonathan Steffen born October 5th 1958

October 5

The Falcon to the Falconer

Unleash me from your hand
And I will lance the light for you
I'll cut a swordblade on the wind
And pennant it with flight for you
To signal I am yours
If you will free me to be true to you

Unleash me from your hand
And I will mock the sky for you
I'll pull the anger from the air
And make the breezes sigh for you
To show that I am yours
If you will free me to be true to you

Unleash me from your hand
And I will jewel it bright for you
I'll hunt the treasures of the wind
And pluck them into sight for you
To show that I am yours
If you will free me to be true to you

O, cast me from your hand
That I may show my love for you
And throw me to the wind
That I may know my need for you

All darkness on your hand
I'm hooded, pinned and held by you
O, give me back my wings
That they may bring me back to you

Jonathan Steffen
(October 5th 1958 –)

Jonathan Steffen lives in Heidelberg in Germany. This poem was published in *The Spectator* in September 1992.

October 6

- *Shakespeare's father John was appointed as a constable October 6th 1559*
- *New Zealand poet Mary Ursula Bethell born in England October 6th 1874*
- *Alfred, Lord Tennyson died October 6th 1892*
- *American poet Elizabeth Bishop died October 6th 1979*

Crossing the Bar

Sunset and evening star,
   And one clear call for me!
And may there be no moaning of the bar,
   When I put out to sea,

But such a tide as moving seems asleep,
   Too full for sound and foam,
When that which drew from out the boundless deep
   Turns again home.

Twilight and evening bell,
   And after that the dark!
And may there be no sadness of farewell,
   When I embark;

For tho' from out our bourne of Time and Place
   The flood may bear me far,
I hope to see my Pilot face to face
   When I have crost the bar.

Alfred, Lord Tennyson
(August 6th 1809 – October 6th 1892)

Tennyson's son Hallam wrote that this poem was "made in my father's eighty-first year, after his serious illness in 1888-9, on a day in October 1889, while crossing the Solent, as we came from Aldworth to Farringford. When he repeated it to me in the evening, I said, 'That is the crown of your life's work.' He answered, 'It came in a moment.' " It is claimed that the idea for this poem was "planted by his nurse, who told him to stop grumbling; she said he might better offer a hymn of praise to his God."

- *Edgar Allan Poe died October 7th 1849. Four days earlier a group of political hacks had amused themselves during an election by keeping him continuously drunk and sending him back to vote at the polls repeatedly*
- *James Whitcombe Riley, the Indiana-born 'Hoosier poet' who wrote 'Little Orfant Annie', was born October 7th 1849*
- *Black Muslim poet Amiri Baraka born as Everett LeRoi Jones in Newark October 7th 1934*

Jewels in my hand

I hold dead friends like jewels in my hand
Watching their brilliance gleam against my palm
Turquoise and emerald, jade, a golden band

All ravages of time they can withstand
Like talismans their grace keeps me from harm
I hold dead friends like jewels in my hand

I see them standing in some borderland
Their heads half-turned, waiting for my arm
Turquoise and emerald, jade, a golden band

I'm not afraid they will misundertand
My turning to them like a magic charm
I hold dead friends like jewels in my hand
Turquoise and emerald, jade, a golden band.

Sasha Moorsom
(January 25th 1931 – June 22nd 1993)

Sophie Young, Sasha's daughter, writes: "This poem was written in hospital when Sasha was first being treated for cancer, expressing the hope and comfort that is much needed at such times. She faced her illness as she had lived her life: so graceful, so dignified and so unself-concerned that it was a real honour to be in her presence. Not long before she died, she said how important it was to accept whatever happens with equanimity. And this is what she did."

October 8

• On this day in 1865 Hopkins recorded in his journal his speculations about converting to Catholicism and added that he talked "about Dr Newman at dinner etc in a foolish way likely to produce unhappiness and pain"

Heaven–Haven
A nun takes the veil

I have desired to go
　　Where springs not fail,
To fields where flies no sharp and sided hail
　　And a few lilies blow.

And I have asked to be
　　Where no storms come,
Where the green swell is in the havens dumb,
　　And out of the swing of the sea.

Gerard Manley Hopkins
(July 28th 1844 – June 8th 1889)

This poem was probably drafted in 1864 at a time when Hopkins, an undergraduate at Balliol College, Oxford, was first attracted to Catholicism and the priesthood.

• Poet and novelist Miguel de Cervantes baptised in Alcalá de Henares
  October 9th 1547
• Poet Leopold Senghor, President of Senegal, born October 9th 1906

Kind of an Ode to Duty

O Duty,
Why hast thou not the visage of a sweetie or a cutie?
Why glitter thy spectacles so ominously?
Why art thou clad so abominously?
Why art thou so different from Venus
And why do thou and I have so few interests mutually in common
  between us?
Why art thou fifty per cent martyr
And fifty-one per cent Tartar?

Why is it thy unfortunate wont
To try to attract people by calling on them either to leave undone
  the deeds they like, or to do the deeds they don't?
Why art thou so like an April post-mortem
Or something that died in the ortumn?
Above all, why dost thou continue to hound me?
Why art thou always albatrossly hanging around me?

Thou so ubiquitous,
And I so iniquitous.
I seem to be the one person in the world thou art perpetually
  preaching at who or to who;
Whatever looks like fun, there art thou standing between me and it,
  calling you-hoo.
O Duty, Duty!
How noble a man should I be hadst thou the visage of a sweetie or
  a cutie!
But as it is thou art so much forbiddinger than a Wodehouse hero's
  forbiddingest aunt
That in the words of the poet, When Duty whispers low, Thou must,
  this erstwhile youth replies, I just can't.

Ogden Nash
(August 19th 1902 – May 19th 1971)

Ogden Nash, American's most popular comic poet, described himself as a "wersifier". In the 1930s, he gave up trying to write serious verse, and settled for his own brew, where, as Archibald MacLeish remarked, "Nothing ... suggests the structure of verse but the rhymes". Nash retired from his job at the *New Yorker* to give himself more time to write, and concluded that "When I consider how my life is spent, / I hardly ever repent".

October 10

• *Donne awarded MA by Oxford University October 10th 1610*
• *Charles Madge born October 10th 1912*
• *Poet David Gascoyne born in Harrow October 10th 1916*

Solar Creation

The sun, of whose terrain we creatures are,
Is the director of all human love,
Unit of time, and circle round the earth,

And we are the commotion born of love
And slanted rays of that illustrious star,
Peregrine of the crowded fields of birth,

The crowded lane, the market and the tower.
Like sight in pictures, real at remove,
Such is our motion on dimensional earth.

Down by the river, where the ragged are,
Continuous the cries and noise of birth,
While to the muddy edge dark fishes move,

And over all, like death, or sloping hill,
Is nature, which is larger and more still.

Charles Madge
(October 10th 1912 –)

Charles Madge was born in Johannesburg and educated at Winchester and Magdalene College, Cambridge. His first wife was Kathleen Raine and his first poetry collection, in which 'Solar Creation' appeared, was *The Disappearing Castle* (1937). The 52 year gap between his second volume, *Father Found* (1941) and the third *Of Love, Time and Places* (1993) is explained in part by his work as a sociologist, founding Mass Observation in 1937 and publishing works with titles such as *Survey Before Development in Thai Villages* and *Art Students Observed*.

They Flee From Me

They flee from me that sometime did me seek
With naked foot stalking in my chamber.
I have seen them gentle, tame, and meek
That now are wild and do not remember
That sometime they put themselves in danger
To take bread at my hand; and now they range
Busily seeking with a continual change.

Thankèd be Fortune, it hath been otherwise
Twenty times better; but once in special,
In thin array after a pleasant guise,
When her loose gown from her shoulders did fall,
And she me caught in her arms long and small;
Therewith all sweetly did me kiss,
And softly said, 'Dear heart, how like you this?'

It was no dream: I lay broad waking.
But all is turnèd, thorough my gentleness,
Into a strange fashion of forsaking;
And I have leave to go of her goodness,
And she also to use newfangleness.
But since that I so kindly am servèd,
I would fain know what she hath deservèd.

Sir Thomas Wyatt
(1503 – October 11th 1542)

Wyatt was twice imprisoned during his career: in 1536, when Henry VIII executed Anne Boleyn's other lovers and merely put Wyatt in the Tower; and in 1541, for alleged treason. Nevertheless, he was despatched by the king to Falmouth on October 3rd 1542 to welcome and escort a Spanish envoy to London. "Having more regard for the royal mandate than his own health," wrote Mason, "in consequence of hard riding with a relay of horses, and the extreme heat, he was seized with a most violent fever, of which in a few days he died in the thirty-eighth year of his age." He died in Sherborne in Dorset and was buried in the great church there.

October 12

• Tennyson was buried in Westminster Abbey October 12th 1892
• Poet and translator Robert Fitzgerald born in Geneva, New York, October 12th 1920
• Sylvia Plath wrote 'Daddy' October 12th 1962

Son and Heir

He's up. And off, a tipsy
    tightrope turn
juggling with gravity.
    The ascent of man
starts here. Like one spotlit

he makes his stand
on the brink of a big-top
    drop. The ground
sways. One false step
    and . . .

Will he take it stonily
    like Sitting Bull?
Like holy Job? Or melancholy
    Charlie, fall-
guy to the old joke? Will he

heck! He's baby-bald
Khrushchev, blamming a shoe
    on the diplomatic table –
'WE WILL BURY YOU . . .'

No joke. He will.

Philip Gross
(February 27th 1952 –)

On this day in 1960 at the United Nations in New York, Khrushchev waved his shoe in the air and slammed it down on the desk, calling the Philippine delegate "this jerk, this American stooge". The sessions were eventually dissolved in chaos. Macmillan had suffered the same behaviour from Khruschchev on a previous occasion. Khrushchev remarked later: "Some people did not seem to understand this unparliamentary method."

Philip Gross comments: "When I wrote this in the mid 1980's, part of the irony was that Khrushchev was already part of history, succeeded as Soviet leader several times over. Today even the words 'Soviet' and 'Cold War' have a historical ring. And yet the world seems just as frightening a place, and much more unpredictable, for this baby (now an adolescent) to step into. You can't beat history itself for irony, however clever you try to be!"

- *Shakespeare's brother Gilbert baptised October 13th 1561*
- *Scottish poet Allan Ramsay born in Leadhills, Lanarkshire, October 13th 1686*
- *W. J. Turner born October 13th 1889*
- *Scottish poet Charles Hamilton Sorley, who spent six happy months in Germany just before the start of the war, was killed at the battle of the Loos October 13th 1915*

Romance

When I was but thirteen or so
  I went into a golden land;
Chimborazo, Cotopaxi
  Took me by the hand.

My father died, my brother too,
  They passed like fleeting dreams,
I stood where Popocatapetl
  In the sunlight gleams.

I dimly heard the master's voice
  And boys far-off at play;
Chimborazo, Cotopaxi
  Had stolen me away.

I walked in a great golden dream
  To and fro from school –
Shining Popocatapetl
  The dusty streets did rule.

I walked home with a gold dark boy
  And never a word I'd say;
Chimborazo, Cotopaxi
  Had taken my speech away:

I gazed entranced upon his face
  Fairer than any flower –
O shining Popocatapetl,
  It was thy magic hour:

The houses, people, traffic seemed
  Thin fading dreams by day;
Chimborazo, Cotopaxi,
  They had stolen my soul away!

W. J. Turner
(October 13th 1889 – November 18th 1946)

Turner was born in Melbourne, Australia, and educated there and in Munich and Vienna. His creative output included: a novel *The Duchess of Popocatapetl*, a play *The Man who ate the Popomack* and three books of poetry. He was also a drama critic, music critic and literary editor.

October 14

• e. e. cummings born in Cambridge, Massachusetts, October 14th 1894
• American critic, poet and children's writer Randall Jarrell was killed by a car whilst out walking, October 14th 1965

i thank You God for most this amazing

i thank You God for most this amazing
day:for the leaping greenly spirits of trees
and a blue true dream of sky;and for everything
which is natural which is infinite which is yes

(i who have died am alive again today,
and this is the sun's birthday; this is the birth
day of life and of love and wings:and of the gay
great happening illimitably earth)

how should tasting touching hearing seeing
breathing any – lifted from the no
of all nothing – human merely being
doubt unimaginable You?

(now the ears of my ears awake and
now the eyes of my eyes are opened)

e. e. cummings
(October 14th 1894 – September 3rd 1962)

e. e. cummings wrote to his sister Elizabeth in 1954: "if you take Someone Worth Worshipping (alias 'God') away from human beings, they'll (without realizing what they're doing) worship someone-unworthy-of-worship); e.g.; a Roosevelt or Stalin or Hitler – alias themselves."

In the Introduction to his *Collected Poems* e. e. cummings wrote (and the punctuation is his): "Life,for mostpeople,simply isn't. What do mostpeople mean by 'living'? They don't mean living. They mean the latest and closest plural approximation to singular prenatal passivity which science,in its finite but unbounded wisdom,has succeeded in selling their wives ... With you I leave a remembrance of miracles:they are by somebody who can love and who shall be continually reborn,a human being."

- Roman poet Virgil born in Andes, near Mantua, Cisalpine Gaul, October 15th 70BC
- Robert Herrick, poet and priest, died October 15th 1674
- Scottish poet William Soutar, who was handicapped with spondylitis from the age of 25, died October 15th 1943

Delight in Disorder

A sweet disorder in the dress
Kindles in clothes a wantonness:
A lawn[1] about the shoulders thrown
Into a fine distraction:
An erring lace, which here and there
Enthrals the crimson stomacher:
A cuff neglectful, and thereby
Ribbons to flow confusedly:
A winning wave, deserving note,
In the tempestuous petticoat:
A careless shoe-string, in whose tie
I see a wild civility:
Do more bewitch me than when art
Is too precise in every part.

Robert Herrick
(August 24th 1591 – October 15th 1674)

"Herrick's verse," Louis Untermeyer wrote, is "never rowdy, often lascivious, but seldom rudely lecherous." His life was of a piece with his verse, for as Herrick himself reassured the reader:

Wantons we are; and though our words be such,
Our lives do differ from our lines by much.

1. A light scarf.

• *Georg Büchner, German poet, playwright and revolutionary, the author of* Woyzeck, *born October 16th 1813*
• *Oscar Wilde born in Dublin October 16th 1854*

Bagpipe Music

It's no go the merrygoround, it's no go the rickshaw,
All we want is a limousine and a ticket for the peepshow.
Their knickers are made of crêpe-de-chine, their shoes are made of python,
Their halls are lined with tiger rugs and their walls with heads of bison.

John MacDonald found a corpse, put it under the sofa,
Waited till it came to life and hit it with a poker,
Sold its eyes for souvenirs, sold its blood for whiskey,
Kept its bones for dumb-bells to use when he was fifty.

It's no go the Yogi-Man, it's no go Blavatsky,
All we want is a bank balance and a bit of skirt in a taxi.

Annie MacDougall went to milk, caught her foot in the heather,
Woke to hear a dance record playing of Old Vienna.
It's no go your maidenheads, it's no go your culture,
All we want is a Dunlop tyre and the devil mend the puncture.

The Laird o' Phelps spent Hogmanay declaring he was sober,
Counted his feet to prove the fact and found he had one foot over.
Mrs Carmichael had her fifth, looked at the job with repulsion,
Said to the midwife 'Take it away; I'm through with over-production'.

It's no go the gossip column, it's no go the ceilidh,
All we want is a mother's help and a sugar-stick for the baby.

Willie Murray cut his thumb, couldn't count the damage,
Took the hide of an Ayrshire cow and used it for a bandage.
His brother caught three hundred cran when the seas were lavish,
Threw the bleeders back in the sea and went upon the parish.

It's no go the Herring Board, it's no go the Bible,
All we want is a packet of fags when our hands are idle.

It's no go the picture palace, it's no go the stadium,
It's no go the country cot with a pot of pink geraniums,
It's no go the Government grants, it's no go the elections,
Sit on your arse for fifty years and hang your hat on a pension.

It's no go my honey love, it's no go my poppet;
Work your hands from day to day, the winds will blow the profit.
The glass is falling hour by hour, the glass will fall for ever,
But if you break the bloody glass you won't hold up the weather.

Louis MacNeice
(September 12th 1907 – September 3rd 1963)

- *Sir Philip Sidney died October 17th 1586*
- *American feminist writer Julia Ward Howe died October 17th 1910*
- *Poet and novelist George MacKay Brown, a native of the Orkney Islands, born October 17th 1921*
- *Les A. Murray, author of the novel in verse* The Boys Who Stole the Funeral, *born in Nabiac, New South Wales, October 17th 1938*
- *'Language poet' S. J Perelman died October 17th 1979*

From The Countess of Pembroke's Arcadia

My true love hath my heart, and I have his,
By just exchange one for the other given.
I hold his dear, and mine he cannot miss:
There never was a better bargain driven.
His heart in me keeps me and him in one;
My heart in him his thoughts and senses guides;
He loves my heart, for once it was his own;
I cherish his, because in me it bides.
His heart his wound receivèd from my sight;
My heart was wounded with his wounded heart;
For as from me on him his hurt did light,
So still, methought, in me his hurt did smart;
　　Both equal hurt, in this change sought our bliss:
　　My true love hath my heart, and I have his.

Sir Philip Sidney
(November 30th 1554 – October 17th 1586)

Immoderately favoured with high birth, influence, charm and success, Sidney is remembered as a paragon of nobility – an extreme example of his behaviour came during an attack on Spanish forces at Zutphen. He is reported to have left his thigh armour off so as not to be better protected than his subordinates. The musket ball wound which ensued quickly became infected and he died within three weeks. As he was being carried from the battlefield, he refused a cup of water, preferring to give it to a dying soldier with the words: "Thy necessity is yet greater than mine."

October 18

• Poet and novelist Thomas Love Peacock, who wrote caricatures of
the Romantic poets, was born in Weymouth October 18th 1785
• William Blake's wife Catherine died October 18th 1831 [1]

Eternity

He who binds to himself a joy
Does the wingèd life destroy;
But he who kisses the joy as it flies
Lives in eternity's sun rise.

William Blake
(November 28th 1757 – August 12th 1827)

Blake believed that a bigger force than himself worked through him. He held the pen, the graver or the brush. He was its agent, never its master, the possessed rather than the possessor.

1. On October 18th 1831, four years after her husband's death, Catherine Blake died at 17 Upper Charlotte Street, Fitzroy Square. In this last home, a contemporary report states, she called "continually to her William, as if he were in the next room, to say she was coming to him and would not be long now".

Abou Ben Adhem

Abou Ben Adhem (may his tribe increase!)
Awoke one night from a deep dream of peace,
And saw, within the moonlight in his room,
Making it rich, and like a lily in bloom,
An angel writing in a book of gold:—
Exceeding peace had made Ben Adhem bold,
And to the presence in the room he said,
'What writest thou?' The vision raised its head,
And with a look made of all sweet accord,
Answered, 'The names of those who love the Lord.'
'And is mine one?' said Abou. 'Nay, not so,'
Replied the angel. Abou spoke more low,
But cheerly still; and said, 'I pray thee, then,
Write me as one that loves his fellow men.'
The angel wrote, and vanished. The next night
It came again with a great wakening light,
And showed the names whom love of God had blest,
And lo! Ben Adhem's name led all the rest.

Leigh Hunt
(October 19th 1784 – August 28th 1859)

Leigh Hunt was born in Southgate, the son of a poor immigrant American preacher. He became a great editor and encourager of talent – helping Keats, Tennyson, Shelley, Byron and others. Imprisoned for two years (1813-1815) for libelling the Prince Regent, he was visited in jail by Bentham and Byron. Dickens caricatured his sunny optimism in the early character of Harold Skimpole in *Bleak House*.

'Abou Ben Adhem' appeared in an anthology, the *Book of Gems*, in 1838. Hunt was proud of this poem, admitting that he was "not unwilling to be judged by 'Ben Adhem' ... and by one or two others of the smallest pieces".

October 20

• Shakespeare's father, John, applied for a coat of arms October
  20th 1596
• Arthur Rimbaud born in Charleville October 20th 1854
• Alfred Lord Tennyson wrote 'Ulysses' October 20th 1833
• Poet Andrew Motion born in London October 20th 1952

Ulysses

It little profits that an idle king,
By this still hearth, among these barren crags,
Match'd with an aged wife, I mete and dole
Unequal laws unto a savage race,
That hoard, and sleep, and feed, and know not me.
I cannot rest from travel; I will drink
Life to the lees. All times I have enjoy'd
Greatly, have suffer'd greatly, both with those
That loved me, and alone; on shore, and when
Thro' scudding drifts the rainy Hyades
Vext the dim sea. I am become a name;
For always roaming with a hungry heart
Much have I seen and known—cities of men
And manners, climates, councils, governments,
Myself not least, but honour'd of them all—
And drunk delight of battle with my peers,
Far on the ringing plains of windy Troy.
I am a part of all that I have met;
Yet all experience is an arch wherethrough
Gleams that untraveled world, whose margin fades
For ever and for ever when I move.
How dull it is to pause, to make an end,
To rust unburnished, not to shine in use!
As tho' to breathe were life! Life piled on life
Were all too little, and of one to me
Little remains: but every hour is saved
From that eternal silence, something more,
A bringer of new things; and vile it were
For some three suns to store and hoard myself,
And this gray spirit yearning in desire
To follow knowledge like a sinking star,
Beyond the utmost bound of human thought.
    This is my son, mine own Telemachus
To whom I leave the sceptre and the isle—
Well-loved of me, discerning to fulfil
This labour, by slow prudence to make mild
A rugged people, and through soft degrees
Subdue them to the useful and the good.
Most blameless is he, centred in the sphere

[Continued]

Of common duties, decent not to fail
In offices of tenderness, and pay
Meet adoration to my household gods,
When I am gone. He works his work, I mine.
    There lies the port; the vessel puffs her sail;
There gloom the dark broad seas. My mariners,
Souls that have toiled, and wrought, and thought with me,
That ever with a frolic welcome took
The thunder and the sunshine, and opposed
Free hearts, free foreheads—you and I are old;
Old age hath yet his honour and his toil.
Death closes all; but something ere the end,
Some work of noble note, may yet be done,
Not unbecoming men that strove with gods.
The lights begin to twinkle from the rocks;
The long day wanes; the slow moon climbs; the deep
Moans round with many voices. Come, my friends,
'Tis not too late to seek a newer world.
Push off, and sitting well in order smite
The sounding furrows; for my purpose holds
To sail beyond the sunset, and the baths
Of all the western stars, until I die.
It may be that the gulfs will wash us down;
It may be we shall touch the Happy Isles,
And see the great Achilles, whom we knew.
Though much is taken, much abides; and though
We are not now that strength which in old days
Moved earth and heaven; that which we are, we are;
One equal temper of heroic hearts,
Made weak by time and fate, but strong in will
To strive, to seek, to find, and not to yield.

Alfred, Lord Tennyson
(August 6th 1809 – October 6th 1892)

Written less than three weeks after Tennyson received the painful news of the death of Arthur Hallam,
'Ulysses' is, according to the poet, a more immediate outpouring of grief for his friend than *In Memoriam*:
"There is more about myself in 'Ulysses' ... It was more written with the feeling of his loss upon me
than many poems in *In Memoriam*" ... "It gives the feeling about the need of going forward and braving
the struggle of life." Sir Robert Peel, on reading this poem, decided to give Tennyson a pension of £200
a year.

October 21

• Poet and politician Edmund Waller born in Coleshill October 21st 1687
• Samuel Taylor Coleridge born in Devon October 21st 1772
• Gerard Manley Hopkins received into Catholic Church by Henry Newman October 21st 1886
• Patrick Kavanagh born in Inniskeen October 21st 1904
• SF writer and poet Ursula Le Guin born in Berkeley October 21st 1929
• Writer and poet Maureen Duffy born October 21st 1933

Kubla Khan
Or, A Vision in a Dream. A Fragment

In Xanadu did Kubla Khan
A stately pleasure-dome decree:
Where Alph, the sacred river, ran
Through caverns measureless to man
  Down to a sunless sea.
So twice five miles of fertile ground
With walls and towers were girdled round:
And here were gardens bright with sinuous rills,
Where blossomed many an incense-bearing tree;
And here were forests ancient as the hills,
Enfolding sunny spots of greenery.

But oh! that deep romantic chasm which slanted
Down the green hill athwart a cedarn cover!
A savage place! as holy and enchanted
As e'er beneath a waning moon was haunted
By woman wailing for her demon-lover!
And from this chasm, with ceaseless turmoil seething
As if this earth in fast thick pants were breathing,
A mighty fountain momently was forced:
Amid whose swift half-intermitted burst
Huge fragments vaulted like rebounding hail
Or chaffy grain beneath the thresher's flail:
And 'mid these dancing rocks at once and ever
It flung up momently the sacred river.
Five miles meandering with a mazy motion
Through wood and dale the sacred river ran,
Then reached the caverns measureless to man,
And sank in tumult to a lifeless ocean:
And 'mid this tumult Kubla heard from far
Ancestral voices prophesying war!

  The shadow of the dome of pleasure
  Floated midway on the waves;
  Where was heard the mingled measure
  From the fountain and the caves.
It was a miracle of rare device,
A sunny pleasure-dome with caves of ice!

[Continued]

A damsel with a dulcimer
In a vision once I saw:
It was an Abyssinian maid,
And on her dulcimer she played,
Singing of Mount Abora.
Could I revive within me
Her symphony and song,
To such a deep delight 'twould win me,
That with music loud and long,
I would build that dome in air,
That sunny dome! those caves of ice!
And all who heard should see them there,
And all should cry, Beware! Beware!
His flashing eyes, his floating hair!
Weave a circle round him thrice,
And close your eyes with holy dread,
For he on honey-dew hath fed,
And drunk the milk of Paradise.

Samuel Taylor Coleridge
(October 21st 1772 – July 25th 1834)

From Coleridge's preface to this poem: ·
"In the summer of the year [1798], the Author, then in ill health, had retired to a lonely farm-house between Porlock and Linton, on the Exmoor confines of Somerset and Devonshire. In consequence of a light indisposition, an anodyne had been prescribed [two grains of opium], from the effects of which he fell asleep in his chair at the moment when he was reading the following sentence, or words of the same substance, in 'Purchas's Pilgrimage': 'Here the Khan Kubla commanded a palace to be built, and a stately garden thereunto. And thus ten miles of fertile ground were inclosed with a wall.' The Author continued for about three hours in a profound sleep, at least of the external senses, during which time he has the most vivid confidence, that he could not have composed less than from two to three hundred lines; if that indeed can be called composition in which all the images rose up before him as *things*, with a parallel production of the correspondent expressions, without any sensation or consciousness of effort. On awaking he appeared to himself to have a distinct recollection of the whole, and taking his pen, ink, and paper, instantly and eagerly wrote down the lines that are here preserved. At this moment he was unfortunately called out by a person on business from Porlock, and detained by him above an hour, and on his return to his room, found, to his no small surprise and mortification, that though he still retained some vague and dim recollection of the general purport of the vision, yet, with the exception of eight or ten scattered lines and images, all the rest had passed away like the images on the surface of a stream into which a stone has been cast, but, alas! without the after restoration of the latter!"

October 22

• The poet Lord Alfred Douglas (whom Oscar Wilde failed in court to establish as a platonic friend) born October 22nd 1870
• Timothy Leary born in West Point, New York, October 22nd 1920. He was expelled from West Point military academy, expelled from a Harvard professorship, imprisoned, escaped, and 'kidnapped' by Eldridge Cleaver in Algeria and by the CIA in Afghanistan. His autobiography is entitled Flashbacks.

All Things Pass

All things pass
A sunrise does not last all morning
All things pass
A cloudburst does not last all day
All things pass
Nor a sunset all night
All things pass
What always changes?

Earth . . . sky . . . thunder . . .
    mountain . . . water . . .
    wind . . . fire . . . lake . . .

These change
And if these do not last

Do man's visions last?
Do man's illusions?

Take things as they come

All things pass

Lao-Tzu
(6th century BC)
from translations adapted by Timothy
Leary
(October 22nd 1920 – May 31st 1996)

This version appears in Leary's *Psychedelic Prayers* (Academy Editions, London 1972). Leary had half a dozen English translations to work from. In the foreword, he writes that "these translations from English to psychedelese were made while sitting under a bamboo tree on a grassy slope of the Kumaon Hills overlooking the snow peaks of the Himalayas ... The first draft version would then be put under the psychedelic microscope. For several years I have pursued the yoga of one LSD session every seven days ... When you are in a psychedelic state—out beyond symbols—game communication seems pointless ... But there are those transition moments of terror, of isolation, of reverence, of gratitude ... when there comes that need to communicate ...

At that time you must be ready to pray
When you have lost the need to pray ...
You are a dead man in a world of dead symbols.
Pray for life.
Pray for life."

• *Poet Laureate Robert Bridges, who befriended Hopkins, born in Walmer, October 23rd 1844*
• *Douglas Dunn born in Renfrewshire October 23rd 1942*
• *Pasternak awarded Nobel prize for literature October 23rd 1958*
• *Gavin Ewart died October 23rd 1995*

The Sun Rising

Busy old fool, unruly Sun,
Why dost thou thus,
Through windows, and through curtains, call on us?
Must to thy motions lovers' seasons run?
Saucy pedantic wretch, go chide
Late school-boys and sour prentices°,   *apprentices*
Go tell court-huntsmen that the king will ride,
Call country ants to harvest offices°;   *duties*
Love, all alike, no season knows nor clime,
Nor hours, days, months, which are the rags of time.

Thy beams so reverend and strong
Why should'st thou think?
I could eclipse and cloud them with a wink,
But that I would not lose her sight so long.
If her eyes have not blinded thine,
Look, and to-morrow late tell me,
Whether both th' Indias of spice and mine
Be where thou left'st them, or lie here with me.
Ask for those kings whom thou saw'st yesterday
And thou shalt hear, 'All here in one bed lay.'

She's all states, and all princes I:
Nothing else is;
Princes do but play us; compared to this,
All honour's mimic°, all wealth alchemy°.   *fake; a fraud*
Thou, Sun, art half as happy as we,
In that the world's contracted thus;
Thine age asks ease, and since thy duties be
To warm the world, that's done by warming us.
Shine here to us, and thou art everywhere;
This bed thy centre is, these walls thy sphere.

John Donne
(c. June 1572 – March 31st 1631)

On this day in 1584, Donne was admitted to Hart Hall, Oxford University, aged 12, which was exceptionally young even for the time. In his twenties, Donne enjoyed independence of means, popularity at court and a degree of sexual promiscuity, reflected in his early lyrics. Jonson told Drummond that after 1615 Donne "repented highly, and sought to destroy all his poems".

October 24

• Poet and anthologist Francis Turner Palgrave died October 24th 1897
• Denise Levertov born October 24th 1923
• Poet, translator and novelist Elaine Feinstein born in Bootle October 24th 1930
• Adrian Mitchell, who wrote 'The Oxford Hysteria of English Poetry', born in London October 24th 1932

From Matins

V

Stir the holy grains, set
the bowls on the table and
call the child to eat.

While we eat we think,
as we think an undercurrent
of dream runs through us
faster than thought
towards recognition.

Call the child to eat,
send him off, his mouth
tasting of toothpaste, to go down
into the ground, into a roaring train
and to school.

His cheeks are pink
his black eyes hold his dreams, he has left
forgetting his glasses.

Follow down the stairs at a clatter
to give them to him and save
his clear sight.

Cold air
comes in at the street door.

Denise Levertov
(October 24th 1923 –)

Denise Levertov writes: "That same child, Nikolai Goodman, when he had grown up, suffered a catastrophic illness – a near-lethal tumor, from which however he slowly recovered. Today he is a visual artist and (so far unpublished) writer. The poem was written in New York City when he was about 10. Incidentally, he only needed to wear glasses for about a year ..."

- *Geoffrey Chaucer died October 25th 1400. He was the first poet to be honoured by burial in Westminster Abbey*
- *Shelley wrote 'Ode to the West Wind' in Florence on October 25th 1811*
- *The ill-fated Charge of the Light Brigade took place on October 25th 1844. (See December 2nd in this book, the date that Tennyson composed his poem about the event)*
- *John Berryman born John Smith in Oklahoma October 25th 1914*

From The Princess
Tears, Idle Tears

Tears, idle tears, I know not what they mean,
Tears from the depth of some divine despair
Rise in the heart, and gather to the eyes,
In looking on the happy autumn-fields,
And thinking of the days that are no more.

Fresh as the first beam glittering on a sail,
That brings our friends up from the underworld,
Sad as the last which reddens over one
That sinks with all we love below the verge;
So sad, so fresh, the days that are no more.

Ah, sad and strange as in dark summer dawns
The earliest pipe of half-awakened birds
To dying ears, when unto dying eyes
The casement slowly grows a glimmering square;
So sad, so strange, the days that are no more.

Dear as remembered kisses after death,
And sweet as those by hopeless fancy feigned
On lips that are for others; deep as love,
Deep as first love, and wild with all regret;
O Death in Life, the days that are no more!

Alfred, Lord Tennyson
(August 6th 1809 – October 6th 1892)

Tennyson wrote: "This song came to me on the yellowing autumn-tide [of October 1834, in the Wye Valley] at Tintern Abbey, full for me of its bygone memories. It is the sense of the abiding in the transient ... It is what as a boy I called the 'passion of the past'. And it is so always with me now; it is the distance that charms me in the landscape, the picture and the past, and not the immediate to-day in which I move."

October 26

• Baroness Carolina Nairne, Jacobite songwriter ('Charlie is my darling') died October 26th 1845

O Western Wind

O western wind, when wilt thou blow
    That the small rain down can rain?
Christ, if my love were in my arms,
    And I in my bed again.

Anonymous
(early 16th century)

On this day in 1529, Henry VIII appointed Sir Thomas More, the poet and author of *Utopia*, as his Lord Chancellor, against More's strongest wish. Henry VIII had him beheaded six years later.

• Poet George Barker died October 27th 1913
• Dylan Thomas born in Swansea October 27th 1914
• Poet Sylvia Plath born in Boston October 27th 1932
• Pasternak expelled from Union of Soviet Writers October 27th 1958

The Force that Through the Green Fuse Drives the Flower

The force that through the green fuse drives the flower
Drives my green age; that blasts the roots of trees
Is my destroyer.
And I am dumb to tell the crooked rose
My youth is bent by the same wintry fever.

The force that drives the water through the rocks
Drives my red blood; that dries the mouthing streams
Turns mine to wax.
And I am dumb to mouth unto my veins
How at the mountain spring the same mouth sucks.

The hand that whirls the water in the pool
Stirs the quicksand; that ropes the blowing wind
Hauls my shroud sail.
And I am dumb to tell the hanging man
How of my clay is made the hangman's lime.

The lips of time leech to the fountain head;
Love drips and gathers, but the fallen blood
Shall calm her sores.
And I am dumb to tell a weather's wind
How time has ticked a heaven round the stars.

And I am dumb to tell my lover's tomb
How at my sheet goes the same crooked worm.

Dylan Thomas
(October 27th 1914 – November 9th 1953)

Dylan Thomas was born in Swansea, though both his parents came from rural Carmarthenshire. His father had worked on the Great Western Railway and had himself written poetry as a young man. Dylan attended Swansea Grammar School where his father was a teacher.

Dylan Thomas wrote this poem when he was 19, wishing to demonstrate "that the blood in my lungs is the blood that goes up and down in a tree". It was published the next year in *18 Poems*, a collection that established his reputation.

October 28

• Ella Wheeler Wilcox, American journalist and author of Poems of Passion, died October 28th 1919
• 'Concrete poet' Ian Hamilton Finlay born October 28th 1925

When You Are Old

When you are old and gray and full of sleep
   And nodding by the fire, take down this book,
   And slowly read, and dream of the soft look
Your eyes had once, and of their shadows deep;

How many loved your moments of glad grace,
   And loved your beauty with love false or true;
   But one man loved the pilgrim soul in you,
And loved the sorrows of your changing face.

And bending down beside the glowing bars,
   Murmur, a little sadly, how love fled
   And paced upon the mountains overhead,
And hid his face amid a crowd of stars.

William Butler Yeats
(June 13th 1865 – January 28th 1939)
based on a French sonnet by Pierre De Ronsard
(September 11th 1524 – December 27th 1585)

This poem was written for the beautiful Irish revolutionary Maud Gonne in October 1891. Both Maud Gonne and later her daughter Iseult turned down offers of marriage from Yeats. The poem is based on Ronsard's sonnet "Quand vous serez bien vielle" in which an old woman by the graveside regrets her proud refusal of the poet's love.

- *Sir Walter Raleigh executed October 29th 1618. Facing death he is reported to have said of the axe, "This is sharp medicine, but it is a sure cure for all diseases"*
- *Shelley wrote to Marianne Hunt on October 29th 1820 from Pisa: "Where is Keats now? I am anxiously expecting him in Italy … I intend to be the physician both of his body and his soul … I am nourishing a rival who will far surpass me"*
- *Polish poet Zbigniew Herbert born in Lvov October 29th 1924*
- *Sylvia Plath completed 'Lazarus' October 29th 1962*

Sonnet 73

That time of year thou mayst in me behold,
When yellow leaves, or none, or few do hang
Upon those boughs which shake against the cold,
Bare ruin'd choirs, where late the sweet birds sang.
In me thou see'st the twilight of such day,
As after sunset fadeth in the west,
Which by and by black night doth take away,
Death's second self that seals up all in rest.
In me thou see'st the glowing of such fire,
That on the ashes of his youth doth lie,
As the death bed, whereon it must expire,
Consum'd with that which it was nourish'd by.
　　This thou perceiv'st, which makes thy love more strong,
　　To love that well, which thou must leave ere long.

William Shakespeare
(April 23rd 1564 – April 23rd 1616)

One of Shakespeare's editors has suggested that "to love that well" in the last line of this sonnet refers to loving not only the poet but the beholder's own youth.

October 30

• Adelaide Anne Procter, whose sentimental poetic works carried a foreword by Dickens, was born October 30th 1825
• French poet and writer Paul Valéry born in Sète, near Montpellier, October 30th 1871
• Poet and critic Ezra Pound born in Hailey, Idaho, October 30th 1885

Ancient Music

Winter is icummen in,
Lhude sing Goddamm,
Raineth drop and staineth slop,
And how the wind doth ramm!
                    Sing: Goddamm.
Skiddeth bus and sloppeth us,
An ague hath my ham.
Freezeth river, turneth liver,
                    Damn you, sing: Goddamm.
Goddamm, Goddamm, 'tis why I am, Goddamm,
                    So 'gainst the winter's balm.
Sing goddamm, damm, sing Goddamm,
Sing goddamm, sing goddamm, DAMM.

Ezra Pound
(October 30th 1885 – November 1st 1972)

Renowned both for his arrogance and his erudition, Pound irritated some and stimulated others in roughly equal measure. He was a great influence on Yeats, his senior by twenty years, he championed the writing of avant-garde modernists such as James Joyce, and T. S. Eliot credited him with being "more responsible for the 20th Century revolution in poetry than any other individual". His literary reputation suffered from being overshadowed by his identification with Italian fascism during the Second World War, and, as T. S. Eliot put it, from being seen as at once "objectionably modern" *and* "objectionably antiquarian".

October 31

On First Looking into Chapman's Homer [1]

Much have I travelled in the realms of gold,
  And many goodly states and kingdoms seen;
  Round many western islands have I been
Which bards in fealty° to Apollo hold.   *allegiance*
Oft of one wide expanse had I been told
  That deep-browed Homer ruled as his demesne°;   *domain*
  Yet did I never breathe its pure serene°   *atmosphere*
Till I heard Chapman speak out loud and bold:
Then felt I like some watcher of the skies
  When a new planet swims into his ken;
Or like stout Cortez when with eagle eyes
  He stared at the Pacific—and all his men
Looked at each other with a wild surmise—
  Silent, upon a peak in Darien.

John Keats
(October 31st 1795 – February 23rd 1821)

Keats was the oldest son of a livery stables manager. His father died in a fall from a horse when Keats was eight, and his mother of tuberculosis when he was 14. Apprenticed to an Edmonton surgeon, Keats cancelled his apprenticeship at 19 and moved to London.

This sonnet was written in October 1816, after a night spent reading aloud translations from Homer with his old school friend Cowden-Clarke. At daybreak, Keats parted from Clarke and walked over London Bridge back to Dean Street, and at once wrote this sonnet. They parted, said Clarke, "at daystring, yet he contrived that I should receive the poem from a distance of, may be, two miles by ten o'clock". In 1816 Leigh Hunt included this sonnet in a survey of young poets in *The Examiner*, and Hunt introduced Keats to Shelley, Coleridge and Wordsworth.

1. Translations from Homer by George Chapman (? 1559 – 1634) completed in 1616.

November 1

• William Whiting, hymn-writer ("Eternal father, strong to save ...") was born November 1st 1825
• Stephen Crane born November 1st 1871
• Edmund Blunden born November 1st 1896
• Naomi Mitchison born November 1st 1897
• Ezra Pound died November 1st 1972

From The Tempest
Act IV Scene i

Prospero. Be cheerful, sir:
Our revels now are ended. These our actors,
As I foretold you, were all spirits and
Are melted into air, into thin air:
And, like the baseless fabric of this vision,
The cloud-capp'd towers, the gorgeous palaces,
The solemn temples, the great globe itself,
Yea, all which it inherit[1], shall dissolve
And, like this insubstantial pageant faded,
Leave not a rack[2] behind. We are such stuff
As dreams are made on, and our little life
Is rounded with a sleep.

William Shakespeare
(April 23rd 1564 – April 23rd 1616)

The first mention of *The Tempest* is in the royal Account Books of the Revels Office: On Hallowmass night, November 1st 1611, "a play called the Tempest" was performed before that most cultured of kings, James I.

W. Raleigh commented in his book *Shakespeare* (1907) that "*The Tempest* was probably his last play— in the sense, at least, that he designed it for his farewell to the stage. The thought which occurs at once to almost every reader of the play, that Prospero resembles Shakespeare himself, can hardly have been absent from the mind of the author ... In all the work of Shakespeare there is nothing more like himself than those quiet words of parting—'Be cheerful, sir: our revels now are ended.' "

1. ie. occupy it.
2. cloud.

• Greek Nobel prize-winning poet Odysseus Elytis, author of The
  Axion Esti, born October 2nd 1911
• Émile Cammaerts, a Belgian poet who settled in England, died
  November 2nd 1953

From A Shropshire Lad
xxxi

On Wenlock Edge[1] the wood's in trouble;
  His forest fleece the Wrekin[2] heaves;
The gale, it plies the saplings double,
  And thick on Severn snow the leaves.

'Twould blow like this through holt and hanger[3]
  When Uricon[4] the city stood:
'Tis the old wind in the old anger,
  But then it threshed another wood.

Then, 'twas before my time, the Roman
  At yonder heaving hill would stare:
The blood that warms an English yeoman,
  The thoughts that hurt him, they were there.

There, like the wind through woods in riot,
  Through him the gale of life blew high;
The tree of man was never quiet:
  Then 'twas the Roman, now 'tis I.

The gale, it plies the saplings double,
  It blows so hard, 'twill soon be gone:
To-day the Roman and his trouble
  Are ashes under Uricon.

A. E. Housman
(March 26th 1859 – April 30th 1936)

This poem was first drafted in November 1895. In 1934 Housman wrote: "I am Worcestershire by birth:
Shropshire was our western horizon, which made me feel romantic about it. I do not know the county well,
except in parts, and some of my topographical details are wrong and imaginary. The Wrekin is wooded, and
Wenlock Edge along the western side."

1. A range of hills in Shropshire.
2. A prominent hill in Shropshire, to the East of Shrewsbury.
3. 'Holt and hanger' are 'wood and wooded slope'.
4. Uriconium – a Roman town which stood on the site of the modern town of Wroxeter in Shropshire.

November 3

• American poet and journalist *William Cullen Bryant* born in Cummington, Massachusetts, November 3rd 1794
• *Oodgeroo of the Noonuccal* born November 3rd 1920

Song

Life is ours in vain
Lacking love, which never
Counts the loss or gain.
But remember, ever
Love is linked with pain.

Light and sister shade
Shape each mortal morrow
Seek not to evade
Love's companion, Sorrow,
and be not dismayed.

Grief is not in vain,
It's for our completeness.
If the fates ordain
Love to bring life's sweetness
Welcome too its pain.

Oodgeroo of the Noonuccal
(November 3rd 1920 – September 16th 1993)

Oodgeroo of the Noonuccal was born on North Stradbroke Island, Queensland, Australia, and described her Aboriginal Noonuccal tribe heritage in the autobiographical *Stradbroke Dreaming* (1970). Her first poetry collection *We Are Going* (1964) has been a best-seller in Australia. Her other publications include *The Dawn is at Hand* (1966), *My People* (1970) and *Quandamooka: The Art of Kath Walker* (1985). She changed her name from Kath Walker in 1988 in protest at the bicentennial year of the European invasion. As Kath Walker, she had been awarded the MBE in 1971 for services to her people.

- *Augustus Montague Toplady, who wrote the hymn 'Rock of Ages', was born November 4th 1740*
- *Scottish poet James Montgomery, twice jailed for seditious behaviour, born in Irvine November 4th 1771*
- *Wilfred Owen killed in action November 4th 1918*
- *Poet Patricia Beer born in Exmouth into a Plymouth Brethren family November 4th 1924*

Greater Love

Red lips are not so red
  As the stained stones kissed by the English dead.
Kindness of wooed and wooer
Seems shame to their love pure.
O Love, your eyes lose lure
  When I behold eyes blinded in my stead!

Your slender attitude
  Trembles not exquisite like limbs knife-skewed,
Rolling and rolling there
Where God seems not to care;
Till the fierce Love they bear
  Cramps them in death's extreme decrepitude.

Your voice sings not so soft,—
  Though even as wind murmuring through raftered loft,—
Your dear voice is not dear,
Gentle, and evening clear,
As theirs whom none now hear,
  Now earth has stopped their piteous mouths that coughed.

Heart, you were never hot,
  Nor large, nor full like hearts made great with shot;
And though your hand be pale,
Paler are all which trail
Your cross through flame and hail:
  Weep, you may weep, for you may touch them not.

Wilfred Owen
(March 18th 1893 – November 4th 1918)

Owen here is reacting to a Swinburne poem about a beautiful woman looking into a mirror which begins "White rose in red rose-garden / Is not so white ...".

Owen died in an assault over the Sambre and Oise canal, near Cambrai in north-east France. His biographer Jon Stallworthy writes that "he was at the water's edge, giving a hand with some duckboards, when he was hit and killed. In Shrewsbury, the Armistice bells were ringing when the Owen's front door bell sounded its small chime, heralding the telegram that [they] had dreaded for two years."

November 5

• The American poet Ella Wheeler Wilcox ("Laugh and the world laughs with you ...") was born November 1st 1856
• Poet James Elroy Flecker born in Lewisham November 5th 1884
• Art critic, novelist and poet John Berger, who gave half his Booker Prize winnings to the Black Panthers, was born in London November 5th 1926

From The Princess

The splendour falls on castle walls
    And snowy summits old in story:
The long light shakes across the lakes,
    And the wild cataract leaps in glory.
Blow, bugle, blow, set the wild echoes flying,
Blow, bugle; answer, echoes, dying, dying, dying.

    O hark, O hear! how thin and clear,
        And thinner, clearer, farther going!
    O sweet and far from cliff and scar
        The horns of Elfland faintly blowing!
Blow, let us hear the purple glens replying:
Blow, bugle; answer, echoes, dying, dying, dying.

    O love, they die in yon rich sky,
        They faint on hill or field or river:
    Our echoes roll from soul to soul,
        And grow for ever and for ever.
Blow, bugle, blow, set the wild echoes flying,
And answer, echoes, answer, dying, dying, dying.

Alfred, Lord Tennyson
(August 6th 1809 – October 6th 1892)

On this day in 1850, Tennyson was offered the honour of becoming Poet Laureate (after it had been declined by Samuel Rogers). Tennyson accepted, as long as he was not required to write birthday odes. Of this song Tennyson noted that it was "written after hearing the echoes at Killarney in 1848. When I was there I heard a bugle blown beneath the 'Eagle's Nest', and eight distinct echoes."

• *Poet Laureate Colley Cibber, actor, playwright and manager at the Theatre Royal, born in London November 6th 1671*

Egyptian Poem

Death is before me to-day,
Like the recovery of a sick man,
Like going forth into a garden after sickness;
Death is before me to-day,
Like the odour of myrrh,
Like sitting under the sail on a windy day;

Death is before me to-day,
Like the odour of lotus flowers,
Like sitting on the shore of drunkenness;
Death is before me to-day,
Like the course of the freshet,
Like the return of a man from the war-galley to his house,
When he has spent years in captivity.

Anonymous

On this day in 1956, the United States backed the United Nations in its condemnation of the British bombing of Egyptian airfields and bases and its airborne assault on Port Said.
Aldous Huxley selected this 'Egyptian Poem' as one of his favourite poems on death and dying for his anthology *Texts and Pretexts* (1932).

November 7

• Poet Ruth Pitter, whose collections include A Mad Lady's Garland (with an introduction by Belloc), The Rude Potato (she was an enthusiastic gardener) and The Ermine, born in Ilford November 7th 1897

The Great Day

Hurrah for revolution and more cannon-shot!
A beggar upon horseback lashes a beggar on foot.
Hurrah for revolution and cannon come again!
The beggars have changed places, but the lash goes on.

William Butler Yeats
(June 13th 1865 – January 28th 1939)

On this day in 1793, at the height of the period of Terror in Paris, with Christianity under attack and Notre Dame turned into a Temple of Reason, the Bishop of Paris was forced to resign and to announce that in future "there should be no other public cult than liberty and equality". 25,000 people were guillotined in France during these years, in the name of liberty and equality.

On this day in 1917 (October 25th Old Style), the Bolshevik Red Guards staged a coup, storming the Winter palace and ousting Kerensky's cabinet.

Yeats himself was vigilant in defence of human rights and liberties under the new Irish Free State. In a speech to the Senate in 1925 he said: "I think it tragic that within three years of this country gaining its independence, we should be discussing a measure [on divorce] which the [Protestant] minority considers grossly oppressive".

• *John Milton died between November 8th and 10th 1674*
• *Dermot O'Byrne (pseudonym of Sir Arnold Bax) poet and composer of Celtic songs, born November 8th 1883*
• *Journalist and poet G. S. Fraser, friend of Lawrence Durrell, born in Glasgow November 8th 1915. His memoirs are entitled* A Stranger and Afraid.

Sonnet xix
On His Blindness

When I consider how my light is spent
Ere half my days in this dark world and wide,
And that one talent which is death to hide
Lodged with me useless, though my soul more bent
To serve therewith my Maker, and present
My true account, lest He returning chide;
'Doth God exact day-labour, light denied?'
I fondly ask. But Patience, to prevent
That murmur, soon replies, 'God doth not need
Either man's work or his own gifts. Who best
Bear his mild yoke, they serve him best. His state
Is kingly: thousands at his bidding speed,
And post o'er land and ocean without rest;
They also serve who only stand and wait.'

John Milton
(December 9th 1608 – c. November 8th 1674)

By 1651 Milton was totally blind. He believed that his blindness had been brought on by his labours in writing treatises such as *Aereopagitica*, his defence of freedom of the press and his *Defence of the English People*. As he put in it Sonnet xxii 'To Cyrick Skinner', he lost his eyes "overplied / In liberty's defence, my noble task, / Of which all Europe talks from side to side". This Sonnet xix was only given the title 'On His Blindness' in 1752. It is probably as much concerned with Milton's feeling that his prose works had caused him to neglect his true talent for poetry.

Louis Untermeyer recounts how his older daughters, Anne and Mary, rebelled against the drudgery of reading aloud to their blind father, cheated him, and disposed of many of his books: "When Milton, at fifty-four, married his third wife, Elizabeth Minshull, twenty-four, Mary remarked that a wedding was no news, but 'if she could hear of his death that would be something' ... In his old age, the disappointed poet, 'on evil days fallen and evil tongues', made a kind of peace with the world and himself. He refused to argue; he declined to attend church and permitted no religious observances in his home ... At sixty-six he died 'in a fit of gout, long troubled with the disease'." His death was so peaceful "that the time of his expiring was not perceived by those in the room".

November 9

• Harriet Westbrook, Shelley's abandoned first wife, drowned herself
  in the Serpentine in London on November 9th 1816. She had
  two children by Shelley and was pregnant by another man
• French poet Guillaume Apollinaire died November 9th 1918
• Poet and novelist James Schuyler born in Chicago November 9th
  1923
• Poet Anne Sexton born in Newton November 9th 1928
• Dylan Thomas died November 9th 1953
• Liverpool poet Roger McGough born November 9th 1954

And Death Shall Have No Dominion

And death shall have no dominion.
Dead men naked they shall be one
With the man in the wind and the west moon;
When their bones are picked clean and the clean bones gone,
They shall have stars at elbow and foot;
Though they go mad they shall be sane,
Though they sink through the sea they shall rise again;
Though lovers be lost love shall not;
And death shall have no dominion.

And death shall have no dominion.
Under the windings of the sea
They lying long shall not die windily;
Twisting on racks when sinews give way,
Strapped to a wheel, yet they shall not break;

Faith in their hands shall snap in two,
And the unicorn evils run them through;
Split all ends up they shan't crack:
And death shall have no dominion.

And death shall have no dominion.
No more may gulls cry at their ears
Or waves break loud on the seashores;
Where blew a flower may a flower no more
Lift its head to the blows of the rain;
Though they be mad and dead as nails
Heads of the characters hammer through daisies;
Break in the sun till the sun breaks down,
And death shall have no dominion.

Dylan Thomas
(October 27th 1914 – November 9th 1953)

This pantheistic early poem first appeared in his 1933 notebook and was finally revised for *Twenty-Five Poems,* published in 1936, the year of his marriage to Caitlin Macnamara. Dylan, an alcoholic, described himself at the age of 35 as "old, small, dark, intelligent, and daring-doting-dotting eyed ... balding and toothlessing". In 1953, during his fourth lecture tour in America, he was living in New York on a diet of raw eggs and booze; in the early hours of November 4th he checked out of the Chelsea Hotel and into a bar, went into a coma and died on November 9th, a few days after his 39th birthday. He was buried in Laugharne Churchyard in Wales.

- *Playwright, novelist and poet Oliver Goldsmith born in Pallasmore, Ireland, November 10th 1728*
- *Dramatist, historian and poet Friedrich von Schiller born in Marbach November 10th 1759*
- *Vachel Lindsay born in Springfield, Illinois, November 10th 1879*
- *Arthur Rimbaud died in Marseilles November 10th 1891, having given up poetry and literature at the age of 19*

The Leaden-Eyed

Let not young souls be smothered out before
They do quaint deeds and fully flaunt their pride.
It is the world's one crime its babes grow dull,
Its poor are ox-like, limp and leaden-eyed.

Not that they starve, but starve so dreamlessly,
Not that they sow, but that they seldom reap,
Not that they serve, but have no gods to serve,
Not that they die but that they die like sheep.

Vachel Lindsay
(November 10th 1879 – December 5th 1931)

As a young man Lindsay tramped throughout the Mid-West and Southern States of the US on a mission to spread poetry. An extraordinary figure with a strong puritan streak, part minstrel, part missionary, and wholly in love with the figure of the pioneer, he carried a pamphlet called *Rhymes to be Traded for Bread* which he took to the door of every farmhouse. There he would relate stories, recite poetry and entertain children in return for a night's bed and food.

Lindsay became a national figure famous for his inspired poetry performances, but gradually he began to despise his audiences believing they were responsible for turning him from a visionary into an entertainer. As he grew older in extreme poverty, self-doubt developed into a mental turmoil of hallucination, hearing voices and imagining persecution from every quarter. On December 5th 1931, aged 52, he committed suicide by drinking lysol.

November 11

• American poet Alicia Ostriker born November 11th 1937. Her collections include The Imaginary Lover and Green Age, and she edited Blake's complete works.

Gethsemane
1914-18

The Garden called Gethsemane
In Picardy it was,
And there the people came to see
The English soldiers pass.
We used to pass—we used to pass
Or halt, as it might be,
And ship our masks in case of gas
Beyond Gethsemane.

The Garden called Gethsemane,
It held a pretty lass,
But all the time she talked to me
I prayed my cup might pass.
The officer sat on the chair,
The men lay on the grass,
And all the time we halted there
I prayed my cup might pass.

It didn't pass—it didn't pass—
It didn't pass from me.
I drank it when we met the gas
Beyond Gethsemane.

Rudyard Kipling
(December 30th 1865 – January 18th 1936)

The armistice ending the First World War was signed on November 11th 1918. Kipling's son John was killed in the Battle of Loos on September 27th 1915.

• Sir Percy Shelley, the only one of Shelley's six children to survive
him, was born on November 12th 1819
• Poet and writer William Hayley, biographer of Cowper and
Milton, died November 12th 1820

From The Circus Animals' Desertion

Those masterful images because complete
Grew in pure mind, but out of what began?
A mound of refuse or the sweepings of a street,
Old kettles, old bottles, and a broken can,
Old iron, old bones, old rags, that raving slut
Who keeps the till. Now that my ladder's gone,
I must lie down where all the ladders start,
In the foul rag-and-bone shop of the heart.

William Butler Yeats
(June 13th 1865 – January 28th 1939)

'Circus Animals' Desertion' was composed in the last year or so of Yeats' life. For Yeats, the "circus animals" were his own early works.

November 13

• Robert Louis Stevenson born in Edinburgh November 13th 1850
• Poet and anti-capitalist Arthur Hugh Clough, commemorated by
  Arnold in the poem 'Thyrsis', died November 13th 1861
• Poet and opium addict Francis Thompson died November 13th
  1907

Requiem

Under the wide and starry sky
Dig the grave and let me lie:
Glad did I live and gladly die,
  And I laid me down with a will.

This be the verse you grave for me:
Here he lies where he long'd to be;
Home is the sailor, home from sea,
  And the hunter home from the hill.

Robert Louis Stevenson
(November 13th 1850 – December 3rd 1894)

Stevenson's grandfather invented the 'intermittent' lights for lighthouses, and planned or constructed 23 lighthouses. Robert Louis Stevenson was prevented by ill health from becoming a lighthouse engineer in his turn. He suffered all his life from haemorrhages and a bronchial condition and travelled in an attempt to find a healthy climate. He met a divorcée Fanny Osbourne in France, and pursued her by emigrant ship and train to California. With her and his stepson Lloyd, he settled for the last five years of his life in Western Samoa where he was known as "Tusitala", 'The Story Teller'. According to various accounts, he was either making mayonnaise or fetching wine from the cellar, when he collapsed from a brain haemorrhage. Sixty natives carried him to a peak overlooking the Pacific and carved this Requiem on a tablet as his epitaph.

- Blake was "in a way to do well" as an engraver, wrote his artist friend Flaxman on November 14th 1805, "if he will only condescend to give that attention to his worldly concerns which every one does that prefers living to Starving." In the event, Blake remained poor all his life
- Scottish poet Norman MacCaig ("My only country / is six feet high / and whether I love it or not / I'll die for its independence") born in Edinburgh November 14th 1910

The Tyger

Tyger, tyger, burning bright
In the forests of the night,
What immortal hand or eye
Could frame thy fearful symmetry?

In what distant deeps or skies
Burnt the fire of thine eyes?
On what wings dare he aspire?
What the hand dare seize the fire?

And what shoulder and what art
Could twist the sinews of thy heart?
And, when thy heart began to beat,
What dread hand and what dread feet?

What the hammer? What the chain?
In what furnace was thy brain?
What the anvil? What dread grasp
Dare its deadly terrors clasp?

When the stars threw down their spears,
And water'd heaven with their tears,
Did He smile His work to see?
Did He who made the lamb make thee?

Tyger, tyger, burning bright
In the forests of the night,
What immortal hand or eye
Dare frame thy fearful symmetry?

William Blake
(November 28th 1757 – August 12th 1827)

Of Blake and his poem Charles Lamb wrote: "There is one [poem] to a tiger ... which is glorious ... I must look on him as one of the most extraordinary persons of the age."

'The Tyger' was written in 1793 when the French Revolution was consuming "the forests of the night" i.e. the French Church and State. It has a Gnostic background, viz. that there are two Gods. The first, Jehovah, the inadequate author of an imperfect creation and, beyond him, the ultimate divinity. To explain himself Blake invented his own mythology but wrote no key to it. It was not until our own time that his code was broken - see S. Foster Damon's *A Blake Dictionary*. The tyger, symbol of wrath, is the product of *Urizen*, the spirit of calculating rationality and materialism. *Urizen* is a fallen titan engaged in a historic struggle with *Los* who is the spirit of imagination and the arts. Their ultimate reconciliation is the climactic moment that makes *Jerusalem* possible. Blake equates the Lamb (Jesus) with spirituality i.e. the arts.

November 15

- William Cowper, depressed and twice nearly suicidal hymn-writer and poet, born November 15th 1731
- Marianne Moore born in Kirkwood, a suburb of St Louis, Missouri, November 15th 1887
- Charlotte Mew born in London November 15th 1889
- Sir Sacheverell Sitwell, whose poems were issued with an introduction by his sister Edith, was born November 15th 1897

The Call

From our low seat beside the fire
   Where we have dozed and dreamed and watched the glow
  Or raked the ashes, stopping so
We scarcely saw the sun or rain
  Above, or looked much higher
Than this same quiet red or burned-out fire.
      To-night we heard a call,
      A rattle on the window-pane,
      A voice on the sharp air,
And felt a breath stirring our hair,
  A flame within us: Something swift and tall
Swept in and out and that was all.
Was it a bright or a dark angel? Who can know?
  It left no mark upon the snow,
    But suddenly it snapped the chain
    Unbarred, flung wide the door
    Which will not shut again;
And so we cannot sit here any more.
    We must arise and go:
    The world is cold without
    And dark and hedged about
    With mystery and enmity and doubt,
    But we must go
    Though yet we do not know
· Who called, or what marks we shall leave upon the snow.

Charlotte Mew
(November 15th 1869 – March 24th 1928)

Hardy said of Charlotte Mew that she was "the least pretentious but undoubtedly the best woman poet of our day", a judgment he backed by securing her a civil list pension. Nevertheless, increasing financial problems combined with protracted family difficulty to make life unbearable and at 58 she committed suicide by drinking lysol. To the doctors who tried to treat her she said: "Don't keep me; let me go."

Moon Compasses

I stole forth dimly in the dripping pause
Between two downpours to see what there was.
And a masked moon had spread down compass rays
To a cone mountain in the midnight haze,
As if the final estimate were hers;
And as it measured in her calipers,
The mountain stood exalted in its place.
So love will take between the hands a face...

Robert Frost
(March 26th 1874 – January 29th 1963)

Frost maintained a fierce belief in the integrity of poetic vision: "A poem is never a put-up job, so to speak. It begins as a lump in the throat, a sense of wrong, a homesickness, a lovesickness. It is never a thought to begin with. It is at its best when it is a tantalizing vagueness ... It finds its thought or *makes* its thought."

November 17

• Hardy's poems Satires of Circumstances *published on this day in 1914. Their contents were to confront Feh with her lack of success as his wife*

I May, I might, I must

If you will tell me why the fen
appears impassable, I then
will tell you why I think that I
can get across it if I try.

Marianne Moore
(November 15th 1887 — February 5th 1972)

Marianne Moore was born in St Louis, Missouri, taught stenography for five years at the government Indian school in Carlisle, Pennsylvania, and edited the *Dial* magazine in New York until it closed in 1929. In her amusing poem that begins "Poetry / I too dislike it: there are things that are important beyond / all this fiddle ...", she asserts that poets should present for inspection "imaginary gardens with real toads in them".

- Sir W. S. Gilbert, librettist of the Gilbert and Sullivan operas, born in London November 18th 1836
- Novelist and poet Margaret Atwood, author of the feminist dystopian novel The Handmaid's Tale, born in Ottawa November 18th 1939
- Australian poet, critic and novelist W. J. Turner died November 18th 1946

Invictus[1]

Out of the night that covers me,
  Black as the Pit from pole to pole,
I thank whatever gods may be
  For my unconquerable soul.

In the fell clutch of circumstance
  I have not winced nor cried aloud.
Under the bludgeonings of chance
  My head is bloody, but unbowed.

Beyond this place of wrath and tears
  Looms but the horror of the shade,
And yet the menace of the years
  Finds, and shall find me, unafraid.

It matters not how strait the gate,
  How charged with punishments the scroll,
I am the master of my fate:
  I am the captain of my soul.

W. E. Henley
(August 23rd 1849 – June 11th 1903)

On this day in 1898, W. E. Henley wrote to Charles Whibley, after yet another operation: "They say I'm bettering and perhaps I am. It may be that a magnificent but grisly cut by Henry Dean is responsible. I know not. In the meantime the pain is considerable, the inconvenience almost beyond bearing ... also often a passion of itching ... a mass of blisters." Henley suffered from tubercular arthritis from childhood (he had an amputated foot). "Every day for the last years of his life," wrote J. M. Barrie, "he woke to more physical pain than the years before."

Of this poem, which dates from 1875, at the end of a two year stay in hospital, Stan Smith writes that "Henley often expresses a desperate carefree nihilism ... yet even when attitudinising about 'the fell clutch of circumstance' or 'the bludgeonings of chance', he preserves a sententious, overwrought dignity that aches with the pain of real feeling."

1. Latin for 'Unconquered'

November 19

- Poet Laureate and dramatist Thomas Shadwell, much ridiculed by Dryden, died November 19th 1692
- Poet and critic Allen Tate born in Winchester, Kentucky, November 19th 1899
- Romantic poet W. S. Graham born in Greenock on the Clyde November 19th 1918
- Sharon Olds born November 19th 1942

The Connoisseuse of Slugs

When I was a connoisseuse of slugs
I would part the ivy leaves, and look for the
naked jelly of those gold bodies,
translucent strangers glistening along the
stones, slowly, their gelatinous bodies
at my mercy. Made mostly of water, they would shrivel
to nothing if they were sprinkled with salt,
but I was not interested in that. What I liked
was to draw aside the ivy, breathe the
odor of the wall, and stand there in silence
until the slug forgot I was there
and sent its antennae up out of its
head, the glimmering umber horns
rising like telescopes, until finally the
sensitive knobs would pop out the ends,
delicate and intimate. Years later,
when I first saw a naked man,
I gasped with pleasure to see that quiet
mystery reenacted, the slow
elegant being coming out of hiding and
gleaming in the dark air, eager and so
trusting you could weep.

Sharon Olds
(November 19th 1942 –)

Sharon Olds comments: "What I notice as I read this for the first time in a while is the beat, out of the Episcopal hymnal, of the four-beat lines; the dangling-ivy-tendril appearance of the right-hand margin; & the number of trochees & dactyls at the left-hand margin, a column made mostly not of prepositions but of *naked, stones, odor, head, mystery*. And I certainly notice the dash after the 1942!"

Sharon Olds was brought up in California but has since lived in New York. Her selected poems were published in London in 1991 under the title *The Sign of Saturn* and a new volume *The Father* the following year. Sharon Olds has written of paying attention to the small beauties of the physical world "as if it were our duty to / find things to love, to bind ourselves to this world".

- *Thomas Chatterton, whom Keats described as "the purest writer in the English language", born November 20th 1752*
- *Henry Francis Lyte died November 20th 1847, having written the hymn 'Abide with me' a few weeks previously*
- *Arthur Guiterman born November 20th 1871*

On the Vanity of Earthly Greatness

The tusks that clashed in mighty brawls
Of mastodons, are billiard balls.

The sword of Charlemagne the Just
Is ferric oxide, known as rust.

The grizzly bear whose potent hug
Was feared by all, is now a rug.

Great Caesar's bust is on the shelf,
And I don't feel so well myself.

Arthur Guiterman
(November 20th 1871 – January 11th 1943)

Arthur Guiterman was born in Vienna of American parents. *The Laughing Muse* is his collection of mock-heroic ballads, parodying the ballads of chivalry. He also initiated the concept of reviews in rhyme, for *Life* magazine; wrote *Ballads of New York* about the quaint, historical side of New York; translated *L'Ecole des Maris*, a play by Molière into rhymed verse for the American stage; and wrote the lyrics and libretto for the opera *The Man Without a Country*.

• Sir Arthur Quiller-Couch, poet, writer and editor of the Oxford Book of English Verse, born in Bodmin, Cornwall, November 21st 1863

To a Mouse (On turning her up in her nest with the Plough, November, 1785)

Wee, sleekit°, cow'rin', tim'rous beastie,   *sleek*
O what a panic's in thy breastie!
Thou need na start awa sae hasty,
      Wi' bickering brattle°!   *hurrying scamper*
I wad be laith° to rin an' chase thee,   *loath*
      Wi' murd'ring pattle°!   *ploughstaff*

I'm truly sorry man's dominion
Has broken Nature's social union,
An' justifies that ill opinion
      Which makes thee startle
At me, thy poor earth-born companion,
      An' fellow-mortal!

I doubt na, whiles°, but thou may thieve;   *sometimes*
What then? poor beastie, thou maun° live!   *must*
      A daimen-icker in a thrave°   *the odd corn-ear from a bundle*
      'S a sma' request:
I'll get a blessin' wi' the lave°,   *rest*
      And never miss 't!

Thy wee bit housie, too, in ruin!
Its silly° wa's the win's are strewin'!   *frail*
An' naething, now, to big° a new ane,   *build*
      O' foggage° green!   *moss*
An' bleak December's winds ensuin',
      Baith snell° an' keen!   *bitter*

Thou saw the fields laid bare and waste,
An' weary winter comin' fast,
An' cozie here, beneath the blast,
      Thou thought to dwell,
Till crash! the cruel coulter° past   *ploughshare*
      Out-thro' thy cell.

[Continued]

That wee bit heap o' leaves an' stibble°   *stubble*
Hast cost thee mony a weary nibble!
Now thou's turned out, for a' thy trouble,
   But house or hald°,   *Without house or holding*
To thole° the winter's sleety dribble,   *endure*
   An' cranreuch° cauld!   *hoar-frost*

But, Mousie, thou art no thy lane°,   *alone*
In proving foresight may be vain:
The best laid schemes o' mice an' men
   Gang aft a-gley°,   *Go often astray*
An' lea'e us nought but grief an' pain
   For promised joy.

Still thou art blest, compared wi' me!
The present only toucheth thee:
But oh! I backward cast my e'e
   On prospects drear!
An' forward tho' I canna see,
   I guess an' fear!

Robert Burns
(January 25th 1759 – July 21st 1796)

According to his brother Gilbert's version of this incident, Robert Burns "was ploughing at Mossgiel with John Blane, the hired servant, as gaudsman carrying the pattle. Blane was running after the mouse to kill it when Burns checked him, but not angrily, asking what the poor mouse had ever done to him. The poet then seemed to his driver to grow very thoughtful and, during the remainder of the afternoon, he spoke not. In the night-time he woke Blane, who slept with him, and reading the poem, which had in the meantime been composed, asked what he thought of the mouse now."

November 22

• On this day in 1802 Blake wrote to a friend: "I have traveld thro Perils & Darkness not unlike a Champion. I have Conquerd, and shall Still Go On Conquering." But it was a struggle for him living away from London in Felpham

From the Introduction to Songs of Experience

Hear the voice of the Bard!
Who Present, Past, & Future sees,
Whose ears have heard
The Holy Word
That walk'd among the ancient trees;

Calling the lapsèd Soul
And weeping in the evening dew;
That might controll
The starry pole,
And fallen fallen light renew!

"O Earth O Earth return!
Arise from out the dewy grass;
Night is worn,
And the morn
Rises from the slumberous mass.

Turn away no more:
Why wilt thou turn away
The starry floor
The watry shore
Is giv'n thee till the break of day."

William Blake
(November 28th 1757 – August 12th 1827)

Notice the imperative first line, that marks the poet as prophet. The Bard is Blake himself. Bards were Celtic poet-prophets (not to be confused with Druids). Their craft was destroyed in Wales by Edward III and in Ireland by the Plantation of the seventeenth century. Blake sought the restoration of the bardic tradition.

Crabb Robinson quotes Wordsworth as saying of Blake: "There is no doubt this poor man was mad, but there is something in the madness of this man which interests me more than the sanity of Lord Byron and Walter Scott!"

- *Poet James Thomson born in Port Glasgow, the son of a merchant seaman, November 23rd 1834. He was educated at the Royal Caledonian Asylum orphanage and dismissed from the army for alcoholism*
- *Poet Paul Celan born in Czernowitz (then in Romania) November 23rd 1920.*
- *Christopher Logue born in Portsmouth November 23rd 1926*
- *Poet Derek Mahon born in Belfast November 23rd 1941*

Buffalo Bill's

Buffalo Bill's
defunct
                who used to
                ride a watersmooth-silver
                                        stallion
and break onetwothreefourfive pigeonsjustlikethat
                                                Jesus

he was a handsome man
                            and what i want to know is
how do you like your blueeyed boy
Mister Death

e. e. cummings
(October 14th 1894 – September 3rd 1962)

Rebecca Cummings, the poet's mother, wrote to him on this day in 1917 that "Poor Father" was staggered by the newspaper reports of the torpedoing of the Antilles by a submarine, and that according to the passenger list, "Cummings, casual civilian" was lost at sea. "Nothing will persuade him that it is not you – I never saw a man change as he had done in these last two days of intense anxiety." In fact, during this period Cummings was in jail in France, as a result of pacifist letters home that had been seen by the censor.

William Frederick Cody, known as Buffalo Bill, was born in 1846 and died on January 10th 1917, and Cummings had read the report of his death in the *New York Sun* next day. An army scout and pony express rider, Buffalo Bill got his nickname from shooting 5,000 buffalo for a contract to supply meat for workers on the Kansas Pacific Railway. In the manuscript version of the poem, Cummings writes of Buffalo Bill "with his long hair like reindeer moss on the old stone of his face".

November 24

• Comte de Lautréamont (Isidore-Lucien Ducasse), writer of prose poems admired by the Surrealists, died November 24th 1870
• Paul Blackburn, whose Collected Poems were published in 1985, was born in St Albans, Vermont, November 24th 1926

Louisa
After accompanying her on a mountain excursion

I met Louisa in the shade,
And, having seen that lovely Maid,
Why should I fear to say
That, nymph-like, she is fleet and strong;
And down the rocks can leap along
Like rivulets in May?

And she hath smiles to earth unknown;
Smiles, that with motion of their own
Do spread, and sink, and rise;
That come and go with endless play,
And ever, as they pass away,
Are hidden in her eyes.

She loves her fire, her cottage-home;
Yet o'er the moorland will she roam
In weather rough and bleak;
And, when against the wind she strains,
Oh! might I kiss the mountain rains
That sparkle on her cheek.

Take all that's mine 'beneath the moon',
If I with her but half a noon
May sit beneath the walls
Of some old cave, or mossy nook,
When up she winds along the brook
To hunt the waterfalls.

William Wordsworth
(April 7th 1770 – April 23rd 1850)

On this day in 1815, Sara Hutchinson (the sister of Wordsworth's wife, Mary) wrote that Thomas De Quincey had been up all night with William at Elleray, dosing himself with opium and drinking like a fish.

The poem 'Louisa' was composed in 1802. The last line is echoed in Dorothy Wordsworth's Journal for October 11th 1802: "A beautiful day. We walked to the Easedale hills to hunt waterfalls. William and Mary left me sitting on a stone on the solitary mountains."

- *Hymn-writer Isaac Watts died November 25th 1748*
- *Painter and poet Isaac Rosenberg born in Bristol, the son of poor Eastern European Jewish immigrants, November 25th 1890. In the war he was sent to a special 'Bantam' unit for under-sized soldiers and was killed on April 1st 1918. His poems include 'Break of Day in the Trenches' ("Droll rat, they would shoot you if they knew / Your cosmopolitan sympathies …")*

To Hell with Commonsense

More kicks than pence
We get from commonsense
Above its door is writ
All hope abandon. It
Is a bank will refuse a post
Dated cheque of the Holy Ghost.
Therefore I say to hell
With all reasonable
Poems in particular
We want no secular
Wisdom plodded together
By concerned fools. Gather
No moss you rolling stones
Nothing thought out atones
For no flight
In the light.
Let them wear out nerve and bone
Those who would have it that way
But in the end nothing that they
Have achieved will be in the shake up
In the final Wake Up
And I have a feeling
That through the hole in reason's ceiling
We can fly to knowledge
Without ever going to college.

Patrick Kavanagh
(October 21st 1905 – November 30th 1967)

Patrick Kavanagh did not go to college. He was born in the parish of Inniskeen, attended Kednaminsha National School till the age of 12, and carried on his father's trade of cobbler and small farmer on the "stony grey soil of Monaghan". At the age of 35 he left for Dublin ("the worst mistake I made in my life") where he published a long poem, *The Great Hunger*, about Ireland and the harsh realities of peasant life ("locked in a stable with pigs and cows forever"), a poem that was subversive enough to gain him the attentions of the police. In 1953 he developed lung cancer, but lived for another 14 years. He was awarded a pension once he was declared incurable ("like a prize each year until I die"). He married Katharine Moloney in the year of his death.

November 26

• Poet and hymn-writer William Cowper, son of the rector of Great Berkhamsptead, born November 26th 1731

From King Lear
Act III Scene ii

Lear. Blow, winds, and crack your cheeks! rage! blow!
You cataracts and hurricanoes, spout
Till you have drench'd our steeples, drown'd the cocks!
You sulphurous and thought-executing fires,
Vaunt-couriers to oak-cleaving thunderbolts,
Singe my white head! And thou, all-shaking thunder,
Strike flat the thick rotundity o' the world!
Crack nature's moulds, all germens° spill at once   *germs or forms*
That make ingrateful man!

   Rumble thy bellyful! Spit, fire! spout, rain!
Nor rain, wind, thunder, fire, are my daughters:
I tax not you, you elements, with unkindness;
I never gave you kingdom, call'd you children,
You owe me no subscription: then, let fall
Your horrible pleasure; here I stand, your slave,
A poor, infirm, weak, and despis'd old man.
But yet I call you servile ministers,
That have with two pernicious daughters join'd
Your high-engender'd battles 'gainst a head
So old and white as this. O! O! 'tis foul.

William Shakespeare
(April 23rd 1564 – April 23rd 1616)

King Lear was entered on the Stationer's Register on this day in 1607.

"... to see Lear acted –" wrote Lamb in his *On the tragedies of Shakespeare* "to see an old man tottering about the stage with a walking stick, turned out of doors by his daughters on a rainy night, has nothing in it but what is painful and disgusting. We want to take him in to shelter and relieve him. That is all the feeling which the acting of Lear ever produced in me. But the Lear of Shakespeare cannot be acted."

- *Roman poet and satirist Horace, whose father was a manumitted slave, died November 27th 8BC*
- *Donne elected dean of St Paul's November 27th 1621 — he got a house fit for a bishop with two courtyards and a gate house*
- *On November 27th 1786 Burns left Mossgiel on a borrowed pony for the bright lights of Edinburgh, which he reached next day*

Sonnet 29

When, in disgrace with fortune and men's eyes,
　　I all alone beweep my outcast state,
And trouble deaf heaven with my bootless cries,
　　And look upon myself, and curse my fate,
Wishing me like to one more rich in hope,
　　Featured like him, like him with friends possessed,
Desiring this man's art and that man's scope,
　　With what I most enjoy contented least;
Yet in these thoughts myself almost despising,
　　Haply I think on thee, and then my state,
Like to the lark at break of day arising
　　From sullen earth, sings hymns at heaven's gate;
　　　For thy sweet love remembered such wealth brings
　　　That then I scorn to change my state with kings.

William Shakespeare
(April 23rd 1564 – April 23rd 1616)

On this day in 1582, a marriage licence was issued to Shakespeare and Anne Hathaway. He married at the age of 18; she was eight years his senior.

November 28

• On November 28th 1582, two sureties pledged £40 each to disclose any lawful impediment to Shakespeare's marriage to Anne Hathaway
• Preacher, writer and poet John Bunyan, author of The Pilgrim's Progress, born in Elstow, near Bedford and baptised November 28th 1628
• William Blake born November 28th 1757 [1]

Infant Sorrow

My mother groan'd! my father wept.
Into the dangerous world I leapt:
Helpless, naked, piping loud:
Like a fiend hid in a cloud.

Struggling in my father's hands,
Striving against my swadling bands,
Bound and weary I thought best
To sulk upon my mother's breast.

William Blake
(November 28th 1757 – August 12th 1827)

Many of Blake's *Songs of Innocence* pair with those of *Experience*. This one pairs with 'Infant Joy' (qv). But now the child is self-aware, with a will of its own, capable of defying both parents. He, or she, has entered "experience", potential alienation.

1. Blake was born at 28 Broad Street in London, the third son of a hosier and haberdasher. From the start he disliked discipline and his father decided not to send him to school, "thinking it most prudent to withhold from him the liability of receiving punishment". Before the age of ten, Blake saw a vision of angels in a tree, "bright angelic wings bespangling every bough like stars".

• Christian writer C. S. Lewis, who wrote the long narrative poem
'Dymer', born in Belfast November 29th 1898
• George Szirtes, painter and poet, whose poetry (in English)
includes Metro and Bridge Passages, was born in Hungary
November 29th 1948

I Think Continually of Those Who Were Truly Great

I think continually of those who were truly great.
Who, from the womb, remembered the soul's history
Through corridors of light where the hours are suns
Endless and singing. Whose lovely ambition
Was that their lips, still touched with fire,
Should tell of the Spirit clothed from head to foot in song.
And who hoarded from the Spring branches
The desires falling across their bodies like blossoms.

What is precious is never to forget
The essential delight of the blood drawn from ageless springs
Breaking through rocks in worlds before our earth.
Never to deny its pleasure in the morning simple light
Nor its grave evening demand for love.
Never to allow gradually the traffic to smother
With noise and fog the flowering of the spirit.

Near the snow, near the sun, in the highest fields
See how these names are fêted by the waving grass
And by the streamers of white cloud
And whispers of wind in the listening sky.
The names of those who in their lives fought for life
Who wore at their hearts the fire's center.
Born of the sun they traveled a short while towards the sun,
And left the vivid air signed with their honor.

Stephen Spender
(September 28th 1909 –)

Sir Stephen Spender once said: "One must look for a constructive idea. If one has the sense of despair and of evil, then one must look for the sense of hope and of good with which to confront despair and evil." He lived through evil times. His mother was of German-Jewish descent, and he lived for a while in Germany before the war. He recorded his impressions of Germany after the war in *European Witness* (1946). A Communist in the 30s, and a friend of Auden, Isherwood and MacNeice at Oxford, he wrote propaganda in Spain for the Republicans during the Civil War, served in the National Fire Service in London during the Second World War, but by the 50s had come full circle, as co-editor of Encounter, an anti-Communist monthly that was initially financed by the CIA.

The poem 'I Think Continually of Those Who Were Truly Great' comes from his early collection, *Poems*, published in 1933.

November 30

• Sir Philip Sidney, author of Arcadia, born November 30th 1554
• Poet and satirist Jonathan Swift born in Belfast November 30th 1667
• John McCrae, the Canadian who wrote 'In Flanders' Fields', born November 30th 1872
• Oscar Wilde died November 30th 1900
• Irish poet and writer Patrick Kavanagh died November 30th 1967

From The Ballad of Reading Gaol
6

In Reading gaol by Reading town
    There is a pit of shame,
And in it lies a wretched man
    Eaten by teeth of flame,
In a burning winding-sheet he lies,
    And his grave has got no name.

And there, till Christ call forth the dead,
    In silence let him lie:
No need to waste the foolish tear,
    Or heave the windy sigh:
The man had killed the thing he loved,
    And so he had to die.

And all men kill the thing they love,
    By all let this be heard,
Some do it with a bitter look,
    Some with a flattering word,
The coward does it with a kiss,
    The brave man with a sword!

Oscar Wilde
(October 16th 1854 – November 30th 1900)

The Marquis of Queensbury, father of Wilde's companion Lord Alfred Douglas, left a card at Wilde's club 'To Oscar Wilde posing as a Somdomite (sic)'. Wilde took him to court for libel, lost the action, and was tried and sentenced to two years in jail for homosexual offences. He was released in 1897, went into exile in France, and published *The Ballad of Reading Gaol* in 1898 under the pseudonym Sebastian Melmoth, a martyr character in a novel by his great-uncle.

Oscar Wilde died in Paris from cerebral meningitis, and was buried as a Roman Catholic in the Bagneux cemetery on the outskirts of Paris, with Lord Alfred Douglas in attendance as chief mourner.

Sea Fever

I must go down to the seas again, to the lonely sea and the sky,
And all I ask is a tall ship and a star to steer her by;
And the wheel's kick and the wind's song and the white sail's shaking,
And a grey mist on the sea's face, and a grey dawn breaking.

I must go down to the seas again, for the call of the running tide
Is a wild call and a clear call that may not be denied;
And all I ask is a windy day with the white clouds flying,
And the flung spray and the blown spume, and the sea-gulls crying.

I must go down to the seas again, to the vagrant gypsy life,
To the gull's way and the whale's way where the wind's like a whetted knife;
And all I ask is a merry yarn from a laughing fellow-rover,
And quiet sleep and a sweet dream when the long trick's over.

John Masefield
(June 1st 1878 – May 12th 1967)

On December 1st 1902, Masefield wrote to his brother-in-law Harry Ross: "Speaking quite impartially, I think the book deserves the recognition of a maritime people. It is something new, said newly." He was referring to *Salt Water Ballads,* published 1902, in which this poem features, although earlier he had written more self-critically to Robert Trevelyan: "They are a rough and tumble lot of ballads dealing with life at sea and drunken sailors, and I can't say there's much romance about them." At that stage he had not been hopeful about their chances of selling, but the 500 copies, at 3s 6d each, were sold out by the end of the year.

December 2

• Shakespeare's sister Margaret baptised December 2nd 1562
• Alfred, Lord Tennyson composed 'The Charge of the Light Brigade' December 2nd 1854
• Poet Jon Silkin born in London December 2nd 1930
• Poet Philip Larkin died December 2nd 1985, having refused the Poet Laureateship a year earlier

The Charge of the Light Brigade

Half a league, half a league,
  Half a league onward,
All in the valley of Death
  Rode the six hundred.
'Forward, the Light Brigade!
Charge for the guns!' he said;
Into the valley of Death
  Rode the six hundred.

'Forward, the Light Brigade!'
Was there a man dismayed?
Not tho' the soldier knew
  Some one had blundered:
Their's not to make reply,
Their's not to reason why,
Their's but to do and die:
Into the valley of Death
  Rode the six hundred.

Cannon to right of them,
Cannon to left of them,
Cannon in front of them
  Volleyed and thundered;
Stormed at with shot and shell,
Boldly they rode and well,
Into the jaws of Death,
Into the mouth of Hell
  Rode the six hundred.

Flashed all their sabres bare,
Flashed as they turned in air,
Sabring the gunners there,

Charging an army, while
  All the world wondered:
Plunged in the battery-smoke
Right thro' the line they broke;
Cossack and Russian
Reeled from the sabre-stroke
  Shattered and sundered.
Then they rode back, but not,
  Not the six hundred.

Cannon to right of them,
Cannon to left of them,
Cannon behind them
  Volleyed and thundered;
Stormed at with shot and shell,
While horse and hero fell,
They that had fought so well
Came thro' the jaws of Death
Back from the mouth of Hell,
All that was left of them,
  Left of six hundred.

When can their glory fade?
O the wild charge they made!
  All the world wondered.
Honour the charge they made!
Honour the Light Brigade,
  Noble six hundred!

Alfred, Lord Tennyson
(August 6th 1809 – October 6th 1892)

The Charge of the Light Brigade took place on October 25th 1854. One of the most infamous blunders in British military history, during which 247 men out of 637 were killed or wounded owing to a misunderstood order, it formed part of the Crimean War fought against Russia in a scramble for control over the remnants of the Ottoman Empire.

Tennyson composed his poem in a few minutes, after reading in *The Times* the phrase 'some one had blundered' – from which he took the metre of his poem. It was 'not a poem on which I pique myself', he said, and he considered omitting it from his collected poems.

• Robert Louis Stevenson died in Western Samoa December 3rd 1894
• Craig Raine born December 3rd 1944

A Martian Sends a Postcard Home

Caxtons are mechanical birds with many wings
and some are treasured for their markings—

they cause the eyes to melt
or the body to shriek without pain.

I have never seen one fly, but
sometimes they perch on the hand.

Mist is when the sky is tired of flight
and rests its soft machine on ground:

then the world is dim and bookish
like engravings under tissue paper.

Rain is when the earth is television.
It has the property of making colours darker.

Model T is a room with the lock inside—
a key is turned to free the world

for movement, so quick there is a film
to watch for anything missed.

But time is tied to the wrist
or kept in a box, ticking with impatience.

In homes, a haunted apparatus sleeps,
that snores when you pick it up.

If the ghost cries, they carry it
to their lips and soothe it to sleep

with sounds. And yet, they wake it up
deliberately, by tickling with a finger.

Only the young are allowed to suffer openly.
Adults go to a punishment room

with water but nothing to eat.
They lock the door and suffer the noises

alone. No one is exempt
and everyone's pain has a different smell.

At night, when all the colours die,
they hide in pairs

and read about themselves—
in colour, with their eyelids shut.

Craig Raine
(December 3rd 1944 –)

Craig Raine was born in Shildon, County Durham, the son of an ex-boxer and faith-healer. He was educated at Exeter College, Oxford, became poetry editor at Faber and is now Fellow in English at New College, Oxford. In 1972 he married Ann Pasternak Slater with whom he has four children. His book of poetry, *A Martian Sends a Postcard Home*, was published in 1979. John Carey wrote in his review that Raine "has set himself the mammoth task of visual retrieval, forcing us to see for the first time things we have been looking at all our lives. The poems which accomplish this are as compact as bullets. No word idles. I can't think of anyone else writing today whose every line is so unfailingly exciting. Whatever he touches, he transforms."

James Fenton described Raine as the founder of the Martian school of poetry, one that views "the commonplace with wonder and innocence". Raine has acknowledged being influenced by the witty riddles in William Golding's novel *The Inheritors*. His latest book is a novel in verse entitled *History: The Home Movie* (Penguin, 1994).

December 4

• John Gay died December 4th 1732. His Westminster Abbey epitaph reads: "Life is a jest, and all things show it / I thought so once, and now I know it"
• Austrian lyric poet Rainer Maria Rilke born in Prague December 4th 1875
• Art historian Sir Herbert Read born in Yorkshire December 4th 1893. His war poetry is in Naked Warriors (1919)

Sonnets to Orpheus
IV

O you lovers that are so gentle, step occasionally
into the breath of the sufferers not meant for you,
let it be parted by your cheeks,
it will tremble, joined again, behind you.

You have been chosen, you are sound and whole,
you are like the very first beat of the heart,
you are the bow that shoots the arrows, and also their target,
in tears your smile would glow forever.

Do not be afraid to suffer, give
the heaviness back to the weight of the earth;
mountains are heavy, seas are heavy.

Even those trees you planted as children
became too heavy long ago—you couldn't carry them now.
But you can carry the winds . . . and the open spaces . . .

Rainer Maria Rilke
(December 4th 1875 – December 29th 1926)
translated by Robert Bly
(December 23rd 1926 –)

Rainer Maria Rilke, an Austrian, was born in Prague and deserted the military academy there to study art history. He was influenced by Tolstoy, whom he met in Russia, and by Rodin, whose pupil, Klara Westhoff, he married in 1901. Rilke became Rodin's secretary in Paris, publishing *Das Rodin-Buch* in 1907. *Die Sonnette an Orpheus*, published in 1923, is seen as some of Rilke's finest work.

- Poet Christina Rossetti born in London December 5th 1830
- Poet and writer Flora Thompson, author of Lark Rise to Candleford, born December 5th 1877
- Anglo-Irish poet Thomas William Rolleston died December 5th 1920
- Vachel Lindsay committed suicide by drinking lysol December 5th 1931
- Novelist and poet Adam Thorpe, author of Ulverton, born in Paris December 5th 1956. He founded the Equinox Travelling Theatre

December 5

Against

Against the bolts and welder's bloom of rhetoric
chamfer the waggon, scoop and shave the grain
to serviceable lightness, take the rein.

Against the packs of fighters shocking screes to fall
gaze on the heron, watch the wings yield their long
elegance over the water, echo the call.

Against the precipitate action of the angry father
loosen the mother, wait for the snow, hold
in a gloved finger his gloved hand, walk the lane.

Adam Thorpe
(December 5th 1956 –)

Adam Thorpe comments: "I wrote this in our first year in France, during the Gulf War. It's about all kinds of aggression, though, including one's own."

December 6

- *Syrian-American Kahlil Gibran, author of* The Prophet, *born December 6th 1883*
- *Poet Alfred Joyce Kilmer born December 6th 1886, killed in World War I*
- *Sir Osbert Sitwell, poet, satirist, playwright, autobiographer, born December 6th 1892*
- *Sylvia Townsend Warner born at Harrow School December 6th 1893*
- *Ira Gerschwin, American songwriter, born December 6th 1896*

He Wishes For The Cloths Of Heaven

Had I the heavens' embroidered cloths,
Enwrought with golden and silver light,
The blue and the dim and the dark cloths
Of night and light and the half-light,
I would spread the cloths under your feet:
But I, being poor, have only my dreams;
I have spread my dreams under your feet;
Tread softly because you tread on my dreams.

W. B. Yeats
(June 13th 1865 – January 28th 1939)

"Yeats remarked of this defeatist pre-Raphaelite poem that it was the way to lose a lady" (Norman Jeffares).

On this day in 1921, the Anglo-Irish treaty was signed creating an Irish Free State with dominion status within the British Empire. Yeats wrote about the treaty to Mrs Shakespeare: "I am in deep gloom about Ireland ... I see no hope of escape from bitterness, and the extreme party may carry the country. When men are very bitter, death and ruin draw them on as a rabbit is supposed to be drawn on by the dancing of the fox." He was wondering whether Dublin would be a safe place to bring up his children, but he soon returned and was full of plans for a State Theatre, an Irish Academy of Letters and the creation of a Ministry of Fine Arts.

• *Poet, writer and journalist Willa Cather born on a farm in Virginia December 7th 1873*
• *Robert Graves died December 7th 1985*

Down, wanton, down!

Down, wanton, down! Have you no shame
That at the whisper of Love's name,
Or Beauty's, presto! up you raise
Your angry head and stand at gaze?

Poor bombard-captain, sworn to reach
The ravelin and effect a breach—
Indifferent what you storm or why,
So be that in the breach you die!

Love may be blind, but Love at least
Knows what is man and what mere beast;
Or Beauty wayward, but requires
More delicacy from her squires.

Tell me, my witless, whose one boast
Could be your staunchness at the post,
When were you made a man of parts
To think fine and profess the arts?

Will many-gifted Beauty come
Bowing to your bald rule of thumb,
Or Love swear loyalty to your crown?
Be gone, have done! Down, wanton, down!

Robert Graves
(July 24th 1895 – December 7th 1985)

In later years, Robert Graves wrote how over-reliance on physical passions and lusts and "the blood sports of desire" leave a person trapped in a hellish and deadened world.

December 8

• Roman poet and satirist Horace born near Venusia in Southern
  Italy December 8th 65 BC
• Thomas Flatman died December 8th 1688
• Poet and critic Delmore Schwarz born in Brooklyn December 8th
  1913. His In Dreams Begin Responsibilities (1937) was
  praised by Eliot. He suffered from paranoia in later years
• Surrealist poet James Tate born in Kansas City December 8th
  1943

An Appeal to Cats in the Business of Love

Ye cats that at midnight spit love at each other,
Who best feel the pangs of a passionate lover,
I appeal to your scratches and your tattered fur,
If the business of love be no more than to purr.
Old Lady Grimalkin with her gooseberry eyes
Knew some thing when a kitten, for why she was wise;
You find by experience, the love-fit's soon o'er,
Puss! Puss! lasts not long, but turns to *Cat-whore*!

    Men ride many miles,
    Cats tread many tiles,
Both hazard their necks in the fray;
    Only cats, when they fall
    From a house or a wall,
Keep their feet, mount their tails, and away!

Thomas Flatman
(February 21st 1637 – December 8th 1688)

Thomas Flatman was born in London and educated at Winchester and New College, Oxford. He became a barrister in 1626, but also acquired a reputation as a painter of miniatures – a self-portrait done when he was 38 is kept in the Victoria and Albert Museum. His *Poems and Songs* were published when he was 39 and include 'The Dying Christian to his Soul', a poem which Alexander Pope later imitated.

- *John Milton born in Bread St, Cheapside, December 9th 1608*
- *Poet and writer James Hogg, who described himself as "the king of the Mountain and Fairy School", born December 9th 1770. Known as the "Ettrick Shepherd", he tended sheep in his youth and was given a farm by the Duchess of Buccleuch*
- *On this day in 1781, in the 'Lounger', a review of Burns' poems calls him a "heaven-sent ploughman" – at which point he is welcomed into high society by the Duchess of Gordon and co*
- *Edith Sitwell died December 9th 1964*

Sonnet vii
How Soon Hath Time

How soon hath Time, the subtle thief of youth,
    Stolen on his wing my three and twentieth year!
My hasting days fly on with full career,
    But my late spring no bud or blossom shew'th°.   *showeth*
Perhaps my semblance° might deceive the truth,   *appearance*
    That I to manhood am arrived so near,
    And inward ripeness doth much less appear,
    That some more timely-happy spirits endu'th°.   *endoweth*
Yet be it less or more, or soon or slow,
    It shall be still in strictest measure even°   *corresponding*
    To that same lot, however mean or high,
Toward which Time leads me, and the will of Heaven;
    All is, if I have grace to use it so,
    As ever in my great Taskmaster's eye.

John Milton
(December 9th 1608 – November 8th 1674)

This sonnet was probably composed on or about December 9th 1632, Milton's 24th birthday. Milton transcribed it at the bottom of a letter to a former Cambridge tutor, in which he defended his love of learning and his reluctance to get a job or take holy orders.

Milton's father was a usurer, who made his money from loans and property. He supported Milton in years of study at home, after leaving Cambridge. In a Latin poem to his father, Milton wrote: "So I, who already have a place, though a low one, in the ranks of the learned, shall one day sit among those who wear the ivy and laurels of victory. Now I shall no longer mix with the brainless mob: my steps will shun the sight of common eyes." Milton had been unpopular at Cambridge, where the undergraduates nicknamed him "The Lady of Christ's". He thought that he may have alienated them by "a certain niceness of nature, an honest haughtiness".

December 10

- *Emily Dickinson born in Amherst, Mass., December 10th 1830*
- *Yeats received the Nobel prize for literature in Stockholm December 10th 1923*
- *Poet, translator and editor Carol Rumens born in London December 10th 1944*
- *T. S. Eliot received the Nobel prize for literature December 10th 1948*

This World is not Conclusion

This World is not Conclusion.
A Species stands beyond –
Invisible, as Music –
But positive, as Sound –
It beckons, and it baffles –
Philosophy – don't know –
And through a Riddle, at the last –
Sagacity, must go –
To guess it, puzzles scholars –
To gain it, Men have borne
Contempt of Generations
And Crucifixion, shown –
Faith slips – and laughs, and rallies –
Blushes, if any see –
Plucks at a twig of Evidence –
And asks a Vane, the way –
Much Gesture, from the Pulpit –
Strong Hallelujahs roll –
Narcotics cannot still the Tooth
That nibbles at the soul –

Emily Dickinson
(December 10th 1830 – May 15th 1886)

Dickinson described her art with typical, striking economy: "If I read a book and it makes my whole body so cold I know no fire can ever warm me, I know that is poetry. If I feel physically as if the top of my head were taken off, I know that is poetry. These are the only ways I know it. Is there any other way?"

• Poet and playwright Alfred De Musset, who wrote the Nuits
poem cycle after his unhappy love affair with George Sand, born
in Paris December 11th 1810
• 'Ethno-poet' Jerome Rothenberg, whose A Seneca Journal was
written whilst he was an honorary member of an American Indian
tribe, born December 11th 1931

From Vacillation

III

Get all the gold and silver that you can,
Satisfy ambition, animate
The trivial days and ram them with the sun,
And yet upon these maxims meditate:
All women dote upon an idle man
Although their children need a rich estate;
No man has ever lived that had enough
Of children's gratitude or woman's love.

No longer in Lethean foliage caught
Begin the preparation for your death
And from the fortieth winter by that thought
Test every work of intellect or faith,
And everything that your own hands have wrought,
And call those works extravagance of breath
That are not suited for such men as come
Proud, open-eyed and laughing to the tomb.

William Butler Yeats
(June 13th 1865 – January 28th 1939)

On this day in 1920, the British Government declared martial law in Ireland, less than a fortnight before ceding Home Rule to Ireland. Yeats was appointed a Senator by the new Free State – but less thanks to his poetry or his work at the Abbey Theatre than to his previous membership of the Irish Republican Brotherhood.

Yeats wrote 'Vacillation' in his late sixties.

December 12

• *Robert Browning died December 12th 1889* [1]
• *Tennyson buried in Westminster Abbey on this day in 1892, with Hardy commenting that the grand scene was "less penetrating than a plain country interment would have been"*

Prospice

Fear death? – to feel the fog in my throat,
    The mist in my face,
When the snows begin, and the blasts denote
    I am nearing the place,
The power of the night, the press of the storm,
    The post of the foe;
Where he stands, the Arch Fear in a visible form,
    Yet the strong man must go:
For the journey is done and the summit attained,
    And the barriers fall,
Though a battle's to fight ere the guerdon be gained,
    The reward of it all.
I was ever a fighter, so – one fight more,
    The best and the last!
I would hate that death bandaged my eyes, and forbore,
    And bade me creep past.
No! let me taste the whole of it, fare like my peers
    The heroes of old,
Bear the brunt, in a minute pay glad life's arrears
    Of pain, darkness and cold.
For sudden the worst turns the best to the brave,
    The black minute's at end,
And the elements' rage, the fiend-voices that rave,
    Shall dwindle, shall blend,
Shall change, shall become first a peace out of pain,
    Then a light, then thy breast,
O thou soul of my soul! I shall clasp thee again,
    And with God be the rest!

Robert Browning
(May 7th 1812 – December 12th 1889)

1. Browning died in Venice at the Palazzo Rezzonico. "It was an unexpected blow," his sister wrote, "he seemed in such exuberant spirits." Browning was buried in Westminster Abbey, once it was established that the cemetery where Elizabeth Barrett Browning had been interred 28 years earlier had since been closed to further burial.

Nice Day for a Lynching

The bloodhounds look like sad old judges
In a strange court. They point their noses
At the Negro jerking in the tight noose;
His feet spread crow-like above these
Honourable men who laugh as he chokes.

I don't know this black man.
I don't know these white men.

But I know that one of my hands
Is black, and one white. I know that
One part of me is being strangled,
While another part horribly laughs.

Until it changes,
I shall be forever killing; and be killed.

Kenneth Patchen
(December 13th 1911 – January 8th 1972)

Kenneth Patchen was born and educated in Ohio, and attended, for one year only, the Experimental College at the University of Wisconsin, where he excelled as an athlete. He held a succession of jobs until the success of his first poetry collection *Before the Brave* in 1936 led him to focus on his (thereafter prolific) writing – the flavour of which is indicated by the title of his 1945 collection *An Astonished Eye Looks Out of the Air: Being Some Poems Old and New Against War and in Behalf of Life*. Some of his books were hand-bound and hand-painted and he exhibited "talismanic wall-hangings warning Fear and Stupidity that Love is in town and well-armed". For the last twenty years and more of his life, he had a spinal ailment and was cared for and protected by his wife Miriam (née Oikemus). Eliot, Auden and others gave money to help support this widely admired poet.

December 14

• Andrew Marvell matriculated from Trinity College, Cambridge, on December 14th 1633
• Poet, writer, playwright, spy, Aphra Behn, author of Oroonokoo, baptised in Wye, Kent, December 14th 1640, and brought up in Surinam

Everness

One thing does not exist: Oblivion.
God saves the metal and he saves the dross,
And his prophetic memory guards from loss
The moons to come, and those of evenings gone.
Everything *is*: the shadows in the glass
Which, in between the day's two twilights, you
Have scattered by the thousands, or shall strew
Henceforward in the mirrors that you pass.
And everything is part of that diverse
Crystalline memory, the universe;
Whoever through its endless mazes wanders
Hears door on door click shut behind his stride,
And only from the sunset's farther side
Shall view at last the Archetypes and the Splendors.

Jorge Luis Borges
(August 24th 1889 – June 14th 1986)
translated by Richard Wilbur
(March 1st 1921 –)

Richard Wilbur comments: "This translation was done with the linguistic and other advice of Norman Thomas di Giovanni, who was putting together a bilingual *Selected Poems* (1971) of Jorge Luis Borges. Borges went over all of the translations done, by various hands, for that book, and delighted me by saying that, in one line of another sonnet, I had improved on the original. I am sure that, in so saying, Borges was merely giving further proof of his notorious love of the English language."

• Poet and playwright Margaret Cavendish, Duchess of Newcastle,
  whom Pepys criticised as "mad, conceited and ridiculous", died
  December 15th 1673
• Politically active feminist poet Muriel Rukeyser ("No more masks!")
  born in New York December 15th 1913

December 15

Woman to Child

You who were darkness warmed my flesh
where out of darkness rose the seed.
Then all a world I made in me;
all the world you hear and see
hung upon my dreaming blood.

There moved the multitudinous stars,
and coloured birds and fishes moved.
There swam the sliding continents.
All time lay rolled in me, and sense,
and love that knew not its beloved.

O node and focus of the world;
I hold you deep within that well
you shall escape and not escape —
that mirrors still your sleeping shape;
that nurtures still your crescent cell.

I wither and you break from me;
yet though you dance in living light
I am the earth, I am the root,
I am the stem that fed the fruit,
the link that joins you to the night.

                                   Judith Wright
                                 (May 31st 1915 –)

Judith Wright once commented that she wrote "as an Australian whose family on both sides were early
comers to a country which was one of the last to be settled by the whites, and were from the beginning
farmers and pastoralists ... The images I use and also my methods no doubt reflect my ties to the landscape
I live in. I tend to use 'traditional' – i.e., biological – rhythms more than free or new forms ... As a woman
poet, the biological aspect of feminine experience has naturally been of importance in my work also.
I expect my poetry is of a kind which no urban technological society will produce again."

December 16

• Philosopher, poet, novelist and autobiographer George Santayana
born in Madrid December 16th 1863. He spent his last years in a
convent in Rome
• Composer, actor, playwright and poet Sir Noel Coward born in
Teddington December 16th 1899

The Last Word

Creep into thy narrow bed,
Creep, and let no more be said!
Vain thy onset! all stands fast;
Thou thyself must break at last.

Let the long contention cease!
Geese are swans, and swans are geese.
Let them have it how they will!
Thou art tired; best be still!

They out-talk'd thee, hiss'd thee, tore thee.
Better men fared thus before thee;
Fired their ringing shot and pass'd,
Hotly charged—and broke at last.

Charge once more, then, and be dumb!
Let the victors, when they come,
When the forts of folly fall,
Find thy body by the wall.

Matthew Arnold
(December 24th 1822 – April 15th 1888)

Arnold wrote to his mother regarding his prospects as a poet: "I have less poetical sentiment than
Tennyson and less intellectual vigour and abundance than Browning. Yet because I have more of a
fusion than either of them, and have more regularly applied that fusion to the main line of modern
development, I am likely to have my turn."
On Arnold's death, Browning wrote: "I shall hold in veneration – to my own dying day – the memory
of one of the noblest and best men I ever knew and ever loved."

• *John Greenleaf Whittier, the American poet and abolitionist, born December 17th 1807*
• *Novelist and editor Ford Madox Ford, author of* The Good Soldier *and founder of the Transatlantic Review, born in Merton December 17th 1873. His poems 'Buckshee' express an old man's gratitude for a young woman's love*

Upon Julia's Clothes

Whenas in silks my Julia goes,
Then, then methinks, how sweetly flows
That liquefaction of her clothes!

Next, when I cast mine eyes and see
That brave vibration each way free;
O how that glittering taketh me!

Robert Herrick
(August 24th 1591 – October 15th 1671)

Though he flirted wildly with his sweethearts, real and imaginary, the vicar of Dean Prior lived as a bachelor, excepting his brief and uncharacteristically impetuous affair with Tomasin Parsons. He filled his house with pets, including a tame pig which would drink from a tankard to the delight of Herrick's visitors.

December 18

• Hymn-writer Charles Wesley born December 18th 1707
• Poet Samuel Rogers, who had a sharp tongue but a generous
  purse, born in Stoke Newington December 18th 1855
• Francis Thompson, who wrote 'The Hound of Heaven', was born
  in Preston, the son of a Roman Catholic doctor, December 18th
  1859. Failing to become either a priest or a doctor, he drifted as a
  homeless opium addict until befriended by the Meynells
• Verse dramatist Christopher Fry born December 18th 1907
• Sasha Moorsom married Michael Young December 18th 1961

From Contemplation[1]

From stones and poets you may know,
Nothing so active is, as that which least seems so.

For he, that conduit running wine of song,
Then to himself does most belong,
When he his mortal house unbars
To the importunate and thronging feet
That round our corporal walls unheeded beat;
Till, all containing, he exalt
His stature to the stars, or stars
Narrow their heaven to his fleshly vault:
When, like a city under ocean,
To human things he grows a desolation,
And is made a habitation
For the fluctuous universe
To lave° with unimpeded motion.   bathe
He scarcely frets the atmosphere
With breathing, and his body shares
The immobility of rocks;
His heart's a drop-well of tranquillity;
His mind more still is than the limbs of fear,
And yet its unperturbed velocity
The spirit of the simoon[2] mocks.
He round the solemn centre of his soul
Wheels like a dervish, while his being is
Streamed with the set of the world's harmonies,
In the long draft of whatsoever sphere
He lists the sweet and clear
Clangour of his high orbit on to roll,
So gracious is his heavenly grace;
And the bold stars does hear,
Every one in his airy soar,
For evermore
Shout to each other from the peaks of space,
As thwart ravines of azure shouts the mountaineer.

                                        Francis Thompson
                    (December 18th 1859 – November 13th 1907)

1. Lines 46 - 78
2. An oppressively hot desert wind

- *Philip Freneau died, lost in a snowstorm near his home, December 19th 1832*
- *Emily Brontë died aged 30 December 19th 1848*
- *Ted Hughes appointed Poet Laureate in succession to John Betjeman, December 19th 1984*

Museum Piece

The good grey guardians of art
Patrol the halls on spongy shoes,
Impartially protective, though
Perhaps suspicious of Toulouse.

Here dozes one against the wall,
Disposed upon a funeral chair.
A Degas dancer pirouettes
Upon the parting of his hair.

See how she spins! The grace is there,
But strain as well is plain to see.
Degas loved the two together:
Beauty joined to energy.

Edgar Degas purchased once
A fine El Greco, which he kept
Against the wall beside his bed
To hang his pants on while he slept.

Richard Wilbur
(March 1st 1921 –)

Richard Wilbur writes: "The concluding anecdote of this 1947 poem is true, and may be found in the art–dealer Vollard's memoir of Degas. What the poem conveys, I hope, is that artists are less gravely reverential about art than its custodians are. The usual shorter form of Toulouse-Lautrec is Lautrec rather than Toulouse, but 'Lautrec' has the defect of not rhyming with 'shoes'."

December 20

The World Is Too Much With Us

The world is too much with us; late and soon,
Getting and spending, we lay waste our powers:
Little we see in nature that is ours;
We have given our hearts away, a sordid boon!
This Sea that bares her bosom to the moon;
The Winds that will be howling at all hours,
And are up-gathered now like sleeping flowers;
For this, for everything, we are out of tune;
It moves us not.—Great God! I'd rather be
A Pagan suckled in a creed outworn;
So might I, standing on this pleasant lea,
Have glimpses that would make me less forlorn;
Have sight of Proteus coming from the sea;
Or hear old Triton blow his wreathèd horn.

William Wordsworth
(April 7th 1770 – April 23rd 1850)

On this day in 1799, William Wordsworth and his sister Dorothy reached their new home, Dove Cottage, after overnight stays at Sedbergh and Kendall. Beset by the wintry weather, they were soon to fall ill with colds. It was left to Dorothy to do her best to make the damp and empty house comfortable.

• *Giovanni Boccaccio died December 21st 1375*
• *Poet Richard Hugo, author of* 31 Letters and 13 Poems *(1977)*
  born in Seattle December 21st 1923

December 21

The Good-morrow

I wonder by my troth, what thou and I
Did, till we loved? were we not weaned till then?
But sucked on country pleasures, childishly?
Or snorted we in the seven sleepers' den?
'Twas so; but this[1], all pleasures fancies be.
If ever any beauty I did see,
Which I desired, and got, 'twas but a dream of thee.

And now good-morrow to our waking souls,
Which watch not one another out of fear;
For love all love of other sights controls,
And makes one little room an everywhere.
Let sea-discoverers to new worlds have gone,
Let maps to others, worlds on worlds have shown,
Let us possess one world, each hath one, and is one.

My face in thine eye, thine in mine appears,
And true plain hearts do in the faces rest;
Where can we find two better hemispheres
Without sharp North, without declining West?
What ever dies, was not mixed equally;
If our two loves be one, or thou and I
Love so alike that none do slacken, none can die.

John Donne
(c. June 1572 – March 31st 1631)

On this day in 1614, Donne wrote to his friend Sir Henry Goodere to tell him he would be printing "forthwith" a collection of his poems "not for much public view, but at mine own cost, a few copies".

Ben Jonson, his contemporary, thought Donne "the first poet in the World in some things" but one who wrote "all his best pieces ere he was twenty-five years old". Once ordained as a minister, Donne was to dismiss his earlier poetry as "light flashes", "evaporations" and "love-song weeds", and wrote of moving into "a graver course than of a poet, into which (that I may also keep my dignity) I would not seem to relapse".

1. Except for this.

December 22

• Playwright and poet Jean-Baptiste Racine, author of Phèdre, born in La Ferté-Milan December 22nd 1639
• Poet Edwin Arlington Robinson, author of The Man Who Died Twice, born in Maine December 22nd 1869
• Kenneth Rexroth, poet and translator (from Chinese and Japanese), born in Indiana December 22nd 1905

I Never Even Suggested It

I know lots of men who are in love and lots of men who are married and lots
    of men who are both,
And to fall out with their loved ones is what all of them are most loth.
They are conciliatory at every opportunity,
Because all they want is serenity and a certain amount of impunity.
Yes, many the swain who has finally admitted that the earth is flat
Simply to sidestep a spat,
Many the masculine Positively or Absolutely which has been diluted to an If
Simply to avert a tiff,
Many the two-fisted executive whose domestic conversation is limited to a
    tactfully interpolated Yes,
And then he is amazed to find that he is being raked backwards over a bed of
    coals nevertheless.
These misguided fellows are under the impression that it takes two to make a
    quarrel, that you can sidestep a crisis by nonaggression and
    nonresistance,
Instead of removing yourself to a discreet distance.
Passivity can be a provoking *modus operandi*:
Consider the Empire and Gandhi.
Silence is golden, but sometimes invisibility is golder,
Because loved ones may not be able to make bricks without straw but often
    they don't need any straw to manufacture a bone to pick or blood in
    their eye or a chip for their soft white shoulder.
It is my duty, gentlemen, to inform you that women are dictators all, and I
    recommend to you this moral:
In real life it takes only one to make a quarrel.

Ogden Nash
(August 19th 1902 – May 19th 1971)

One of Ogden Nash's verse collections is entitled *Marriage Lines: Notes of a Student Husband* (1964). He himself married in 1931 at the age of 29, and his poetry collections *Hard Lines* and *Free Wheeling* appeared in the same year.

- On this day in 1614, Stratford corporation drafted a letter seeking Shakespeare's help against enclosure of common lands
- Michael Drayton died December 23rd 1631
- Critic and poet Charles Sainte-Beuve (friend of Victor Hugo until his affair with Madame Hugo) born in Boulogne December 23rd 1804
- Poet and translator Robert Bly born on a farm in Minnesota December 23rd 1926
- Poet and playwright Carol Ann Duffy, one of whose poetry collections is Standing Female Nude (1985), born in Glasgow December 23rd 1955

From Idea
61

Since there's no help, come let us kiss and part:
Nay, I have done; you get no more of me,
And I am glad, yea, glad with all my heart,
That thus so cleanly I myself can free;
Shake hands for ever, cancel all our vows,
And when we meet at any time again,
Be it not seen in either of our brows
That we one jot of former love retain.
Now at the last gasp of love's latest breath,
When, his pulse failing, passion speechless lies,
When faith is kneeling by his bed of death,
And innocence is closing up his eyes,
Now, if thou wouldst, when all have given him over,
From death to life thou mightst him yet recover.

Michael Drayton
(1563 – December 23rd 1631)

Michael Drayton was born in Hartshill, Warwickshire. It is conjectured that he became a page in the household of Sir Henry Goodere and that his *Idea* sonnet sequence is addressed to Ann, Sir Henry's younger daughter. The sonnets were first published in 1594, but this particular sonnet was not added until the publication of *Ideas Mirrour* in 1619.

The authorities took offence at Drayton's first published work, metrical paraphrases from the Bible, entitled *The Harmony of the Church* (1592), and gave orders for it to be destroyed. Drayton went on to write odes, dramas, mythological poems, historical tales and patriotic poems such as 'The Battle of Agincourt'. His *Poems, Lyric and Pastoral* (c. 1606) contained the poem 'Fair Stood the Wind for France'. His mammoth multi-volume poem, *Poly-olbion*, aimed to provide "a chronological description of all the tracts, rivers, mountains, forests, and other parts of Great Britain".

He died in relative poverty, and it was left to Lady Anne Clifford, countess of Dorset, to sponsor the construction and installation of his monument in Westminster Abbey.

December 24

• Poet George Crabbe born in Aldeburgh December 24th 1754
• Poet and critic Matthew Arnold born December 24th 1822
• William Makepeace Thackeray died in his newly completed home in Bayswater, London, December 24th 1863
• Poet Juan Ramón Jiménez born in Helva December 24th 1881

The Ballad of Bouillabaisse

A street there is in Paris famous,
    For which no rhyme our language yields,
Rue Neuve des Petits Champs its name is—
    The New Street of the Little Fields;
And here's an inn, not rich and splendid,
    But still in comfortable case;
The which in youth I oft attended,
    To eat a bowl of Bouillabaisse.

This Bouillabaisse a noble dish is—
    A sort of soup or broth, or brew,
Or hotchpotch of all sorts of fishes,
    That Greenwich never could outdo;
Green herbs, red peppers, mussels, saffern,
    Soles, onions, garlic, roach, and dace;
All these you eat at Terré's tavern,
    In that one dish of Bouillabaisse.

Indeed, a rich and savoury stew 'tis;
    And true philosophers, methinks,
Who love all sorts of natural beauties,
    Should love good victuals and good drinks.
And Cordelier or Benedictine
    Might gladly, sure, his lot embrace,
Nor find a fast-day too afflicting
    Which served him up a Bouillabaisse.

I wonder if the house still there is?
    Yes, here the lamp is, as before;
The smiling red-cheeked écaillère is
    Still opening oysters at the door.
Is Terré still alive and able?
    I recollect his droll grimace;
He'd come and smile before your table,
    And hope you liked your Bouillabaisse.

We enter—nothing's changed or older.
    'How's Monsieur Terré, waiter, pray?'
The waiter stares and shrugs his shoulder—
    'Monsieur is dead this many a day.'
'It is the lot of saint and sinner,
    So honest Terré's run his race.'
'What will Monsieur require for dinner?'
    'Say, do you still cook Bouillabaisse?'

'Oh oui, Monsieur,' 's the waiter's answer;
    'Quel vin Monsieur désire-t-il?'
'Tell me a good one.'—'That I can, Sir:

[Continued]

The Chambertin with yellow seal.'
'So Terré's gone,' I say, and sink in
     My old accustomed corner-place;
'He's done with feasting and with drinking,
     With Burgundy and Bouillabaisse.'

My old accustomed corner here is,
     The table still is in the nook;
Ah! vanished many a busy year is,
     This well-known chair since last I took.
When first I saw ye, *cari luoghi°*,   *dear places*
     I'd scarce a beard upon my face,
And now a grizzled, grim old fogy,
     I sit and wait for Bouillabaisse.

Where are you, old companions trusty,
     Of early days, here met to dine?
Come, waiter! quick, a flagon crusty—
     I'll pledge them in the good old wine.
The kind old voices and old faces.
     My memory can quick retrace;
Around the board they take their places,
     And share the wine and Bouillabaisse.

There's Jack has made a wondrous marriage;
     There's laughing Tom is laughing yet;
There's brave Augustus drives his carriage;
     There's poor old Fred in the Gazette;
On James's head the grass is growing:
     Good Lord! the world has wagged apace
Since here we set the Claret flowing,
     And drank, and ate the Bouillabaisse.

Ah me! how quick the days are flitting?
     I mind me of a time that's gone,
When here I'd sit, as now I'm sitting,
     In this same place—but not alone.
A fair young form was nestled near me,
     A dear, dear face looked fondly up,
And sweetly spoke and smiled to cheer me.
     —There's no one now to share my cup.

I drink it, as the Fates ordain it.
     Come, fill it, and have done with rhymes:
Fill up the lonely glass, and drain it
     In memory of dear old times.
Welcome the wine, whate'er the seal is;
     And sit you down and say your grace
With thankful heart, whate'er the meal is.
     —Here comes the smoking Bouillabaisse!

William Makepeace Thackeray
(July 18th 1811 – December 24th 1863)

December 25

- Poet William Collins born in Chichester December 25th 1721
- Dorothy Wordsworth, the diarist and sister of William Wordsworth, born December 25th 1771
- Henry James wrote to Grace Norton on this day in 1897 that Kipling's talent was "quite diabolically great ... Almost nothing civilised, save steam and patriotism"

Innocent's Song

Who's that knocking on the window,
Who's that standing at the door,
What are all those presents
Lying on the kitchen floor?

Who is the smiling stranger
With hair as white as gin,
What is he doing with the children?
And who could have let him in?

Why has he rubies on his fingers,
A cold, cold crown on his head,
Why, when he caws his carol,
Does the salty snow run red?

Why does he ferry my fireside
As a spider on a thread,
His fingers made of fuses
And his tongue of gingerbread?

Why does the world before him
Melt in a million suns,
Why do his yellow, yearning eyes
Burn like saffron buns?

Watch where he comes walking
Out of the Christmas flame,
Dancing, double-talking:

Herod is his name.

Charles Causley
(August 24th 1917 –)

Charles Causley comments: "I wrote this poem for a private Christmas card at the time of the Cold War when such phrases as 'the peaceful use of atomic energy' for me rang particularly thin. There is a clear reference to the Christian Feast of the Holy Innocents (28 December) or Childermass. I also wanted to build a poem in which a succession of images dissolved one into another in the manner of a film dissolve."

Nicholas Albery adds: "I remember my friend Maya enthusiastically reciting this poem by heart when she was three and a half years old."

- King Lear *was played to the Court on December 26th 1606*
- *Poet Thomas Gray born in London December 26th 1716*
- *Patric Dickinson born December 26th 1914*
- *Poet Ivor Gurney, gassed at Ypres in 1917, died December 26th 1937, having spent his last years in an asylum*
- *Liz Lochhead, author of* Bagpipe Muzak, *born in Lanarkshire December 26th 1947*

Jodrell Bank

Who were they, what lonely men
Imposed on the fact of night
The fiction of constellations
And made commensurable
The distances between
Themselves, their loves, and their doubt
Of governments and nations?
Who made the dark stable

When the light was not? Now
We receive the blind codes
Of spaces beyond the span
Of our myths, and a long dead star
May only echo how
There are no loves nor gods
Men can invent to explain
How lonely all men are.

Patric Dickinson
(December 26th 1914 – January 28th 1994)

Patric Dickinson was born in Nasirabad, India, and educated at St Catharine's College, Cambridge, to which he won an exhibition. His father was killed early on in the First World War and he himself was invalided out of the Second in 1940.

For three years after the war he was Poetry Editor for the BBC Home Service. His poetry collections include *This Cold Universe* (1949) and *Selected Poems* (1968). He was also a playwright and a translator and with his wife Sheila Shannon edited anthologies such as *Poems to Remember* (1958). His autobiographical study is entitled *The Good Minute* (1965).

December 27

- *French poet Pierre de Ronsard died December 27th 1585*
- *Charles Lamb, poet, friend of Coleridge and author of* Tales from Shakespeare, *died December 27th 1834*
- *Thomas Carlyle described Tennyson, his dinner companion of this day, 1843, as a "right hearty talker" and "one of the powerfullest smokers" he has ever "worked along with in that department"*
- *Charles Olson born in Worcester, Mass., December 27th 1910*
- *Poet John Cornford born in Cambridge December 27th 1915*
- *Alfred Percival Graves, Irish poet and songwriter, father of Robert Graves, died December 27th 1931*
- *Osip Mandelstam died in a transit camp December 27th 1938*

From Variations Done for Gerald Van De Wiele[1]

what soul
isn't in default?

can you afford not to make
the magical study

which happiness is? do you hear
the cock when he crows? do you know the charge,

that you shall have no envy, that your life
has its orders, that the seasons

seize you too, that no body and soul are one
if they are not wrought

in this retort? that otherwise efforts
are efforts? And that the hour of your flight

will be the hour of your death?

Charles Olson
(December 27th 1910 – January 10th 1970)
based around 'Le Bonheur' by Arthur Rimbaud
(October 20th 1854 – November 10th 1891)

Charles Olson was born in Chicago, the son of a postman, and educated at the university there. He married twice and had four children. Towards the end of his life he concentrated on his long poem *Maximus* (he himself was Maximus, all 6 feet 8 inches of him). He died of cancer at the age of 56.

He is identified as a Black Mountain poet, having been rector at this experimental Black Mountain College in North Carolina, influencing the poets Robert Creeley and Denise Levertov amongst others. In his advocacy for open or 'projective verse', sound is more important than sense, and sense is conveyed not by rational argument but by shifts of perception.

Arthur Rimbaud, the son of an army captain, was brought up in Charleville, Ardennes, by a religious and strict widowed mother. He was a model pupil until the age of 15, at which stage in his life he deliberately set out to debauch himself and "become God" by transcending the world through sin and suffering. The older poet Verlaine invited him to Paris and shot at and wounded him at the end of their affair. At 19, Rimbaud, disappointed at the reception of his *Saison en Enfer*, burnt his manuscripts and wandered the world as trader, gun-runner and soldier. His leg was amputated in Marseilles, and he died there.

1. From Section II, *The Charge*, lines 55 to 67.

Sonnet 129

The expense of spirit in a waste of shame
Is lust in action; and till action, lust
Is perjur'd, murderous, bloody, full of blame,
Savage, extreme, rude, cruel, not to trust;
Enjoy'd no sooner but despis'd straight;
Past reason hunted; and no sooner had,
Past reason hated, as a swallow'd bait,
On purpose laid to make the taker mad:
Mad in pursuit, and in possession so;
Had, having, and in quest to have, extreme;
A bliss in proof,—and prov'd, a very woe;
Before, a joy propos'd; behind, a dream.
    All this the world well knows; yet none knows well
    To shun the heaven that leads men to this hell.

William Shakespeare
(April 23rd 1564 – April 23rd 1616)

On this day in 1594, Queen Elizabeth I watched Shakespeare, William Kemp and Richard Burbage act in an unidentified comedy. The three actors received £20 by "waye of her Majesties rewarde".

December 29

• *Christina Rossetti died of Graves's disease December 29th 1894*
• *Austrian lyric poet Rainer Maria Rilke died December 29th 1926*

Song

When I am dead, my dearest,
   Sing no sad songs for me;
Plant thou no roses at my head,
   Nor shady cypress tree:
Be the green grass above me
   With showers and dewdrops wet;
And if thou wilt, remember,
   And if thou wilt, forget.

I shall not see the shadows,
   I shall not feel the rain;
I shall not hear the nightingale
   Sing on, as if in pain:
And dreaming through the twilight
   That doth not rise nor set,
Haply I may remember,
   And haply may forget.

Christina Rossetti
(December 5th 1830 – December 29th 1894)

This poem was written on December 12th 1848, just after Christina Rossetti's 18th birthday, as an engagement present to the painter James Collinson. She broke off the engagement when he returned to the Catholic faith – and never married. "Grown old before my time," as she put it, she suffered from ill-health most of her life, and was operated on for cancer. She died later, according to one report, whilst "in the act of prayer".

- *Shelley married his second wife, Mary Godwin, on December 30th 1816, his long-since abandoned first wife Harriet having committed suicide the previous month*
- *Rudyard Kipling born in Bombay, where his father was an architectural sculptor, December 30th 1865. Kipling's parents had first met at Rudyard Lake in Staffordshire, hence his name*

If—

If you can keep your head when all about you
    Are losing theirs and blaming it on you,
If you can trust yourself when all men doubt you,
    But make allowance for their doubting too;
If you can wait and not be tired of waiting,
    Or being lied about, don't deal in lies,
Or being hated, don't give way to hating,
    And yet don't look too good, nor talk too wise:

If you can dream—and not make dreams your master;
    If you can think—and not make thoughts your aim;
If you can meet with Triumph and Disaster
    And treat those two impostors just the same;
If you can bear to hear the truth you've spoken
    Twisted by knaves to make a trap for fools,
Or watch the things you gave your life to, broken,
    And stoop and build 'em up with worn-out tools:

If you can make one heap of all your winnings
    And risk it on one turn of pitch-and-toss,
And lose, and start again at your beginnings
    And never breathe a word about your loss;
If you can force your heart and nerve and sinew
    To serve your turn long after they are gone,
And so hold on when there is nothing in you
    Except the Will which says to them: 'Hold on!'

If you can talk with crowds and keep your virtue,
    Or walk with Kings—nor lose the common touch,
If neither foes nor loving friends can hurt you,
    If all men count with you, but none too much;
If you can fill the unforgiving minute
    With sixty seconds' worth of distance run,
Yours is the Earth and everything that's in it,
    And—which is more—you'll be a Man, my son!

Rudyard Kipling
(December 30th 1865 – January 18th 1936)

Kipling based this masculine ideal on Dr Jameson, leader of the fiasco which came to be known as the Jameson raid (December 29th 1895 to January 2nd 1896). The raid was intended to surprise the Transvaal Boers but ended ignominiously with Jameson being led off to a Pretoria jail in tears.

December 31

• Shakespeare's youngest brother Edmund buried in Southwark at
St Saviour's Church December 31st 1607
• On this day in 1792 Burns told Mrs Dunlop that hard drinking
was "the devil to him"
• 'Spasmodic' poet Alexander Smith born in Kilmarnock December
31st 1830

Auld Lang Syne

Should auld acquaintance be forgot,
  And never brought to min'?
Should auld acquaintance be forgot,
  And auld lang syne?

For auld lang syne, my dear.
  For auld lang syne,
We'll tak a cup o' kindness yet,
  For auld lang syne.

We twa hae run about the braes,
  And pu'd the gowans° fine;   *daisies*
But we've wandered mony a weary foot
  Sin' auld lang syne.

We twa hae paidled° i' the burn,   *paddled*
  From morning sun till dine;
But seas between us braid hae roared
  Sin' auld lang syne.

And there's a hand, my trusty fiere°,   *comrade*
  And gie's a hand o' thine;
And we'll tak a right guid-willie waught°, *hearty draught*
  For auld lang syne.

And surely ye'll be your pint-stowp,
  And surely I'll be mine;
And we'll tak a cup o' kindness yet
  For auld lang syne.

Robert Burns
(January 25th 1759 – July 21st 1796)

Burns contributed this song to James Thomson's Scots Musical Museum, writing to Thomson in September 1793 that it was "the old song of olden times, and which has never been in print, nor even in manuscript, untill I took it down from an old man's singing". This reference to the old man singing may have been made "merely in a playful humour," says one editor, for "the song offers evidence of our Bard himself being the author". In which case, Burns had again been playful when he sent this song to Mrs Dunlop on December 17th 1788, with a letter to say: "Light be the turf on the breast of the Heaven-inspired poet who composed this glorious fragment. There is more fire of native genius in it than in half a dozen Modern English Bacchanalians."

Acknowledgements

The Natural Death Centre is grateful to Wendy Cope, Peter Ratcliffe, Matthew Mezey, Christine Mills, Emma Whiting, Peter Cadogan, Gillian Rathbone, John-David Papworth, Merlyn Albery, Josefine Speyer and Yvonne Ackroyd for their work on this book; to Richard Doust for his design help; to David Owen for his comment for the back cover; and to the many people and organisations that contributed poems, suggestions or research, including Heather Albery, Anne Ashworth, Tim Beaumont, Judith Becque-Rowley, Rosemary Bett, Dr Irene Campbell, Betsy Cook, Theo Dorgan, Marie Louise Grennert, Karen McCosker, Yvonne Malik, Marianne Nault, Marcelle Papworth, John Rowan, Pattie Powell, Diana Senior, Guida Swan, Janet Whitaker, Heathcote Williams and Valerie Yule.

Much of the source material for the biographical information on the poets was compiled from the following reference works, to which the reader is directed for further information: *The Oxford Companion to English Literature* (Drabble, OUP), *The Oxford Companion to Twentieth Century Poetry in English* (Hamilton, OUP), *Contemporary Poets* (Vinson, St James Press), *Chamber's Biographical Dictionary* (Magnusson, Chambers) and *The Dictionary of National Biography* (OUP). The Natural Death Centre is also grateful to help from librarians at the British Museum, the London Library, the Poetry Library, the Bodleian Library and the Kensington and Chelsea Library.

The Natural Death Centre gratefully acknowledges the following for their patient help and for their most generous permission to reproduce copyright material (and is apologetic for any errors or omissions – this was our first venture into the minefield of poem permissions):

Virago Press Ltd for a poem by Maya Angelou from *And Still I Rise* ©1978; Faber and Faber Ltd and Simon Armitage for a poem by Simon Armitage; Faber and Faber Ltd for 'Lullaby' and 'Stop all the clocks' by W.H. Auden from *Collected Poems*; Faber and Faber Ltd for 'To My Mother' by George Barker from *Collected Poems*; Peters Fraser & Dunlop for a poem by Hilaire Belloc; Faber and Faber Ltd for 'Sonnet 117' by John Berryman from *Collected Poems 1937-1971*; Duncan Cotterill & Co on behalf of the Estate of Ursula Bethell for a poem by Ursula Bethell; John Murray (Publishers) Ltd for poems by John Betjeman from *Collected Poems*; Earle Birney for a poem from *The Collected Poems of Earle Birney* (McClelland & Stewart Ltd); Farrar, Straus & Giroux, Inc for 'Casabianca' and 'One Art' by Elizabeth Bishop from *The Complete Poems 1927-1979* ©1979, 1983 by Alice Helen Methfessel; Robert Bly for his translations of poems by Antonio Machado, Rainer Maria Rilke, Kabir and Juan Ramón Jiménez; Grove/Atlantic Inc for a poem by Raymond Carver from *A New Path to the Waterfall* published by The Atlantic Monthly Press ©1989; TRO Essex Music Ltd for a song by Leonard Cohen ©1966 Leonard Cohen Stranger Music Inc USA, London for UK and Commonwealth (ex Canada), Republics of Ireland and South Africa. All rights reserved. Used by permission; David Higham Associates for a poem by Charles Causley from *Collected Poems* published by Macmillan; Faber and Faber Ltd and Wendy Cope for 'Summer Vilanelle' and 'Giving up Smoking' from *Making Cocoa for Kingsley Amis*, and 'Bloody Men' from *Serious Concerns,* both books by Wendy Cope; Random House UK Ltd and the estate of Frances Cornford for a poem from her *Collected Poems* (Cresset Press); Marion Boyars Publishing Ltd for a poem by Robert Creeley; W.W. Norton and Company for poems by e.e. cummings ©1951, 1975, 1976, 1976, 1976 by the trustees of the e.e. cummings trust; Anvil Press Ltd for '6 A.M. Thoughts' by Dick Davis from *Dick Davis: Devices and Desires* (Anvil Press Poetry

Index

Poetry Marathon

Organise a Poetry Marathon in your area!

Reciting poems for charity

Organise a Poetry Marathon in your area! Learn a poem for charity! It's such a simple idea: You get your friends and relatives to sponsor you to learn one or more poems for the charity of your choice. You have to recite this to an audience.

It's great fun! Victoria Zinovieff wrote about the 1995 London Poetry Marathon: "I felt proud and happy and amazed to find myself up on stage reciting a poem to an audience. I also enjoyed the other poems. It was such a good atmosphere." Sheila Thomson wrote: "We enjoyed it very much – particularly the liveliness and variety and the feeling that everybody there was having a good time." Diana Senior wrote: "As a spectator sport, it worked much better than I expected. The highlights for me were: Marvell in a Yorkshire accent; Burns in a proper Scottish accident; and the delighted faces of each person who had successfully completed their poem – the lineaments of gratified desire. All the people I persuaded to come went away inspired."

You may recite any poem you like, including your own poetry, as long as you have learnt it by heart.

Some organisational tips:

• Have a prompter able to help people who forget their lines – ask people to bring printed copies of their poems, to lend to the prompter.

• Warn reciters that, after 5 minutes, they may be halted if they make a mistake, so as to allow others a go on stage.

• Publicise the event with poems hung from trees like Tibetan prayer flags. Engrave poems into pavements.

• Get newspapers, radio and TV to interview star poets who are attending – they can say, for instnace, which poems they are reciting and why they like them.

• Give free entry to those who are under 18 or unemployed.

In 1995, for the Poetry Marathon held in London, some 200 people came, including 45 children. The longest poem recited was the complete Highwayman by Noyes. Yeats and Shakespeare were the most popular poets chosen by reciters. But modern poets chosen included Seamus Heaney, Charles Causley, Rah X, Denise Levertov and Elizabeth Bishop. Over £4,000 was raised for a varied list of charities. A number of schools organised their own mini-Poetry Marathons – one school raised £2,150.

The Poetry Marathon in London is on the second Sunday in October each year.

So, get training and exercise those brain cells! There is big money to be earned!

Please contact The Poetry Marathon, 20 Heber Road, London NW2 6AA, UK (tel 0181 208 2853; fax 0181 452 6434; e-mail: <rhino@dial.pipex.com>) for further details; and for a sponsorship form and a performance certificate, both of which can be photocopied.

Charity newsletters

Help your favourite charity! Please send a copy of the item below to the Newsletter Editor at the main address of any charity you particularly support, asking the editor to adapt it for reprinting – the editor may edit it freely, adding in the relevant charity's name where appropriate.

PLEASE REPRINT THIS:

Reciting poems for charity

Nicholas Albery, Director of the Poetry Marathon

The Poetry Marathon hopes that each year your charity's supporters will take part in the Poetry Marathon, which happens in London on the second Sunday in October (phone 0181 208 2853 to book a place and for sponsorship forms). Several individuals raised over £2,000 last year this way for their favourite charities. It's good fun for all ages – and it makes a pleasant change for a marathon to be exercising the brain rather than the body!

The event just involves getting friends and relatives to sponsor you to learn a poem by heart (any poem, old or new, your own or someone else's) and to recite it at the Marathon – or to recite it where you live, you don't have to come to the London venue. The only rule is that there must be an audience of some kind.

It is also a good way to gather funds for your favourite charity, since each person says on stage who they are raising money for, and why.

Or you might be able to get your local school to run a similar event, with all the pupils taking part.

For the London event, except for those who are unemployed or under 18, entrants must already possess or must buy a copy of the 400-page book *Poem for the Day* (Sinclair-Stevenson, £9-99) as this book is helping to fund the event. It contains 366 poems old and new, one for every day of the year, with each one worth learning by heart and many suitable for all ages.

If you want a poem to learn that would suit you, it might anyway be a good book to consult in advance.

For further details of how to organise an event like this or for more about the Poem for the Day *book, please send an SAE to the Poetry Marathon, 20 Heber Road, London NW2 6AA (tel 0181 208 2853).*

Fund-raising for schools

PLEASE SEND A COPY OF THIS TO THE ENGLISH TEACHER AT YOUR LOCAL PRIMARY OR SECONDARY SCHOOL

Organise a Poetry Marathon in *your* school

This simple idea is for the pupils and teachers to get sponsored by their family and friends to raise money for charity by reciting in public a poem that they have learnt by heart.

It can be any poem, and any charities, and the event can be any date in any term. It can take place over a week-long period, or it can be a single assembly. It can be run any way you fancy.

School raises £2,150 for charity by reciting poems!

Elizabeth Howard of St Catherine's School writes:

Inspired by your brilliant idea of a Poetry Marathon, our school, St Catherine's, decided to have a 'Poetry Happening'. Every child in the school from age 3 to 13 (240 children) chose and recited a poem for charity. We devoted a whole week to this project.

One class recited a poem all together. A group of teachers recited and mimed 'Albert the Lion'.

The children recited their poems to other classes and, at our final assembly of the term, one child from each class recited their poem to the whole school – stage, lights, the works – a great success.

Parents and children all loved the whole project, said they enjoyed looking through poetry books, selecting their poem and actually found it fun and pleasure to learn a poem by heart. Some children amazed us by the length of their poems. The teachers all participated with enthusiasm. We had a display of poetry books in the school entrance. Many of the children wrote out and illustrated their poems, which were also on display around the school. The older children organised the whole event, including collecting and counting the money! We raised the staggering sum of £2,150.

We intend to make this an annual event. We would like to include a reading by a poet and maybe have an evening to which the parents could be invited. The money will be divided between four charities which we, as a school, support.

We also gave each child a certificate saying they had recited their poem successfully.

We all thank you for this wonderful idea which was a total success in every way.

Please contact Poetry Marathons International, 20 Heber Road, London NW2 6AA, (tel 0181 208 2853; fax 0181 452 6434; e-mail: <rhino@dial.pipex.com>) for further details; and for a sponsorship form and performance certificate that can be photocopied.

The Poetry Marathon is supported by the anthology Poem for the Day – 366 Poems Old and New Worth Learning by Heart, *which was reviewed in the School Librarian magazine as 'Yes, fitting for bedside and classroom'.*

The Natural Death Centre

The Befriending Network and inexpensive, 'Green' Funerals

The Natural Death Centre is an educational charity which is receiving all the royalties from this book. As an introduction to the work of the Centre, here are brief answers to the questions that The Natural Death Centre is most frequently asked (the figures are correct for 1996):

Why is it called The Natural Death Centre? It is not, as some assume, a centre for euthanasia. The name was chosen in analogy to the natural birth movement which advocated the possibility of childbirth at home – the Centre is in effect a society for supporting those who are dying at home, and many of the consultants are people involved in the hospice movement. The Centre feels that NHS priorities and funds need redirecting to make it possible for more people to die at home rather than in hospitals.

What do you actually do? The Befriending Network, started by the Centre, offers trained volunteers who can go to the home of someone who is critically ill (not necessarily dying) in order to help the person or their carer, with anything from errands to just being there as a relief for the carer. More volunteers prepared to offer about two hours a week of their time are needed. Those who have done so report feeling enriched by the experience.

You were in the media in connection with cardboard coffins and green burials. What is that about? The Centre offers advice on inexpensive, Green and family-arranged funerals. The average price of a conventional funeral is over £1,000. A 'd-i-y' family-arranged one can cost under £350. The Centre has started an Association of Nature Reserve Burial Grounds, run by farmers and local authorities, where people can be buried for about £300 and where, instead of a headstone, a tree is planted. All these sites also make available either cardboard coffins or ordinary coffins or sometimes just shrouds, for those who are not using funeral directors. The Centre has information on cardboard coffins available by mail order from £52, and chipboard ones, fully fitted, at about £125 including delivery, and also information on which are the most helpful funeral directors, cemeteries and crematoria nationwide.

What about the stories of burial in the back garden? The Centre advises careful thought before going for this perfectly legal option, unless the people concerned have a very large garden and the inheritors are not worried at a possible drop in the value of the property as a result. More feasible in many cases is burial on farmland, with the permission of the farmer. No planning permission is required at present for a limited number of uncommercial burials of this nature.

What else do you offer? The Centre has workshops for nurses and the general public ('Living with Dying' workshops for instance), and informal Salons on various topics; it has a Living Will people can fill in specifying how much high tech medical intervention they want when dying; it also has book listings, organisation listings, and much more.

How do I find out more? An information pack costs six first class stamps (to help cover the cost of photocopying the leaflets). *The Natural Death Handbook* covers friends and family organising a funeral themselves (making the coffin, laying out the body, etc) and caring for a dying person at home. It is available from the Centre for £10-95 including p&p. A set of forms (Living Will, Values Statement, Advance Funeral Wishes Form and Death Plan) costs four first class stamps.

The Natural Death Centre, 20 Heber Road, London NW2 6AA (tel 0181 208 2853; fax 0181 452 6434; e-mail: <rhino@dial.pipex.com>). Its publications are available free on the Internet at the location: <http://newciv.org/naturaldeath.html >.